T0192133

Lecture Notes in Computer Science 13424

More information about this series at https://link.springer.com/bookseries/558

Cristina Carmona-Duarte · Moises Diaz ·
Miguel A. Ferrer · Aythami Morales (Eds.)

Intertwining Graphonomics with Human Movements

20th International Conference
of the International Graphonomics Society, IGS 2021
Las Palmas de Gran Canaria, Spain, June 7–9, 2022
Proceedings

Editors
Cristina Carmona-Duarte ⓘ
Universidad de Las Palmas de Gran Canaria
Las Palmas de Gran Canaria, Spain

Moises Diaz ⓘ
Universidad de Las Palmas de Gran Canaria
Las Palmas de Gran Canaria, Spain

Miguel A. Ferrer ⓘ
Universidad de Las Palmas de Gran Canaria
Las Palmas de Gran Canaria, Spain

Aythami Morales ⓘ
Universidad Autónoma de Madrid
Madrid, Spain

ISSN 0302-9743   ISSN 1611-3349 (electronic)
Lecture Notes in Computer Science
ISBN 978-3-031-19744-4   ISBN 978-3-031-19745-1 (eBook)
https://doi.org/10.1007/978-3-031-19745-1

This Springer imprint is published by the registered company Springer Nature Switzerland AG
The registered company address is: Gewerbestrasse 11, 6330 Cham, Switzerland

Preface

After 20 editions, the conference of the International Graphonomics Society (IGS) has become a key research event, and the most important in the graphonomics community. The travel restrictions imposed during the COVID-19 outbreak caused the IGS 2021 conference to be held in 2022.

The IGS conference has always been an open international event, and this year received submissions from more than 14 countries. In this edition, the biggest presence was from Italy, but there was also a strong good presence from Spain, Canada, and the Czech Republic.

IGS 2021 received 41 submissions. The review process for IGS 2021 was diligent and required the careful consideration of 67 reviewers who spent significant time and effort in reviewing the papers, with a minimum of three reviews per paper. In the end, 36 papers were accepted for the conference and 26 for publication in this Springer LNCS volume, which is an 87% and 63% rate of acceptance, respectively. To form the final program, 20 papers were selected for oral presentations (48% of all submissions), 17% for the poster session, and 22% for special sessions.

The program was comprised of six oral sessions on the following topics: historical documents, forensic handwriting examinations, handwriting learning and development, and motor control. One additional poster session included papers on all previous topics, and three special sessions included papers on neurodegenerative disorders. All the papers, including the ones submitted by organizers, went through the same revision procedure. To avoid any bias in favor of the organizers' papers, objective rules were followed. The IGS 2021 program was enhanced by three keynotes by eminent speakers: Miguel Ángel Ferrer, José Manuel Vilar, and José Juan Quintana.

The graphonomics community is witnessing a deep transformation, now increasingly dominated by advances occurring in the industry in machine learning, computer vision, and related fields around Artificial Intelligence. We hope that these proceedings will result in a fruitful reference for the graphonomic research community. Finally, we would like to thank all who made this possible, especially the authors, the reviewers, and the IGS community at large.

May 2022

Cristina Carmona-Duarte
Moises Diaz
Miguel A. Ferrer
Aythami Morales

Organization

Local Committee President

Miguel A. Ferrer — Universidad de Las Palmas de Gran Canaria, Spain

General Chairs

Cristina Carmona-Duarte — Universidad de Las Palmas de Gran Canaria, Spain

Moises Diaz — Universidad de Las Palmas de Gran Canaria, Spain

Steering Committee

Claudio De Stefano — Università di Cassino e del Lazio Meridionale, Italy

Angelo Marcelli — University of Salerno, Italy

Réjean Plamondon — Ecole Polytechnique Montreal, Canada

Hans-Leo Teulings — Neuroscript, USA

Arend Van Gemmert — Louisiana State University, USA

Céline Rémi — LAMIA, Guadeloupe

Andreas Fischer — University of Applied Sciences and Arts Western, Switzerland

Ana Rita Matias — University of Évora, Portugal

Erika Griechisch — Cursor Insight, Hungary

Sara Rosenblum — University of Haifa, Israel

Heidi Harralson — East Tennessee State University, USA

Publication Chair

Aythami Morales Moreno — Universidad Autónoma de Madrid, Spain

Local Organizing Committee

José J. Quintana — Universidad de Las Palmas de Gran Canaria, Spain

Jesús Bernardino Alonso — Universidad de Las Palmas de Gran Canaria, Spain

Program Committee

Serena Starita	Università degli Studi di Trieste, Italy
Donato Impedovo	UNIBA, Italy
Andreas Fischer	University of Fribourg, Switzerland
Josep Llados	Computer Vision Center, Spain
Nina Hosseini	University of Luxembourg, Luxembourg
Liat Hen-Herbst	Ariel University, Israel
Mateusz Dubiel	University of Strathclyde, UK
Remi Celine	Université des Antilles, Guadeloupe
Réjean Plamondon	École Polytechnique de Montréal, Canada
Mathias Seuret	University of Fribourg, Switzerland
Arend Van Gemmert	Louisiana State University, USA
Isabelle Marthot-Santaniello	University of Basel, Switzerland
Najla Al-Qawasmeh	Concordia University, Canada
Thiago Borduqui	Federal District Civil Police, Brazil
Kyungsoo Kim	Kyung Hee University, South Korea
Asma Bensalah	Universitat Autònoma de Barcelona, Spain
Nicole Vincent	Universite de Paris, France
Deborah Watson	Mississippi State University, USA
Nicole Dalia Cilia	Sapienza University of Rome, Italy
Antonio Parziale	University of Salerno, Italy
Vincent Christlein	University of Erlangen-Nuremberg, Germany
Carina Fernandes	NCForenses, Portugal
Miguel Ferrer	Universidad de Las Palmas de Gran Canaria, Spain
Ruben Vera-Rodriguez	Universidad Autonoma de Madrid, Spain
Marie Anne Nauer	Institute for Handwriting Sciences, Switzerland
Ana Matias	University of Évora, Portugal
Adolfo Santoro Natural	Intelligent Technologies S.R.L., Italy
Hans-Leo Teulings	NeuroScript, USA
Zhujun Pan	Mississippi State University, USA
Bence Kovari	Budapest University of Technology and Economics, Hungary
Erika Griechisch	Cursor Insight, Hungary
Bereket Abera Yilma	Luxembourg Institute of Science and Technology, Luxembourg
Mohammad Saleem	Budapest University of Technology and Economics, Hungary
Elias Zois	TEI of Athens, Greece
Christopher Aiken	New Mexico State University, USA
Chawki Djeddi Larbi	Tebessi Uinversity, Algeria
Jan Mucha	Brno University of Technology, Czech Republic

Contents

Motor Control

Handwriting for Neurodegenerative Disorders

Handwriting Verification

Forensic Handwriting Examination at IGS Conferences: A Review by Numbers

Angelo Marcelli⬥ and Antonio Parziale(✉)⬥

DIEM, University of Salerno, 84084 Fisciano, SA, Italy
{amarcelli,anparziale}@unisa.it

Abstract. We review the number of contributions to the advancements in handwriting analysis for forensic applications that were presented at the biennial conferences of the International Graphonomics Society through its 20 editions. We introduce a taxonomy for the systematic analysis of the literature, propose a way to evaluate the overall interest and relevance of the topic in the context of the conference editions, as well as the interest and relevance of each category of the taxonomy. We discuss past and current trends emerging from the quantitative analysis and outline some future possible developments.

Keywords: Forensic Handwriting Examination · Graphonomics

1 Introduction

The biennial conferences of the International Graphonomics Society have been the most relevant scientific events organized to fulfill the Society's mission of promoting the advancement of research in the field of graphonomics. The term graphonomics was introduced during the first conference to denote the scientific and technological effort for unveiling relationships between the planning and generation of handwriting and drawing movements, the resulting spatial traces of writing and drawing instruments (either conventional or electronic), and the dynamic features of these traces. Thus, it highlights the multidisciplinary and interdisciplinary nature of the entire research field, which encompasses motor control, experimental psychology, neuroscience, pattern recognition and artificial intelligence. The cross-fertilization between such diverse disciplines aims at understanding how handwriting is learned and executed, to which extent the handwriting characteristics vary under the influence of the neural, psychological, and biomechanical conditions of the writer, and to which extent the handwriting behavior can be explained in terms of patterns appearing in a given set of quantitative features derived from handwriting statistical and/or computational models.

Forensic handwriting examination (hereinafter referred as FHE) pertains to the analysis of handwriting for evaluating to which extent the specimen under investigation can be attributed to a given writer or to a writer among a set of them, by comparing the questioned samples to the genuine ones. It is therefore not surprising that forensic handwriting examination has deeply rooted in graphonomics, its goal being that of finding

© Springer Nature Switzerland AG 2022
C. Carmona-Duarte et al. (Eds.): IGS 2021, LNCS 13424, pp. 3–10, 2022.
https://doi.org/10.1007/978-3-031-19745-1_1

the characteristics of handwriting to evaluate and defining a measure of the similarity between two handwritten samples.

In this context, we survey the works that have been presented at the 20 biennial conferences over 40 years, from 1982 to 2022. The purpose is to identify the dimensions of forensic handwriting examination that have been addressed, how they have developed during this time-lapse, and to which extent they reflect the general trends in the field as observed from a broad perspective.

For sake of space, in this short paper, we will not discuss the major contributions of each paper, but rather how the number of papers falling in each of the categories varied over the years, with the aim of detecting their quantitative trends. For the same reason, the reference section includes only the proceedings and other publications that follow from the conferences. These goals will be pursued in a future extended version of the survey.

The remaining of the paper is organized as it follows. In Sect. 2 we will present the rationale behind the taxonomy we have adopted to present the literature, while in Sect. 3 we will outline the trends that we have observed, and suggest possible reasons related to changes in the field due to new methodological paradigms and/or technological developments. In Sect. 4 we briefly highlight what could be the future trends and the concluding section attempts to highlight some open issues and challenges that remain to be addressed.

2   A Taxonomy of Forensic Handwriting Examination Literature

In order to dissect how the different aspects of handwriting have contributed to the interest and the relevance of the topic, we have grouped the works on FHE that were presented at the IGS conferences into six categories:

- Methodologies
- Signature Verification
- Writer verification/identification
- Disguising writer identification
- Tools
- Case report

The *Methodologies (MET)* category includes papers that present either theories or experimental works aimed at finding the handwriting characteristics that reflect at the best the handwriting of a subject or a group of subjects and how they should be compared. The papers in this category look at handwriting generation and execution by adopting a motor control perspective to formulate hypotheses about the sources of the variability exhibited by the samples produced by different subjects or by the same subjects in different occasions, and by designing experiments rooted in the framework of experimental psychology for supporting the hypotheses or to unveil quantitative relation between the considered aspects of handwriting. Some of the papers included in this category, moreover, addressed the more general problem of defining the operative procedure forensic experts should follow during handwriting examination, from document collection to final opinion formulation, in order to make the whole process easy to reproduce by different experts, while leaving the forensic expert to exert their expertise in putting the data into context and formulating the final answers to the specific questions for whom the examination has been requested.

Signatures are among the oldest and certainly the longest-lived means of authorship identification. Originally produced by ink and paper, the development of digitizing tablets capable of acquiring the temporal information of the trajectory has been deployed and used to collect signatures, opening new challenges to forensic experts, due to the intertwining of the handwriting execution and its digital representation and storage. As signatures are among the most automated handwriting movements, and because they are not meant to convey a message to the reader, but rather to link the writer to a graphical representation of its name, they raise specific issues and offer peculiar characteristics to be exploited, and then we have introduced the *Signature Verification (SV)* category.

The papers included in the *Writer identification/verification (WI/WV)* category describe the efforts to the general problem of assessing an individual identity through the analysis of the handwriting production. As such, they include mostly experimental studies adopting feature sets derived from the findings of investigations on handwriting learning and execution or exploiting properties of the digital representation of handwriting execution, and then processing them by some kind of statistical analysis, often implemented by a computer model of the probability distribution function, to achieve the final goal.

Disguising writer identification (Disguising) aims at detecting handwriting produced by a subject that intentionally modifies its handwriting behavior for eventually denying the authorship of a handwritten sample. It differs from the previous category because in writer identification/verification forensic experts aim to detect differences and weight their relevance with respect to similarity, in the latter they look for similarities and weight their relevance with respect to differences.

Papers belonging to the *Tools* category somehow complement those belonging to the previous ones, as they presented tools that have been developed for evaluating handwriting characteristics and put the obtained values in a statistical framework to have a quantitative profile of the handwriting, and eventually to evaluate the similarities/differences among samples.

The *Case Report (CR)* category, eventually, includes paper that describe the forensic examination of "extra-ordinary" cases, i.e. cases that deviate from the ordinary casework either for the relevance of the case itself (as it happens when new findings are reported to clarify previously disputed or questionable conclusion) or because they adventure in unexplored territories (as in case of the handwritings produced by subject with personality or motor disorders), so opening new technology-driven avenues or addressing challenging issues beyond the current state of the art and best practices.

3   FHE by Numbers

A preliminary analysis of the proceedings [1], as well as of the journal special issues and the books containing extended versions of selected papers presented at the various editions [2], allowed us to extract 164 papers that explicitly refer to FHE out of 907

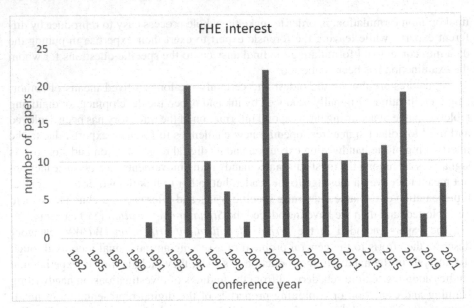

Fig. 1. The interest in FHE at IGS conferences, measured as the number of papers addressing the general topic of FHE at each edition of the IGS conference.

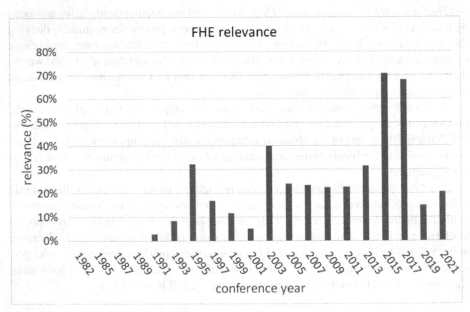

Fig. 2. The relevance of FHE at IGS conferences, measured as the percentage of papers addressing the general topic of FHE with respect to the total number of papers presented at each edition of the IGS conference.

papers presented at the conferences. Figure 1 shows the interest in the topic, expressed by the number of FHE papers presented at the different editions of the conference, while Fig. 2 shows the relevance of the topic within the conferences, defined as the percentage of FHE papers with respect to the total number of papers presented at each conference.

The histogram in Fig. 1 shows that starting from the 5th edition of the conference, FHE has been one of the topics addressed in every following conference, with a mean relevance of 18.1%. It also shows that the conference editions with the higher number of FHE papers have been the 7th, 11th and 18th editions with 20, 22 and 19 papers, respectively.

The 7th and 11th editions of the conference were organized in conjunction with the annual symposium of the Association of the Forensic Document Examiners and that had the effect of a significant increase of FHE papers with respect to the previous editions. The interest in forensic handwriting examination at IGS conferences surged again at the 11th edition and it remains stable until the 17th and 18th editions, when it accounts for roughly 70% of the total number of papers. The lasting interest in FHE since 2003 may reflect the reaction of forensic experts and scientists to several rulings of the US Supreme Court that questioned forensic document examination expertise as scientific expertise: Daubert et al. v. Merrell Dow Pharmaceuticals, U.S. v. Starzecpyzel cases, General Electric Co., et al. v. Joiner et al., Kumho Tire Co., Ltd., et al. v. Carmichael et al. and United States v. Paul ruled out in November 1993, April 1995, December 1997, March 1999 and May 1999, respectively.

The 18th edition of the conference, which was held in Italy, exhibited a renovated interest in FHE as an effect of the implementation of European directives about the legal effect of electronic signature and the following diffusion of commercial solutions for signing over a tablet in public offices. Many papers were submitted by Italian associations of forensic experts that in the years just before the conference had started a reconsideration and transformation of the procedures for handwritten document examination adopted by their affiliates.

In the last two editions, however, the interest decreases again, possibly because of the rather narrow focus of the 19th edition and the effects of the pandemics on the overall participation for the 20th edition.

To decide what category reflects to the best the content of the papers we have used author statements, experimental results evaluation and, as a last resort for a few cases, our judgement. So, while there maybe papers that could have been ascribed to a different category, we believe that the trends we have observed, as it will be described next, will not be affected by our choices.

After including each paper in its category, we have computed the interest and relevance of each category we have adopted. Figures 3 and 4 show the interest and relevance of each category with respect to the total number of FHE papers.

The histogram in Fig. 3 shows that each of the MET and SV categories accounts for more than 30% of the total number of FHE papers, and that together with the *WI/WV* category they include almost 85% of all the FHE papers presented at the 20 editions of the IGS conference. This is, at the same time, a piece of good and bad news. On the good side, the large number of papers addressing the methodological issues show that IGS conferences have been a primary place for the exchange of ideas between forensic experts and scientists coming from the diverse disciplines envisaged by graphonomics to either get support for (or critics on) the foundations and best practice in FHE, or to offer other disciplines challenging issues. On the bad side, they show that disguising writer identification has been only marginally addressed at the conferences. This reflects a general trend in the field. A search on Scopus for the keyword "disguised handwriting" in title, abstract and keyword showed 49 documents, while a similar search for the keyword "writer identification/verification" returned 635 documents.

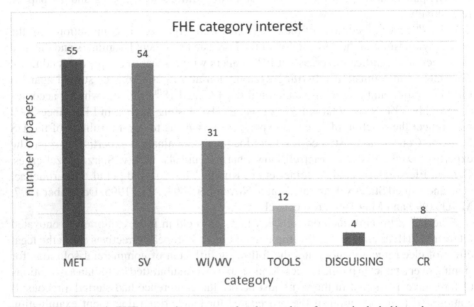

Fig. 3. The interest in FHE categories, measured as the number of papers included in each category presented at all the editions of the IGS conference.

The histogram in Fig. 4 shows that the distribution of the papers included in the MET category resembles very closely that of Fig. 3: roughly speaking, papers addressing methodological issues covers between 25% and 35% of the total number of FHE papers presented at each conference, confirming the observations we made by looking at the interest in the category. It also shows that the relevance of the SV increased a lot at the 11th edition and remained almost constant for the following seven editions. The large increment at the 11th edition was driven by two main factors: the widespread use of tablets, which raised new issues for FHE, and the availability of public datasets of genuine and forged signatures, which make it possible a fair comparison between competing approaches (and forensic experts as well) on a common ground. Eventually, the relevance of the TOOLS category reached its maximum at the 6th and 7th editions, but it has almost disappeared afterward. The main reasons for that could have been the establishment of the International Workshop on Frontiers in Handwriting Recognition, which was deemed more appropriate for presenting handwriting analysis tools by their designer since most of them were computer scientists, and the availability of powerful and versatile tools, such as MovAlyzeR and CEDAR-FOX.

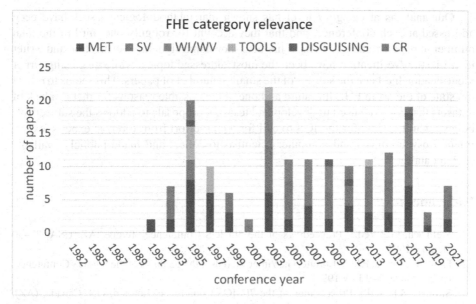

Fig. 4. The relevance of FHE categories, measured as the number of papers included in each category presented at each edition of the IGS conference.

4 Future Trends

In the last years, researchers that regularly attend IGS conferences are mainly interested in investigating how ageing and neurodegenerative disorders affect the planning and generation of handwriting. It is reasonable to expect that at the next IGS conferences FHE papers will focus on methods and experimental works aimed at considering the ageing of the neuromuscular system and the onset of neurodegenerative disorders during the assessment of authorship of a handwritten document.

Moreover, it is worth noting that the transition from handwriting on paper to handwriting on a tablet is still ongoing and both modalities will coexist still for many years. Therefore, we expect that at the next IGS conferences some papers will be focused on device interoperability, i.e. comparing online handwriting samples coming from different tablet devices, and mixed tool investigations, i.e. comparing handwriting samples written on a sheet of paper and on a screen.

5 Conclusions

We presented a quantitative review of the papers addressing the topic of forensic handwriting examination presented at the 20 editions of IGS conferences. At a glance, they show that forensic handwriting examination is a topic that has been addressed since the 5th edition and in each of the following ones. We have also discussed the factors that may have been the main causes of the "waves" of increasing/decreasing interest in the topic.

Our analysis at category level has shown that methodological issues have been addressed at each conference, and that they account for roughly one-third of the total number of papers related to FHE. It has also shown that signature verification and writer identification/verification have been the most addressed topics, while disguising writer identification has been the subject of the smallest number of papers. This seems to reflect the state of the art in FHE literature and one of the possible reasons for that is a lack of datasets that could be used to develop and test new proposals to address the subject. We believe that it is time for the IGS to call for a joint effort from forensic experts, experimental psychologists and computer scientists to collect and made publicly available such a data set.

References

1. Stelmach, G.E. (ed.): Proceedings of the 5th IGS Conference, Tempe, AZ, USA, 27–30 October 1991
2. Faure, C., Keuss, P.J.G., Lorette, G., Vinter, A. (eds.): Proceedings of the 6th IGS Conference, Paris, France, 7–9 July 1993
3. Simner, M.L. (ed.): Proceedings of the 7th IGS Conference, London, ON, Canada, (AZ), 6–10 August 1995
4. Colla, A.M., Masulli, F., Morasso, P. (eds.): Proceedings of the 8th IGS Conference, Genova, Italy, 24–29 August 1997
5. Leedham, C.G., Leung, M., Sagar, V., Xuhong, X. (eds.): Proceedings of the 9th IGS Conference, Singapore, 28–30 June 1999
6. Meulenbroek, R.G.J., Steenberger, B. (eds.): Proceedings of the 10th IGS Conference, Nijmegen, The Netherlands, 6–8 August 2001
7. Teulings, H.-L., Van Gemmert, A.W.A. (eds.): Proceedings of the 11th IGS Conference, Scottsdale, AZ, USA, 2–5 November 2003
8. Marcelli, A., De Stefano, C. (eds.): Proceedings of the 12th IGS Conference, Salerno, Italy, 26–29 June 2005
9. Phillips, J.G., Rogers, D., Ogeil, R.P. (eds.): Proceedings of the 13th IGS Conference, Melbourne, Australia, 27–30 October 2007
10. Vinter, A., Velay, J.-L. (eds.): Proceedings of the 14th IGS Conference, Dijon, France, 13–16 September 2009
11. Grassi, E., Contreras-Vidal, J.L. (eds.): Proceedings of the 15th IGS Conference, Cancun, Mexico, 12–15 June 2011
12. Nakagawa, M., Liwicki, M., Zhu, B. (eds.): Proceedings of the 16th IGS Conference, Nara, Japan, 10–13 June 2013
13. Remi, C., Prevost, L., Anquetil, E. (eds.): Proceedings of the 17th IGS Conference, Guadeloupe, France, 21–25 June 2015
14. De Stefano, C., Marcelli, A. (eds.): Proceedings of the 18th IGS Conference, Gaeta, Italy, 18–21 June 2017
15. 19th IGS Conference, Cancun, Mexico, 9–13 June 2019. https://igs2019-boa.egr.uh.edu/schedule
16. Carmona-Duarte, C., Diaz, M., Ferrer, M.A. (eds.): Proceedings of the 20th IGS Conference, Las Palmas de Gran Canarias, Spain, 6–9 June 2021

Impact of Writing Order Recovery in Automatic Signature Verification

Moises Diaz[1]([⊠]) [iD], Gioele Crispo[2] [iD], Antonio Parziale[3] [iD], Angelo Marcelli[3] [iD], and Miguel A. Ferrer[1] [iD]

[1] Institute IDeTIC, Universidad de Las Palmas de Gran Canaria, Municipality of Las Palmas, Spain
{moises.diaz,miguelangel.ferrer}@ulpgc.es
[2] NTT DATA Italia S.p.A., Via Calindri 4, 20143 Milano, Italy
gioele.crispo@nttdata.com
[3] DIEM, University of Salerno, Via Giovanni Paolo II 132, 84084 Fisciano, SA, Italy
{anparziale,amarcelli}@unisa.it

Abstract. In signature verification, spatio-temporal features offer better performance than the ones extracted from static images. However, estimating spatio-temporal or spatial sequences in static images would be advantageous for recognizers. This paper studies recovered trajectories from skeleton-based images and their impact in automatic signature verification. To this aim, we propose to use a publicly available system for writing order recovery trajectory in offline signatures. Firstly, 8-connected recovered trajectories are generated from our system. Then, we evaluate their impact on the performance of baseline signature verification systems to the original trajectories. Our observations on three databases suggest that verifiers based on distributions are more suitable than those that requiring the exact order of the signatures for the off-2-on challenge.

Keywords: Signature verification · Writing order recovery · Spatial sequences · Function-based features

1 Introduction

The main difference between on-line and off-line signature recognition is the type of the templates. While the on-line signatures include the spatio-temporal information of the executed specimen, off-line ones are static images, which contain the result of an inked pen deposited on a paper. This main characteristic can explain a better performance in automatic systems that use on-line signatures. To this aim, it would be desirable extracting the spatio-temporal features from the off-line signatures.

This extraction has been named *off-2-on* conversion, which consists in developing an on-line counterpart using the image-based signature as seed. In order to measure the performance of an off-2-on conversion, the generated signature should be compared to an original on-line signature as a sort of ground truth.

© Springer Nature Switzerland AG 2022
C. Carmona-Duarte et al. (Eds.): IGS 2021, LNCS 13424, pp. 11–25, 2022.
https://doi.org/10.1007/978-3-031-19745-1_2

Therefore, on-line and off-line signatures acquired simultaneously are necessary for such comparison purposes. Public signature databases, such as the ones used during the SigComp2011 competition [17] or BiosecurID [13], among others, may be helpful for researchers in this task.

The off-2-on idea is not new. There are several contributions and competitions in the field [14]. However, acceptable and competitive results for signature verification systems remain an open issue. Probably, there are some non-solved challenges in the stages involved in the off-2-on procedure [7].

One of the critical aspects is the quality of the images. For example, blur and dust images, low resolution in the sensor, noise in the acquisition, or pattern background make it harder to initiate the procedure. These initial drawbacks directly impact the quality of the final estimated signature.

Next, extracting the skeleton from inked traces is another pivotal role in this procedure. A mistake in this extraction would have a negative impact since losing or adding unreal pixels in the skeleton would modify the shape of the original trajectory [19].

Recovering the order of a traced signature from the skeleton is another crucial stage. This stage will be more demanding when the signature is composed of long flourishes or other aesthetic characteristics, creating ambiguous zones and crosses.

In the context of signature verification, an 8-connected ordered sequence of (x, y) pixels is not considered an on-line signature because of the lack of temporal aspects. Accordingly, another essential stage is estimating temporal features such as velocity or acceleration. Success in this estimation implies a correct sampling of the ordered interpolated trajectory. The kinematic theory of rapid movements would be helpful in this purpose [11]. In any case, as pointed-out in [15], it is challenging to estimate dynamic information from static images.

Regarding the intermediate stages of the writing order recovery, in a previous study of this work, published in [4,8], we designed an automatic system to recover the (x, y) trajectories in signatures. The input of the system is a black and white skeleton of signatures, whereas the output is an estimated 8-connected and ordered (x, y) trajectory. It was evaluated by comparing the real and the recovery trajectories in terms of Root Mean Square Error (RMSE) or the Signal-to-Noise-Ratio (SNR).

This paper aims to assess the impact of the recovering specimens on the verification performances, comparing the performances to real tracings. Note that the output of our approach was neither static nor dynamic features but spatial sequences. As such, we work out the performance of on-line verifiers that use these (x, y) 8-connected sequences. Instead of using original spatio-temporal features, these verifiers will use the spatial sequences estimated by our writing recovery system [4,8] as input.

As a baseline, the same experiments will be repeated with the real spatial sequences drawn by the signer. Our goal is to compare the performances in both cases. The closeness of the performance is another additional metric to evaluate the writing order recovered system and its impact on signature recognition.

Note that we are not interested in beating the state-of-the-art performances by this work. We notice that our spatial sequences, (x, y), are not as powerful as real spatio-temporal ones used in on-line verifiers. Instead, we aim to quantify the impact of the trace errors. To this end, we compute the similarity between the performance with real and our recovered signatures under the same experimental conditions.

The rest of the paper is organized as follows: Sect. 2 briefly describes the used method to recover the order of the signatures. Then, Sect. 3 is devoted to the experimental setup with verifiers that use spatio-temporal sequences as features, whereas Sect. 4 shows the study results. Finally, the article is concluded in Sect. 5.

2   Proposed System to Recover Signature Trajectories

In this section, we briefly review our system to estimate the writing order recovery of signatures [4,8]. Also, we describe the used performance metrics to compute the quality of the recovered spatial sequences.

2.1   Reconstruction Quality Evaluation

To evaluate the reconstruction quality of the writing order, the estimated trace is compared to the real one in the 8-connected space. The online data of the specimen is interpolated to generate an 8-connected trajectory with the Bresenham line drawing algorithm [3]. The metrics used are the Root Mean Square Error (RMSE) and the Signal-to Noise-Ratio (SNR), defined as follows:

$$
\text{RMSE} = \sqrt{\frac{1}{n}\left(\sum_{i=1}^{n}(x_i - \widehat{x}_i)^2 + \sum_{i=1}^{n}(y_i - \widehat{y}_i)^2\right)}
\tag{1}
$$

$$
\text{SNR} = 10\log\left(\frac{\sum_{i=1}^{n}\left((x_i - \overline{x}_i)^2 + (y_i - \overline{y}_i)^2\right)}{\sum_{i=1}^{n}\left((x_i - \widehat{x}_i)^2 + (y_i - \widehat{y}_i)^2\right)}\right)
\tag{2}
$$

where (x, y) and $(\widehat{x}, \widehat{y})$ are the points belonging to the real and recovered trajectories, respectively.

2.2   Recover Trajectories Algorithm

The algorithm is composed of three stages. It first scans the image to find the fundamental signature points, such as isolated ones and agglomeration of pixels, also known as *clusters*. This phase is called *Point Classification*. Subsequently, the *Local Examination* stage performs a local analysis to classify the clusters and understand the direction of tracing. The clusters are generated in correspondence of intertwined writing strokes. Therefore, correctly estimating the tracing direction of the clusters allows to isolate the writing strokes, also called pen-downs or *writing components*. Finally, the *Global Reconstruction* phase combines the information computed in the previous phase to reconstruct the writing order. One of the most critical challenges of this step is identifying the order of the writing components; this requires that the clusters are classified accurately and the components are isolated correctly.

Algorithm 1 shows how to process an 8-connected thin line representation of a handwriting image. The algorithm uses two inputs: an image path of the skeletonized signature and a binary flag. Such a flag is used to visualize the estimated 8-connected trajectory order over the input signature. The procedure uses some configuration parameters to perfom heuristic-based geometric evaluations. The thresholds and parameters are fixed as in [8]. The outputs are the estimated (x, y) trajectory and additional information such as the location of end points, among others. This information is contained in the *wor_results* variable. In the function, M denotes the matrix of pixels, which are labeled through the adjacent pixels number and C the clusters.

Algorithm 1. Main stages of the writing order recovery algorithm

---

1: **function** WOR($imagepath, flag_v$)
2:     $opt \leftarrow$ configuration()   ▷ Thresholds were fixed in [8]
3:     $data \leftarrow$ loadData($imagepath, opt$)
4:     $[M, C] \leftarrow$ pointClassification($data, opt$)
5:     $[M, C] \leftarrow$ localExamination(M, C, opt)
6:     $[x, y, wor\_results] \leftarrow$ globalReconstruction($M, C, data, opt$)
7:     **if** $flag_v$ **then**
8:         visualization($x, y, data$)
9:     **return** $[x, y, wor\_results]$

To determine whether the written order is estimated correctly, the estimated trace is compared to the online one, containing details of how real signers wrote the trajectory. A visual demonstration is shown in Fig. 1.

It can be seen that the components[1] are isolated correctly through the end points detection. Thus, the reconstructed order follows the real one for the first two components (a), (b), (e); the clusters and their output branches are correctly associated (c), (d). The reconstruction metrics, SNR and RMSE, remain good until the faulty component is chosen (f). From this point, the values start to drop, and the reconstruction error is propagated to the end of trace (g), (h).

Although the correct association of branches in clusters is the first step, the choice of the component plays an essential role in the reconstruction. Furthermore, few errors can lead to an overall error in estimating the order of the trajectory.

---

[1] By component, we mean a piece of a continuous trajectory without lifting the pen. It is also known as pen-downs or surface trajectories on the literature.

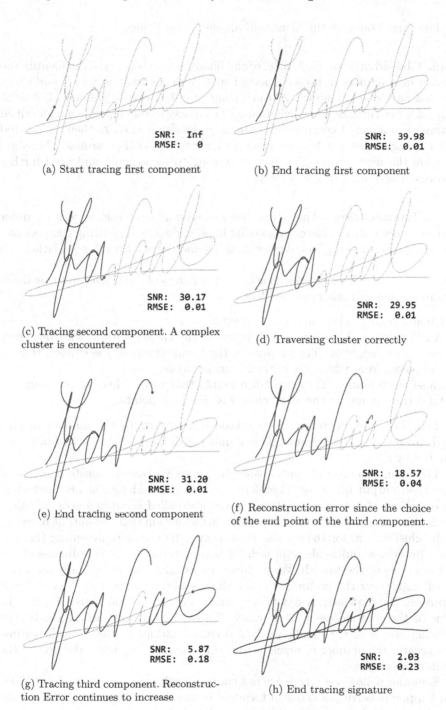

(a) Start tracing first component

(b) End tracing first component

(c) Tracing second component. A complex cluster is encountered

(d) Traversing cluster correctly

(e) End tracing second component

(f) Reconstruction error since the choice of the end point of the third component.

(g) Tracing third component. Reconstruction Error continues to increase

(h) End tracing signature

Fig. 1. Tracing of a signature, made up of 4 components and different clusters, after the recovery of the trajectory.

The three stages of the algorithm are described below.

Point Classification. Each pixel of the binary image is analyzed to identify the number of neighbors in its 8-connected space and is classified as: (1) *end point*, if it has only one neighbor; (2) *trace point*, if it has two neighbors; (3) *branch point*, if it has three or more neighbors. The adjacent branch points are identified through a connected components searching algorithm and are then aggregated under a single cluster. Clusters represent intertwined writing strokes. Therefore, they are the most challenging part of writing to reconstruct and need further analysis, described in the next step.

Local Examination. This stage plays a fundamental role in writing order recovery since correct cluster processing implies identifying writing components. It is composed of two parts: cluster analysis and output branch association.

Cluster Analysis. First, a classification of the points of the cluster must be done. Different types of points can be identified:

- Cluster points. They are branch points.
- Anchor points. They are branch points of the cluster with at least one trace point as a neighbor. They represent the terminations of the cluster, that is, the points from which the output branches arise.
- False trace points. They are trace points that have other cluster points or false trace points of the same cluster as adjacent points.

Therefore, the clusters can be classified according to the number of output branches or anchor points. This number is defined as the cluster rank and denoted by r.

The main objective of this classification is to analyze the clusters and associate their output branches. Therefore, geometric considerations are made, and the directions of the branches of the cluster, also called *external angles* are calculated. With branch directions, we define the inclination that the output branches of the cluster form for the x axis. To calculate the vector representing the outgoing branch, a multiscale approach [5] is used through the coordinates of the first n points of the branch. We perform the `atan2d` operation to obtain a vector of angles over the vector of the coordinates obtained through the multiscale approach. Subsequently, a `circular mean` is carried out on it to compute the value of the external angle of a branch. This value indicates where the branch is facing and is used to make analytical considerations for the branch pairing. The greater the number of pixels n used and the scale to obtain the vector, the greater the precision.

Sometimes, however, there are not enough pixels on the output branch. This can happen in correspondence of terminal branches or when the image does not have a very high resolution. The *internal angles* are another good indicator, which allows overcoming the lack of precision of the external angles. We need to define the cluster center of gravity to compute internal angles. It is defined as the arithmetic mean of the anchor points coordinates. Internal angles are computed through a circular mean of the difference of the first n points of the branch from the center of gravity.

Another great indicator is the curvature of the output branches of a cluster, taken two by two. To calculate the curvature, the circular mean of the coordinates of the previous s and subsequent t points is calculated for each point of the curve. The set of values obtained in this way is used to compute the curvature value by making arithmetic mean. This approach is sufficient to represent the curvature since the considered curves are composed of few pixels. The curvature is a value that goes from $0°$, when the curve is straight, to 180, when it is folded back on itself.

Output Branch Association. To associate the output branches of a cluster, we rely on rules based on the criteria of good continuity derived from Gestalt theory and the principle of energy minimization. The Gestalt theory [1] states that all elements of sensory input are perceived as belonging to a coherent and continuous whole. The principle of energy minimization is supported by the studies of motor control theory [18] and is particularly suitable in the case of fluid and rapid movements, such as writing. From an analytical point of view, the idea is to associate a pair of (i, j) branches that best satisfy the following conditions: (1) their external, (α_i, α_j), and internal, (β_i, β_j), angles with respect to the x axis have a difference close to $180°$; (2) their curvature value, $c_{i,j}$, is close to 0. This corresponds to affirm that the more the two branches form a straight, continuous curve, without interruptions or sudden changes of direction, the more suitable it is to be taken into consideration to associate the two output branches that form it. Although conceptually, the two conditions are very similar, it is often necessary to combine the three measures to obviate noise and imperfections related to image resolution and thus stabilize the result. To this aim, these conditions are averaged with three weights, $(\omega_{ext}, \omega_{int}, \omega_{cur})$, already defined in [8]. Thus, we define the weighted angle direction, $\pi_{i,j}$, as follows:

$$\pi_{i,j} = \omega_{ext} \cdot |\alpha_i - \alpha_j| + \omega_{int} \cdot |\beta_i - \beta_j| + \omega_{cur} \cdot c_{i,j} \tag{3}$$

It is worth highlighting that we iteratively choose the smallest $\pi_{i,j}$ for final paring branches.

However, some considerations must be made on the rank of a cluster: managing clusters of even rank, being the associations made two by two, is not very complex. Those of odd rank higher than three can be treated in the following way: the output branches are associated in pairs until there are three remainings. The remaining branches constitute a new 3-rank cluster. A rank equal to 3 is the most challenging cluster to manage. It represents different write situations and therefore deserves additional classification. We have identified 4 cases:

- **T-pattern:** they are clusters whose shape is very similar to a "T". The writer forms this pattern with two separate strokes. The condition for determining whether a 3-rank cluster is a T-pattern is that one of the internal angles β is approximately $180°$, and the other two, are approximately $90°$. The branch perpendicular to the head of the "T" is isolated and treated as a terminal stroke, while the other two are associated as a continuous line.

– **Retraced:** Appears in correspondence to closed handwritten loops. The writer passes through a branch of the cluster, stops the pen at an output branch, and then retraces that branch to proceed on the opposite side. Therefore, the condition for identifying this type of cluster is that there is an end point as the termination of an output branch of a 3-rank cluster. The retraced branch is associated with one branch and once with the other.

– **Coupled:** They are 3-rank clusters that do not satisfy the conditions of the two classes described above. To be classified as such, two clusters must share an output branch, and the other branches must respect the criteria of good continuity. If verified, they are associated as you would for a 4-rank cluster.

– **Normal:** 3-rank clusters that do not meet any of the conditions discussed are treated independently, and the following rule is applied: the two branches that best match according to the association rules described above are paired; the other branch is isolated and treated as a terminal stroke.

A complete overview of the cluster types and their classification is shown in Fig. 2. It is worth pointing out that 3-rank clusters must be treated last and that whenever a branch is "detached" from a cluster, it is necessary to reanalyze the clusters, since that terminal branch could be a retracing trait for some other cluster. Therefore, the procedure we implement is the following: first, the clusters of even rank are analyzed, and their output branches are associated, then the clusters of odd rank higher than three are treated, associating the branches that best respect the criteria of good continuity and isolating the remaining 3-rank clusters. Finally, rank 3 clusters are analyzed and classified until no branches are detached from a cluster. This allows being more precise in identifying the components. Indeed, their identification depends significantly on the correct classification and management of the 3-rank clusters, which hide closed loops and overlapping traits made by the writer.

Global Reconstruction. Once the clusters have been classified and associated with their output branches, it is possible to reconstruct the entire trajectory. To this end, it is first necessary to define how to traverse the cluster given its output branches. Then, we determine how to choose the starting points of each component to be traced and their order.

Traversing Clusters. Assuming that a cluster is composed of p pixels, it is possible to define an adjacency matrix A, of dimensions $p \times p$, which represents the positions of the pixels in the cluster and the interconnections between them. The idea is to calculate the minimum path; the adjacency matrix A is processed by the Dijkstra [10] algorithm. We have given greater weight to the oblique connections always to prefer, if possible, the more linear ones, even at the local level. This choice is in line with the principles of energy minimization, the theories of Gestalt and rapid movements, and thus respect the criteria of good continuity.

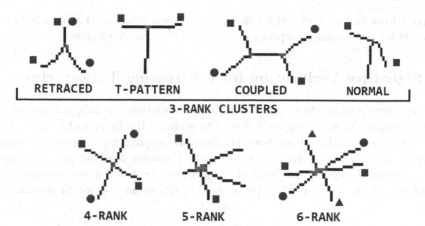

Fig. 2. Clusters of different ranks. Dark Red points are anchor points; gray are cluster ones. The geometric shapes, squares, circles, and triangles, show how the branches are paired. Those left without markers are detached branches. In the 5-rank cluster, the unpaired branches form a new cluster of rank 3, which requires further processing. (Color figure online)

Choosing First Component. To choose the first component to trace, we collected all the starting points coordinates of the signatures databases. Then, we used them to model, in two dimensions, a Gaussian function that would indicate a more occurrent starting point.

The Gaussian function generates an ellipse of size equal to the mean and the two standard deviations. It is experimentally located in the upper left part of the images, particularly at 0.15 w and 0.35 h, with h and w being the height and the width of the image. If there are no end points inside the ellipse, the leftmost end point is selected as the starting point. It is typically the most common area in western handwriting.

Next Component Selection. Once the first component has been recovered, the following ones are chosen through a proximity criterion: the starting point of the closest component not yet traced is chosen in terms of Euclidean distance. The choice reflects the principle of energy minimization.

Our previous work results indicated that adopting the Dijkstra algorithm for choosing a path inside a cluster is a good approximation. Nevertheless, sometimes a few pixels remain outside the tracing, and thus there is a slight deviation on the SNR and RMSE values.

Furthermore, the results indicated that choosing the component looking at the Euclidean distance from the last plotted point is not the best choice. This can be explained by assuming that a writer learns and memorizes the execution of a writing stroke independently of the others. Therefore, there is room to improve this decision, which was initially based on heuristic observations. Finally, the interested reader can find further details of this algorithm in [4,8] and download the code for researching purposes at www.github.com/gioelecrispo/wor.

3   Signature Verification for the Tracing Trajectories

The recovered 8-connected trajectories (x, y) are used as the unique input feature in two verifiers. This strategy is followed to evaluate the impact of recovered trajectories. These verifiers have been traditionally applied to dynamic signatures. However, the output of the recovering writing system does not offer estimated spatio-temporal signatures. Instead, it provides an 8-connected sequence per signature, which is expected to be ordered in the same way as the original signatures.

3.1   Databases

Three publicly on-line signature databases are used in this work. They are briefly described as follows:

- SigComp2009 [2]. It includes 1552 on-line specimens in the Western script. In average terms, each of 79 users gave 12 genuine signatures. Also, the database contains 620 skilled forgeries in total, but not available for all users.
- The SUSIG-Visual [16] corpus has 94 users with 20 genuine signatures acquired in two sessions. They also included 10 fake signatures per writer.
- SVC-Task2 [23]. This database contains signatures produced in Oriental and Western scripts. There are 40 subjects with 20 genuine and 20 skilled forgeries per signer.

We generated binary images from these on-line signatures. To this aim, we used Bresenham's line drawing algorithm [3], which draws skeletons set up to 600 dpi of resolution. It is worth pointing out that any further processing [20] is applied to the on-line signatures for our purposes.

The chosen databases contain long and complex signatures. In the context of this paper, it means that they have many ambiguous zones and crosses [9], which make harder the writing order estimation. However, our previous research confirmed that the writing order estimation was satisfactorily measured [4,8].

3.2   Signature Verifiers

We have selected two automatic signature verifiers (ASVs) for our experiments. To this end, we quantify the extent to which the traced trajectory looks like the real one in on-line ASVs. Specifically, we compare the performance of real 8-connected signatures and signatures recovered to our system [4,8]. These two state-of-the-art on-line ASVs consider the (x, y) trajectories as function-based features. They are described as follows:

- Dynamic Time Warping (DTW): The trajectories of enrolled signatures and questioned signatures are compared using the DTW algorithm by optimizing the Euclidean distance of the (x, y) trajectories [12]. The nearest distance normalized by both the warping path and the average DTW of the enrolled signature is used as the score.
- Manhattan Distance-Based (MAN): The features of this ASV include histograms of absolute and relative frequencies [21]. The comparison between an enrolled and a questioned signature is performed in terms of Manhattan distance. We used our implementation of this system, which was introduced in [7].

On average, the 8-connected (x, y) sequences, which were generated by our system, have around 5200 ± 2500 points. As this means the sequences are too long, we speed up the verification process by a uniform resampling. For this purpose, we take one out of fifteen points. As the data downsampling was applied after estimating the trajectories, this stage does not influence the verification rates. It is worth raising that this resampling does not create on-line specimens with realistic velocity or acceleration. This goal would require a more complex resampling of an 8-connected trajectory [11], which is not approached in this work.

3.3   Evaluation Protocol

We follow a standard benchmark for signature verification proposed in [23], which has continued to be applied over the years in the latest competitions [6, 22]. For the training, Tr random genuine signatures are used. Next, we use the remaining genuine signatures to test and compute the False Rejection Rate (FRR) curve. Then, we carry out two typical experiments in signature verification: random forgery (RF) and skilled forgeries (SF) [6]. In the case of RF, we use the first testing signature drawn by all the other users to design the False Acceptance Rate (FAR) curve. In the case of SF, all skilled forgeries signatures of a signer are used to build the FAR curve. Then, the performance of the ASV is measured based on the Equal Error Rate (EER), which represents the operative point when the FRR and FAR errors coincide. Finally, all experiments are repeated ten times, and the final performance is averaged.

4   Experimental Results

The objective of this paper was not to highlight the utility of spatio-temporal information in signature verification. Instead, we study and compare how our recovered trajectories impact the performance of two common ASVs [6].

Figure 3 shows the results in a 3-by-3 grid. The first column gives the performance of the SigComp2009 corpus using three, five, or seven signatures per user to train. The second and third columns depict the results for the SUSIG-Visual and SVC-Task2 databases. Each bar plot represents four pairs of performances in

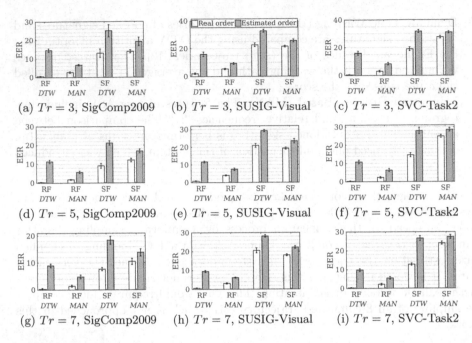

Fig. 3. Signature verification results with two automatic signature verifiers (MAN) and (DTW) for random forgeries (RF) and skilled forgeries (SF). Tr denotes the number of genuine signatures to train per user.

terms of EER regarding the two ASVs and the RF and SF experiments. We see the performance with real (x, y) order in white color, whereas gray bars show the performance with estimated order. All bars include the error bars, which represent the standard deviation of the EER after the ten repetitions in each case.

We can see in Fig. 3 that although the performances obtained with estimated trajectories are not equal to those from real ones, in all cases, our system can mimic the EER tendency. Moreover, we also observe coherent results with all estimated trajectories since the greater the number of training signatures, the better the results. Besides, better performances have been achieved in RF, which is logical since the difficulty of verifying this kind of questioned signature is not as high as in SF.

For RF, we observe that in the SVC-Task2 dataset, the EER with traced signatures is quite close to real ones. However, the most significant differences can be seen in SigComp2009. One reason is that the signatures in the latter database have more complex and lengthy pen-downs. In SF, the EER of the MAN system is reduced by three points versus the real one for the SVC-Task2, by four points for SUSIG-Visual, and by five points for SigComp2009. Generally, these observations are independent of the values of Tr.

The DTW system seems to be more sensitive to the estimated trajectories than the MAN one regarding the ASV used. The main reason is that the DTW processes the sequence following the sequence point order. Mistakes in the order are propagated along with the whole data points in the sequences. Accordingly, while the DTW is an optimal option in signature verification, this distance measure penalizes the tracing order mistakes more than the differences usually observed among trajectories executed by the same subject.

One weak point of our system is choosing the next component to recover. It can be seen in the DTW signature verifier, which penalizes these kinds of mistakes since it evaluates the sequence of features.

On the other hand, we observed that the MAN system did not perform well with the real order. This may be expected since this is not the most robust distance measure to be used for signature verification, despite competitive results found in the prior literature [21]. However, the MAN system focused more on the distribution of derivative input sequences. Probably, this property compensates for the errors produced in the estimated trajectory order. In the words of our previous work [7], this system tries to mitigate the order selection of components and the assignation of the start and end points. However, the classifier does not solve errors in the branches when the trace is recovered.

As a result, we can observe similar performance with real and recovery signatures when the MAN system is used as a verifier. For this reason, the MAN system seems to be a better option for the recovered trajectories. More investigation on systems that observe the derivative properties rather than the strict order to trace the signature is a better option for the off-2-on signature verification challenge.

5   Conclusions

This paper studies the performance of the writing order recovery process in signature verification. A recent writing order recovery system is used to get (x, y) 8-connected sequences, which estimates the order in which a signature was executed. The generated trajectories are used as spatial function features in two on-line automatic signature verifiers. Results are compared to original trajectories under the same conditions. We know that the obtained performances are not so attractive to use this system in a final application. However, our purpose is to study the impact of these trajectories on ASV. The impact of our experiments suggests that ASVs based on histograms of the features are more suitable, like the Manhattan-based one. However, this kind of system does not dramatically penalize errors in choosing the starting points of the non-traced components.

Regarding the off-2-on signature verification challenge, more investigation in ASVs based on the distribution of the features seems to be more suitable, according to the observations of this paper.

We plan to resample these trajectories in our future works using the kinematic theory of rapid movement. It would imply a more realistic scenario regarding this study. Indeed, new insights would be analyzed for this off-2-on problem. However, the findings observed here suggest that the MAN-based verifier is more suitable for the use of estimated trajectories. Furthermore, this ASV reported closer performances comparing our estimated trajectories with real ones. Towards replicability research, we expect that the research community use our algorithm[2] for further benchmarks in the off-2-on challenge.

References

1. Allport, F.H.: Theories of Perception and the Concept of Structure: A Review and Critical Analysis with an Introduction to a Dynamic-Structural Theory of Behavior. Wiley (1955). https://doi.org/10.1037/11116-000
2. Blankers, V.L., et al.: ICDAR 2009 signature verification competition. In: 10th International Conference on Document Analysis and Recognition, pp. 1403–1407. IEEE (2009). https://doi.org/10.1109/ICDAR.2009.216
3. Bresenham, J.E.: Algorithm for computer control of a digital plotter. IBM Syst. J. **4**(1), 25–30 (1965). https://doi.org/10.1147/sj.41.0025
4. Crispo, G., Diaz, M., Marcelli, A., Ferrer, M.A.: Tracking the ballistic trajectory in complex and long handwritten signatures. In: 16th International Conference on Frontiers in Handwriting Recognition, pp. 351–356 (2018). https://doi.org/10.1109/ICFHR-2018.2018.00068
5. De Stefano, C., Garruto, M., Marcelli, A.: A saliency-based multiscale method for on-line cursive handwriting shape description. Int. J. Pattern Recogn. Artif. Intell. **18**(6), 1139–1156 (2004). ISSN: 0218-0014
6. Diaz, M., Ferrer, M.A., Impedovo, D., Malik, M.I., Pirlo, G., Plamondon, R.: A perspective analysis of handwritten signature technology. ACM Comput. Surv. (CSUR) **51**(6), 1–39 (2019). https://doi.org/10.1145/3274658
7. Diaz, M., Ferrer, M.A., Parziale, A., Marcelli, A.: Recovering western on-line signatures from image-based specimens. In: 2017 14th IAPR International Conference on Document Analysis and Recognition (ICDAR), pp. 1204–1209. IEEE (2017). https://doi.org/10.1109/ICDAR.2017.199
8. Diaz Cabrera, M., Crispo, G., Parziale, A., Marcelli, A., Ferrer Ballester, M.A.: Writing order recovery in complex and long static handwriting. Int. J. Interact. Multimed. Artif. Intell. (2022). In press
9. Diaz-Cabrera, M., Ferrer, M.A., Morales, A.: Modeling the lexical morphology of western handwritten signatures. PLoS ONE **10**(4), 1–22 (2015). https://doi.org/10.1371/journal.pone.0123254
10. Dijkstra, E.W.: A note on two problems in connexion with graphs. Numer. Math. **1**(1), 269–271 (1959). https://doi.org/10.1007/BF01386390
11. Ferrer, M.A., Diaz, M., Carmona-Duarte, C., Plamondon, R.: Generating off-line and on-line forgeries from on-line genuine signatures. In: 2019 International Carnahan Conference on Security Technology (ICCST), pp. 1–6. IEEE (2019)
12. Fischer, A., Diaz, M., Plamondon, R., Ferrer, M.A.: Robust score normalization for DTW-based on-line signature verification. In: 2015 13th International Conference on Document Analysis and Recognition (ICDAR), pp. 241–245. IEEE (2015). https://doi.org/10.1109/ICDAR.2015.7333760

---

[2] Our algorithm is freely available for research purposes at www.github.com/gioelecrispo/wor.

13. Galbally, J., et al.: On-line signature recognition through the combination of real dynamic data and synthetically generated static data. Pattern Recogn. **48**(9), 2921–2934 (2015)
14. Hassaine, A., Al Maadeed, S., Bouridane, A.: ICDAR 2013 competition on handwriting stroke recovery from offline data. In: Proceedings of the International Conference on Document Analysis and Recognition, ICDAR (2013). https://doi.org/10.1109/ICDAR.2013.285
15. Justino, E.J., El Yacoubi, A., Bortolozzi, F., Sabourin, R.: An off-line signature verification system using HMM and graphometric features. In: Proceedings of the 4th International Workshop on Document Analysis Systems, pp. 211–222. Citeseer (2000)
16. Kholmatov, A., Yanikoglu, B.: SUSIG: an on-line signature database, associated protocols and benchmark results. Pattern Anal. Appl. **12**(3), 227–236 (2009). https://doi.org/10.1007/s10044-008-0118-x
17. Liwicki, M., et al.: Signature verification competition for online and offline skilled forgeries (SigComp2011). In: 2011 International Conference on Document Analysis and Recognition, pp. 1480–1484 (2011). https://doi.org/10.1109/ICDAR.2011.294
18. Marcelli, A., Parziale, A., Senatore, R.: Some observations on handwriting from a motor learning perspective. In: 2nd International Workshop on Automated Forensic Handwriting Analysis, pp. 6–10 (2013)
19. Nguyen, V., Blumenstein, M.: Techniques for static handwriting trajectory recovery: a survey. In: Proceedings of the 9th IAPR International Workshop on Document Analysis Systems, pp. 463–470. ACM (2010). https://doi.org/10.1145/1815330.1815390
20. Qiao, Y., Nishiara, M., Yasuhara, M.: A framework toward restoration of writing order from single-stroked handwriting image. IEEE Trans. Pattern Anal. Mach. Intell. **28**(11), 1724–1737 (2006). https://doi.org/10.1109/TPAMI.2006.216
21. Sae-Bae, N., Memon, N.: Online signature verification on mobile devices. IEEE Trans. Inf. Forensics Secur. **9**(6), 933–947 (2014). https://doi.org/10.1109/TIFS.2014.2316472
22. Tolosana, R., et al.: SVC-onGoing: signature verification competition. Pattern Recogn. **127**, 108609 (2022). https://doi.org/10.1016/j.patcog.2022.108609
23. Yeung, D.-Y., et al.: SVC2004: first international signature verification competition. In: Zhang, D., Jain, A.K. (eds.) ICBA 2004. LNCS, vol. 3072, pp. 16–22. Springer, Heidelberg (2004). https://doi.org/10.1007/978-3-540-25948-0_3

Spiral Based Run-Length Features for Offline Signature Verification

Walid Bouamra[1,2(✉)], Moises Diaz[2], Miguel Angel Ferrer[2], and Brahim Nini[1]

[1] Larbi ben M'hidi University, Oum El Bouaghi, Algeria
{walid.bouamra,b.nini}@univ-oeb.dz
[2] Institute IDeTIC, Universidad de Las Palmas de Gran Canaria, Las Palmas, Spain
Walid.bouamra101@alu.ulpgc.es, {moises.diaz,
miguelangel.ferrer}@ulpgc.es

Abstract. Automatic signature verification is one of the main modes to verify the identity of the individuals. Among the strategies to describe the signature in the verifiers, run-length features have attracted the attention of many researchers. This work aims to upgrade the classical run-length distribution as an additional representation for off-line signatures. Specifically, we add a fifth direction to the four classical directions of run-length features. Such fifth direction runs the signature in a spiral way providing an outside to inside view of the signature. This paper evaluates the performance of the new run-length direction combined with the classical ones. For classification purposes, we used a one-class support vector machine. Additionally, we study how to combine the new direction with the previous four original ones at both feature and score levels. Our results validate the use of this novel direction in run-length features in our own experiments and external international competition in signature verification.

Keywords: Spiral run-length features · Four-directions run-length features · Offline signature verification · OC-SVM · Feature fusion · Score fusion · Signature verification competition

1 Introduction

Biometrics has become more and more an important need for automatically verifying individuals and evenly for the security of enterprises. Nowadays, among the different modalities of biometrics, the signature remains a very confident, lawfully, and socially accepted modality for verifying identities [1].

To design an Automatic Signature Verifier (ASV), the literature proposes to use two approaches: Writer-Dependent and Writer-Independent [1]. In the first approach, the samples of each individual are trained by a classifier separately from others, whereas in the Writer-Independent approach, only one classifier is used to train all the writers' signatures. In both cases, the aim is to verify whether a questioned signature is genuine or forgery.

Since the texture remains one of the main discriminant characteristics to extract useful information from the images, many ASV systems are based on textural features

C. Carmona-Duarte et al. (Eds.): IGS 2021, LNCS 13424, pp. 26–41, 2022.
https://doi.org/10.1007/978-3-031-19745-1_3

for the signature image analysis and pattern recognition process. In our work, we propose to use a novel handcrafted feature for off-line signature verification based on both textural properties and run-length distributions.

The run-length features have been a favored method in several fields of image processing. They present one of the used features for image classification [2, 3], writer identification [4], and in our case, for offline signature verification. In the latter domain, they give a powerful spatial presentation of pixels, and under the concept of runs [2]. Typically, such spatial distribution is achieved by counting the runs in four directions: horizontal, vertical, and two diagonal directions.

However, a major problem is the well-known high intra-class variability of a user signature. It could be mainly due to changes in shape, size, or other visual aspects, which causes a spatial distribution distortion within the image signature of a user. All this limits the classic run-length features performance.

The main contribution of this paper is the definition of a new direction in the framework of run-length features. This new direction is named spiral direction, which adds a new representation of the image. Moreover, we combine this new direction to the classical four directions to improve the representation of the run-length features. Our work aims to study the efficiency of run-length features when adding the spiral direction for off-line ASV.

It is expected that this new direction will expand the run-length limitations due to its flexibility within the orientation and the size of the scanned lines, which raises its robustness regarding the intra-class variability, and compensates the static of each direction of the run-length features, that traverses the image line by line in only one given direction.

The paper is organized as follows: Sect. 2 includes some related works on run-length features in off-line signature verification. Section 3 defines the previous run-length features whereas the proposed spiral run-length feature is given in Sect. 4. Section 5 is devoted to the experiments and results. We close the paper by the conclusion in Sect. 6.

2   Related Works on Run-Length Features

Many techniques have been used for image texture analysis in signature verification [1, 2]. Run-length features are one of the textural descriptors basing on the lengths of runs. A run can be explained as a set of consecutive pixels in a given direction having the same value [3]. The length of the run is the number of pixels composing this run.

As a consequence, we work out the run-length histograms, which are composed of the numbers of runs of different lengths. This process is generalized for the four principal directions, Horizontal (0°), Vertical (90°), right-diagonal (45°) and left diagonal (135°). As a result, it gives four feature vectors comprising the four directions.

In 1975, Galloway [3] applied the run-length features to a set of textures representing nine terrain types, each one with six samples. He arranged two adjustments on the run-length technique to obtain numerical texture measures: the first one was based on all diagonal run lengths should be multiplied by $\sqrt{2}$, while the second one was the short-run emphasis function. The classification results were quite promising.

The use of run-length features has been spread frequently in the field of texture analysis. Further, they have been adopted for purposes related to handwriting, such as writing or writer identification and verification and, more specifically, the verification of off-line handwritten signatures.

Djeddi et al. [5] applied the run-length and the 2D autoregressive coefficient features in signature verification. They used 521 writers from the GPDS960 dataset and the Support Vector Machine as the classifier. They performed the run-length on black pixels which correspond to the ink trace of the signatures and considered only runs of a maximum of 100 pixels for each direction (0°, 45°, 90°, 135°). A final vector of 400 values was obtained as a feature vector of 100 values per direction.

Serdouk et al. [6] proposed a combination of two data features, the orthogonal combination of local binary patterns and the Longest Run Features (LRF). The LRF calculated the connected pixels through the four principal directions: horizontal, vertical, right diagonal and left diagonal. For each direction, the longest run of the signature pixels was selected, the total sum of these numbers (lengths) constituted the LRF value in the given direction. This procedure was repeated for the remaining directions in order to get four LRF features. Finally, the four LRF features were combined with the other features to define each image-based signature. The proposed features were employed on GPDS300 and CEDAR databases, using SVM classifiers for the automatic verification task.

In Bouamra et al. [2], a new off-line ASV was designed by using run-length features. They were applied to black and white pixels, which corresponded to the signature and the background, respectively. The four run-length vectors for each color contained 400 values and the black and white output feature vector had, therefore, 800 values. They used only genuine signatures for training and employing the 881 writers of the GPDS960 (281 users for generating signature models and choosing optimal threshold, and 600 for the evaluation step). The One-Class Support Vector Machine (OC-SVM) was used for the classification phase. Some standard metrics were used to quantify the performance of the system, obtaining competitive performances.

In another work related to the prior one, Bouamra et al. [8] implemented multidirectional run-length features for automatic signature verification. The new features were based on the standard run-length features [2], with four supplementary angles added to the four primary directions: horizontal, vertical, left-diagonal, and right-diagonal direction; each angle is enhanced by its neighborhood to generate a composite one formed by three adjacent angles. Finally, eight composite angles are obtained as explicit orientations for scanning the signature image. The researchers employed the OC-SVM as a classifier to apply their features on the GPDS960 database.

The run-length features were also used on off-line ASV by Ghanim and Nabil [7]. In their study, they used different features including run-length, slant distribution, entropy, the histogram of gradient features and geometric features. Then, they applied machine learning techniques on the computed features like bagging trees, rand forest and support vector machines. The study aimed to calculate the accuracy of different approaches and to design an accurate system for signature verification and forgery detection. The Persian Offline Signature Data-set was utilized for evaluating the system, and the obtained results were satisfactory.

3   Classical Run-Length Features

Let be assumed a binarized image-based signature, in run-length histograms, $RL_b(i|\theta)$ is the (i)th element describing the number of runs with black values and length i, occurring in the image along an angle θ. Thus, $RL_w(j|\theta)$ is the (j)th element describing the number of runs with white value and length j occur in the image along angle θ.

Let's indicate the following notations:

- RL_b is the number of black run lengths in the image.
- RL_w is the number of white runs lengths in the image.
- N_B is the black run-length histograms for the four directions.
- N_W is the white run-length histograms for four directions.
- RL_4D is the Global black and white Run-Length histograms for four directions.

The black and white run-length histograms are defined, respectively, as:

$$RL_b(\theta) = \sum_{i=1}^{RL_b} N_b(i|\theta) \tag{1}$$

$$RL_w(\theta) = \sum_{j=1}^{RL_w} N_w(j|\theta) \tag{2}$$

$$\forall\ 1 \le i \le N_b\ and\ 1 \le j \le N_w.$$

The black and white run-length histograms for a given direction are concatenated as

$$RL(\theta) - [RL_b(\theta), RL_w(\theta)] \tag{3}$$

According to the pixel color, the black and white run-length histograms for the four directions are processed as:

$$RL_B = \left[RL_b(0°), RL_b(45°), RL_b(90°), RL_b(135°)\right] \tag{4}$$

$$RL_W = \left[RL_w(0°), RL_w(45°), RL_w(90°), RL_w(135°)\right] \tag{5}$$

where the final feature vector based on run-length histograms are concatenated as [2]:

$$RL_{4D} = [RL_B, RL_W] = [RL_b(0°), RL_b(45°), RL_b(90°), RL_b(135°), RL_w(0°), \atop RL_w(45°), RL_w(90°), RL_w(135°)] \tag{6}$$

In our work, we vectorized the 2D image to get a single long line. At this level, the run-lengths are calculated for both black and white pixels. This procedure is applied to the other three directions, i.e. vertical, right-diagonal and left-diagonal. In another meaning, before calculating the lengths of runs, we juxtaposed the lines of the image in the desired direction, line by line in a way to form a single vector that denotes a new different presentation of the image. On this vector, we apply the same algorithm to calculate the Run-Length distributions for this given direction, and so for the other directions.

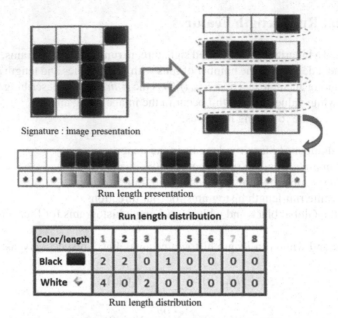

Run length distribution

Color/length	1	2	3	4	5	6	7	8
Black	2	2	0	1	0	0	0	0
White	4	0	2	0	0	0	0	0

Run length distribution

Fig. 1. Run-length distribution for the horizontal direction

In Fig. 1 we illustrated a toy example of this procedure for the horizontal direction. In the black pixels, we observed that there is no run of length one, two runs of length two, one run of length three and one run of length four, as indicated in the first row. A similar observation can be made for white pixels. As such, the final horizontal vector is about 800 values (400 + 400 for black and white pixels, respectively). The procedure is repeated for the remaining directions. The resultant run-length feature vector has 3200 values due to the final concatenation of the four directions.

4 Spiral Run-Length Features

In this section, we describe first the proposed spiral run-length feature. Next, we propose two combinations to fuse the new feature with the previous four directions.

4.1 Spiral Feature Vector

A uniform displacement describes it on a rotating line until reaching a final center point. This way, the spiral run-length feature traverses the entire image in a spiral counter-clockwise curve starting from the first pixel at the upper left corner of the image. Then it moves away more and more towards a last central point. This spiral movement rotates between the horizontal and the vertical directions. The procedure is shown in Fig. 2.

It could be said that the spiral feature treats four orthogonal directions differently, as shown in Fig. 2. The movement hither is done permanently, starting with a horizontal direction with an angle $\theta_1 = 0°$, followed by a descending vertical scan with an angle $\theta_2 = -90°$. On reaching the end of the vertical column, the direction changes again moving towards the horizontal direction but on the contrary direction to the first angle with an angle of $\theta_3 = 180°$. The last direction to progress is the vertically upward direction by exploring the entire column from bottom to top on an angle $\theta_4 = 90°$. This round of four directions is iterated until browsing the entire signature image.

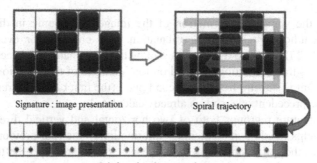

Signature : image presentation   Spiral trajectory

Spiral run-length presentation

Color\Length	1	2	3	4	5	6	7	8
Spiral Run Length distribution								
Black	2	3	1	0	0	0	0	0
White	4	1	1	0	0	0	0	0

Spiral run-length distribution

Fig. 2. New run-length direction: spiral based feature.

For counting the length of runs, the same procedure described in Sect. 3 is applied to the resulting vector of the spiral function. Accordingly, the final spiral vector size contains 800 values (400 for black pixels + 400 for white ones).

We consider the next notations:

- SP_B is the number of black run lengths in the image.
- SP_W is the number of white runs lengths in the image.
- N_b is the black run-length histograms in spiral direction.
- N_w is the white run-length histograms in spiral direction.
- SP is the global black and white run-length histograms in spiral direction.
- θ_k is the browsing spiral angle:

$$\theta_1 = 0°, \theta_2 = -90°, \theta_3 = 180°, \theta_4 = 90°.$$

The black and white run-length histograms are defined, respectively, as follows:

$$SP_B = \sum_{i=1}^{SP_B} \sum_{k=1}^{4} N_b(i|\theta_k) \tag{7}$$

$$SP_W = \sum_{j=1}^{SP_W} \sum_{k=1}^{4} N_w(j|\theta_k) \tag{8}$$

$$\forall \ 1 \le i \le SP_B \ and \ 1 \le j \le SP_W.$$

The global Spiral Run-Length histograms are then concatenated as

$$SP = [SP_B, SP_W] \tag{9}$$

Therefore, the spiral transformation of the image is dynamic in direction (two changes: vertical/horizontal) and in orientation (two changes for every direction: ($\rightarrow$, $\leftarrow$) and ($\uparrow$, $\downarrow$)). It is also dynamic in size; with every change of direction, we subtract a pixel. This transformation is based on four changes of the directions, and every current movement is starting from the second pixel (the first of this current movement is the last of the precedent one, so it is already calculated).

The spiral feature regroups both of two horizontal and vertical directions at the same time. It helps to add complementary information to the four previous run-length directions. Thus, the spiral run-length feature can be considered as the fifth direction.

Algorithm 1. Spiral vector extraction

Input
Read_image;
Initialize
[M, N] ← Image_size;
i←1; j←1;
SP ←[]; % Spiral vector
While (i < =M) and (j<=N) do
  Begin
  image=image(i:M,j:N);
  [M, N] ← Image_size;
  If i=M % the current image zone is composed of one row (or one pixel)
  SP ← [SP, first_row(j:N │ 0°)];
    Else if j=N % the current image zone is composed of one column (with more than one pixel)
      SP ← [SP, first_row(j:N │ 0°), last_column(i+1:M │ -90°)];
      Else if i=M-1 % the current image zone is composed of two lignes (with more than one column)
        SP←[SP, first_row(j:N │ 0°), last_column(i+1:M │ -90°), last_row(N-1:j:-1 │ 180°)];
          Else % General case
            SP←[SP, first_row(j:N│ 0°),last_column(i+1:M│ -90°),last_row(N-1:j:-1│ 180°), first_column(M-1:i+1:-1│ 90°)];
    End_If
    i++;j++; M--, N --;
    End;
  End While;

The steps of the proposed feature are highlighted in the pseudo-code Algorithms 1 and 2. They describe the spiral vector extraction and the spiral run-length features, respectively.

Algorithm 2. Spiral run-length features extraction

Input
Read_image;
Initialize
$i \leftarrow 1; j \leftarrow 1;$
$[M, N] \leftarrow Image\_size;$
Spiral_Black_Hist $\leftarrow$ *zeros (1,400); % Black Histograms*
Spiral_White_Hist $\leftarrow$ *zeros (1,400); % White Histograms*
Spiral_Hist $\leftarrow$ *zeros (1,800); % Spiral_Histograms*
   Read(SP); % Spiral vector outcoming from image by spiral transformation.
   For current_pixel = 1: Length(Spiral_Vector) **do**
      Begin
      Score $\leftarrow$ *0;*
      If current_pixel=0
         REPEAT
         score ++;
         Go to next pixel;
         UNTIL *(current_pixel_value* **different from** *next_pixel_value) or (score ==*
      400)
         Spiral_Black_Hist(score)= Spiral_Black_Hist(score)+1;
      Else
         REPEAT
         score ++;
         Go to next pixel,
         UNTIL *(current_pixel_value* **different from** *next_pixel_value) or (score ==*
      400)
         Spiral_White_His(score)= Spiral_White_Hist(score)+1;
      End_If
   End_For
Spiral_Hist=[Spiral_Black_Hist,Spiral_White_Hist];

4.2 Combining Spiral with the Previous Directions

Two combinations are proposed to use the new spiral feature along with the previous run-length features. Specifically, they consist of combining the run-lengths features at the feature and score level.

On the feature level, the combination consists of concatenating the four run-length features and the spiral feature. On the one hand, we concatenate all the five black run-length histograms and, on the other hand, the five white run-length histograms. This way, the combined histograms contain the five directions. Let RL_5D be the combined run-length histograms, it is defined as follows:

$$RL\_5D = [RL_B, SP_B, RL_W, SP_W]$$

$$RL_{5D} = [RL_b(0°), RL_b(45°), RL_b(90°), RL_b(135°), SP_B,$$
$$RL_w(0°), RL_w(45°), RL_w(90°), RL_w(135°), SP_W] \tag{10}$$

On the score level combination, this fusion is concerned by the scores generated by classifiers. The global score is a combination of the two scores of the previous four run-length features and the spiral one. A weight sum of the two scores performs the combination:

$$Sc = \alpha.Sc_1 + (1 - \alpha).Sc_2 \tag{11}$$

Sc being the final score, Sc_1 being the score of four directions run-length features and Sc_2 being the score of the spiral one, we heuristically set α in 0.5. In both cases of features, we process the black and white pixel distribution.

The experiments are carried out on each of the two levels of combination, with further details provided in the next passage.

5   Experiments

In this section, we present the used databases, the experimental protocol and the experiments with the two types of combinations: at both feature and score level when run-length features are used in ASV.

5.1   Database

We used the following two databases to evaluate our system:

GPDS75 Database.   This database was introduced by Ferrer et al. [9]. It contains the first 75 writers; each one has 24 genuine signatures and 30 skilled forgeries.

CEDAR Database.   IT is one of the most frequently used database for off-line ASV [10]. This database comprises a total of 55 signatures of different signers. Each individual signed 24 genuine signatures and has a total of 24 forged specimens.

5.2   Preprocessing

Our experiments necessitated the preprocessing phase since both GPDS75, and CEDAR datasets contain greyscale signatures, whereas our system's application relies mostly on binary signatures.

The signatures were first extracted from the datasets, then binarized using Otsu's method [17, 23], which involved determining a global threshold from the greyscale signature image. The threshold was accordingly employed to transform the greyscale signature into a binary signature by reducing the intra-class variance of the thresholded pixels.

5.3 One-Class Support Vector Machine

The availability of positive and negative training examples is one of the criteria of a classic Support Vector Machine (SVM) classifier.

The OC-SVM classifier employs only the genuine signatures for the training. The target class is discriminated from all other classes using only training data from the target class. The objective is to achieve a border that separates the target class examples from the rest of the space, a barrier that takes as many examples as possible targets [2, 11]. This border is defined by a decision function that is positive within a class S but negative outside of S: ($\overline{S}$) as described in Fig. 3.

$$f(x) = \begin{cases} +1 \ if \ x \in S \\ -1 \ if \ x \in \overline{S} \end{cases}$$

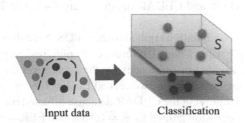

Input data   Classification

Fig. 3. One-class SVM classification

The parameters to be determined for the OC-SVM include the proportion of outliers ($\vartheta \in [0\ 1]$) and the radial basis function kernel parameter ($\gamma \in [0\ 1]$). The RBF kernel was chosen after experimenting with several kernel functions [2].

5.4 Experimental Protocol

Our signature verification system comprises four steps: selecting a set of signers, building the signature models, locating the optimal decision threshold, and finally achieving the classification step.

The set of signers to be selected includes the first five (R5) and ten (R10) genuine signatures that are kept as reference signatures in the training stage. Then, the testing stage is conducted by employing the next ten genuine samples (g6...g15 in the case of R5, and g11...g20 in the case of R10) and the first ten skilled forgeries (f1...f10) for the experiments in both databases.

The optimal decision threshold is deduced from the false rejection rate (FRR) and the false acceptance rate (FAR) curves using the equal error rate (EER) [24, 25], as described in the next figure. The choice of the (EER) metric, which is defined as the system error rate when FRR = FAR [24], was chosen since it has been used in a variety of relevant studies (Fig. 4).

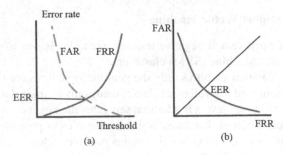

Fig. 4. EER performance measure

5.5 Results

We discuss here the combination at two levels: feature level and score level. The results of such fusions on GPDS75 and CEDAR databases are shown in Table 1 and Table 2, respectively.

For the feature level combination applied to the GPDS75 database, we gained EER = 9.24% and EER = 8.26% using 5 and 10 reference samples, respectively. Whereas, using the same database and number of references for the score level combination generated EER = 7.98% and as the best outcome we earned EER = 6.86%.

On the other hand, employing the CEDAR database affected the results illustrated in Table 2. The feature level fusion gained EER = 0.55% and EER = 0.36%, respectively, with 05 and 10 reference samples, while the results attained are EER = 0.73% and EER = 0.18% performing the score level fusion. This last outcome (EER = 0.18%) is the best value obtained operating the score level combination with 10 reference samples.

For both types of fusion, the experimental results in Tables 1 and 2 reveal that fusing the features raises the rate and improves system performance.

Table 1. Results in EER (%) on GPDS75 by combining at feature and score level.

System	GPDS-75	
	R5	R10
Basic RL (RL)	10.78	9.38
Spiral RL (SP)	12.88	11.62
[4RL, SP]*: Feature level	**9.24**	**8.26**
[4RL, SP]*: Score level	**7.98**	**6.86**

*[4RL, SP]: Combination of the classical run-length (4RL) features with the spiral one.

Table 2. Results in EER (%) on CEDAR by combining at feature and score level.

System	CEDAR	
	R5	R10
Basic RL (RL)	0.73	0.55
Spiral RL (SP)	0.91	0.55
[4RL, SP]*: Feature level	**0.55**	**0.36**
[4RL, SP]*: Score level	**0.73**	**0.18**

*[4RL, SP]: Combination of the classical run-length (4RL) features with the spiral one.

Furthermore, we compare our results with previous works. Table 3 shows different works that have used the GPDS75 database. We can observe that our performances are in line with state of the art. For instance, Maergner et al. obtained the best EER = 6.49%, while in another work they got an EER = 6.84%. When we combine the five run-length features at the score level, our best performance was 6.86% on GPDS75.

According to Table 4, our results were competitive compared with previous works in CEDAR database. We observe a gap getting two minimal rates: EER = 0.18% and EER = 0.36%, followed by Hamadene et al. with AER = 2.10%, then Hafemann et al. with EER = 4.63% accompanied by Sharif et al. with EER = 4.67%. We conclude that our system was more performant with CEDAR database than GPDS75 database.

Table 3. Results on GPDS75 – comparison between the state-of-the-art and our system.

Reference	Samples/user	EER %
Maergner et al. [12]	10	6.84
Maergner et al. [13]	10	9.42
Maergner et al. [14]	10	6.49
Ferrer et al. [15]	10	16.01
This work (score level)	**5**	**7.98**
This work (score level)	**10**	**6.86**

Table 4. Results on CEDAR – comparison between the state-of-the-art and our system.

Reference	Samples/user	EER %
Guerbai et al. [11]	12	5.6
Sharif et al. [16]	12	4.67
Hafemann et al. [17]	12	4.63 ($\pm$0.42)
Hamadene et al. [18]	5	2.10
This work (feature level)	**10**	**0.36**
This work (score level)	**10**	**0.18**

5.6 Spiral Run-Length Features in External Competition

The evaluation of spiral run-length features against other handwritten signature verification systems was a critical step. For this reason, we submitted our features to the international competition on Short answer Assessment and Thai Student Signature and Name Components Recognition and Verification (SASIGCOM 2020) [19] which was organized in conjunction with the 17th International Conference on Frontiers in Handwriting Recognition (ICFHR 2020).

In the competition, six tasks were prepared for the competitors including the signature verification task, the thai student signature dataset was employed for this task shown in Table 5. Three type of forgery were adopted: simple, skilled and random forgeries. The Equal Error Rate (EER) was employed as the judge the different participating systems performance.

Table 5. Signature verification dataset (SASIGCOM 2020).

Dataset	No. of users	Train	Test		
		Gn*	Gn*	Skld*	Smpl*
Thai student signature dataset	100	5	25	12	12

*Gn: Number of genuine samples/user. *Skld: Number of skilled samples/user.
*Smpl: Number of simple samples/user.

Our system based on the spiral run-length feature get EER $= 0.1108\%$ for the random forgeries, EER $= 0.2045\%$ for the skilled forgeries and an EER $= 0.1459\%$ for simple forgeries with an average of 0.1537%. The results cited in Table 6 show also that the classical run-length features get EER $= 0.1308\%$, EER $= 0.2145\%$ and EER $= 0.1599\%$ for random, skilled and simple forgeries, while the multidirectional run-length feature obtained an average of 0.1415%. The first ranking was for a learned system with EER $= 0.0019\%$, EER $= 0.0710\%$ and EER $= 0.0090\%$ for the same forgeries types respectively with an average of 0.0273%.

Table 6. Results of the signature verification task (SASIGCOM 2020).

Rank	Algorithm	EER %			
		Random forgeries	Skilled forgeries	Simple forgeries	AVG
1	SCUT-CNN [20]	0.0019	0.0710	0.0090	0.0273
2	LTP + oBIFs [21]	0.0109	0.1091	0.0712	0.0637
3	ERL [2]	0.0302	0.1780	0.0955	0.1012
4	oBIFs [21]	0.0444	0.1876	0.1010	0.1110
5	LTP [21]	0.0511	0.1901	0.1105	0.1172
6	MDRL [8]	0.0986	0.2000	0.1258	0.1415
7	SPIRAL-RL	0.1108	0.2045	0.1459	0.1537
8	RL400 [2]	0.1308	0.2145	0.1599	0.1686
9	RL [4]	0.1308	0.2145	0.1599	0.1686
	Benchmark [22]	0.0201	0.1108	0.0031	0.0447

According to Tables 3, 4, and 6, we notice that the different systems' results obtained by using the GPDS75 database are more elevated than those acquired by using the CEDAR and the SASIGCOM databases.

More clearly, our system could reach very lowered EER values using the CEDAR database; this differentia is due to the system-dataset ratio. How the system scrutinizes the signature, the characteristic of each database, and how the signatures were pre-processed before including them in the database. For instance, the GPDS75 dataset is greyscaled, whereas the SASIGCOM database signatures are already binarized. Also, the background of the GPDS database is almost similar, whereas we find a difference in the CEDAR signatures background between the genuine and the forged signatures.

6 Conclusion

In this work, we propose a new direction for run-length features based on the signature's spiral path. We observe performance improvements by combining the previous well-known four directions in run-length features with the proposal spiral direction. Thus, the spiral run-length feature can be understood as the fifth direction, which is more robust to intra-class variability and get better results than using only the four run-length features. In this work, we show results when combining the run-length features at the feature and score level, obtaining better performances at score level combination.

In our future works, we seek to improve the performance of automatic signature verification by applying other techniques of fusion and combination. In addition, we study other methods to process the run-length features and to extend its use in on-line signatures.

References

1. Diaz, M., Ferrer, M.A., Impedovo, D., Malik, M.I., Pirlo, G., Plamondon, R.: A perspective analysis of handwritten signature technology. ACM Comput. Surv. (CSUR) **51**(6), 117 (2019)
2. Bouamra, W., Djeddi, C., Nini, B., Diaz, M., Siddiqi, I.: Towards the design of an offline signature verifier based on a small number of genuine samples for training. Expert Syst. Appl. **107**, 182–195 (2018)
3. Galloway, M.M.: Texture analysis using gray level run lengths. Comput. Graph. Image Process. **4**(2), 172–179 (1975)
4. Djeddi, C., Siddiqi, I., Souici-Meslati, L., Ennaji, A.: Text-independent writer recognition using multi-script handwritten texts. Pattern Recogn. Lett. **34**(10), 1196–1202 (2013)
5. Djeddi, C., Siddiqi, I., Al-Maadeed, S., Souici-Meslati, L., Gattal, A., Ennaji, A.: Signature verification for offline skilled forgeries using textural features. In: 11th International Conference on Signal-Image Technology & Internet-Based Systems (SITIS), pp. 76–80. IEEE (2015)
6. Serdouk, Y., Nemmour, H., Chibani, Y.: Combination of OC-LBP and longest run features for off-line signature verification. In: Conference: Proceedings - 10th International Conference on Signal-Image Technology and Internet-Based Systems, SITIS 2014 (2015). https://doi.org/10.1109/SITIS.2014.36
7. Ghanim, T., Nabil, A.: Offline signature verification and forgery detection approach. In: 13th International Conference on Computer Engineering and Systems (ICCES) (2018). https://doi.org/10.1109/ICCES.2018.8639420
8. Bouamra, W., Díaz, M., Ferrer, M.A., Nini, B.: Off-line signature verification using multidirectional run-length features. In: ICIST 2020, vol. 43, pp. 1:8–43:8 (2020)
9. Ferrer, M.A., Travieso, C., Alonso, J.: Off-line handwritten signature GPDS-960 corpus. In: Ninth International Conference on Document Analysis and Recognition, ICDAR 2007, vol. 2, pp. 764–768. IEEE (2007)
10. Kalera, M.K., Srihari, S., Xu, A.: Offline signature verification and identification using distance statistics. Int. J. Pattern Recogn. Artif. Intell. **18**(07), 1339–1360 (2004). https://doi.org/10.1142/S0218001404003630
11. Guerbai, Y., Chibani, Y., Hadjadji, B.: The effective use of the one-class SVM classifier for handwritten signature verification based on writer-independent parameters. Pattern Recogn. **48**(1), 103–113 (2015). https://doi.org/10.1016/j.patcog.2014.07.016
12. Maergner, P., Howe, N., Riesen, K., Ingold, R., Fischer, A.: Offline signature verification via structural methods: graph edit distance and inkball models. In: ICFHR 2018, pp. 163–168 (2018)
13. Maergner, P., Riesen, K., Ingold, R., Fischer, A.: A structural approach to offline signature verification using graph edit distance. In: Proceedings of International Conference on Document Analysis and Recognition (ICDAR), pp. 1216–1222. IEEE (2017)
14. Maergner, P., et al.: Offline signature verification by combining graph edit distance and triplet networks. In: Bai, X., Hancock, E.R., Ho, T.K., Wilson, R.C., Biggio, B., Robles-Kelly, A. (eds.) S+SSPR 2018. LNCS, vol. 11004, pp. 470–480. Springer, Cham (2018). https://doi.org/10.1007/978-3-319-97785-0_45
15. Ferrer, M.A., Vargas, J.F., Morales, A., Ordonez, A.: Robustness of offline signature verification based on gray level features. IEEE Trans. Inf. Forensics Secur. **7**(3), 966–977 (2012)
16. Sharif, M., Khan, M.A., Faisal, M., Yasmin, M., Fernandes, S.L.: A framework for offline signature verification system. Best features selection approach. Pattern Recogn. Lett. **139**, 50–59 (2018). https://doi.org/10.1016/j.patrec.2018.01.021

17. Hafemann, L.G., Sabourin, R., Oliveira, L.S.: Learning features for offline handwritten signature verification using deep convolutional neural networks. Pattern Recogn. **70**, 163–176 (2017)
18. Hamadene, A., Chibani, Y.: One-class writer-independent off-line signature verification using feature dissimilarity thresholding. IEEE Trans. Inf. Forensics Secur. **11**(6), 1 (2016). https://doi.org/10.1109/TIFS.2016.2521611
19. Das, A., Suwanwiwat, H., Pal, U., Blumenstein, M.: ICFHR 2020 Competition on Short answer ASsessment and Thai Student SIGnature and Name COMponents Recognition and Verification (SASIGCOM 2020), ICFHR 2020, pp. 222–227 (2020)
20. Zhu, Y., Lai, S., Li, Z., Jin, L.: Point-to-set similarity based deep metric learning for offline signature verification. In: ICFHR 2020 (2020)
21. Hadjadj, I., Gattal, A., Djeddi, C., Ayad, M., Siddiqi, I., Abass, F.: Offline signature verification using textural descriptors. In: Morales, A., Fierrez, J., Sánchez, J.S., Ribeiro, B. (eds.) IbPRIA 2019. LNCS, vol. 11868, pp. 177–188. Springer, Cham (2019). https://doi.org/10.1007/978-3-030-31321-0_16
22. Das, A.: Face recognition in reduced Eigen-plane. In: Proceedings of the 2012 International Conference on Communications, Devices and Intelligent Systems, CODIS 2012, pp. 620–623. IEEE (2012)
23. Otsu, N.: A threshold selection method from gray-level histograms. IEEE Trans. Syst. Man Cybern. **9**(10), 62–66 (1979). https://doi.org/10.1109/TSMC.1979.4310076
24. Impedovo, D., Pirlo, G.: Automatic signature verification: the state of the art. IEEE Trans. Syst. Man Cybern. Part C (Appl. Rev.) **38**(5), 609–635 (2008)
25. Wirtz, B.: Technical evaluation of biometric systems. In: Chin, R., Pong, T.-C. (eds.) ACCV 1998. LNCS, vol. 1351, pp. 499–506. Springer, Heidelberg (1997). https://doi.org/10.1007/3-540-63930-6_160

Historical Documents

Transcript Alignment for Historical Handwritten Documents: The MiM Algorithm

Giuseppe De Gregorio[1,2(✉)], Ilaria Citro[1], and Angelo Marcelli[1,2]

[1] DIEM, University of Salerno, Via Giovanni Paolo II 132, 84084 Fisciano, SA, Italy
{gdegregorio,amarcelli}@unisa.it, i.citro4@studenti.unisa.it
[2] CINI, National Laboratory of Artificial Intelligence and Intelligent Systems,
University of Salerno Unit, Fisciano, SA, Italy

Abstract. Libraries contain a large number of digital images of handwritten documents of historical and cultural interest, and digital transcriptions are also available for some of them. The ability to trace back to the portion of the image that contains the handwritten text starting from the transcription can be essential for the study of the document by scholars in humanities, as well as for the development of modern technologies that greatly facilitate the search, indexing, and transcription of ancient documents.

We propose a method to perform the transcription alignment automatically. The method analyzes images of handwritten text lines together with the corresponding transcription and performs alignment by analyzing the line alternatively from left to right and from right to left, making the method language-independent. Experiments on the Bentham Collection dataset have shown that the method can correctly align more than 75% of the text. We also show that, by using a GUI we have designed for the purpose, our method reduces the time for error-free alignment by more than 47% compared to the time required for manual alignment.

Keywords: Historical document processing · Handwritten text alignment · Performance evaluation

1 Introduction

In recent years, digital libraries [1] have gained considerably in importance and are meeting with growing interest, not only from historians and scholars. The digitisation of libraries allows easy access to the contents of preserved collections, and makes the knowledge they contain quickly and easily available to the general public. This new form of library enables the automatic processing of native digital documents with a variety of built-in tools that facilitate the user's search, annotation or any other manipulation of the document or its content [8].

When documents are available as digital images of the original paper form, in order to fully exploit the potential of digital tools, it is necessary to accompany

© Springer Nature Switzerland AG 2022
C. Carmona-Duarte et al. (Eds.): IGS 2021, LNCS 13424, pp. 45–60, 2022.
https://doi.org/10.1007/978-3-031-19745-1_4

the images of the handwritten documents with the digital transcription of their content. For this reason, the transcription of handwritten documents of historical interest is an ongoing process that attracts the attention of various branches of research [7]. Progress is constantly being made in the development of tools for the recognition of handwritten texts, so that today transcriptions exist for various documents, increasingly produced by automatic tools whose results are eventually validated by specialised personnel. However, by its very nature, the digital transcription is not linked to the handwritten image of the document, making it difficult to locate the parts of a handwritten document image that correspond to a piece of text of the digital transcription. So the problem arises of aligning the digital transcription with the parts of the handwritten document image to which it refers, in such a way that the digital transcription is linked to the images of the words in the manuscript [2] as shown in Fig. 1.

Fig. 1. Example of a transcription aligned with the original image of a text line extracted from the Bentham dataset.

The ability to link the page image to the transcription of its contents can facilitate the work of scholars and historians who often have to work with handwritten versions of documents. A first advantage of alignment is the improvement of archiving and indexing capacity. One of the most important features of digital libraries is the almost instantaneous process of searching and indexing a digital text. The alignment process makes it possible to transfer this immediacy to the handwritten version as well, making it possible to search a handwritten document in the same way as a digital document and then easily and quickly access the handwritten version of interest.

Another advantage of the alignment process is that it makes reading the document easier. This process is particularly interesting when working with old documents of historical interest, because handwritten documents are often complicated to read, whether because of the difficulty of interpreting the author's handwriting, the stylistic rules of the time in which the document was written, or the precarious state of preservation of some old documents. These factors often make it difficult to read a handwritten text, especially for an inexperienced and untrained eye. The availability of digital transcription overcomes all these complications and makes the content of the document easily interpretable without losing sight of the original handwritten version. Another application of the result of alignment is the study of dissimilarity between different handwritten versions of the same document. In the past, the different copies of the same text were made by hand by scribes copying an entire text page by page. Hand copying is not a perfect process, and sometimes there can be inconsistencies between the different copies due to copying errors, omissions or additions of parts of the text, or changes in the text that were necessary to adapt the manuscripts to different language canons. The result of the comparison can help scholars to identify and analyse the differences between the various copies.

As mentioned earlier, the transcription of handwritten documents is attracting the attention of the scholarly community, and solutions for automatic transcription are now in the interest of researchers. Modern machine learning techniques are widely used in this field, and more and more solutions are being proposed that use this paradigm to present methods and applications to simplify and speed up the transcription process. Solutions based on machine learning require a learning process that starts from a large amount of correctly labelled data. The creation of ground truth data is a time-consuming process that is often done by hand [9]. In this direction, alignment results can quickly and easily provide a good amount of labelled data, making the preparation of training data easier and, more importantly, faster than manual.

We present here an alignment algorithm that, starting from a word-level segmentation of the line of text, estimates the extent to which the size of a word image and the intended transcription match, and uses this information to deal with over- and under-segmentation errors scanning alternately the line of text along the direction of writing and vice versa. Once detected, the over-segmentation errors are corrected by merging the word images, while the under-segmentation errors are corrected by merging the transcripts.

In the remaining of the paper, Sect. 2 is devoted to reviewing the related literature, Sect. 3 introduces the proposed algorithm, and Sect. 4 presents the setup and the results of the experiments we have performed. In Sect. 5 we summarize the motivation and rationale for the proposed method, discuss the current limitations and outline our future investigations on this topic

2   State of the Art

In the literature, the problem of aligning handwritten text is divided into two categories: *Image-Image Alignment* and *Image-Text Alignment*. The first category involves aligning two different copies of the same document to highlight any differences that may occur. Te second, on the other hand, is about aligning the digital transcription of the document with the corresponding images of the handwritten document.

2.1   Image-Image Alignment

In the context of image-image matching, Kassis et al. [4] propose a method based on convolutional Siamese neural networks to detect whether two images contain the transcription of the same text. The method involves an initial training phase in which a certain number of pages must be annotated by hand. The method achieves alignment accuracy between 96% and 97% on the different test sets.

2.2   Image-Text Alignment

One of the first examples of image-text alignment is proposed by Tomai et al. [15]. The proposed method works with documents segmented at the level of text lines, which are segmented at the word level to obtain different segmentation hypotheses. A text recognizer is then used to obtain the transcription of each segmented word, restricting the dictionary of the recognizer to the words present in the transcription. Finally, a dynamic programming algorithm suggests the best pairing between images and transcripts, achieving a percentage of 72% correct alignment. The text recognizer is not trained on the pages of the collection to be matched, and performance is highly dependent on the recognition module used.

In the method proposed by Kornfield et al. [5], the authors segment the document at the word level and consider the sequence of segmented words and the sequence of words in the transcription as temporal sequences, and then they apply a Dynamic Time Wrapping algorithm to perform the alignment. The method achieves 75.40% correct alignment when working with lines of text.

Rothfeder et al. [11] tackle the alignment problem as a problem of alignment between two sequences. Once the document is segmented at the word level, they use a linear Hidden Markov Model (HMM) solved by applying the Viterbi algorithm to obtain alignment, achieving a percentage of 72.80% correct alignment.

Toselli et al. [16] also use a Viterbi decoded approach to handwriting recognition based on an HMM, in this case, using a forced-recognition approach that restricts the possible transcriptions to the words present in the text line, and in their best results, they can reach more than 90% of correct alignment.

Indermuehle et al. [3] propose a procedure for aligning the transcription with the images using an HMM recognizer and working with individual lines of text. Feature vectors are calculated for the alignment process using an HMM. Therefore, the method requires a training phase to enable the calculation of the features. The method achieves the best results with a training set of 2500 words, which is about 65% correctly aligned. Finally, a model trained on the public IAM dataset is tested. By merging the results with the previous system, a correct alignment of almost 95.5% is achieved. However, this result requires a training phase with a dataset of words from the collection to be aligned.

In the method proposed by Zinger et al. [17], the images of the handwritten documents are segmented into lines that are used for matching with the transcription. The matching is based on a word segmentation of the line achieved by analyzing the longest spaces between parts of the handwriting. A gap metric is defined that considers the relative length of the word. This results in a cost function that must be minimized to obtain correct alignment. The results yield a percentage of 69% correct alignment.

Stamatopoulos et al., in their works [13,14], propose an alignment technique that involves segmenting the lines of text based on the Hough transform and the number of lines obtained from the digital transcription. Each line is then segmented at the word level using a gap classification technique based on the number of words in the text line. In [14] A manual correction phase is performed at the end of the automated process to obtain an error-free alignment. The authors show that their method saves 90% of the time compared to manual labeling and results in a percentage of 97.21% correctly aligned words. In [13] the authors add an extra step that works at character level to correct segmentation errors, so the result reaches 99.48% correct alignment.

Leydier et al. [6] propose a segmentation-free and learning-free alignment method. The method involves extracting signature strings representing a whole line of text and then aligning them to the digital transcription by calculating the Levenshtein distance transformation matrix. The rate of correct alignment of the method is almost 73%.

Romero-Gòmez et al. [10] propose an alignment method that uses dynamic programming to obtain the best alignment between the image of a line of text and its entire transcription. The method automatically segments the document at the text line level and then uses an HMM-based text recognizer to obtain a transcription estimate. Alignment confidence is then calculated by computing the Levenshtein distance between the recognition result and the transcript lines, reaching a correct alignment percentage about of 75.5%.

2.3   Not Handwritten Documents

Ziran et al. [18] propose an image-text alignment method that can be applied to early printed documents and uses deep models in combination with a dynamic programming algorithm. The method involves using a recurrent convolutional neural network to search for words within a line based on the number of words present in the line. A second model searches for certain landmark words that serve as a reference to align the transcript using a dynamic programming algorithm.

3   The Proposed Method

However, the proposed method assumes that the images of the text lines are segmented at the word level. Although there are many algorithms, none of them is able to provide error-free segmentation, so the performance of the alignment method depends on the specific segmentation algorithm. To avoid the impact of the strengths/weaknesses of the segmentation algorithm on the performance evaluation, we have included a word-level segmentation step in our method, as is common in this field. To this end, our segmentation algorithm calculates the vertical histogram, i.e. the number of black pixels in each column of the image, of the text line image, and then looks for spaces between words, i.e. a sequence of consecutive 0's. These sequences are then sorted according to their length, and only those whose length is greater than a certain threshold ν, whose value depends on the average length of the sequences estimated for all the text lines of a page, are finally retained as those corresponding to the actual spaces between two consecutive words.

After performing a word-level segmentation, the image of a text line is represented by the ordered list W of word images, starting from the leftmost one, extracted from the text line image:

$$W = < w_1, w_2, \ldots, w_m >$$

where m is the number of word images extracted from the text line. From now on, we will refer to each word image w_j with the term box. Analogously, the transcription of a line of text T is the sequence of the transcription of the words of which it is composed:

$$T = < t_1, t_2, \ldots, t_n >$$

where n is the total number of words that compose the text line, and t_i denotes the transcription of the i-th word in the line of text. So, solving the alignment problem means linking each w_j to its correct transcription t_i. If there were no segmentation errors, i.e. $m = n$ and each box contained a single word, the final alignment would be easily achieved by linking each box w_j to its corresponding transcriptions t_i, where $i = j$. Since the assumption of error-free segmentation is unrealistic, we have built a consistency check into the algorithm that performs the linkage between a transcript and a box, as described below.

3.1   Image and Transcript Linking

After word segmentation, there are m boxes that need to be linked to n transcripts. In the case $m = n$, the method assumes that the segmentation is error-free, and therefore the desired alignment is achieved by linking each box w_j to the corresponding transcripts t_i, where $i = j$. In the case $m > n$, the method assumes that there were over-segmentation errors. So the method successively removes the spaces that are in the image of the text line, starting with the shortest, until $m = n$. Then the alignment is done as before. In the case of $m < n$, the method assumes that there are sub-segmentation errors. Since it is very difficult, if not impossible, to decide which box to split and how, we circumvent the problem by allowing the algorithm to associate the transcriptions of multiple words with one box. For this purpose, we calculate for each line of text the average character width (ACW), defined as:

$$ACW = \frac{\sum_W (Word\ image\ width\ (pixels))}{\sum_T (Number\ of\ characters)}$$

and the smallest value m_{th} and the largest value M_{th} of the ACWs computed over all the text line images of the page. Then, the method checks the consistency between the width of the box w_j and the number of characters of the transcription t_i by computing the ACW of the characters of the box, called ACW_{box} as:

$$ACW_{box} = \frac{width\ of\ w_i}{character\ number\ of\ t_j}$$

and comparing it with m_{th} and M_{th}. The following cases can be distinguished:

1. $ACW_{box} < m_{th}$ - the size of the box w_i is too small to contain the number of characters of transcription t_j;

2. $ACW_{box} > M_{th}$ - the size of the box w_i is too large to contain the number of characters of transcription t_j;
3. $m_{th} < ACW_{box} < M_{th}$ - the size of the box w_i is consistent with the number of the characters of the transcription t_j.

f the consistency test yields case 1., an over-segmentation error has occurred and therefore the box w_j is merged with the nearest contiguous box w_k and m is decreased. In this way, the size of the box increases, which may lead to coherence between the merged box w_{ik} and the transcription t_i. If the coherence test gives case 2., an under-segmentation error has occurred, and then the transcript t_j is merged with a neighboring transcript t_k and n is decreased.In this way, the size of the box w_i could become consistent with the merged transcript t_{jk}. Finally, if the consistency test yields case 3., the box w_i is merged with the transcription t_j. Algorithm 1 contains the pseudo-code of the algorithm that performs the described alignment method for a single box w_i to be analyzed.

Algorithm 1: The word alignment algorithm

Data: list of line transcriptions T, list of segmented word images W, index of Wi, index of Tj, threshold values m_{th} and M_{th}

Result: aligned images a_i, *Failure* in case no alignment is possible

1 $X \leftarrow width(\{w_i \in W\})$;
2 $L \leftarrow length(\{t_j \in T\})$;
3 $ACW_{box} \leftarrow X/L$
4 **if** *($ACW_{box} < m_{th}$)* **then**
5    $pre \leftarrow distance(w_i, w_{i-1})$;
6    $post \leftarrow distance(w_i, w_{i+1})$;
7   **if** *(pre is None AND post is None)* **then**
8 | **return** *Failure*
9    $w_{min} \leftarrow min(pre, post)$;
10   $w_i \leftarrow mergeBox(w_i, w_{min})$;
11   $a_i \leftarrow ncwAlignment(w_i, t_j)$;
12 **else if** *($ACW_{box} > M_{th}$)* **then**
13   **while** *($ACW_{box} > M_{th}$)* **do**
14   **if** *(t_{next} is None)* **then**
15 | **return** *Failure*
16    $new_t \leftarrow mergeTranscription(t_j, t_{next})$;
17    $ACW_{box} \leftarrow X_{newt}/L_{newt}$;
18   **end**
19   $a_i \leftarrow newAlignment(w_i, new_t)$;
20 **else**
21 | $a_i \leftarrow newAlignment(w_i, t_j)$;
22 **return** a_i;

3.2   Text Line Alignment

As for the order in which the sequence of boxes w_j and transcriptions t_j are analyzed, it would be most natural to follow the order of writing, i.e. from left to right or vice versa, depending on the language. However, we have considered that segmentation errors that are not properly detected and handled during the consistency check at the beginning of the sequence would spread to the following boxes/transcriptions along the line, causing errors or even messing up the whole alignment. To avoid this "avalanche effect", we have therefore chosen a strategy called *Meet in the Middle (MiM)*, which looks at the boxes/transcripts alternately from both sides of the line of text, starting with the one furthest to the left, then the one furthest to the right, then the one furthest to the left, then the one furthest to the right, and so on.

Algorithm 2 shows the pseudo-code of the MiM alignment algorithm for selecting the sequence of boxes w_i to be analyzed.

4   Experimental Results

4.1   The Dataset

Experiments were conducted on selected handwritten documents from the Bentham Collection dataset. This dataset consists of images of manuscripts by the English reformer and philosopher Jeremy Bentham (1748–1832). Currently, the transcription of the entire collection is being carried out by volunteers as part of the crowdsourcing initiative "Transcribe Bentham"[1], thanks to which it is possible to access both the images of the documents and the associated transcripts. 433 pages selected from the entire collection represent the dataset used in the ICFHR-2014 HTRtS competition [12], this subset contains 11,473 lines, nearly 110,000 words, and a vocabulary of more than 9,500 different words. Figure 2 shows an example of a document from the collection.

From the Bentham data used in ICFHR-2014, a set of 20 page images was selected and used as the data set to perform the experiments. An initial subset consisting of 5 pages was used during an exploratory phase to compute the values of ACW, m_{th} and M_{th}, and for setting up the value of the threshold ν. For the calculation of the threshold, the lengths of all the white spaces between words detected in the lines of text were considered according to the number of words contained in the line of text. The mean value of the length of the whitespace between words was then used to define the threshold ν. The whole 20 page data set was then used for performance assessment. The 5-pages data set consists of 77 lines whose transcripts contain 805 words, while the 20-pages test set consists of 431 lines and 3,698 words. We have performed the experiments by using two versions of the proposed method, one adopting the left-to-right (hereinafter denoted as *forward*) strategy, the other by using the newly proposed *MiM* strategy.

---

[1] https://blogs.ucl.ac.uk/transcribe-bentham/.

Algorithm 2: The complete alignment algorithm

Data: list of line transcriptions **T**, list of segmented word images for each line
W

Result: aligned images

1 $x \leftarrow AvgCharacterWitdh()$;
2 $m_{th} \leftarrow MinimumThreshold(x)$;
3 $M_{th} \leftarrow MaximumThreshold(x)$;
4 $allAligns \leftarrow []$;
5 **foreach** $W_i \in \mathbf{W}$ **do**
6     $forwardAlign \leftarrow []$;
7     $backwardsAlign \leftarrow []$;
8     $MiMAlign \leftarrow []$;
9     $T_i \leftarrow correspondTranscription(W_i)$;
10    $i_w \leftarrow 0; j_w \leftarrow length(W_i) - 1$;   // W_i **indices**
11    $i_t \leftarrow 0; j_t \leftarrow length(T_i) - 1$;   // T_i **indices**
12    $remain_{wi} \leftarrow length(W_i)$;   // **number of alignments to perform**
13   **while** *($remain_{wi} > 0$)* **do**
14      $align \leftarrow alignAlgorithm(W_i, T_i, i_w, i_t, m_{th}, M_{th})$;
15   **if** *align Failure* **then**
16 | skip to next row W_{i+1}
17   **end**
18      $forwardAlign[] \leftarrow align$;
19      $remain_{wi} \leftarrow remain_{wi} - -$;
20      $i_w \leftarrow i_w + +$;
21      $i_t \leftarrow i_t + +$;
22   **if** *($remain_{wi} > 1$)* **then**
23        $align \leftarrow alignAlgorithm(W_i, T_i, j_w, j_t, m_{th}, M_{th})$;
24   **if** *align Failure* **then**
25 | skip to next row W_{i+1}
26   **end**
27        $backwardsAlign[] \leftarrow align$;
28        $remain_{wi} \leftarrow remain_{wi} - -$;
29        $j_w \leftarrow j_w - -$;
30        $j_t \leftarrow j_t - -$;
31   **end**
32   **end**
33    $MiMAlign[] \leftarrow forwardAlign[] + backwardsAlign[]$;
34    $allAligns[] \leftarrow MimAlign[]$
35 **end**
36 **return** $allAligns[]$;

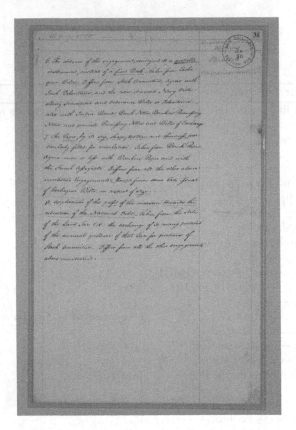

Fig. 2. Example of a page of the Bentham Collection.

4.2   Validation Tool

To evaluate the performance of the proposed method, a validation phase of the alignment results is required. The validation phase must be performed manually by an operator who analyses all images and verifies that the associated transcriptions are correct, discarding or correcting any errors. This can be a delicate and time-consuming process, so it is important to make this process quick and easy. We have therefore implemented a validation software tool that allows us to check the results of the alignment system. The tool allows us to identify all correct alignments and collects the set of words that consists only of valid alignments. In addition, the tool provides functions to correct alignment errors. Figure 3 shows the user interface of the tool. The validation process must be as fast as possible. For this reason, we have kept the operations that the user has to perform to a minimum. The user interface shows all the alignments created with the method and the user only has to select the erroneous ones. The tool then assumes that all the alignments are correct and it is up to the user to identify only the wrong ones by marking them with a simple mouse click on the misaligned image. The tool also allows for the correction of misalignments. Once an alignment is marked as wrong, you can insert the correct caption by typing it with the keyboard, while the tool suggests possible correct alignments by analysing the characters entered and the transcription of the current line of text. The user must make the decision whether to validate or correct. It should be noted that the pure validation process is faster than the correction, but results in correctly labelled sets consisting of fewer elements.

One of the main problems that led us to define a method for word alignment is the need for a method to quickly and easily obtain correctly labelled data sets that can be used to train automatic handwriting recognition systems. In order for these data sets to be used correctly and profitably, they must be error-free; in our case, each word image must be correctly labelled with its actual transcription. The validation tool makes it possible to obtain a correctly labelled dataset starting from the output of the *MiM* algorithm, which makes the process faster and easier than a completely manual labelling.

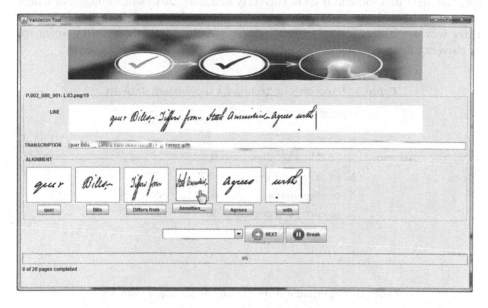

Fig. 3. The user interface of the validation tool. The figure shows how to select an incorrect alignment by clicking on the image of the word that contains the error. Once an incorrect image has been selected, it is possible to enter the correct transcription by pasting it into the appropriate text box at the bottom of the interface.

4.3   Method Evaluation

The results of the experiments on the 5-pages data set are reported in Table 1, while Table 2 reports those achieved on the 20-page data set. They show that:

- the performance exhibit the same trends on both the data sets, thus confirming that a few pages are enough to reliably estimate the value of ν, and that the *ACW* is a simple yet effective metric for evaluating the consistency between the box width and the number of character of the transcript;
- the MiM strategy is actually better than the forward one, as it is capable of processing more lines;
- the consistency check allows to deal properly with segmentation errors, as independently of the strategy, more than 83% of the boxes are correctly associated with their transcripts.

It is essential to highlight that in the tables above an alignment is considered correct even if it is not at the word level; a box may contain two (or more) words, and the alignment is correct if the transcripts of all the words in the box are linked to it. The number of alignments then indicates how good the word segmentation is; the closer this number to the total number of words in the dataset, the better the word-level segmentation. In the case of the 20-page data set, the MiM method succeeds in correctly assigning 2645 word images, of which 2497 contain a single word, 142 contain two words, and 6 contain more than three words, yielding a total of 2801 correctly assigned words, with a percentage of correct alignment of 75.93%.

Table 1. Experimental results on the 5-pages data set.

	Forward	MiM
N. of lines	77	
N. of words to align	805	
N. of processed lines	65	77
N. of alignments	607	689
N. of correct alignments	501	590

Table 2. Experimental results on the 20-pages data set.

	Forward	MiM
N. of lines	431	
N. of words to align	3689	
N. of processed lines	365	428
N. of alignments	2686	3196
N. of correct alignments	2233	2645

4.4 Time Evaluation

In order to evaluate the time efficiency of the proposed method, after running the alignment method with the MiM strategy, the validation tool presented in Sect. 4.2 was used for recording the time spent by the user for validating the correct alignments and correcting the wrong ones. Validation and correction were performed by alternating a 20-min working session with a 5-min resting session, as is common in these cases to avoid fatigue effects. For comparison, we also recorded the time spent by the user, alternating working and resting session as in the previous case, to manually segment and align the same data. Table 3 shows the time needed for validating and correcting the processed lines, and thus the total time to achieve an error-free alignment for the 20-pages data set using the MiM algorithm, and the total time required for a fully manual alignment. The data reported in the table show that by using the proposed method, we recorded a reduction of 47.73% of the time for achieving an error-free alignment.

Table 3. Time spent by the user to achieve an error-free alignment of the processed text lines for the 20-pages data set using the proposed method and performing a full manual alignment.

	MiM algorithm	Manual alignment
Total time (min)	98.97	189.35
Validation time (min)	41.12	N/A
Correction time (min)	57.83	N/A

4.5 Results Comparison

Several methods in the literature have tried to address a similar problem, Table 4 reports a summary view of these works. The methods considered all use different datasets from the Bentham Collection, however, works [5,11,15] use datasets somewhat similar to the dataset used for these work. [15] uses as a dataset a manuscript letter from the American politician and scientist Thomas Jefferson, while the works [5] and [11] test their method on the George Washington archive. The documents in these datasets are contemporary to those of the Bentham collection, and they are all written in cursive English. Furthermore, the works [15] and [5] admit that the alignment also occurs with an image that contains more than one word, in the same way as the proposed method. Among all the works, [6] and [18] use the most different datasets with respect to the dataset used. [6] tests the method on the dataset 'These of the saint Grail', a dataset from the 13th century, while [18] develops a methodology for carrying out an alignment on early printed documents and tests on the Gutenberg Bible.The remaining datasets contain documents either written in languages other than English or with a modern style of handwriting.

Table 4. Comparison between the methods used in literature and the different datasets used.

Reference	Dataset	Dataset dimension	Results
[15]	Thomas Jefferson Letter - 1787	249 words	72% correct alignment
[5]	George Washington's archive - GW100	100 pages	75.40% correct alignment
[11]	George Washington's archive - GW100	100 pages	72.80% correct alignment
[16]	Corpus Cristo Salvador	53 pages 1172 lines	92.80% correct alignment
[3]	The Swiss Literary Archives Handwritten poetry by Gerhard Meier	145 pages 1640 lines	94.66% word mapping rate (require training for feat extraction)
[17]	Kabinet van de Koningin (KdK) collection	100 lines	69% correct alignment
[13]	ICDAR2009 test set	200 documents 29717 words	99.48% detection rate (extension of [14])
[14]	ICDAR2009 test set	200 documents 29717 words	97.04% detection rate (requires manual validation)
[10]	C5 Hattem Manuscript	303 pages	75.50% Correct alignment
[6]	Queste del saint Graal (no coursive)	120 double-columned pages	72.90% correct alignment
[18]	Gutenberg Bible (incunambula)	37 pages	94.30% correct alignment
Proposed	Bentham Collection	20 pages 431 lines	75.93% correct alignment

The proposed method can reach a percentage of correct alignment of 75.93%. Comparing this result with those in Table 3, it is possible to note that the performance is comparable with those of the methods tested on datasets similar to the one used performing slightly better. However a direct comparison between all the methods is difficult, since all the methods are tested on different datasets with very different dimensions and characteristics.

5   Conclusion

We have presented a method for automatically aligning the transcription of handwritten historical documents with the digital document images. We then implemented a tool to validate the alignment results, saving all the correct alignments or correcting the misleading ones. The tool allowed us to record the time taken for the process. It was found that using the proposed method to obtain datasets with correctly labelled handwritten word images compared favourably with the time required for manual labeling the dataset. The experimental results showed that our method was able to correctly match 75.93% of the words in the dataset. The results reported here cannot be directly compared with the results of other methods proposed in the literature, as they were obtained with different data and under different assumptions. Nevertheless, they show that the performance of our method is comparable to the state of the art and its complexity is much lower than that of the best performing competitors. Moreover, the method reduces the time needed for the user to perform the alignment manually by more than 47%.

The method allows us to obtain good results, but we believe that it is possible to improve the performance of the system and we are working in this direction. To this end, we have discovered some potential weaknesses in the system and are thinking about solutions to improve performance. Currently, the method calculates a threshold ν before the alignment step and keeps this value constant for all analysed lines, but it is possible to estimate a different threshold for each line of text. The calculation of the ACW_{box} value is based on purely geometric and spatial considerations. During the alignment process, it is possible to track the size of the boxes of the previously aligned words. This information can be used to improve the estimation of the ACW_{box} value, assuming that the size of the same handwritten characters remains constant throughout the document.

The promising results reported here, and the idea of using the results of the system to simplify the labelling of handwritten records, have led us to believe that the process of transcription alignment could be of considerable interest and have prompted us to continue our investigations for future developments.

References

1. Fox, E.A.: The digital libraries initiative: update and discussion, Chap. 26. In: Bulletin of the American Society for Information Science and Technology (2003)
2. Hobby, J.D.: Matching document images with ground truth. Int. J. Doc. Anal. Recogn. **1**(1), 52–61 (1998)
3. Indermühle, E., Liwicki, M., Bunke, H.: Combining alignment results for historical handwritten document analysis. In: 2009 10th International Conference on Document Analysis and Recognition, pp. 1186–1190. IEEE (2009)
4. Kassis, M., Nassour, J., El-Sana, J.: Alignment of historical handwritten manuscripts using Siamese neural network. In: 2017 14th IAPR International Conference on Document Analysis and Recognition (ICDAR), vol. 01, pp. 293–298 (2017). https://doi.org/10.1109/ICDAR.2017.56
5. Kornfield, E., Manmatha, R., Allan, J.: Text alignment with handwritten documents. In: 2004 Proceedings of the First International Workshop on Document Image Analysis for Libraries, pp. 195–209 (2004). https://doi.org/10.1109/DIAL. 2004.1263249
6. Leydier, Y., Églin, V., Brès, S., Stutzmann, D.: Learning-free text-image alignment for medieval manuscripts. In: 2014 14th International Conference on Frontiers in Handwriting Recognition, pp. 363–368 (2014). https://doi.org/10.1109/ICFHR. 2014.67
7. Lombardi, F., Marinai, S.: Deep learning for historical document analysis and recognition-a survey. J. Imag. **6**(10), 110 (2020)

8. Marchionini, G., Geisler, G.: The open video digital library. D-Lib Mag. **8**(12), 1082–9873 (2002)
9. Parziale, A., Capriolo, G., Marcelli, A.: One step is not enough: a multi-step procedure for building the training set of a query by string keyword spotting system to assist the transcription of historical document. J. Imag. **6**(10), 109 (2020)
10. Romero-Gómez, V., Toselli, A.H., Bosch, V., Sánchez, J.A., Vidal, E.: Automatic alignment of handwritten images and transcripts for training handwritten text recognition systems. In: 2018 13th IAPR International Workshop on Document Analysis Systems (DAS), pp. 328–333. IEEE (2018)
11. Rothfeder, J., Manmatha, R., Rath, T.M.: Aligning transcripts to automatically segmented handwritten manuscripts. In: Bunke, H., Spitz, A.L. (eds.) DAS 2006. LNCS, vol. 3872, pp. 84–95. Springer, Heidelberg (2006). https://doi.org/10.1007/11669487_8
12. Sánchez, J.A., Romero, V., Toselli, A.H., Vidal, E.: ICFHR 2014 competition on handwritten text recognition on transcriptorium datasets (HTRtS). In: 2014 14th International Conference on Frontiers in Handwriting Recognition, pp. 785–790. IEEE (2014)
13. Stamatopoulos, N., Gatos, B., Louloudis, G.: A novel transcript mapping technique for handwritten document images. In: 2014 14th International Conference on Frontiers in Handwriting Recognition, pp. 41–46 (2014). https://doi.org/10.1109/ICFHR.2014.15
14. Stamatopoulos, N., Louloudis, G., Gatos, B.: Efficient transcript mapping to ease the creation of document image segmentation ground truth with text-image alignment. In: 2010 12th International Conference on Frontiers in Handwriting Recognition, pp. 226–231. IEEE (2010)
15. Tomai, C.I., Zhang, B., Govindaraju, V.: Transcript mapping for historic handwritten document images. In: Proceedings Eighth International Workshop on Frontiers in Handwriting Recognition, pp. 413–418. IEEE (2002)
16. Toselli, A.H., Romero, V., Vidal, E.: Viterbi based alignment between text images and their transcripts. In: Proceedings of the Workshop on Language Technology for Cultural Heritage Data (LaTeCH 2007), pp. 9–16 (2007)
17. Zinger, S., Nerbonne, J., Schomaker, L.: Text-image alignment for historical handwritten documents. In: Document Recognition and Retrieval XVI, vol. 7247, p. 724703. International Society for Optics and Photonics (2009)
18. Ziran, Z., Pic, X., Innocenti, S.U., Mugnai, D., Marinai, S.: Text alignment in early printed books combining deep learning and dynamic programming. Pattern Recogn. Lett. **133**, 109–115 (2020)

Improving Handwriting Recognition for Historical Documents Using Synthetic Text Lines

Martin Spoto[1], Beat Wolf[1], Andreas Fischer[1,2],
and Anna Scius-Bertrand[1,2,3($\boxtimes$)]

[1] iCoSys, HES-SO, Fribourg, Switzerland
{martin.spoto,beat.wolf,andreas.fischer,anna.scius-bertrand}@hefr.ch
[2] DIVA, University of Fribourg, Fribourg, Switzerland
[3] EPHE-PSL, Paris, France

Abstract. Automatic handwriting recognition for historical documents is a key element for making our cultural heritage available to researchers and the general public. However, current approaches based on machine learning require a considerable amount of annotated learning samples to read ancient scripts and languages. Producing such ground truth is a laborious and time-consuming task that often requires human experts. In this paper, to cope with a limited amount of learning samples, we explore the impact of using synthetic text line images to support the training of handwriting recognition systems. For generating text lines, we consider lineGen, a recent GAN-based approach, and for handwriting recognition, we consider HTR-Flor, a state-of-the-art recognition system. Different meta-learning strategies are explored that schedule the addition of synthetic text line images to the existing real samples. In an experimental evaluation on the well-known Bentham dataset as well as the newly introduced Bullinger dataset, we demonstrate a significant improvement of the recognition performance when combining real and synthetic samples.

Keywords: Handwriting recognition · Synthetic handwriting · Meta-learning strategies · Linegen · HTR-Flor

1 Introduction

The state of the art in handwritten text recognition (HTR) for historical documents has improved greatly in the past decade, leading to relatively robust systems for automated transcription and keyword spotting [3]. However, the main limitation of such systems is the need to access thousands of annotated training samples, which have to be produced by human experts for each script and handwriting style anew.

A promising approach to alleviate this limitation is to support the training of the recognition system with synthetic samples. Recent progress include the use

C. Carmona-Duarte et al. (Eds.): IGS 2021, LNCS 13424, pp. 61–75, 2022.
https://doi.org/10.1007/978-3-031-19745-1_5

of Generative Adversarial Network (GANs) for generating synthetic handwriting based on examples of existing handwriting styles.

In this paper, we aim to investigate whether or not synthetic handwriting samples can help to improve the recognition performance for historical documents when only few real labeled samples are available. To the best of our knowledge, this question has not been addressed comprehensively so far. We consider a recent GAN-based approach, lineGen [2], for style transfer and synthesis of text line images, and use the synthetic learning samples for training a state-of-the-art recognition system, HTR-Flor [14]. Several meta-learning strategies are investigated to schedule the addition of synthetic samples to the real ones.

Two datasets are considered for experimental evaluation. First, the well-known Bentham collection [5], which contains a single-writer collection of English manuscripts from the 18th and early 19th century. Secondly, the newly introduced Bullinger dataset, a work in progress that aims to make the letter correspondence of Heinrich Bullinger, a Swiss reformer, available in an electronic edition. The letters were written in Latin and German in the 16th century and encompass a considerable number of writers who are represented with only one or few letters in the collection. Handwriting synthesis is particularly interesting in this scenario, as it may allow to adapt a handwriting recognition system to the particular writing styles of these letters.

In the following, we discuss related work, describe the handwriting datasets, introduce the synthesis and recognition methods as well as the meta-learning strategies, and present the experimental results. The paper is concluded with an outlook to future work.

1.1 Related Work

We found relatively few examples of using synthetic handwriting data to help with the training of HTR systems. One recent example is TrOCR [9]. It uses a transformer-based architecture as well as pre-trained image and text transformers to achieve state-of-the-art recognition performance on both printed and handwritten text datasets. One issue of transformer-based architectures is that they require huge amount of training data. The solution implemented by TrOCR is to use synthetic data to augment existing datasets. They did not however use a handwriting generator, but instead generated training data using publicly available fonts with both printed and handwritten style.

There have been several attempts at handwritten text generation in recent years since the introduction of Generative Adversarial Networks [6], but only in a few cases, the resulting synthetic data has been used to train an HTR system.

To the best of our knowledge, Alonso et al. [1] is the first attempt at generating handwritten text images by using a Generative Adversarial Networks (GAN) [6] trained on offline data. While it is able to generate legible French and Arabic words, it suffers from several limitations. It is only able to generate fixed width images with consequently a fixed character count. It is also unable to properly disentangle style from content, making it impossible to control the style of the generated images. Despite these limitations, the generated images were used to augment the IAM dataset with 100k new entries and train a handwritten text recognition system, but to no noticeable improvements.

ScrabbleGAN [4] improves on Alonso et al. [1] by using a fully convolutional generator and a filter bank to handle character style. These improvements allow for variable word length and control over the generated style, but the character width is still fixed, making generated cursive text look unrealistic. Generated data was evaluated by mixing 100k images to existing datasets of modern handwriting, specifically IAM and RIMES, and retraining the HTR system. A improvement of around 1% was measured on both datasets. More interestingly, they highlighted the possibility of using such a generation system in domain adaptation scenarios.

GANWriting [8] improves on ScrabbleGAN [4] by removing the character width limitation, and therefore showing huge improvements in generation quality for cursive and tight handwriting styles. Unfortunately, they did not evaluate their data for HTR system training.

SmartPatch [10] is the latest improvement of GANWriting [8]. Custom patch discriminators are used to improve generation quality by removing some common artifacts produced by GANWriting. In a human evaluation, SmartPatch was thought to look better than GANWriting 70.5% of the time, and it even seemed more real than the true real data 54.4% of the time. They did not however evaluate their results on a HTR model either.

LineGen [2] is based on Alonso et al. [1]. It works directly on entire lines and is capable of extracting style information from only a few samples. It uses an additional spacing network to allow much better variation in character output width. It makes use of an autoencoder like architecture to introduce perceptual and pixel-wise reconstruction loss, enabling for high-fidelity results. However, we find once again no evaluation of the results on a HTR model.

In this paper, we consider lineGen for generating synthetic handwriting because of convincing visual results and its ability to generate complete text lines, which are the standard input for current HTR systems. The synthetic training samples are studied in the context of handwriting recognition with HTR-Flor [14], a relatively lightweight convolutional recognition system with state-of-the-art performance.

2   Data

2.1   Bentham

The Bentham collection [5,13] is a set of manuscripts images written by the English philosopher Jeremy Bentham during the 18th and early 19th centuries. It is therefore a single writer dataset. It contains 433 pages of scanned letters, totaling 11,473 lines. The scans are of high quality, with a clearly legible black ink on grey background handwriting, as can be seen in Fig. 1.

The dataset comes as either directly the pages or the lines, along with a ground truth indicating what is written on each image. There is no word-level

Fig. 1. Example of a line from the Bentham dataset.

isolation available. That means that, as can be seen on Fig. 1, the entire lines are cut from the pages. The skew, i.e. the inclination of the text lines, is not corrected, so some of the lines are not perfectly horizontal and may have a slight upward or downward angle.

2.2 Bullinger

The Bullinger dataset is a novel, work-in-progress dataset originating from the Bullinger Digital project[1]. This project aims to scan and associate transcriptions to letters sent by and to the Swiss reformer Heinrich Bullinger (1504–1575), which leads to the presence of different handwriting styles. While the scans are of high quality, the dataset itself is a challenge for handwriting recognition. It features 16th century style handwriting with ink on paper that is often hard to read even for a human observer. It is also a multi-language dataset, featuring letters mostly in Latin but also in German. A line example is shown in Fig. 2.

Fig. 2. Example of a line from the Bullinger dataset.

The dataset is composed of a set of scanned letters with the line location information.

As the dataset is still a work in progress, we did not have access to all the data at once. We therefore used two distinct releases. The first release, the small Bullinger dataset, is composed of 1,488 lines after preprocessing. The second release, the large Bullinger dataset, is composed of 18,925 lines.

There are also some caveats with the provided ground truth and segmentations. While some of the content and segmentations have been proofread and are human-verified, most of the data comes from a Transkribus [7] based transcription alignment system. Although transcription alignment has a very high precision, the resulting ground truth still contains a few errors. In particular, some abbreviations that are commonly used in handwritten Latin text may be written out in full. While this makes sense when providing a transcription of a

---

[1] https://www.bullinger-digital.ch/.

letter to a human reader, it is not ideal for training an HTR system, because it leads to a mismatch between the abbreviation character visible in the image and the word written out in full in the transcription. Nevertheless, an experimental evaluation of this dataset is still feasible, since we only compare relative HTR performances measured on the same data.

3 Methods

In this section, we describe our choice of methods for evaluating the impact of synthetic training data. First, the GAN-based approach to generate synthetic text lines using lineGen, secondly, the HTR system, and finally the meta-learning strategies for mixing real and synthetic data.

3.1 Text-Line Image Generation

To generate new text-line images we use lineGen [2]. It works directly on entire lines and is capable of extracting style information from only a few samples of the target style. It uses an additional spacing network to allow much better variation in character output width. It makes use of an autoencoder-like architecture to introduce perceptual and pixel-wise reconstruction loss, enabling for high-fidelity results.

The network is composed of six components: a style extractor, a space predictor, a pre-trained HTR system, a generator, a discriminator and a pre-trained encoder. The style extractor takes a single image as input and outputs a style vector. The space predictor takes a line of text and the style vector as input and outputs spaced text. Both the style vector and the spaced text are then fed to the generator which outputs a generated image that should have the content of the given line of text with the style of the given image example.

Three loss functions are considered. First, the generated image is used by the pre-trained HTR system to compute a Connectionist Temporal Classification (CTC) loss. Second, the discriminator computes an adversarial loss and, third, the pre-trained encoder computes a perceptual and pixel-wise reconstruction loss.

We use this network on two datasets described below, Bentham and Bullinger. The data is split randomly into independent sets for training, validation, and testing, respectively. The exact split is indicated in Table 2 in the experiments Sect. 4.1.

Bentham. To generate synthetic text lines for the English Bentham dataset, we write lines from *The Lord of the Rings* in the style of the Bentham dataset. We successively trained the encoder (25'000 iterations), the internal HTR system (15'000 iterations), and the generator (50'000 iterations). Figure 3 shows the results obtained after this training process. Visually the lines look like the original database lines. They are legible with relatively few artifacts. Some do appear, especially with characters that go below the baseline like "y" or "g".

We can also see some artifacts appear around punctuation marks like "!" or ",". Some of those artifacts are due to the data, in particular the non-frequent characters. For example, we count only 19 occurrences of "!" in the whole Bentham dataset.

Fig. 3. Example of generated lines using lineGen on the Bentham dataset after 50'000 iterations

The artifacts of letters like "y" and "g" are harder to understand. One possible explanation is that they are somewhat often cut or overlapped in the dataset, due to the segmentation of the lines. One other interesting point regarding those letters is that they seem to share the same defects across sentences. Figure 4 shows a close up of those artifacts from multiple different lines. We can clearly see that the defaults as well as the general shape are similar for each instance. It seems that the generator does not produce enough variations. We tried to add some variations by introducing a normal noise $X \sim \mathcal{N}(0, 0.5)$ to the style vector centered around the mean. We do not observe any significant difference with or without additional noise, hinting that adding noise to the style vector is not enough to fix the variation issues of the generator.

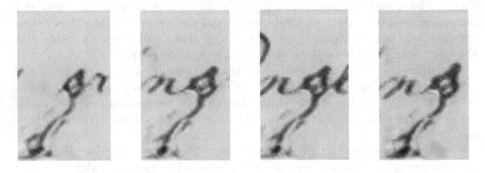

Fig. 4. Example of artefacts in a line generate by lineGen on the Bentham dataset

Bullinger. On the Bullinger dataset, the training was done in two parts. It was first attempted on the small original dataset containing only 1,190 transcribed lines. As the results were not satisfactory, training was then continued on the bigger 17,033 lines dataset.

After training our text-line generator on the small dataset we reach a Character Error Rate lower than 1% on the training data and 30% on the validation data. These results show clearly an overfitting, as should be expected with such a small dataset. Nevertheless, we went ahead with the training of the generator to see how it would perform in such bad conditions. It was trained for 50,000 iterations (about 54 h). As visible in Fig. 5a), the generator struggled to output something coherent, and it took over 40'000 iterations just to start seeing something that was remotely similar to what we would expect. After another 10,000 iterations, the output stabilized to very blurry but still coherent text, as can be seen in Fig. 5b). We can however see that the general look of the generated image matches the expected style of the Bullinger dataset.

After this initial training, we continued on the larger one. The generator was trained for another 10,000 steps. This resulted in a significant improvement in generation quality, as can be seen in Fig. 5c). The text is sharper and mostly legible. We can however observe the same artifacts as on the Bentham dataset, particularly visible on the "y" letter. This effect is amplified here because we generated an English sentence, which has vastly more occurrences of "y" than the original Latin or German languages of the dataset.

As an attempt to further increase the generation quality, both the encoder and internal HTR were also trained on the larger dataset. The encoder was trained for an additional 54,000 iterations, bringing the total to 80,000. The internal HTR was trained for 15,000 more iterations, for a total of 30,000. This renewed training ended up with a Character Error Rate of 6% on the training data and 15% on the validation data, i.e., we see much less overfitting than after the initial training, as it shows on the results obtained on the validation data. Using those new pre-trained parts, the generator was then trained for another 20,000 iterations, reaching a total of 80,000. An example is shown Fig. 5d).

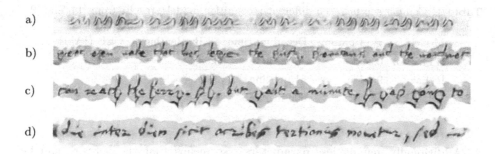

Fig. 5. Example of generated line images using lineGen on the small Bullinger dataset after a) 40'000 iterations, b) 50 000 iterations and on the large one with c) 60'000 and d) 80'000 iterations

While the results may look worse than before at first glance, they are actually closer to the original dataset. This is explained by the fact that the internal HTR got significantly better. Before the additional data and training, it was biased towards "easy to read" characters, and this bias got carried over to the generator. By increasing the ability of the internal HTR, the generator is able to create a wider variety of character styles that are still correctly recognized, and is therefore not incorrectly penalized by the character loss.

Note, however that the final results are overall worse than on the Bentham dataset, with more artifacts appearing. This is easily explainable by the nature of the two datasets. The Bentham dataset being a cleaner, single writer dataset, it is obviously easier than the Bullinger one and its multiple writers with hard to read handwriting, even for an human observer. The synthetic Bullinger style is expected to contain predominant character styles across the whole database but not to mimic one writer in particular, although it will be biased towards the style of Bullinger himself who wrote the largest number of letters.

3.2   Recognition System

To choose the recognition system, three networks were compared on the Bentham and IAM dataset: HTR-Flor [14], TrOCR [9] and PyLaia [12], used in commercial tools like Transkribus [7]. The results of the papers mentioned above have been reported in Table 1. TrOCR has the lowest CER rate but is the network with the largest number of parameters and the longest decoding time. Also, this network needs more training data than the two other networks.

For evaluating the impact of synthetic training samples on the recognition performance, we chose HTR-Flor as our baseline recognition system, because it offers an excellent trade-off between recognition performance and computational effort. It is lightweight, relatively fast, and still manages to outperform other models like PyLaia.

Table 1. Comparison between different recognition models, results from [14] and [9]

Model	# of params	Decoding time	CER (Bentham)	CER (IAM)
HTR-Flor	0.8 M	55 ms/line	3.98%	3.72%
PyLaia	9.4 M	81 ms/line	4.65%	4.94%
TrOCR	558 M	600 ms/line	–	2.89%

Additionally, having less parameters also means that the network can be trained with less data, and with less risks of overfitting when data is scarce. This is also an advantage in our case, since our final use case aims to be able to train the HTR system on as little as a single page of real text for a particular writer.

3.3   Meta-learning Strategy

The standard meta-learning strategy for using synthetic data is to add a fixed number s of synthetic samples to the real samples and then train the system until convergence. Because there is no limit in the number of synthetic text lines that can be produced by the generator, different values for s can be tested. The expectation is that adding some synthetic data will be helpful because of the increased data quantity but adding too much synthetic data leads to a reduced performance because of the decreased data quality when compared with real samples.

We explore also a more detailed meta-learning strategy by gradually adding more synthetic data to the system as the number of training epochs increase. Our intuition is that real data is especially important at the beginning of the training process, in order to find good initial parameters for the HTR system with high-quality data, and that adding synthetic data is especially beneficial at the end of the training process to fine-tune the parameters with high-quantity data.

The suggested meta-learning strategy applies a sequence $L_1, \ldots, L_n$ of learning steps, where each step $L_i = (r_i, s_i, e_i)$ utilizes r_i real samples and s_i synthetic samples for training the HTR system during e_i epochs, with $r_i \geq r_{i+1}$ and $s_i \leq s_{i+1}$ to gradually increase the number of synthetic learning samples. The following strategies are considered in this paper:

- *Real-only.* Use only real samples $L = (r, 0, e)$.
- *Synthetic-only.* Use only synthetic samples $L = (0, s, e)$.
- *Fixed.* Use a fixed amount of real and synthetic samples $L = (r, s, e)$.
- *Increase.* Increase synthetic samples $L_1 = (r, s_1, e_1), \ldots, L_n = (r, s_n, e_n)$.
- *Replace.* Also decrease real samples $L_1 = (r_1, s_1, e_1), \ldots, L_n = (r_n, s_n, e_n)$.

4 Experiments

4.1 Setup

To evaluate the impact of synthetic data for HTR training, the Bentham and Bullinger datasets are first split into independent sets of text lines used for training, validation, and testing, as indicated in Table 2.

Table 2. Distribution of text lines partitions

Dataset	Training	Validation	Test	Total
Bentham	9,198	1,415	960	11,573
Bullinger (large)	17,033	946	946	18,925

After training the lineGen text line generator for the two datasets (see Sect. 3.1), we consider two scenarios for evaluating the HTR system:

- **Medium.** A medium amount of 1000 real text lines from the training set is used to train the HTR-Flor recognition system. Such a situation is encountered when ground truth is available for several pages of a historical manuscript.

– **Low.** A low amount of 200 real text lines is used. Such a situation is encountered when ground truth is prepared only for one or few pages of a historical manuscript.

The HTR system is trained for 75 epochs in total, which is sufficient for convergence. Depending on the meta-learning strategies employed, the 75 epochs are subdivided into several learning steps $L_i = (r_i, s_i, e_i)$ with $\sum_{i=1}^{n} e_i = 75$.

For the **Medium** scenario, the meta-learning strategies are evaluated:

– *Real-only:* 1000 real samples.
– *Synthetic-only:* 1000 synthetic samples.
– *Fixed:* 1000 real and 1000 synthetic samples.
– *Increase:* $(1000, 0, 20), (1000, 500, 10), (1000, 1000, 20), (1000, 2000, 25)$
– *Replace:* $(1000, 0, 25), (750, 250, 25), (500, 500, 15), (0, 1000, 10)$

For the **Low** scenario, the following meta-learning strategies are evaluated:

– *Real-only:* 200 real samples.
– *Synthetic-only:* 200 synthetic samples.
– *Fixed:* 200 real and 200 synthetic samples.
– *Fixed-4k:* 200 real and 4000 synthetic samples.
– *Fixed-8k:* 200 real and 8000 synthetic samples.
– *Increase:* $(200, 0, 20), (200, 200, 10), (200, 500, 20), (200, 1000, 25)$
– *Replace:* $(200, 0, 25), (150, 50, 25), (100, 100, 15), (0, 200, 10)$

In both scenarios, to put the results into context, a baseline is provided, which corresponds to a situation where a large amount of ground truth is created for a historical document collection.

– *Baseline:* Use all the available real training samples (see Table 2).

4.2   Medium Scenario

The recognition results of the **Medium** scenario are summarized in Table 3 in terms of character error rate (CER). The best results on Bentham are achieved with the *Fixed* meta-learning strategy, with a CER of 11.38%, and the best results on Bullinger are achieved with the *Increase* strategy, with a CER of 23.55%. In both cases, the results of the *Fixed* and *Increase* strategies are very similar. When compared with the *Real-only* scenario, significant improvements of 3.39% (Bentham) and 3.24% (Bullinger) are obtained when using synthetic text lines during training. When compared with the *Baseline*, the achieved CER indicates that HTR remains feasible even when ground truth exists only for 1000 text lines.

When comparing the different meta-learning strategies, we can see that both datasets follow the same general trends. While the *Real-only* scenario reaches a solid performance of 14.77% and 26.79% on Bentham and Bullinger, respectively, the *Synthetic-only* one seems to quickly get stuck at 67.70% and 83.37%.

Table 3. Character error rates for the **Medium** scenario. The best results among the different meta-learning strategies are highlighted in bold font.

Medium	Bentham	Bullinger
Baseline	05.01	10.69
Real-only	14.77	26.79
Synthetic-only	67.70	83.37
Fixed	**11.38**	24.09
Increase	11.99	**23.35**
Replace	30.63	55.96

This strongly hints that the HTR model is overfitting on the synthetic training data. The most likely explanation is that the generated images do not have enough variations. As previously shown in Fig. 4 during the generator training, the individual characters do not seem to vary in a meaningful way, suggesting that the HTR model learns the shape of a few particular characters but cannot generalize to real variations present in the handwriting.

Figures 6 and 7 show the evolution of the CER in more detail during training with the different meta-learning strategies. Again, we observe consistent results among the two datasets.

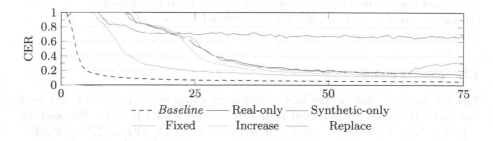

Fig. 6. Training behavior for the **Medium** scenario on the Bentham dataset.

Real-Only and Synthetic-Only. In the **Medium** scenario, training with only real data achieves a reasonable performance but leaves room for improvements when compared with the *Baseline*. Using only synthetic data fails and leads quickly to overfitting.

Fixed. The *Fixed* scenario uses the same amount of real and synthetic images over 75 training epochs. It clearly outperforms the *Real-only* scenario, both learning faster and reaching a lower CER. This is a very encouraging result, as it shows that the additional generated data did indeed help training the HTR model.

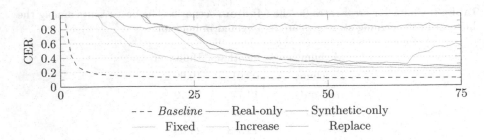

Fig. 7. Training behavior for the **Medium** scenario on the Bullinger dataset.

Increase. The *Increase* scenario gradually adds more synthetic data. As expected, this scenario stays close to the performances of the real-only one until the 20th epoch. It then starts to outperform it as additional generated data is included, reaching a final performance similar to the *Fixed* scenario. These results seem to indicate that it is not necessary to add the synthetic data progressively to "guide" the training.

Replace. The *Replace* scenario both decreases the real data and increases the synthetic data gradually. This scenario is interesting because the training seems to follow the *Real-only* scenario, up to the 65th epoch, where we switch to generated data only. We can then see the CER climbing back up, presumably as the model overfits on the generated data, as theorized previously. It shows that the model overfits very quickly when presented with only synthetic data, even when previously "warmed up" with real data.

4.3   Low Scenario

The recognition results of the **Low** scenario are summarized in Table 4. The best results on Bentham are achieved with *Fixed-4k*, with a CER of 19.78%, and the best results on Bullinger are also achieved with *Fixed-4k*, with a CER of 40.24%. When compared with the *Real-only* scenario, drastic improvements of 61.31% (Bentham) and 47.79% (Bullinger) are observed, highlighting that synthetic data is especially helpful when only very few labeled samples are available in the ground truth, i.e. only a few pages or a single letter in a historical document collection.

Figures 8 and 9 illustrate the evolution of the CER during training. Again, consistent trends are observed among the two datasets.

Real-Only and Synthetic-Only. We see that the real data is not sufficient to train the model in the **Low** scenario. For *Synthetic-only*, the performance remains similar to the **Medium** scenario.

Fixed. The different *Fixed* meta-learning strategies greatly outperform *Real-only* and *Synthetic-only*, demonstrating that a combination of real and synthetic data

Table 4. Character error rates for the **Low** scenario. The best results among the different meta-learning strategies are highlighted in bold font.

Low	Bentham	Bullinger
Baseline	05.01	10.69
Real	81.10	88.03
Generated	68.41	80.71
Fixed	27.03	47.68
Fixed-4k	**19.78**	**40.24**
Fixed-8k	21.29	43.70
Increase	29.02	47.04
Replace	63.30	77.40

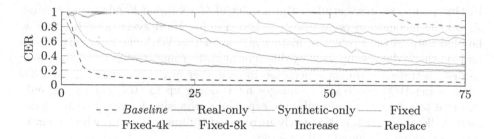

Fig. 8. Training behavior for the **Low** scenario on the Bentham dataset.

is of crucial importance when working in the **Low** scenario. We observe that adding more synthetic data using *Fixed-4k* improves the performance reaching a peak performance. Adding even more synthetic data with *Fixed-8k* does not further improve the result.

Increase. As expected, we see the same "slow start" for *Increase* as with *Real-only*. We then see a rapid improvement as we add more data, the CER continuously decreases until the end of the training. On the Bullinger dataset, the strategy to gradually increase the synthetic data slightly outperforms the fixed combination of the *Fixed* strategies.

Replace. As for the **Medium** scenario, it is again not beneficial to remove the real samples. It leads to an overfitting to the synthetic data after the 65th epoch when all real data is removed. However, unlike the **Medium** scenario, the error rate does not increase significantly after this epoch, it just stops improving.

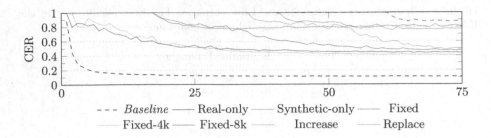

Fig. 9. Training behavior for the **Low** scenario on the Bullinger dataset.

5   Conclusion

In this paper, we have studied the impact of GAN-based handwriting synthesis on the recognition performance, when training HTR systems with only few labeled data in the context of historical documents. With the right mix of real and synthetic data, supported by different meta-learning strategies, we were able to demonstrate a significant decrease in character error rate, ranging from 3% when using 1000 real text line images for training up to 60% when using only 200 real text lines. These results are especially promising for multi-writer document collections, such as the newly introduced Bullinger dataset, which contain a large number of unique writing styles.

There are several lines of future research. First, the handwriting generation system itself also depends on training data to perform a successful style transfer. This might not always be feasible for smaller datasets, as the initial training with the small Bullinger dataset showed. It would be interesting to further investigate the behavior of generators when trained using low quantity of data, or to explore new ways of training the generators, such as transfer learning with fine-tuning.

Secondly, all experiments in this paper have been realized using lineGen. It would be beneficial to test other generators as well, in particular to verify if the same drop in performance is observed when using only synthetic data.

Finally, the synthetically generated samples, although matching the target style well, were lacking some natural variability. Future work should investigate methods to increase the variability and make it as natural as possible. Using the kinematic theory of rapid human movements [11] for this purpose seems especially promising.

Acknowledgements. This work has been supported by the Hasler Foundation, Switzerland. We would like to thank the anonymous reviewers for their detailed and helpful comments.

References

1. Alonso, E., Moysset, B., Messina, R.: Adversarial generation of handwritten text images conditioned on sequences. arXiv:1903.00277 (2019)

2. Davis, B., Tensmeyer, C., Price, B., Wigington, C., Morse, B., Jain, R.: Text and style conditioned GAN for generation of offline handwriting lines. arXiv:2009.00678 (2020)
3. Fischer, A., Liwicki, M., Ingold, R. (eds.): Handwritten Historical Document Analysis, Recognition, and Retrieval - State of the Art and Future Trends. World Scientific (2020)
4. Fogel, S., Averbuch-Elor, H., Cohen, S., Mazor, S., Litman, R.: ScrabbleGAN: semi-supervised varying length handwritten text generation. arXiv:2003.10557 (2020)
5. Gatos, B., et al.: Ground-truth production in the transcriptorium project. In: 2014 11th IAPR International Workshop on Document Analysis Systems, pp. 237–241 (2014). https://doi.org/10.1109/DAS.2014.23
6. Goodfellow, I.J., et al.: Generative adversarial networks. arXiv:1406.2661 (2014)
7. Kahle, P., Colutto, S., Hackl, G., Mühlberger, G.: Transkribus - a service platform for transcription, recognition and retrieval of historical documents. In: 2017 14th IAPR International Conference on Document Analysis and Recognition (ICDAR), vol. 04, pp. 19–24 (2017). https://doi.org/10.1109/ICDAR.2017.307
8. Kang, L., Riba, P., Wang, Y., Rusiñol, M., Fornés, A., Villegas, M.: GAN-writing: content-conditioned generation of styled handwritten word images. arXiv:2003.02567 (2020)
9. Li, M., et al.: TrOCR: Transformer-based optical character recognition with pre-trained models. CoRR abs/2109.10282 (2021). https://arxiv.org/abs/2109.10282
10. Mattick, A., Mayr, M., Seuret, M., Maier, A., Christlein, V.: SmartPatch: improving handwritten word imitation with patch discriminators. In: Lladós, J., Lopresti, D., Uchida, S. (eds.) ICDAR 2021. LNCS, vol. 12821, pp. 268–283. Springer, Cham (2021). https://doi.org/10.1007/978-3-030-86549-8_18
11. Plamondon, R., Marcelli, A., Ferrer, M. (eds.): The Lognormality Principle and its Applications in e-Security, e-Learning and e-Health. World Scientific (2020)
12. Puigcerver, J.: Are multidimensional recurrent layers really necessary for handwritten text recognition? In: 2017 14th IAPR International Conference on Document Analysis and Recognition (ICDAR), vol. 01, pp. 67–72 (2017). https://doi.org/10.1109/ICDAR.2017.20
13. Sánchez, J.A., Romero, V., Toselli, A.H., Vidal, E.: ICFHR 2014 competition on handwritten text recognition on transcriptorium datasets (HTRtS). In: 2014 14th International Conference on Frontiers in Handwriting Recognition, pp. 785–790 (2014). https://doi.org/10.1109/ICFHR.2014.137
14. de Sousa Neto, A.F., Bezerra, B.L.D., Toselli, A.H., Lima, E.B.: HTR-flor: a deep learning system for offline handwritten text recognition. In: 2020 33rd SIBGRAPI Conference on Graphics, Patterns and Images (SIBGRAPI), pp. 54–61 (2020). https://doi.org/10.1109/SIBGRAPI51738.2020.00016

Writer Retrieval and Writer Identification in Greek Papyri

Vincent Christlein[1]($^{\boxtimes}$) [iD], Isabelle Marthot-Santaniello[2] [iD], Martin Mayr[1] [iD], Anguelos Nicolaou[1] [iD], and Mathias Seuret[1] [iD]

[1] Pattern Recognition Lab, Friedrich-Alexander-Universität Erlangen-Nürnberg, Erlangen, Germany
vincent.christlein@fau.de
[2] Departement Altertumswissenschaften, Universität Basel, Basel, Switzerland

Abstract. The analysis of digitized historical manuscripts is typically addressed by paleographic experts. Writer identification refers to the classification of known writers while writer retrieval seeks to find the writer by means of image similarity in a dataset of images. While automatic writer identification/retrieval methods already provide promising results for many historical document types, papyri data is very challenging due to the fiber structures and severe artifacts. Thus, an important step for an improved writer identification is the preprocessing and feature sampling process. We investigate several methods and show that a good binarization is key to an improved writer identification in papyri writings. We focus mainly on writer retrieval using unsupervised feature methods based on traditional or self-supervised-based methods. It is, however, also comparable to the state of the art supervised deep learning-based method in the case of writer classification/re-identification.

Keywords: Writer identification · Writer retrieval · Greek papyri

1 Introduction

The mass digitization of handwritten documents not only makes them accessible to the public, but also accelerates research in the fields of linguistics, history and especially paleography.

An important task is writer[1] identification (scribe attribution), which can provide clues to life in the past and enable further analysis of networks, sizes of writing schools, correspondences, etc. The term writer identification is often used for both *writer retrieval* and *writer classification* (or writer re-identification). Writer retrieval is related to the scenario where a query image with possible known writer identity is given and a dataset of images is ranked according to their similarity to the query image. This can help to pre-sort large corpora. Conversely, writer re-identification has a training set of known identities that

---

[1] "Writer" and "scribe" is used interchangeably throughout the paper.

© Springer Nature Switzerland AG 2022
C. Carmona-Duarte et al. (Eds.): IGS 2021, LNCS 13424, pp. 76–89, 2022.
https://doi.org/10.1007/978-3-031-19745-1_6

can be used to train classifiers that are able to distinguish and classify new samples in these classes.

Writer identification can be obtained at two levels: based on the content of the text or on the appearance of the writing. For the first one, the raw text, i. e., a transcription of the text, is analyzed on the stylistic point of view and the author is attributed. However, the author does not need to be the writer of the text, which could for example be written by a secretary. An appearance analysis can give clues about the person who penned the text, the actual writer. This appearance analysis can be realized in multiple ways. Sometimes the layout can give hints about the scribe, e. g., in charters [20, pp. 40]. However, this depends much on the document type and its tradition quality. Writer identification is traditionally a completely exemplar-based and manual task often accomplished by forensic or paleographic experts. Results obtained by paleographers have often been put in doubt for their subjectivity, the difficulty to produce objective, reproducible arguments. In this paper, we explore an automatic writer identification based upon the script appearance using signed documents, i. e., internal-based evidence of the writer's identity. We enrich our interpretation of the results with paleographic considerations in order to better apprehend the peculiarities of this group of writers.

Script-based writer identification in historical documents gained some attention throughout the last years. A popular group of approaches analyses the textural components of script, e. g., angles or script width, such as the *Hinge* feature [4], which measures at each contour point two different angles. This feature was also applied [3] to a medieval dataset containing 70 document images written by ten writers. Another textural feature is the *Quill* feature [2]. It relates the ink width to the angle at a specific radius. The authors show promising results on historical data consisting of 10–18 writers (depending on the language) using 70–248 document images.

Fiel and Sablating [15] suggest a method based on Scale Invariant Feature Transform (SIFT) and Fisher Vectors [17] to historical Glagolitic documents (oldest known Slavic alphabet) consisting of 361 images written by eight scribes. Therefore, they detect the text by local projection profiles and binarize the document images using the method of Su et al. [33].

Another group of scientists investigate methods for writer identification in historical Arabic documents [1,13,14]. The rejection strategy proposed by Fecker et al. [14] is especially interesting, since it gives information whether a writer is present in the reference dataset or not.

We investigated writer identification for different letter sets of correspondences [9]. We also proposed a deep learning-based approach based on self-supervised learning. It still achieves close to state-of-the-art results on the dataset of letters of the ICDAR'17 competition on historical writer identification [16].

Apart from the technical point of view, writer identification methods were also used in various paleographic analyses. The effort of finding join candidates of the Cairo Genizah collection, which consists of approximately 350 000 fragments, could be reduced drastically by an automatic method for finding join candidates focusing on similar writing [34]. More recently, Shaus et al. [32] analyzed 18 Arad inscriptions (ca. 600 BCE). By means of a forensic expert and statistical methods, they show that the analyzed corpus was written by at least 12 different writers. Popović et al. [28] studied the Bible's ancient scribal culture by analyzing the Great Isaiah Scroll ($1QIsa^a$) of the Dead Sea Scrolls and found a switching point in the column series with a clear phase transition in several columns. This suggests that two main scribes were writing this scroll, showing that multiple scribes worked at the same manuscript.

Papyri manuscripts were studied by Pirrone et al. [27] who investigate self-supervised deep metric learning for ancient papyrus fragments retrieval. Papyri data was also used as a challenging dataset in a competition for segmenting the text (binarization) [29]. A baseline for writer identification of papyri manuscripts was given by Mohammed et al. [23]. It is based on SIFT descriptors evaluated on FAST keypoints classified using a normalized local naive Bayes Nearest Neighbor classifier. The authors also provided a first papyri dataset (GRK-Papyri) consisting of 50 image samples of 10 writers. Cilia et al. [12] used an extended version of this dataset (122 images from 23 writers) and extracted single lines to form the PapyRow dataset that can be used for further investigation. However note that results based on lines are not image-independent anymore and thus could be biased by background artifacts. The GRK-Papyri dataset was also in focus of two further studies [24,25] that focused on writer (re-)identification, i. e., a part of the dataset was used for training and the task was to classify the remainder of the dataset. They showed that a two-step fine-tuning is beneficial for writer identification. In particular, an ImageNet-pretrained network was fine-tuned first on the IAM writer identification dataset [22] before it was fine-tuned a second time on the writers of the papyri training dataset.

In this work, we evaluate two methods for writer identification. Both methods are completely unsupervised, i. e., they do not need known writer identities. One method relies on traditional features and the other one trains a deep neural network in a self-supervised fashion. We evaluate the methods on the GRK-Papyri dataset [23] where we mainly focus on the retrieval scenario because there are no other works apart of a baseline given by Mohammed et al. [23] considering the retrieval case. We show that both methods surpass the baseline by a large margin. In particular, we investigate the critical sampling procedure and show that a good binarization increases the retrieval and re-identification accuracy.

The paper is organized as follows. We first present the methodology used for writer identification in Sect. 2. In Sect. 3, we first discuss the dataset, then present two different evaluation protocols: writer retrieval and writer classification/re-identification, and eventually present and discuss our results before we conclude the paper in Sect. 4.

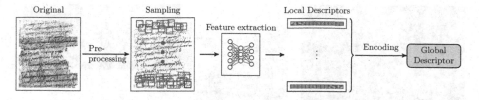

Fig. 1. Writer identification pipeline.

2 Methodology

The writer identification methods we use are based on the work done for the PhD thesis of V. Christlein [6]. It follows a writer identification pipeline based on local features, see Fig. 1. First, the image is pre-processed. This typically involves the binarization of the image. Later, we will see that this is a particular important part of the pipeline. We extract local features at specific sampling points in the image, e.g., from contours of the handwriting or from keypoints. The local descriptors themselves could be generated by a neural network as depicted in Fig. 1. For example in a supervised way by training Convolutional Neural Network (CNN) [8,18]. However, we do not have much training data available. Therefore, we rely on two unsupervised methods to create local descriptors:

(1) We use descriptors based on SIFT [21]. The SIFT descriptors are Dirichlet-normalized, decorrelated and dimensionality-reduced to 64 components by means of PCA-whitening, and eventually ℓ^2-normalized, i.e., the representation is normalized such that its ℓ^2 norm is one. More details are given in [6].
(2) We learn features in a self-supervised fashion [10] using a CNN, i.e., without the need of labeled training data (here the writer information). At SIFT keypoints, SIFT descriptors and 32×32 patches are extracted. This patch size was experimentally shown to work best. The SIFT descriptors are clustered using k-means. The patches are used as input for a CNN. As targets for the CNN, we use the cluster ids of the SIFT clusters. Note that we omit SIFT keypoints and descriptors corresponding to patches that are completely blank. Furthermore, because the image resolution is mostly very large, we downsample the images by a factor of two in each dimension.

From these local descriptors, we create global descriptors to enable a simplified matching. We rely on Vectors of Locally Aggregated Descriptors (VLAD) [19] for encoding the local descriptors into a high dimensional global representation using 100 clusters for k-means clustering. Additionally, we employ Generalized Max Pooling (GMP), which was shown to improve the writer identification performance [5,11] with a regularization parameter $\gamma = 1000$. The global representation is eventually power-normalized with a power of 0.5 and ℓ^2-normalized. This process is repeated five times. These five representations are afterwards jointly PCA-whitened and once more ℓ^2-normalized to further decorrelate the

Fig. 2. Example images of the GRK-Papyri dataset [23]. IDs: Abraamios_3, Andreas_8, Dioscorus_5, Victor_2

global representations [6]. This final representation is eventually used for similarity comparison using Cosine distance, which is a common metric for writer retrieval. If a large enough independent training set would be available, then also Exemplar-SVMs could be used to improve the results further [7].

3 Evaluation

3.1 Data

We use the GRK-papyri dataset [23], see Fig. 2 for some example images. It consists of 50 document images written in Greek on papyri by ten different notaries. For each writer, four to seven samples were cropped from securely attributed texts: sometimes non-overlapping parts of a single long document, sometimes different documents possibly several years apart from one another. They all date from the 6th and early 7th century CE, as can be seen in Fig. 3. The images come from several collections, thus using various digitization parameters.[2] The images contain different artifacts, such as holes, low contrast, etc., and are hence difficult to process.

3.2 Evaluation Protocol

We evaluate our method in two ways:

---

[2] Meta-data on the images are available (reference, date, collection...) at https://d-scribes.philhist.unibas.ch/en/gkr-papyri/.

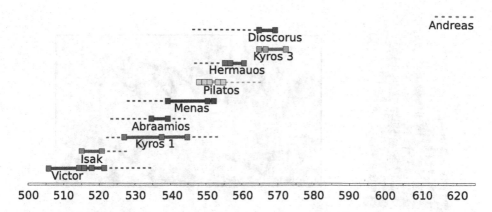

Fig. 3. Period of activity of the ten writers. Squares mark the precisely dated texts included in the GRK-Papyri dataset. Dashed lines mark the maximum extension known thanks to other texts outside the dataset. Note that for Andreas, his only text is securely dated from the period marked with a dotted line.

(1) Leave-one-image-out cross validation. That means, we use each of the 50 images as query image and rank the other 49 images according to their similarity with the query image. These results already allow a detailed pale-ographic interpretation. From these ranks, we can compute different metrics: the Top-1, Top-5, Top-10 identification rate, which denotes the probability that the correct writer is among the first 1, 5, or 10 retrieved, i. e., most similar, images (this is also known as *soft* criterion). Additionally, we give the mean average precision (mAP) which takes into account all predictions by taking the mean over all average precisions.

(2) Classification. For this scenario, we train on 20 samples, two from each writer and test on the remainder.

3.3   Experiments

We evaluate five different methods, where the first four methods only differ in the sampling/pre-processing. As baseline, we extract the SIFT descriptors at SIFT keypoints. Keypoints overlaid over one image of the GRK-Papyri dataset can be seen in Fig. 4. The example shows that many features are lying in the background of the image.

In general, we have two different ways to deal with such a problem: (1) Make the writer identification method robust against noise (artifacts, holes, etc.). This can for example be achieved by using heavy data augmentation during the feature learning process. (2) Remove the noise by means of *binarization*, i. e., a segmentation of the writing.

We follow the second approach and thus try to segment the text in the papyri data.

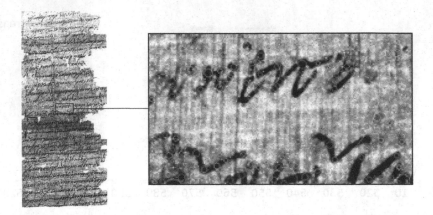

Fig. 4. Example of SIFT keypoints applied on papyri data. Overlay with GRK-Papyri [23], ID: Andreas_8

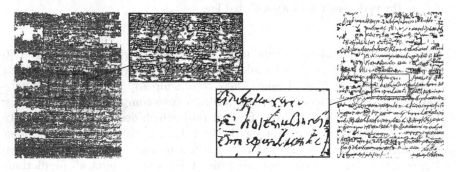

Fig. 5. Su binarization vs. AngU-Net. Image source: GRK-Papyri [23], ID: Abraamios_4.

Binarization. We evaluate two different binarization methods. The first one by Su et al. [33] works commonly well for such purposes. However, on some images, the fiber of the papyri data causes sever artifacts, see for example Fig. 5 (left).

The second binarization method, denoted as *AngU-Net* is based on the popular U-Net [31]. The model was trained on 512 × 512 patches cropped from the training set of the 2017 DIBCO Dataset [30]. The model was specifically trained with augmentations consistent to textual information and designed to simulate material degradation using TorMentor[3] [26]. The effectiveness of this approach is visualized in Fig. 5 (right). For inference, the AngU-Net is used in a fully-convolutional manner.

Given the binarized images, we detect keypoints, extract local features by one of the two presented methods, and compute the global image representations as done in the baseline. As an alternative strategy, we can restrict the SIFT keypoints to lie strictly on dark (here: black) pixels [10]. This can be achieved

---

[3] https://github.com/anguelos/tormentor.

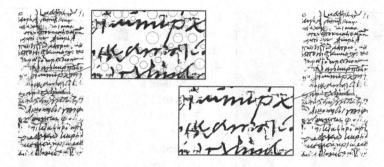

Fig. 6. Common SIFT keypoints (left) vs. restricted SIFT keypoints (right). Image source: GRK-Papyri [23], ID: Victor_5.

Table 1. Writer retrieval results, evaluated by a leave-one-image-out cross-validation.

Method	Top-1	Top-5	Top-10	mAP
Mohammed et al. [23]	30			
SIFT (Baseline)	28	70	84	30.3
Su Binarization + SIFT	40	72	86	30.5
AngU-Net + SIFT	46	**84**	88	36.5
AngU-Net + R-SIFT	48	**84**	92	**42.8**
AngU-Net + Cl-S [10]	**52**	82	**94**	42.2

by restricting the SIFT keypoint extraction such that only minima in the scale space are used. The effect can be seen in Fig. 6.

Retrieval Results. We first focus on the first evaluation protocol, i. e., image retrieval by applying a leave-one-image-out cross-validation. All results are shown in Table 1. The reference method of Mohammed et al. [23] and our baseline approach achieve quite similar results, where our baseline method is slightly worse, i. e., retrieving one less sample, out of the 50, correctly. However, when we apply binarization, the picture alters drastically. The binarization with the method of Su et al. [33] gives already 10 % better results. This can be further improved by using a better segmentation method, e. g., using the proposed AngU-Net. Also restricting the keypoints (R-SIFT) to lie on the writing improves the result slightly. This is interesting since we encountered the contrary in handwritten Latin text [10]. Finally, the Top-1 accuracy can be further improved by using our self-supervised approach to learn robust local features [10].

Based on the document-level heatmap, see Fig. 7a, the best score (smallest number, closest similarity) was achieved between Andreas 5 and 6, i. e., two samples from the same document. Second best was between Kyros3_1 and Kyros3_2, two different texts written only one week apart. Among the best scores are Dioscorus 2 and 3 (recto and versos of the same text) as well as Victor 2 and 3,

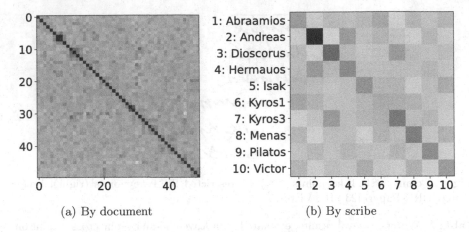

(a) By document   (b) By scribe

Fig. 7. Visualization of AngU-Net + R-SIFT method by heatmaps (the darker the square, the higher the similarity). In (a), the numbers are related to the writer samples in alphabetic order (from Abraamios_1 to Victor_8, Victor _10 being before Victor_2). In (b), the similarity between scribes is displayed as the average of each pair of images; inter-scribe similarity is computed by ignoring comparisons of images with themselves.

which come from the same document but in two different collections, thus two totally different images.

The scribe-level heatmap, in Fig. 7b, shows the inter-scribe similarity, i. e., the average distance between all documents of a scribe and all documents of another one. We can see that texts written by Andreas have the highest similarity among them, while the ones of Kyros1 have the lowest. The homogeneity of Andreas' samples is not surprising since on the one hand Andreas' hand is represented by four samples of the same document, three coming from the same collection, and on the other hand he is a chronological outsider (by far the most recent writer, see Fig. 3). Kyros1 is represented by four different documents, three of which are precisely dated and span over 18 years, which makes his period of activity the longest present in the dataset, cf. Fig. 3. Victor is in a similar situation, since he is represented by 7 samples coming from 6 documents and spanning over 16 years. However, the similarity between his samples is quite high, suggesting that his handwriting has varied less than Kyros1's one over a comparable amount of time.

Classification Results. Finally, we conduct the second evaluation protocol, i. e., we have a train/test split and use two samples of each writer for training. We evaluate two different classifiers: a Nearest Neighbor (NN) approach and a Support Vector Machine (SVM). For the latter approach, we train for each writer an individual SVM using the two samples as positives and the remaining 18 samples as negatives. The two classes are balanced by weighting them indirectly proportionally to the number of respective samples. The classifiers use the

Table 2. Classification results.

Method	Top-1	Top-5
Mohammed et al. [23]	26	
Nasir & Siddiqi [24]	54	
Nasir et al. [25]	**64**	
AngU-Net + SIFT + NN	47	83
AngU-Net + SIFT + SVM	57	**87**
AngU-Net + R-SIFT + NN	53	77
AngU-Net + R-SIFT + SVM	60	80

Table 3. Confusion matrix of the classification result obtained by using AngU-Net + R-SIFT + SVM. Correct ones highlighted in blue, wrong ones in red.

Predicted→	Abraamios	Andreas	Dioscorus	Hermauos	Isak	Kyros1	Kyros3	Menas	Pilatos	Victor
Abraamios	1	0	0	0	0	1	0	0	0	0
Andreas	0	1	0	1	0	0	0	0	0	0
Dioscorus	0	0	2	1	0	0	0	0	0	0
Hermauos	0	0	0	1	0	2	0	0	0	0
Isak	0	0	0	1	1	0	0	0	0	1
Kyros1	0	1	0	0	0	1	0	0	0	0
Kyros3	0	0	0	0	0	1	1	0	0	0
Menas	0	0	0	0	0	0	0	3	0	0
Pilatos	0	0	0	0	1	0	0	0	3	0
Victor	0	0	0	0	0	1	0	1	0	3

True Label (vertical axis label)

global representations computed from local descriptors sampled on normal SIFT keypoints or restricted keypoints (R-SIFT).

The results in Table 2 reflect the same benefit of proper binarization as in the retrieval case. Comparing SIFT and R-SIFT, the latter is beneficial also for classification purposes. Classifier-wise, the use of SVMs is preferable in comparison to a simple nearest neighbor classifier, although the SVMs were only trained with two positive samples. Since the writer classification is fully supervised, we refrain from evaluating the unsupervised CL-S method, which would be needed to be trained on an even smaller training set (30 instead of 50 images) in an unsupervised manner. In future work, it might be worth investigating if an unsupervised pre-training on a large papyri corpus instead of using an ImageNet-pretrained network is beneficial for an additional fine-tuning step similar to the methods proposed by Nasir et al. [24, 25]. The full confusion matrix can be seen in Table 3. Interestingly, the writer who was the least confused with anybody else is the geographic outsider Menas. Indeed, while all the others lived and worked in the same village, Menas' dossier comes from a big city several hundred kilometers north. Another interesting result, which requires an in-depth paleographic analysis, is the confusion between Hermauos and Kyros1 as well as the many false predictions they both have generated. We have already mentioned the variety among Kyros1's samples. Hermauos' results may be due to the important degradation of some of his samples. Future investigations will aim determining if these two writers share specific paleographic features.

In comparison with the state of the art [25], the proposed SIFT-based method does not fully compete to the deep learning based methods that train a CNN on small image patches and then apply a majority vote. While the state-of-the-art method [24] is slightly superior, a drawback of it is that it cannot be used for novel writers, the CNN is tuned towards the writers of the training set and needs to be fine-tuned for each novel writer. In contrast, our method can easily be adapted to more writers by computing a new SVM or just by means of nearest neighbor matching.

4   Conclusion

In this work, we investigated automatic writer identification on the specific historical documents that are the Greek papyri. In particular, we evaluated different binarization and sampling procedures in two different scenarios: retrieval and classification. We show that binarization, especially deep learning-based binarization, improves the writer identification performance by removing the most noise and artifacts introduced by the papyri. We believe that better binarization methods can help to reduce the misclassifications further. Additionally, a sampling that is restricted to the handwriting is beneficial. The obtained results are already stimulating for further paleographic investigations. Some expected results have been confirmed: the geographical and chronological outsiders have distinguished themselves. Some have been refuted: Abraamios was supposed to have a particularly clumsy hand, easy to recognize, but this has not been the case in neither of the two scenarios. For future work, we would like to investigate the possibility of improving writer identification by learning noise-robust descriptors. We would also lead in-depth interpretations of the results in a paleographic perspective to better apprehend and qualify the similarities or at the opposite the originality of the various hands, setting the foundations for sounder scribal attributions on paleographic and computer-assisted grounds.

Acknowledgement. This work was partially supported by the Swiss National Science Foundation as part of the project no. PZ00P1-174149 "Reuniting fragments, identifying scribes and characterizing scripts: the Digital paleography of Greek and Coptic papyri (d-scribes)". This research was supported by grants from NVIDIA and utilized NVIDIA Quadro RTX 6000.

References

1. Asi, A., Abdalhaleem, A., Fecker, D., Märgner, V., El-Sana, J.: On writer identification for Arabic historical manuscripts. Int. J. Doc. Anal. Recogn. (IJDAR) **20**(3), 173–187 (2017). https://doi.org/10.1007/s10032-017-0289-3. https://link.springer.com/10.1007/s10032-017-0289-3
2. Brink, A., Smit, J., Bulacu, M., Schomaker, L.: Writer identification using directional ink-trace width measurements. Pattern Recogn. **45**(1), 162–171 (2012). https://doi.org/10.1016/j.patcog.2011.07.005
3. Bulacu, M., Schomaker, L.: Automatic handwriting identification on medieval documents. In: 14th International Conference on Image Analysis and Processing (ICIAP 2007), no. ICIAP, pp. 279–284. IEEE, Modena, September 2007
4. Bulacu, M., Schomaker, L., Vuurpijl, L.: Writer identification using edge-based directional features. In: Seventh International Conference on Document Analysis and Recognition (ICDAR), Edinburgh, pp. 937–941, August 2003. https://doi.org/10.1109/ICDAR.2003.1227797
5. Christlein, V., Spranger, L., Seuret, M., Nicolaou, A., Král, P., Maier, A.: Deep generalized max pooling. In: 2019 International Conference on Document Analysis and Recognition (ICDAR), pp. 1090–1096, September 2019. https://doi.org/10.1109/ICDAR.2019.00177
6. Christlein, V.: Handwriting analysis with focus on writer identification and writer retrieval. Ph.D. thesis, FAU Erlangen-Nürnberg (2019)
7. Christlein, V., Bernecker, D., Hönig, F., Maier, A., Angelopoulou, E.: Writer identification using GMM supervectors and exemplar-SVMs. Pattern Recogn. **63**, 258–267 (2017). https://doi.org/10.1016/j.patcog.2016.10.005. https://www.sciencedirect.com/science/article/pii/S0031320316303211
8. Christlein, V., Bernecker, D., Maier, A., Angelopoulou, E.: Offline writer identification using convolutional neural network activation features. In: Gall, J., Gehler, P., Leibe, B. (eds.) GCPR 2015. LNCS, vol. 9358, pp. 540–552. Springer, Cham (2015). https://doi.org/10.1007/978-3-319-24947-6_45
9. Christlein, V., et al.: Automatic Writer Identification in Historical Documents: A Case Study. Zeitschrift für digitale Geisteswissenschaften text/html (2016). https://doi.org/10.17175/2016_002. https://www.zfdg.de/2016_002
10. Christlein, V., Gropp, M., Fiel, S., Maier, A.: Unsupervised feature learning for writer identification and writer retrieval. In: 2017 14th IAPR International Conference on Document Analysis and Recognition (ICDAR), Kyoto, vol. 01, pp. 991–997, November 2017. https://doi.org/10.1109/ICDAR.2017.165
11. Christlein, V., Maier, A.: Encoding CNN activations for writer recognition. In: 13th IAPR International Workshop on Document Analysis Systems, Vienna, pp. 169–174, April 2018. https://doi.org/10.1109/DAS.2018.9
12. Cilia, N.D., De Stefano, C., Fontanella, F., Marthot-Santaniello, I., Scotto di Freca, A.: PapyRow: a dataset of row images from ancient Greek papyri for writers identification. In: Del Bimbo, A., et al. (eds.) ICPR 2021. LNCS, vol. 12667, pp. 223–234. Springer, Cham (2021). https://doi.org/10.1007/978-3-030-68787-8_16
13. Fecker, D., et al.: Writer identification for historical Arabic documents. In: 2014 22nd International Conference on Pattern Recognition (ICPR), Stockholm, pp. 3050–3055, August 2014. https://doi.org/10.1109/ICPR.2014.526
14. Fecker, D., Asi, A., Pantke, W., Märgner, V., El-Sana, J., Fingscheidt, T.: Document writer analysis with rejection for historical Arabic manuscripts. In: 2014 14th International Conference on Frontiers in Handwriting Recognition (ICFHR), Heraklion, pp. 743–748, September 2014. https://doi.org/10.1109/ICFHR.2014.130

15. Fiel, S., Hollaus, F., Gau, M., Sablatnig, R.: Writer identification on historical Glagolitic documents. Doc. Recogn. Retr. **9021**, 902102-1–902102-10 (2014). https://doi.org/10.1117/12.2042338

16. Fiel, S., et al.: ICDAR2017 competition on historical document writer identification (historical-WI). In: 2017 14th IAPR International Conference on Document Analysis and Recognition (ICDAR), Kyoto, vol. 01, pp. 1377–1382, November 2017. https://doi.org/10.1109/ICDAR.2017.225

17. Fiel, S., Sablatnig, R.: Writer identification and writer retrieval using the fisher vector on visual vocabularies. In: 2013 12th International Conference on Document Analysis and Recognition (ICDAR), Washington DC, pp. 545–549, August 2013. https://doi.org/10.1109/ICDAR.2013.114

18. Fiel, S., Sablatnig, R.: Writer identification and retrieval using a convolutional neural network. In: Azzopardi, G., Petkov, N. (eds.) CAIP 2015. LNCS, vol. 9257, pp. 26–37. Springer, Cham (2015). https://doi.org/10.1007/978-3-319-23117-4_3

19. Jégou, H., Perronnin, F., Douze, M., Sánchez, J., Pérez, P., Schmid, C.: Aggregating local image descriptors into compact codes. IEEE Trans. Pattern Anal. Mach. Intell. **34**(9), 1704–1716 (2012). https://doi.org/10.1109/TPAMI.2011.235

20. Krafft, O.: Bene Valete: Entwicklung und Typologie des Monogramms in Urkunden der Päpste und anderer Aussteller seit 1049. Eudora-Verlag, Leipzig, September 2010

21. Lowe, D.G.: Distinctive image features from scale-invariant keypoints. Int. J. Comput. Vis. **60**(2), 91–110 (2004). https://doi.org/10.1023/B:VISI.0000029664.99615.94. Nov

22. Marti, U.V., Bunke, H.: The IAM-database: an English sentence database for offline handwriting recognition. Int. J. Doc. Anal. Recogn. **5**(1), 39–46 (2002). https://doi.org/10.1007/s100320200071. https://www.springerlink.com/index/QD6A25KWJE4TU6V7.pdf

23. Mohammed, H., Marthot-Santaniello, I., Märgner, V.: GRK-Papyri: a dataset of Greek handwriting on papyri for the task of writer identification. In: 2019 International Conference on Document Analysis and Recognition (ICDAR), pp. 726–731 (2019). https://doi.org/10.1109/ICDAR.2019.00121

24. Nasir, S., Siddiqi, I.: Learning features for writer identification from handwriting on Papyri. In: Djeddi, C., Kessentini, Y., Siddiqi, I., Jmaiel, M. (eds.) MedPRAI 2020. CCIS, vol. 1322, pp. 229–241. Springer, Cham (2021). https://doi.org/10.1007/978-3-030-71804-6_17

25. Nasir, S., Siddiqi, I., Moetesum, M.: Writer characterization from handwriting on Papyri using multi-step feature learning. In: Barney Smith, E.H., Pal, U. (eds.) ICDAR 2021. LNCS, vol. 12916, pp. 451–465. Springer, Cham (2021). https://doi.org/10.1007/978-3-030-86198-8_32

26. Nicolaou, A., Christlein, V., Riba, E., Shi, J., Vogeler, G., Seuret, M.: Tormentor: deterministic dynamic-path, data augmentations with fractals. In: 26th International Conference of Pattern Recognition (2022, accepted)

27. Pirrone, A., Beurton-Aimar, M., Journet, N.: Self-supervised deep metric learning for ancient papyrus fragments retrieval. Int. J. Doc. Anal. Recogn. (IJDAR) **24**(3), 219–234 (2021). https://doi.org/10.1007/s10032-021-00369-1

28. Popović, M., Dhali, M.A., Schomaker, L.: Artificial intelligence based writer identification generates new evidence for the unknown scribes of the Dead Sea Scrolls exemplified by the Great Isaiah Scroll (1QIsaa). PLOS ONE **16**(4), 1–28 (2021). https://doi.org/10.1371/journal.pone.0249769

29. Pratikakis, I., Zagoris, K., Karagiannis, X., Tsochatzidis, L., Mondal, T., Marthot-Santaniello, I.: ICDAR 2019 competition on document image binarization (DIBCO 2019). In: 2019 International Conference on Document Analysis and Recognition (ICDAR), pp. 1547–1556, September 2019. https://doi.org/10.1109/ICDAR.2019.00249

30. Pratikakis, I., Zagoris, K., Barlas, G., Gatos, B., Blumenstein, M.: ICDAR2017 Competition on Document Image Binarization (DIBCO 2017). In: 2017 14th IAPR International Conference on Document Analysis and Recognition (ICDAR), pp. 1395–1403 (2017). https://doi.org/10.1109/ICDAR.2017.228

31. Ronneberger, O., Fischer, P., Brox, T.: U-Net: convolutional networks for biomedical image segmentation. In: Navab, N., Hornegger, J., Wells, W.M., Frangi, A.F. (eds.) MICCAI 2015. LNCS, vol. 9351, pp. 234–241. Springer, Cham (2015). https://doi.org/10.1007/978-3-319-24574-4_28

32. Shaus, A., Gerber, Y., Faigenbaum-Golovin, S., Sober, B., Piasetzky, E., Finkelstein, I.: Forensic document examination and algorithmic handwriting analysis of Judahite biblical period inscriptions reveal significant literacy level. PLOS ONE 15(9), 1–15 (2020). https://doi.org/10.1371/journal.pone.0237962

33. Su, B., Lu, S., Tan, C.L.: Binarization of historical document images using the local maximum and minimum. In: 9th IAPR International Workshop on Document Analysis Systems, Boston, pp. 159–165, June 2010. https://doi.org/10.1145/1815330.1815351

34. Wolf, L., et al.: Identifying join candidates in the Cairo Genizah. Int. J. Comput. Vis. 94(1), 118–135 (2011). https://doi.org/10.1007/s11263-010-0389-8

Handwriting Learning and Development

Enhanced Physiological Tremor in Normal Ageing: Kinematic and Spectral Analysis of Elderly Handwriting

Serena Starita[1], Monica Guerra[2(✉)], Lorenzo Pascazio[2], and Agostino Accardo[1]

[1] Department of Engineering and Architecture, University of Trieste, Via Valerio, 10, 34127 Trieste, Italy
serena.starita@phd.units.it, accardo@units.it
[2] Geriatric Unit, Department of Medicine, Surgery and Health Sciences, Trieste University Hospital – ASUGI, Piazza dell'Ospitale, 2, 34129 Trieste, Italy
lorenzo.pascazio@asugi.sanita.fvg.it

Abstract. Tremor is a motor phenomenon that occurs in both neurological disorders and normal people. Enhanced physiological tremor can manifest in healthy elderly, as a consequence of age-related normal neurodegeneration, along with an overall decline of motor performance as slowing, decreased coordination, and balance difficulties. Handwriting is a complex neuromotor skill involving fine motor control as well as high-level cognitive processes and its analysis represents a method to investigate motor impairments of the upper limb that occur during the execution of voluntary movements.

In this exploratory and preliminary study, has the aim of selecting features and tasks able to characterize handwriting-related kinetic tremor in the elderly by using a digitizing tablet. 11 healthy elderly (over 70 years old) subjects and 17 healthy younger subjects were enrolled in the trial. Participants were asked to perform an accurate drawing task - Archimedes' Spiral, and three fast drawing tasks - overlapped continuous circles and diagonal ascending/descending lines). Data analysis consisted of integrating classical kinematic analysis with spectral analysis. Results of kinematic analysis show the elderly handwriting is overall slower and more fragmented in spiral and diagonal lines tasks but not in overlapped circles compared to younger subjects. The spectral analysis of velocity and acceleration drawing profiles reveals a significant presence of enhanced physiological tremor in the elderly but only in the accurate spiral task. We assess that, beside the Archimedes' spiral already used in previous research works, fast diagonal lines tasks can be employed for kinematic characterization of elderly handwriting but not for tremor identification. The spiral remains the only handwriting exercise able to reveal the presence of age-related enhanced physiological tremor. We conclude that the nature of the handwriting task influences the emergence of involuntary movement and the strength at which motor impairments arise. This aspect must be considered when performing the feature selection of the variables best suited for the characterization of the elderly handwriting.

Keywords: Handwriting · Kinematic analysis · Spectral analysis · Elderly · Normal ageing · Physiological tremor

© Springer Nature Switzerland AG 2022
C. Carmona-Duarte et al. (Eds.): IGS 2021, LNCS 13424, pp. 93–104, 2022.
https://doi.org/10.1007/978-3-031-19745-1_7

1 Introduction

Tremor, defined as a rhythmic, oscillatory, and involuntary movement of a body part, is a motor phenomenon found in neurological disorders as well as in normal individuals [1]. The first type is referred to as pathological tremor, the latter as physiological tremor [2]. Given tremor complex phenomenology and still unclear origin, diagnosis of tremor-presenting disorders is challenging [1, 3, 4], especially in elderly people. Age-related normal neurodegeneration can manifest as enhanced physiological tremor (also referred to as senile tremor or age-related tremor) and it is not associated to any underlying pathological condition [2, 5, 6]. Tremor aside, the elderly show an overall decline of motor performance manifested as slowing, increased variability, decreased coordination, and balance difficulties [7]. Such impairments are caused by malfunctions in the muscle-tendon, central, and peripheral neural systems [7]. The dopaminergic system appears to have the largest impact: research shows nigrostriatal dopaminergic denervation in ageing results in a decrease of fine movement control, movement slowing, reduced motivation, and compromised working memory [7, 8]. Due to the overall decline in dopaminergic transmission, some authors consider the ageing nervous system as a preclinical continuum of Parkinson's Disease [9].

Handwriting is a complex neuromotor skill involving fine motor control as well as high-level cognitive processes [10] and its analysis represents a method to investigate motor impairments of upper limb that occur during the execution of voluntary movements. Only a few studies focused on this approach, employing a digitizing tablet to collect the written tracks of healthy elderly, and aiming at unraveling the composite relation between handwriting and ageing. The experimental designs mainly concerned sentence writing [11], l-loop writing [12], participant's signature [13] and spiral drawing [14, 15] tasks. Analysis of kinematic features revealed an overall reduction of speed, lower pressure, increased variability, and loss of fluency with ageing. Almeida et al. [14, 15] used frequency analysis to show the presence of kinetic tremor in the elderly. The authors analyzed the frequency range between 4 and 12 Hz (the band of involuntary movement) during the execution of an Archimedes' spiral and introduced a parameter (LDA-value) to quantify physiological tremor and demonstrate its linear correlation with age. To the best of our knowledge, this research group is the only one that addressed tremor quantification in handwriting by using frequency analysis and it only investigated the execution of Archimedes' spiral task.

While assessing if different drawing tasks may be conveniently employed in tremor evaluation and in the analysis of its relationship with age, our study examines new tasks by using spectral analysis of velocity and acceleration signals, alongside classical kinematic parameters, with the aim of identifying features suited to quantify involuntary movements and performance impairment in the elderly.

In our perspective, delving into this research topic is of twofold importance. On one side, providing insight into executive control and motor performance deterioration in normal ageing can be very useful to understand the difference between pathological and physiological tremor, supporting neurologists in their diagnosis and pointing out the importance of selecting age-matched controls when designing an experiment that addresses motor impairments. On the other hand, it allows to better comprehend the implication of central, peripheral, and neuromuscular functional losses with ageing and how those mechanisms are accountable for handwriting-related motor control decline.

2 Materials and Methods

2.1 Subjects and Tasks

This preliminary study encompasses 28 participants, 11 healthy Elderly subjects - hE (aged 70–84, mean 76.5 ± 4.9 years), and 17 healthy Young control subjects - hY (aged 31–68, mean 54.3 ± 11.6 years). Participants were screened for the absence of neurological or motor abnormalities, history of stroke, epilepsy, serious psychiatric illness, arthritis and dementia. They all released their written informed consent. The decision to separate subjects according to the age threshold of 70 is based on previous findings. Caligiuri et al. [13] report that the relationship between age and handwriting movements is likely to be non-linear with the greatest decline occurring after age 70 years. Marzinotto et al. [16] highlight three principal handwriting styles in the elderly where the most common one, characterized by low dynamics, is present in writers over 67 years old. Finally, the systematic review by Macleod et al. [17] reports a meta-analysis of several studies about the incidence of Parkinson's disease and shows that the mean age of onset or diagnosis of the pathology is 70 years old. Healthy subjects over 70 are therefore at higher risk to be misdiagnosed and thus characterizing physiological tremor in this age range may serve as an important support for geriatricians and neurologists.

The subjects performed four different drawing exercises with visual feedback: an ingoing, clockwise Archimedes' Spiral (AS) following a given template, overlapped continuous Circles (C), Ascending diagonal Lines (AL) and Descending diagonal Lines (DL). Subjects were required to draw C, AL, and DL as fast as possible for a duration of 15 s and to execute AS accurately with no time limits. Participants were instructed to complete the exercises without pen lifts and keeping the arm leaned on the table otherwise, the response was excluded from the analysis. 28 C samples (11 hE, 17 hY), 28 AL samples (11 hE, 17 hY), 27 DL samples (11 hE, 16 hY) and 25 AS samples (9 hE, 16 hY) were eventually considered.

2.2 Handwriting Acquisition and Analysis

Handwriting was recorded by means of a commercial digitizing tablet (Wacom, Inc., Vancouver, WA, Model Intuos 3.0), using an ink pen thus providing visual feedback. The pen displacement was sampled at 200 Hz and acquired with a spatial resolution of 0.02 mm. The horizontal and vertical pen positions were filtered separately using a second-order low-pass Butterworth filter (15 Hz cut-off frequency) and the velocity and acceleration profiles were derived. For each test, the handwriting features were calculated and analyzed by using an ad hoc custom program written in MATLAB® [18].

The kinematic parameters were calculated both at whole track level and at stroke level (Table 1). The stroke is defined as the pen track between two successive velocity minima.

Table 1. Kinematic parameters extracted at whole track and at stroke level

Whole track parameters	Stroke parameters
Total track length (L)	Median duration (D_S)
Mean pressure (P)	Median and max horizontal velocity (Vx_S, $maxVx_S$)
Mean horizontal velocity (Vx)	Median and max vertical velocity (Vy_S, $maxVy_S$)
Mean vertical velocity (Vy)	Median and max curvilinear velocity (Vc_S, $maxVc_S$)
Mean curvilinear velocity (Vc)	Stroke number normalized by tot track length (N_S/L)
Execution time (T)[1]	Normalized jerk (N_J)
	Stroke length (L_S)

[1]Only for the accurate task AS.

N_J and Ns/L represent measures of fluidity; the smaller their values, the less fragmented and more fluid a movement is. JN was calculated according to Teulings et al. [19].

Power Spectral Density (PSD) of both velocity and acceleration signals in their horizontal, vertical, and curvilinear components was estimated by using Welch's method [20], with a Hamming window on intervals of 5 s and a 50% overlap. To analyze the power distribution related to different movement-associated phenomena, two frequency bands were selected: a band concerning voluntary Movement Execution required by the task (BME), ranging from 0.2 to 4 Hz, and a band associated with involuntary Tremor (BT), ranging from 4.0 to 12 Hz. The BT frequency range was carefully designed to capture the whole involuntary component in task-specific tremor [15]. For each subject, relative spectral powers were quantified by dividing the absolute power in each frequency band by their sum.

For each task, median value and interquartile range of parameters were calculated in the two groups; the difference between them was assessed by the Wilcoxon Rank sum test, with a significance level of 5%. The statistical analysis did not include any correction for multiple testing since the study is oriented toward features selection. The Bonferroni correction would not offer the flexibility required in such exploratory stage that has the purpose of emphasizing what parameters better characterize the tremor of the two groups rather than evaluating if the groups are different in all tested parameters [20].

3   Results

Median and interquartile range values of kinematic and spectral parameters for hE and hY groups, as well as the p-values of their comparison, are reported in Table 2.

Table 2. Median values and interquartile ranges (iqr) of kinematic and spectral parameters in the two groups (hE and hY) and p‑values of their comparison in the Fast executed tasks (C, AL, DL) and in the Accurate one (AS). (In bold italic the p‑value < 0.05)

	Fast Tasks — C					Fast Tasks — AL					Fast Tasks — DL					Accurate Task — AS				
	hE median	hE iqr	hY median	hY iqr	p-value	hE median	hE iqr	hY median	hY iqr	p-value	hE median	hE iqr	hY median	hY iqr	p-value	hE median	hE iqr	hY median	hY iqr	p-value
Kinematic Analysis																				
D (s)	126,53	100,83	162,19	206,32	0,240	94,78	58,11	142,15	144,38	***0,048***	88,72	62,15	127,20	113,85	***0,017***	30,51	12,97	19,11	13,14	***0,010***
L (cm)	281,83	126,26	346,42	228,16	0,962	194,83	134,08	164,40	154,76	0,778	211,34	175,02	258,45	193,68	0,711	103,52	3,37	102,35	5,15	0,165
P (a.u.)	52,56	41,19	70,02	91,89	0,204	46,33	24,78	68,55	89,99	***0,027***	44,30	31,13	67,92	65,33	***0,007***	340,18	144,55	262,34	126,41	***0,019***
V_x (mm/s)	54,79	44,89	65,78	83,78	0,240	42,52	20,44	62,72	80,42	***0,014***	38,43	27,21	65,32	62,79	***0,007***	23,15	7,99	33,47	21,44	***0,016***
V_y (mm/s)	84,13	67,04	107,84	137,13	0,204	63,04	32,13	94,53	120,31	***0,019***	58,99	41,35	96,13	90,80	***0,007***	23,04	7,29	33,47	21,75	***0,019***
V_c (mm/s)	133,00	13,75	131,00	16,13	0,383	155,00	42,75	199,00	66,25	0,077	141,00	51,88	156,50	94,25	0,570	36,31	12,25	52,57	34,53	***0,016***
D_S (ms)	12,36	10,85	13,20	17,96	0,279	7,63	10,05	18,89	47,72	***0,011***	6,88	8,21	13,73	35,78	***0,013***	131,00	14,25	125,50	16,00	0,393
L_S (mm)	0,07	0,11	0,07	0,07	0,279	0,09	0,05	0,04	0,05	***0,011***	0,14	0,15	0,05	0,05	***0,032***	4,93	1,19	6,61	5,51	***0,034***
N_S/L (mm^{-1})	2,18	1,02	1,97	0,86	0,110	8,12	3,98	9,95	6,24	0,173	5,27	5,01	7,97	6,07	0,289	0,19	0,05	0,14	0,10	***0,019***
N_U																2,62	0,97	1,36	0,95	***0,006***
Spectral Analysis																				
V_x B_{ME}	98,69	1,79	98,75	1,79	0,510	98,72	2,93	98,68	1,17	0,814	97,48	2,11	97,56	2,68	0,748	98,25	1,92	99,49	1,03	***0,019***
V_x B_T	1,31	1,79	1,25	1,54	0,510	1,28	2,93	1,32	1,17	0,814	2,52	2,11	2,44	2,68	0,748	1,75	1,92	0,51	1,03	***0,019***
V_y B_{ME}	98,29	1,97	98,22	1,40	0,605	98,43	2,66	98,49	0,79	0,851	97,51	4,31	97,29	2,39	0,863	97,90	2,32	99,36	0,75	***0,012***
V_y B_T	1,71	1,97	1,78	1,40	0,605	1,52	2,66	1,51	0,79	0,851	2,49	4,31	2,71	2,39	0,863	2,10	2,32	0,64	0,75	***0,012***
V_c B_{ME}	79,15	16,07	72,13	19,04	0,221	96,53	10,99	94,58	27,80	0,371	92,77	11,54	91,53	17,16	0,444	86,60	8,21	94,56	10,20	0,119
V_c B_T	20,85	16,07	27,87	19,04	0,221	3,47	10,99	5,42	27,80	0,371	7,23	11,54	8,47	17,16	0,444	13,40	8,21	5,44	10,20	0,119
A_x B_{ME}	66,05	37,58	72,50	56,96	0,480	59,58	22,04	73,31	20,69	0,158	52,13	47,67	60,88	29,10	0,474	31,25	19,54	52,22	35,92	0,066
A_x B_T	33,95	37,58	27,50	56,96	0,480	40,42	22,04	26,69	20,69	0,158	47,87	47,67	39,12	29,10	0,474	68,75	19,54	47,78	35,92	0,066
A_y B_{ME}	63,64	45,68	72,24	54,14	0,672	54,88	21,10	72,60	25,59	0,110	35,63	38,40	52,26	22,39	0,289	24,29	13,50	35,99	23,13	***0,039***
A_y B_T	36,36	45,68	27,76	54,14	0,672	45,12	21,10	27,40	25,59	0,110	64,37	38,40	47,74	22,39	0,289	75,71	13,50	64,01	23,13	***0,039***
A_c B_{ME}	20,95	9,94	12,67	14,74	0,090	57,80	50,54	53,76	47,34	0,742	43,35	47,87	51,75	36,70	0,742	24,85	20,36	34,22	27,04	0,445
A_c B_T	79,05	9,94	87,33	14,74	0,090	42,20	50,54	36,24	47,34	0,742	56,65	47,87	48,25	36,70	0,742	75,15	20,36	65,78	27,04	0,445

3.1 Kinematic Analysis

The results show that the participants draw significantly slower (lower velocities at both stroke and whole track level) and in a more fragmented fashion in AL, DL and AS tasks. Furthermore, the participants cover a shorter distance in AL and DL tasks, while taking longer time and exerting a higher pressure to complete the spiral. No significant results are found at the C task level.

Figure 1 represents the velocity of strokes in hE and in hY groups during the execution of the four tasks. The results probe what showed by whole track parameters: strokes of the elderly are significatively slower compared to younger participants in all tasks except for C task.

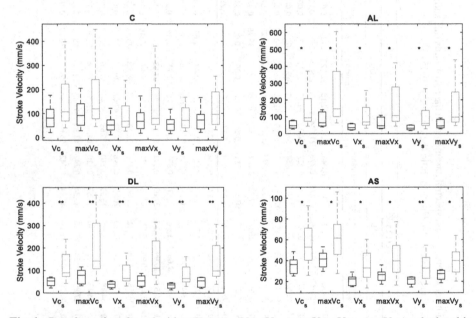

Fig. 1. Boxplots of stroke velocities (Vc_S, $maxVc_S$, Vx_S, $maxVx_S$, Vy_S, $maxVy_S$) calculated in the elderly group (black boxes) and in the younger group (gray boxes), for each task. (* = p-value < 0.05; ** = p-value < 0.01)

3.2 Spectral Analysis

Fast tasks do not allow to differentiate between hE and hY participants in the domain of spectral analysis. In the accurate AS task, the hE subjects present lower power in B_{ME} and higher power in B_T, in horizontal and vertical velocity and in vertical acceleration components, compared to hY controls (Table 2).

Figures 2 and 3 show the PSDs and the time courses of horizontal, vertical, and curvilinear components of velocity and acceleration, respectively. The data are obtained from the execution of AS task by an hE subject and an hY subject (Fig. 4).

The PSDs exemplify the trend observed in the two groups where the elderly have higher power in B_T and lower power in B_{ME} compared to younger controls when performing accurate AS.

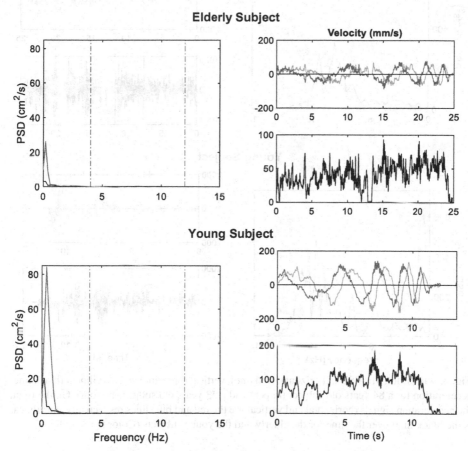

Fig. 2. On the left, the PSD of horizontal (red line), vertical (blue line) and curvilinear (black line) velocity for a 84 years old subject (upper) and a 53 years old subject (bottom). On the right, the velocity signals (horizontal and vertical are the red and blue lines respectively, curvilinear is the black line) over the time for the elderly and the young subjects (Color figure online).

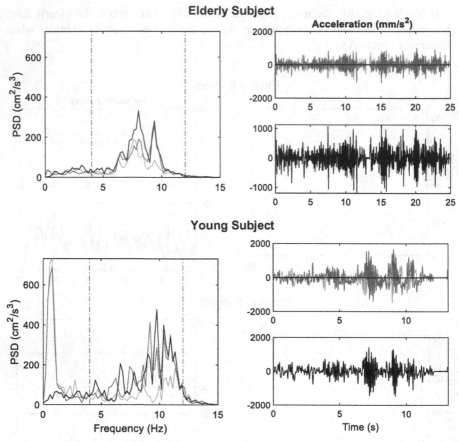

Fig. 3. On the left, the PSD of horizontal (red line), vertical (blue line) and curvilinear (black line) acceleration for a 84 years old subject (upper) and a 53 years old subject (bottom). On the right, the acceleration signals (horizontal and vertical are the red and blue lines respectively, curvilinear is the black line) over the time for the elderly and the young subjects (Color figure online).

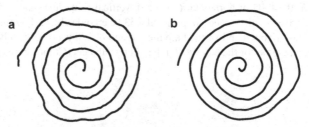

Fig. 4. The tracks of AS task for an elderly (a) and a young (b) participant. The left drawing is visibly tremulous

4 Discussion

The characterization of handwriting in elderly people may provide a useful insight in movement execution deterioration with ageing. Research focusing on digitizing tablets can serve as a complementary low-cost, non-invasive diagnostic tool to support geriatricians and neurologists dealing with tremor-presenting patients. While handwriting kinematics of elderly has been already inquired by previous research, very few studies have focused on the description of physiological tremor associated with the act of writing. Specifically, the drawing task analyzed in the literature is limited to the accurate Archimedes' spiral [13, 14], and to the best of our knowledge, no exercise executed in the fast condition has ever been utilized. The parameter extracted by Almeida et al. [13] to assess tremor, the LDA-value, is able to discriminate the age groups analyzed in the research work and to characterize a linear relationship with age but is complex to calculate; therefore, we evaluate if a simpler and more straightforward approach is as much effective.

In our study, kinematic analysis results confirm previous research outcomes, highlighting a slower and more fragmented performance in the elderly compared to younger subjects. Only circles task does not show significant results in any of the analyzed features (Table 2). We provide two hypotheses to explain this. On one hand, circles execution, differently from diagonal lines, is a continuous task meaning that velocity never reaches the zero value; thus, in this task the influence of movement initiation is minimal. On the contrary, in diagonal lines exercises, the effect of initiating the movement is more evident. Disfunction in movement initiation, also defined as akinesia [22], is a common symptom of Parkinson's disease and is associated with basal ganglia pathophysiology and dopamine denervation [8]. Embracing the perspective of the ageing nervous system as a preclinical continuum of Parkinson's Disease [9], we speculate that akinesia may be present also in normal elderly. In this regard the absence of significative results in the circles task but not in the others, may suggest the presence of akinesia in healthy elderly, especially when executing fast movements. Recalling that dopamine transmission regulates not only fine motor control but also arousal and motivation [7], we theorize that these effects may both be responsible for the impairments here observed in older adults handwriting. On the other hand, the absence of significant results in the circles task may be simply explained by the heterogeneity in the elderly handwriting styles that this exercise is not able to bring out. According to Marzinotto et al. [16], there is not a unique pattern of handwriting change with age; while handwriting of most elderly is slower and more fragmented, a small percentage of these subjects presents a style that is indistinguishable from younger writers.

Concerning other tasks, while stroke duration does not vary between the two groups, the results show a higher fragmentation and reduced stroke size (Table 2) related to ageing. This finding leads to hypothesize that ageing affects velocity of strokes as well as motor programming. Movement becomes less fluid (higher N_s/L and N_J) in the elderly allegedly because of the need to reprogram more frequently the voluntary action as a consequence of dopaminergic loss and its implications on fine motor control and on arousal and motivation, as stated previously [7].

Results on pressure median values represent an exception in respect to previous findings: in our research in fact, pressure does not vary significantly with age in fast tasks while results higher in the hE subjects during accurate AS task execution (Table 2). These findings may be explained by low numerosity and high variability of the hE group, as confirmed by interquartile ranges, as well by heterogeneity of handwriting styles of the elderly [16].

Spectral analysis reveals significant differences between the groups only in the execution of accurate AS task, where the elderly show higher power in B_T and lower power in B_{ME} compared to younger controls, highlighting the presence of physiological tremor in the hE group (Table 2, Figs. 2 and 3). Relative spectral power of horizontal and vertical components of velocity and acceleration, in the 4–12 Hz frequency range, appears to be a simple and straightforward parameter to account for enhanced physiological tremor, but this is true only for accurate tasks. On the contrary, no clear tremor was found through frequency analysis of fast tasks. To explain our finding, we postulate that during fast movement, tremor could be absent or disguised as it superimposes to voluntary movement and the two components of movement may somehow merge into each other. The circles and diagonal lines tasks were executed as fast as possible, but this indication can be interpreted subjectively by each participant and is reasonable to assume that each subject selected a velocity in which the effect of tremor of handwriting could be masked. Since tremor does emerge in AS execution, the nature of the task plays a key role. The execution of accurate movements demands a higher level of fine motor control and the requirement of preferring accuracy over velocity may lead to the occurrence of tremor. Furthermore, our small and highly variable samples may not be able to significantly point out the tremor in fast tasks, as it may be present only in some individuals.

5 Conclusion

The outcomes of this study confirm previous findings on the kinematics of elderly handwriting but also offer a new insight on the feasibility of employing exercise alternative to the already established ones, i.e., Archimedes' Spiral, sentences, and words [11–15].

To the best of our knowledge, this study represents the first attempt to characterize physiological tremor in the elderly during fast drawing tasks and it is necessary to approach our results with caution. Whether the absence of physiological tremor in the elderly during the execution of fast drawings is a solid outcome, not due to the above-mentioned limitations, is an interesting research topic that deserve to be deepened. Appropriate experimental designs and increasing the participant pool may help to verify our findings and to test our suggested interpretation of absence of tremor in fast tasks.

Addressing these topics may also provide a deeper understanding of the mechanisms underlying physiological tremor in handwriting since the nature of central and peripheral influence is still debated [4, 7].

The study highlights that relative spectral power of physiological tremor in the frequency range between 4 and 12 Hz, is a simple parameter for tremor identification in the elderly during the execution of an accurate drawing task. To identify and characterize involuntary movements in the elderly is of crucial importance to support clinical practice and our results suggest that handwriting analysis may develop into a practical, non-invasive and low-cost tool for differential diagnosis between physiological tremor and pathologies exhibiting motor impairments such as Parkinson's Disease and Essential Tremor, that typically present in older adults.

The principal limitations of this exploratory research are the small sample size, the high variability among subjects and the non-equally distributed number of participants in the two analyzed groups. Future work will focus on increasing the sample size of tested subjects to fill the limitations and on selecting the best features able to reveal motor impairment in each task. While these answers will shed light on the mechanisms underlying motor impairments in the elderly, the implementations of this method into clinical praxis will require a confirmatory study aiming at verifying if the elderly differ from the young people in all the tested variables. Another goal would be implementing spectral analysis in order to identify a parameter that, starting from velocity and acceleration PSDs, would be able to not only assess tremor presence, but also to quantify it. Additional topics of interest, well suited to handwriting analysis, would be the characterization of physiological tremor progression with age and the evaluation of risk factors that affect motor impairments in the elderly.

Acknowledgements. Work partially supported by Master in Clinical Engineering, University of Trieste, Italy.

References

1. Saifee, T.A.: Tremor. Br. Med. Bull. **130**, 51–63 (2019)
2. McAuley, J.H., Marsden, C.D.: Physiological and pathological tremors and rhythmic central motor control. Brain **123**, 1545–1567 (2000)
3. Andrade, A.O., et al.: Human tremor: origins, detection and quantification. Practical Applications in Biomedical Engineering, IntechOpen, London (2013)
4. Morales-Briceño, H., Fois, A.F., Fung, V.S.C,; Tremor. Handb. Clin. Neurol. **159**, 283–301 (2018)
5. Louis, E.D., Wendt, K.J., Ford, B.: Senile tremor. What is the prevalence and severity of tremor in older adults? Gerontology **46**, 12–16 (2000)
6. Deuschl, G., Petersen, I., Lorenz, D., Christensen, K.: Tremor in the elderly: essential and aging-related tremor. Mov. Disord. **30**, 1327–1334 (2015)
7. Seidler, R.D., et al.: Motor control and aging: links to age-related brain structural, functional, and biochemical effects. Neurosci. Biobehav. Rev. **34**(5), 721–733 (2010)
8. Rodriguez-Oroz, M.C., et al.: Initial clinical manifestations of Parkinson's disease: features and pathophysiological mechanisms. Lancet Neurol. **8**(12), 1128–1139 (2009)
9. Romero, D.H., Stelmach, G.E.: Motor function in neurodegenerative disease and aging. In: Boller, F., Cappa, S.F. (eds.) Handbook of Neuropsychology. Elsevier Science, Amsterdam (2002)
10. Plamondon, R., O'Reilly, C., Rémi, C., Duval, T.: The lognormal handwriter: learning, performing, and declining. Front. Psychol. **4**, 1–14 (2013)
11. Rosenblum, S., Engel-Yeger, B., Fogel, Y.: Age-related changes in executive control and their relationships with activity performance in handwriting. Hum. Mov. Sci. **32**, 363–376 (2013)
12. Slavin, M.J., Phillips, J.G., Bradshaw, J.L.: Visual cues and the handwriting of older adults: a kinematic analysis. Psychol. Aging **11**, 521–526 (1996)
13. Caligiuri, M.P., Kim, C., Landy, K.M.: Kinematics of signature writing in healthy aging. J. Forensic Sci. **59**, 1020–1024 (2014)
14. Almeida, M.F.S., Cavalheiro, G.L., Pereira, A.A., Andrade, A.O.: Investigation of age-related changes in physiological kinetic tremor. Ann. Biomed. Eng. **38**, 3423–3439 (2010)

15. Almeida, M.F.S., Cavalheiro, G.L., Furtado, D.A., Pereira, A.A., Andrade, A.O.: Quantification of physiological kinetic tremor and its correlation with aging. In: Proceedings of Annual International Conference of the IEEE Engineering in Medicine and Biology Society, EMBS, pp. 2631–2634 (2012)
16. Marzinotto, G., et al.: Age-related evolution patterns in online handwriting. Comput. Math. Methods Med. **2016**, 3246595:1–3246595:15 (2016)
17. Macleod, A.D., Henery, R., Nwajiugo, P.C., Scott, N.W., Caslake, R., Counsell, C.E.: Age-related selection bias in Parkinson's disease research: are we recruiting the right participants? Park. Relat. Disord. **55**, 128–133 (2018)
18. Accardo, A., et al.: A device for quantitative kinematic analysis of children's handwriting movements. In: Proceedings of MEDICON 2007, Lubljiana, pp. 445–448 (2007)
19. Teulings, H.L., Contreras-Vidal, J.L., Stelmach, G.E., Adler, C.H.: Parkinsonism reduces coordination of fingers, wrist, and arm in fine motor control. Exp. Neurol. **146**, 159–170 (1997)
20. Welch, P.: The use of fast Fourier transform for the estimation of power spectra: a method based on time averaging over short, modified periodograms. IEEE Trans. Audio Electroacoust. **15**(2), 70–73 (1967)
21. Bender, R., Lange, S.: Adjusting for multiple testing–when and how? J. Clin. Epidemiol. **54**(4), 343–349 (2001)
22. Spay, C., Meyer, G., Welter, M.L., Lau, B., Boulinguez, P., Ballanger, B.: Functional imaging correlates of akinesia in Parkinson's disease: still open issues. Neuroimage Clin. **21**, 101644 (2019)

Comparison Between Two Sigma-Lognormal Extractors with Primary Schools Students Handwriting

Nadir Faci[1]($\boxtimes$) , Cristina Carmona-Duarte[2] , Moises Diaz[2] ,
Miguel A. Ferrer[2] , and Réjean Plamondon[1]

[1] Ecole Polytechnique, Montreal, Canada
{nadir.faci,rejean.plamondon}@polymtl.ca
[2] Universidad de Las Palmas de Gran Canaria, Las Palmas, Spain
{cristina.carmona,moises.diaz,miguelangel.ferrer}@ulpgc.es

Abstract. In this study, we examine the differences between two Sigma-Lognormal extractors. ScriptStudio is used to extract the Sigma-Lognormal parameters based on the velocity, and iDeLog is used for extracting the parameters based on both the velocity and the trajectory. The iDeLog software is tested with and without smoothing the data. Handwriting data are used to compare both types of extractor (algorithm for parameters extraction). The data consist of triangles drawn on a Wacom Cintiq 13HD by healthy children aged between six and thirteen years old. Globally, ScriptStudio Extract the data with the best SNR for the trajectory (SNRt) and the velocity (SNRv). Moreover, it used slightly more lognormals for the reconstruction than iDeLog with smoothing (iDeLog ws), and nearly half of the number of lognormals used in iDeLog without smoothing (iDeLog ns). Finally, iDeLog without smoothing has a better reconstruction of the velocity and the trajectory than iDeLog with smoothing.

Keywords: Sigma-lognormal model · Kinematic theory of human movements · Kinematic analysis · Fine motor control · Children handwriting · ScriptStudio · iDeLog

1 Introduction

The study of human movements can be useful to understand the impact of some psychophysical conditions on the human motor control as for example in studies dealing with children suffering from Attention Deficit Disorder, with or without Hyperactivity (ADHD) [1, 2]. In that case, different approaches have been proposed in order to model this neurological problem, among these stands the Kinematic Theory of rapid human movements [3–7]. This theory describes the generation of human movements as the results of a synergetic action of a large number of different coupled subsystems organized into neuromuscular systems. The central nervous system plans the movement to be executed by the peripheral system. Overall, the impulse response of a neuromuscular system is described by a lognormal function and the resulting velocity of an activation

© Springer Nature Switzerland AG 2022
C. Carmona-Duarte et al. (Eds.): IGS 2021, LNCS 13424, pp. 105–113, 2022.
https://doi.org/10.1007/978-3-031-19745-1_8

command can be modelled with a vector summation of lognormals. According to the lognormality principle, the Kinematic Theory describes movements executed under an adequate motor control. Thus, during the development of children, these will improve their motor control and will tend to the lognormality while become adult [8].

The Kinematic Theory is the corner stone of the Sigma-Lognormal model that can shape complex and underdeveloped children movements. This model assumes that the velocity of a human movement can be modelled using lognormal functions combined by a time superimposed vector addition. Each lognormal is described by six parameters [9]. Several software have been developed over the years to perform reverse engineering and extract these Sigma-Lognormal parameters from various movements. Among them, there are ScriptStudio [9] and iDeLog [10]. Those two used different approaches to extract the parameters. The first one is mostly based on the velocity analysis, while the second one seeks a trade-off between the velocity and the trajectory to recover the best fitting parameters. In this study, we aim to compare the effectiveness of both software to extract the Sigma-Lognormal parameters from primary school students handwriting who were asked to execute complex movements, some triangles, on a tablet. Thereupon, we will first present two software used in this study in Sect. 2. Afterward, in Sect. 3, the methodology and the dataset used to compare them will be presented. Then, in Sect. 4, the statistical analyses that were carried out and their results will be detailed. Finally, we will examine and discuss those results in Sect. 5, to put the whole work in a more general perspective.

2   The Extractors

2.1   ScriptStudio Algorithm

ScriptStudio [9] is a Sigma-Lognormal reconstruction software based on the velocity that incorporates the Robust XZERO algorithm [11]. This software extracts the Sigma-Lognormal parameters while maximizing the velocity Signal-to-Noise Ratio (SNRv). This performance criterion is calculated between the original and reconstructed velocity. Specifically, this extractor will use a vector combination of lognormals to reconstruct the original velocity. Thus, in a first step, for each velocity maximum peak in the original velocity profile, the software plugs a lognormal. Afterward, in the next steps, smaller lognormals are added to the reconstructed signal in order to increase the SNRv up to a minimum required SNRv specified by the experimenter. The resulting trajectory is reconstructed by integrating the velocity with no further optimization. This software has proven its value as it has been used in a multitude of studies as detection tool for ADHD [12, 13], brain injury [14, 15], Parkinson [16] and more. Furthermore, it was used to monitor the children evolution towards lognormality [8, 17].

2.2   iDeLog Algorithm

iDeLog [10] reconstructs the trajectory and the velocity of a movement at the same time, calculating the angles and lognormal parameters of each stroke. This algorithm is based on motor equivalence theory and the hypothesis of a visual feedback compatible with open-loop motor control. To this end, firstly, the virtual target points and angles are calculated by finding the velocity minimum and using the 8-connected trajectory of a given long and complex movement. In this way the velocity is decomposed as a sum of weighted lognormals, where the spatial and kinematic parameters are extracted separately. Secondly, with this first segmentation procedure, a first velocity reconstruction is obtained. Then, the reconstructed movement is iteratively optimized by moving the virtual target points with the ensuing changes of the angles and lognormal parameters. Finally, a fine optimization of the virtual target point is carried out for each segment by improving the SNRv and SNRt simultaneously.

2.3 Differences Between Both Extractor

Those two ways of extracting the Sigma-Lognormal model parameters present some differences that can impact the results of this study. First of all, ScriptStudio reconstructs the pen tip velocity by overlapping the lognormals composing the reconstructed signal. As a result, errors in the velocity estimation are propagated over the entire movement, resulting in an increased spatial deviation [18]. To avoid this problem and improve the trajectory reconstruction, iDeLog relies on adjusting the trajectory and speed jointly. So, rather than adding new lognormals to improve the reconstruction, iDeLog iteratively moves the target points to improve the adjustment between an original trajectory and its reconstructed counterpart. However, iDeLog may present lower SNRv compared to ScriptStudio but better SNRt.

As ScriptStudio preprocess the raw signal to break down the speed profile into lognormals, the iDeLog includes an option for preprocessing the original signal or not. This option allows to smooth the input signal in the same way that ScriptStudio does. As a difference in the preprocessing, the sampling frequency is not changed in iDeLog.

3 Methodology

The present study is part of a larger project aiming to standardize the data acquisition system developed within the Scribens Lab. This system, called the lognometer [19], could be used as a diagnostic tool in ADHD detection for example [13].

3.1 Participants

Participants were recruited from three different primary schools. In total, 780 children aged from six years to thirteen years old participated in the research, and from 1st grade to the 6th. For each grade, there are at least 120 participants while the maximum is 135 participants. 48% (375) of the children are female. Moreover, 24% (185) of the participants were neuroatypical. For the present comparative study, the neuroatypical participants were excluded. That left 594 participants remaining with at least 90 children per grade.

3.2 Procedures

Participants were asked to rapidly draw, one at a time, 30 triangles on a digitizing tablet (Wacom Cintiq HD13) using a stylus [19]. The instructions for writing a triangle were composed of three points, one starting and ending dot (1), and two crossing points (2 and 3) to be reached in the corresponding sequence: 1,2,3,1. The guide sheet displayed is presented in Fig. 1. An audio cue signal was used to indicate the start of the drawing. The handwritten data were recorded at 200 Hz.

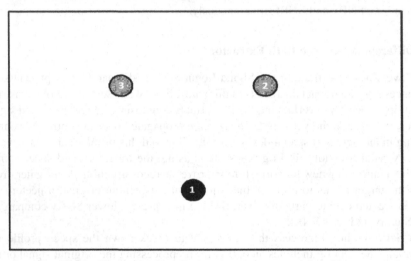

Fig. 1. The guide sheet displayed on the screen of the tablet.

3.3 Sigma-Lognormal Extraction

Before extracting the Sigma-Lognormal parameters, the dataset was cleaned. Thus, the strokes that started before the sound cue or weren't properly executed were removed. Afterward, the three extractors (iDeLog ws, iDeLog ns and ScripStudio) was used to extract the Sigma-Lognormal parameters for each trial. This model allows to extract three global parameters: the number of lognormals (NbLog) and the Signal-to-Noise Ratio for trajectory (SNRt) and for velocity (SNRv). Those parameters are unique for each trial and describe the general state of the neuromotor system. Moreover, we calculated the SNRt/NbLog and SNRv/NbLog. Based on those parameters, we rejected the trials that had a SNRt or SNRv lower than 10 dB, or that required more than 40 lognormals for reconstruction. In those cases, we assumed that the extractors were not able to reconstruct the signal correctly.

4   Results

To compare the three extractors, we analyzed the basic statistics of the above-mentioned global parameters. Table 1 presents the mean and the standard deviation of each parameter for the three extractors. Moreover, the repartition of the parameters is presented in the following boxplots (Fig. 2). We can see that ScriptStudio reconstruct the data with a higher SNRt, SNRv, SNRv\NbLog. iDeLog with smoothing presents the lowest NbLog, SNRt and SNRv. On the other hand, iDeLog with smoothing has the highest SNRt\NbLog. Finally, iDeLog without smoothing has the highest NbLog, and consequently the lowest SNRt\NbLog and SNRv\NbLog. The bold values with upper script "a" and "b" are respectively the highest and lowest value for each parameter.

Table 1. Statistical measures for each extractor.

		Script studio	iDeLog ws	iDeLog ns
NbLog	Mean	8.95	**7.28**[b]	**16.41**[a]
	Std	1.69	1.45	4.09
SNRt	Mean	**30.27**[a]	**24.30**[b]	25.67
	Std	2.52	1.01	1.18
SNRv	Mean	**25.40**[a]	**16.94**[b]	17.87
	Std	0.98	0.98	0.69
SNRt\NbLog	Mean	3.59	**3.65**[a]	**1.80**[b]
	Std	0.55	0.65	0.41
SNRv\NbLog	Mean	**3.05**[a]	2.56	**1.26**[b]
	Std	0.57	0.51	0.32

Table 2. P-value for the statistical tests. First row: the results of the comparison of the 3 algorithms with the non-parametric Kruskal-Wallis test. The following rows: the results of the non-parametric pair comparison with the Mann-Whitney U-test.

	NbLog	SNRt	SNRv	SNRt/ NbLog	SNRv/ NbLog
ScriptStudio iDeLog ws iDeLog ns	2E−267	6E−249	1E−279	2E−245	9E−264
ScriptStudio iDeLog ws	2E−66	2E−173	5E−191	7E−02	8E−44
ScriptStudio iDeLog ns	2E−172	1E−148	5E−191	6E−187	8E−190
iDeLog ws iDeLog ns	5E−187	2E−77	1E−64	5E−185	1E−180

For the statistical tests, the Bonferroni correction was used to counteract the multiple comparison. In that case, the α (0.05) was divided by the number of extracted parameters (3) which brought the corrected α to 0.017. After that, we used a Jarque-Bera test [20] to determine if the extracted parameters are normally distributed. In that case, only the SNRt/NbLog and SNRv/NbLog for ScriptStudio and IDeLog with smoothing has a p-value over 0.05, so those parameters are normally distributed. All the other parameters were not normally distributed. According to this observation, we used the Kruskal-Wallis

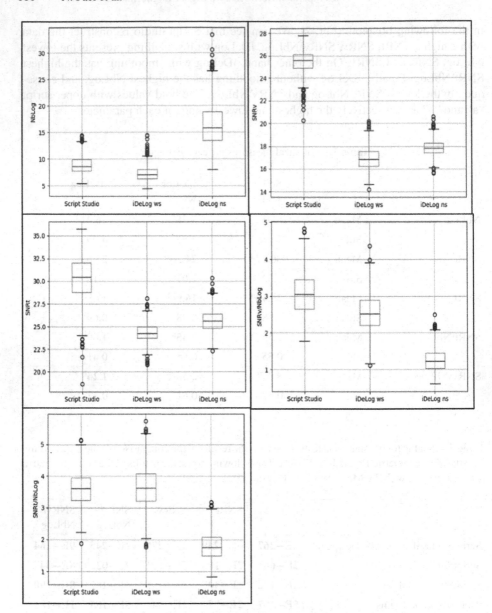

Fig. 2. The boxplot representing the extracted parameters for the three extractors. From top to bottom and left to right: NbLog, SNRt, SNRt\NbLog, SNRv and SNRv\NbLog. In each figure, from left to right: ScriptStudio, iDeLog with smoothing and iDeLog without smoothing.

non-parametric test [21] to evaluate if the three extractors are statistically similar. The extractors are not statistically similar because their p-value lower than the corrected α. When comparing the extractor to each other, we used the non-parametric Mann-Whitney U-test [22]. Thus, there are significant differences between the extractors for all the parameters, except for the SNRt/NbLog between ScriptStudio and iDeLog with smoothing. The p-values and the statistical value of each test are presented in Table 2 and 3. The first row presents the results of the non-parametric Kruskal-Wallis test. The following rows are the results of the non-parametric Mann Whitney U-test. All the bold values in Table 2 represent a p-value lower than the α corrected with Bonferroni (0.017). The statistical value for the Kruskal-Wallis test corresponds to the chi-squared value. The statistical value for the Mann Whitney U-test corresponds to the sum of ranks one samples. For both, the higher the value, the better is the results.

Table 3. The statistical tests value for the non-parametric Kruskal-Wallis test in the first row results of the comparison of the 3 algorithms. The following rows: the results of the non-parametric Mann-Whitney U-test.

	NbLog	SNRt	SNRv	SNRt/NbLog	SNRv/NbLog
ScriptStudio iDeLog ws iDeLog ns	1228	1143	1285	1127	1211
ScriptStudio iDeLog ws	69933	8035	0	159181	88901
ScriptStudio iDeLog ns	8457	20056	2	1810	526
iDeLog ws iDeLog ns	1791	61813	71269	2680	4683

5 Discussion

After those results, it seems that ScriptStudio is more suited to extract the global sigma-lognormal parameters of triangles because it gives back a higher SNR than IDeLog for the velocity and the trajectory, while using a lower number of lognormals. Moreover, the SNR/NbLog for the trajectory and the velocity are better for ScriptStudio since that they needed less NbLog than iDeLog without smoothing and having a higher SNR than the iDeLog with smoothing. It must be kept in mind, that this dataset is composed of triangles executed by children that did not reach their full potential yet. In that case, those children are heading towards the lognormality. Concerning the triangles, those movements can be classified as complex but not as long movement. Moreover, the movements executed by those children may be jerkier and not continuous. In that case, it makes sense that iDeLog have poorer results than ScriptStudio since it adds one lognormal per velocity peak. This founding fits with what was reported in [10] where it was mentioned that iDeLog should have better results for continuous, long and complex movement like signatures.

6 Future Works

In conclusion, this preliminary study shows that that both iDeLog and ScriptStudio could be used as a platform to analyze children movements, but that ScriptStudio is might be more appropriate to do it, when the best reconstruction is a requirement. It would be interesting to examine the results of triangles executed by adult to see if the performance of iDeLog improves when the movements are less jerky but this is beyond the scope of this paper. In future works, we will extend our statistical analyses and investigate the classification performance of the three algorithms. We will add the other Sigma-Lognormal parameters to the analyses: t_0, D, Theta start, theta end, μ and σ. Moreover, we will use those results to explore the possibility of discriminating for example between age groups and gender. Although the performances in terms of signal reconstruction might differ, this does not guarantee that their performances in term of classification and prediction will follow a similar ranking Moreover, in the context of the No Free Lunch Theorem [23], it is expected that fine tuning will be required to adapt and optimize any of these algorithms to any specific studies.

Acknowledgment. This work was supported by NSERC CANADA Discovery Grants RGPIN 2015 06409 to Réjean Plamondon and by a research contract from Institut TransMedTEch, Montréal, Canada and the Spanish government's MIMECO PID2019-109099RB-C41 research project and European Union FEDER program/funds.

References

1. Yan, J.H., Thomas, J.R.: Arm movement control: differences between children with and without attention deficit hyperactivity disorder. Res. Q. Exerc. Sport **73**(1), 10–18 (2002)
2. Rosenblum, S., Epsztein, L., Josman, N.: Handwriting performance of children with attention deficit hyperactive disorders: a pilot study. Phys. Occup. Ther. Pediatr. **28**(3), 219–234 (2008)
3. Plamondon, R., Yu, L.-D., Stelmach, G.E., Clément, B.: On the automatic extraction of biomechanical information from handwriting signals. IEEE Trans. Syst. Man Cybern. **21**(1), 90–101 (1991)
4. Plamondon, R.: A kinematic theory of rapid human movements: part I: movement representation and generation. Biol. Cybern. **72**(4), 295–307 (1995)
5. Plamondon, R.: A kinematic theory of rapid human movements. Part II. Movement time and control. Biol. Cybern. **72**(4), 309–320 (1995)
6. Plamondon, R.: A kinematic theory of rapid human movements: part III. Kinetic outcomes. Biol. Cybern. **78**(2), 133–145 (1998)
7. Plamondon, R., Feng, C., Woch, A.: A kinematic theory of rapid human movement. Part IV: a formal mathematical proof and new insights. Biol. Cybern. **89**(2), 126–138 (2003)
8. Plamondon, R., O'Reilly, C., Rémi, C., Duval, T.: The lognormal handwriter: learning, performing, and declining. Front. Psychol. **4**, 945 (2013)
9. O'Reilly, C., Plamondon, R.: Development of a sigma-lognormal representation for on-line signatures. Pattern Recogn. **42**(12), 3324–3337 (2009)
10. Ferrer, M.A., Diaz, M., Carmona-Duarte, C., Plamondon, R.: iDeLog: iterative dual spatial and kinematic extraction of sigma-lognormal parameters. IEEE Trans. Pattern Anal. Mach. Intell. **42**(1), 114–125 (2018)
11. O'Reilly, C., Plamondon, R.: Automatic extraction of sigma-lognormal parameters on signatures. In: Proceedings of 11th International Conference on Frontier in Handwriting Recognition (ICFHR) (2008)
12. Laniel, P., Faci, N., Plamondon, R., Beauchamp, M.H., Gauthier, B.: Kinematic analysis of fast pen strokes in children with ADHD. Appl. Neuropsychol.: Child 1–16 (2019)

13. Laniel, P., Faci, N., Plamondon, R., Beauchamp, M., Gauthier, B.: Kinematic analysis of fast pen strokes in children with ADHD using the sigma-lognormal model. In: International Conference on Pattern Recognition and Artificial Intelligence: Workshop on the Lognormality Principle and its Applications, Montreal (2018)
14. Faci, N., Désiré, N., Beauchamp, M.H., Gagnon, I., Plamondon, R.: Lognormality in children with mild traumatic brain injury: a preliminary pilot study. In: International Conference on Pattern Recognition and Artificial Intelligence, Montreal (2018)
15. Faci, N., Désiré, N., Beauchamps, M.H., Gagnon, I., Plamondon, R.: Analysing the evolution of children neuromotor system lognormality after mild traumatic brain injury. In: Lognormality Principle: Applications for e-Security, e-Health and e-Learning, World scientific Publishing (2020, in press)
16. Lebel, K., Nguyen, H., Duval, C., Plamondon, R., Boissy, P.: Capturing the cranio-caudal signature of a turn with inertial measurement systems: methods, parameters robustness and reliability. Front. Bioeng. Biotechnol. 5, 51 (2017)
17. Duval, T., Plamondon, R., O'Reilly, C., Remi, C., Vaillant, J.: On the use of the sigma-lognormal model to study children handwriting. In: Nakagawa, M., Liwicki, M., Zhu, B. (eds.) Recent Progress in Graphonomics: Learn from the Past, Nara, Japan (2013)
18. Fischer, A., Plamondon, R., O'Reilly, C., Savaria, Y.: Neuromuscular representation and synthetic generation of handwritten whiteboard note. In: Proceedings of the International Conference on Frontiers in Handwriting Recognition (2014)
19. Faci, N., Boyogueno Bibias, S.P., Plamondon, R., Bergeron, N.: A new experimental set-up to run neuromuscular tests. In: International Conference on Pattern Recognition and Artificial Intelligence: Workshop on the Lognormality Principle and its Applications, Montreal (2018)
20. Jarque, C.M., Bera, A.K.: Efficient tests for normality, homoscedasticity and serial independence of regression residuals. Econ. Lett. 6(3), 255–259 (1980)
21. Kruskal, W.H., Wallis, W.A.: Use of ranks in one-criterion variance analysis. J. Am. Stat. Assoc. 47(260), 583–621 (1952)
22. Mann, H.B., Whitney, D.R.: On a test of whether one of two random variables is stochastically larger than the other. Ann. Math. Stat. 18, 50–60 (1947)
23. Wolpert, D.H., Macready, W.G.: No free lunch theorems for optimization. IEEE Trans. Evol. Comput. 1(1), 67–82 (1997)

Effects of a Graphomotor Intervention on the Graphic Skills of Children: An Analysis with the Sigma-Lognormal Model

Ana Rita Matias[1] ⓘ, Filipe Melo[2(✉)] ⓘ, Helena Coradinho[1] ⓘ,
Orlando Fernandes[1] ⓘ, Guillaume de Broin[3] ⓘ, and Réjean Plamondon[3] ⓘ

[1] Comprehensive Health Research Center (CHRC-UÉ), University of Évora, 7000 Évora,
Portugal
{armatias,hifc,orlandoj}@uevora.pt

[2] Faculty of Human Kinetics, Comprehensive Health Research Center (CHRC-UÉ), Lisbon
University, 1495 Lisbon, Portugal
fmelo@fmh.ulisboa.pt

[3] Laboratoire Scribens, Département de Génie Électrique, Polytechnique Montréal, Montréal,
Canada
{guillaume.seguin-de-broin,rejean.plamondon}@polymtl.ca

Abstract. One of the most discussed issues in handwriting is the question of when young children are (or not) ready to begin handwriting instruction. Several studies highlight the importance of early detection of graphomotor difficulties to better assist and remediate them in the first years of formal school. Also, it is necessary to understand how children control handwriting movements and its learning strategies.

Using the Sigma Lognormal approach, in this study we aim to study the effects of a graphomotor intervention program, in the Graphic Skills according to lognormal parameters.

Fifty-five children attending the last year of pre-school (25 experimental group; 30 control group) performed the first nine figures of Beery-Buktenica Developmental Test of Visual-Motor Integration (6th edition) (Beery VMI) on a digitizing tablet.

To address the issue related with handwriting, forty-one second graders (20 experimental group; 21 control group) performed. The Concise Evaluation Scale for Children's Handwriting (BHK), also on a digitizing tablet. A follow-up assessment has been performed six months after the end of graphomotor intervention program.

Participants from control group benefited from 16 sessions (twice a week) of a graphomotor intervention program, divided in small groups (6–8 children/group). Each session lasted for 30 min.

In general children who benefited from a graphomotor intervention showed better fine movement quality improved with better motor control quality and higher movement fluidity. The maintenance of results after six months was more consistent in preschoolers, because the second-year students are still in a process of handwriting automation.

C. Carmona-Duarte et al. (Eds.): IGS 2021, LNCS 13424, pp. 114–128, 2022.
https://doi.org/10.1007/978-3-031-19745-1_9

Keywords: Handwriting readiness · Preschoolers · Second graders · Process assessment · Kinematic theory · Sigma-Lognormal model · Psychomotor intervention

1 Introduction

1.1 Preschool

Preschool time is a key period for the development of graphomotor skills (Graphic Skills) [1] in which children spend about 42% of the day performing paper and pencil tasks [2] developing handwriting readiness skills [3, 4].

Handwriting readiness refers to a stage of development at which a child has the necessary characteristics to satisfactorily benefit from formal handwriting teaching [2, 3, 5].

The ability to copy geometric forms is considered an indicator of handwriting readiness. Children are not ready to learn handwriting without first correctly copying the first nine pictures of the Beery–Buktenica Developmental Test of Visual-Motor Integration (Beery VMI) [6]. Several studies show that preschool children who copy these forms correctly will copy more letters and present better handwriting quality in the first grade [7–9]. Beery VMI is an internationally recognized test useful for assessing handwriting readiness in 5- and 6-year olds children [10].

Although graphomotor skills are considered a predictor of future school success [3, 10, 11] not all children can develop proficient handwriting [5, 12]. 12% to 30% of children have handwriting difficulties [13], which can bring future problems throughout their academic path [14, 15].

Early identification of handwriting difficulties, should help to develop more effective interventions and may prevent future handwriting difficulties [4, 16, 17].

1.2 2nd Graders

Handwriting skills are crucial for success in school [18, 19] considering that children spend, on average, 33% of their time on fine motor activities (approximately 85% on handwriting) [20]. A significant proportion (12 to 30%) of children have handwriting difficulties [13]. The handwriting difficulties are one of the most common reasons that children receive psychomotor therapy in school age [21], reason why it is important to understand the factors that affect handwriting performance for the early identification of handwriting difficulties and to develop more effective interventions [14, 19, 22].

Formal handwriting instruction is typically introduced at 6–7 years old [23]. Quality of handwriting improves significantly and reaches a plateau at 7–8 years [14, 24, 25] and at 8–9 years there are again improvements in the quality of handwriting, and it becomes more automatic [14, 24, 25]. In addition, the speed of handwriting progressively increases during elementary school [14, 24, 25].

1.3   Intervention in Graphomotor Skills

Although the literature on handwriting readiness skills is limited [11], several skills have been identified that must be mastered before a child can succeed with handwriting [26]. Learning to handwriting can be a real challenge for children who do not master handwriting readiness skills [11], so it is essential to develop and implement interventions at an early age to ensure the proper development of these skills and thus prevent possible handwriting difficulties at a later age [3, 4, 10, 11, 17, 26–30].

At elementary-school children who are identified has having handwriting difficulties (in terms of handwriting legibility and speed) are referred for assessment and intervention [2, 13]. Intervention programs should include handwriting practice [31], sensoriomotor practice and strategies [13].

1.4   Graphic Skill Assessment

The Graphic-motor Skill assessment has evolved towards two complementary approaches: product and process [32–38]. The first one refers to the evaluation of the legibility and speed of the trace left on the paper and is performed using pencil-paper tasks [33, 34, 36, 38]. The second one, concerns the real-time movement evaluation with the aid of a digitizing tablet, a pen and specific software [such as ScriptStudio, 39] and allows collecting of spatial, temporal and kinematic data from the Graphic Skills [32, 33, 35–38]. In the present study, we focus on the process, through the analysis of Sigma-Lognormal parameters, while the complementarity of the two approaches will be discussed in another article. The Sigma-Lognormal parameters come from the reconstruction of a movement captured by pen strokes and based on the Kinematic Theory of rapid human movements [40, 41] and allow us to assess the state of motor control, here specifically on the fluidity of the movement [41] of fine motor skills. The parameters we used in this study are obtained through the segmentation of the movement performed by the children, having been used in other similar studies [42]: i) number of lognormal functions required to reconstruct the signal (nbLog), which is supposed to decrease with fine motor movement improvement [42]; ii) the signal-to-noise ratio between the original speed profile and the reconstructed speed profile of the reconstruction process (SNR), which increases with fine motor movement improvement [42] meaning a better reconstruction [40, 41]; and iii) the ratio between these two variables (SNR/nbLog). The higher SNR/nbLog, the closer the movement is to the ideal lognormal behavior predicted the by the Lognormality Principle [43]. This last parameter can be seen as a global indicator of handwriter performance [41].

The relevance of these parameters in child Graphic Skills assessment is recognized, due to their complementary information [42] not only with typical development children but also with neurodevelopmental population [44]. Therefore, present study focuses on the effects of children's Graphic Skills characterization using process, i.e., analysis through log-normal parameters extracted from the above-mentioned tasks performed on a digitizing tablet.

2 Method

2.1 Participants

Two groups of children were recruited from local kindergartens and primary schools. The first group, 55 preschoolers (24 boys and 31 girls) ranging from 4 to 6 years old, were subdivided in two other groups: control group (CG, 30 children) and experimental group (EG, 25 children). With the second group, 41 second graders (14 boys and 27 girls) ranging 8–9 years old, the same procedure was taken, and two subgroups created: control group (CG, 21 children) and experimental group (EG, 20 children). All children gave their verbal agreement to participate in the study.

2.2 Intervention Program

Intervention program was developed during 16 sessions, twice a week. Each session was developed in group of 6–8 children and lasted 30 min. In the beginning of each session, some reinforcement activities were carried out, so that the children could remember the contents they had experienced in the previous session.

Participants were assessed in three moments: pre, pos intervention and six months after finishing the program (follow-up).

2.3 Tasks

One of the most discussed issues in handwriting is the question of when young children are (or not) ready to begin handwriting instruction. Beyond perceptual readiness, linguistic readiness, and maturity of pencil control, [6] argued that young children are not ready to learn handwriting until they correctly copy the first nine forms of the VMI (Fig. 1), revealing an adequate visuomotor integration. The highest the score, the better visuomotor integration ability.

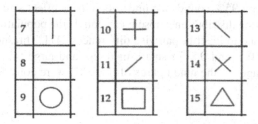

Fig. 1. First nine VMI figures (Numbers refer to the figures number in the test)

The BHK (Portuguese version) was used to measure the legibility (quality) and speed (quantity) of handwriting. It consists of handwriting task that involves a copy of a text in 5 min. Only the first five lines are scored in what legibility is concerned. The higher the total score, the lower the handwriting quality [45].

2.4 Procedures

Preschoolers' participants were asked to perform the Beery VMI while second graders performed BHK copy, on a quiet room. Movements were recorded using a x-y digitizing tablet (WACOM) with an inking pen (WACOM Grip Pen). The tablet had an active surface area of 32.51 cm × 20.32 cm, a device resolution of .0005 cm and a sampling frequency of 100 Hz. Participants were seated in front of the tablet that was centred on the participant's midline in front of the chest. The height of the chair and table was adjusted, and the laptop computer was set aside so that the real-time visual feedback of the child's pen movements was only available to the experimenter.

2.5 Statistical Analysis

After preliminary inspections for distribution and assumptions, data were processed to fit analysis of covariance (ANCOVA, group effect: control and experimental group), with post-test values as the dependent variable and pre-test values as the covariate and after follow-up as dependent variable and post-test values as the covariate. Pairwise differences were assessed with Bonferroni post-hoc. Statistical significance was set at p < 0.05 and calculations were completed using the Jamovi Project [46].

An estimation techniques approach was carried to overcome the shortcomings associated with traditional Neyman-Pearson null hypothesis significance testing [47, 48]. According to the control and experimental group, estimation plots for SNR, nbLog and SNR/nbLog variables were used as descriptive statistics. This graphical representation shows the individual and mean group values for pre-test, post-test and follow-up measures and the difference of mean with 95% of confidence intervals [47, 48]. Also, Cohen's dunbiased (dunb) with 95% confidence intervals (CI) as effect size (ES) (an unbiased estimate has a sampling distribution whose mean equals the population parameter being estimated) was applied to identify pairwise differences [47]. Thresholds for effect size statistics were: 0.2, 0.5, and 0.8 for small, medium, and large [49]. In the preschoolers' group, the averages of the nine figures of the VMI were considered in each of the lognormal variables.

3 Results

3.1 Changes in Lognormal Parameters After Intervention and in Follow-Up Moment

Preeschoolers
The summary of findings from the ANCOVA for group factor is presented in Table 1.

Table 1. Analysis of covariance (ANCOVA) results considering the group factor.

Variables	Control group (CG, n = 30)			Experimental group (EG, n = 25)			Group factor			ANCOVA CG vs EG
	Pre	Post	Fol	Pre	Post	Fol	F	p	$\eta^2 p$	
SNR	25.5 ± 0.91	25.3 ± 1.23	25.6 ± 0.77	25.3 ± 0.91	25.3 ± 1.05	25.6 ± 0.95	0.09	0.77	.00	a.
							0.03	0.87	.05	b.
nbLog	15.7 ± 5.77	16.4 ± 5.98	13.0 ± 3.72	15.3 ± 4.92	15.2 ± 5.36	13.7 ± 4.43	1.11	0.30	.03	a.
							0.12	0.74	.00	b.
SNR/nbLog	1.9 ± 0.66	1.8 ± 0.66	2.1 ± 0.59	1.8 ± 0.56	1.8 ± 0.58	2.1 ± 0.59	0.67	0.42	.01	a.
							0.15	0.71	.00	b.

Values in bold represent significant differences at $p < 0.05$.
a. Pre vs. Post-test; b. Post vs. follow-up-test.

Individual and differences of mean values from pre-test to post-test performance measures are shown in Figs. 1, 2, and 3. The estimation plots present the differences of means as a bootstrap 95% confidence interval on separate but aligned axes. This representation can be observed for each variable and for each group. Complementary, the dunb with 95% confidence intervals are presented in Fig. 5.

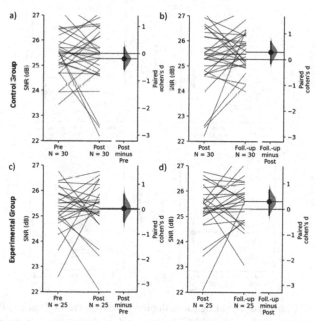

Fig. 2. The paired Cohen's d for SNR (preschoolers) between Pre vs. Post and Post vs. Follow-up for both CG (upper panel, a, b) and EG (lower panel, c, d) are shown in the above Gardner-Altman estimation plots. The groups are plotted on the left axes as a slopegraph: each paired set of observations is connected by a line. The paired Cohen's d is plotted on a floating axis on the right as a bootstrap sampling distribution. The Cohen's d is depicted as a dot; the 95% confidence interval is indicated by the ends of the vertical error bar.

The SNR test did not show significant effects of group factor for the post-test (F = 0.09, p = .77, $\eta^2 p$ = .00) or for the follow-up test (F = 0.03, p = .87, $\eta^2 p$ = .05) (Table 1). For these results, in each group type, post-hoc differences were identified for pairwise comparisons pre-test vs. post-test and post-test vs. follow-up group. For the CG, there was a decrease from pre- to post-test (Cohen's d [95% confidence intervals]: −0.19 [−0.57, 0.22]; with small ES) (Fig. 2a) like what happened in EG (0.30 [−0.512, 0.594]; with small ES) (Fig. 2c). When considering post- to follow-up test, SNR values increased in both CG (0.28 [0.158, 0.695]; with small ES) (Fig. 2b) and EG (0.30 [−0.235, 0.754]; with small ES) (Fig. 2d).

The nbLog test did not show significant effects of group factor for the post-test (F = 1.11, p = .30, $\eta^2 p$ = .03) or for the follow-up test (F = 1.12, p = .74, $\eta^2 p$ = .00) (Table 1). For these results, in each group type, post-hoc differences were identified for pairwise comparisons pre-test vs. post-test and post-test vs. follow-up group. For the CG, there was an increase in nbLog values from pre- to post-test (0.117 [−0.212, 0.452]; with small ES) (Fig. 3a) and the opposite happened in EG (−0.0195 [−0.459, 0.337]; with trivial ES) (Fig. 3c). Although, when observing post- to follow-up test, nbLog values decreased in both groups, CG (−0.678 [−1.03, −0.314]; with medium ES) (Fig. 3b) and EG (0.311 [−0.726, 0.154]; with small ES) (Fig. 3d).

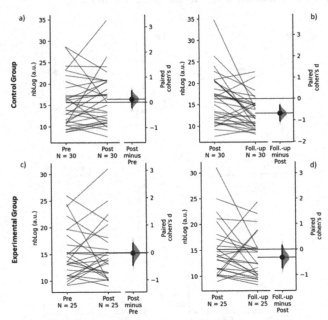

Fig. 3. The paired Cohen's d for nbLog (preschoolers) between Pre vs. Post and Post vs. Follow-up for both CG (upper panel, a, b) and EG (lower panel, c, d) are shown in the above Gardner-Altman estimation plots. The groups are plotted on the left axes as a slopegraph: each paired set of observations is connected by a line. The paired Cohen's d is plotted on a floating axis on the right as a bootstrap sampling distribution. The Cohen's d is depicted as a dot; the 95% confidence interval is indicated by the ends of the vertical error bar.

The SNR/nbLog outcomes promoted similar results. Non-significant effects of group factor (F = 0.67, p = .42, η^2p = .01) for the post-test neither for follow-up (F = 0.15, p = .71, η^2p = .00). A decrease was identified from Pre- to Post-test in CG (−0.147 [−0.471, 0.172]; with small ES) (Fig. 4a) and an increase in EG (0.0491 [−0.347, 0.496]; with small ES) (Fig. 4c). An increased was observed from post- to follow-up test in both groups, with a bigger magnitude in CG (0.594 [0.235, 0.975]) (Fig. 4b) than in EG (0.362 [−0.113, 0.771] (Fig. 4d).

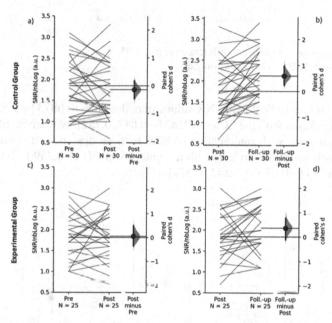

Fig. 4. The paired Cohen's d for SNR/nbLog (preschoolers) between Pre vs. Post and Post vs. Follow-up for both CG (upper panel, a, b) and EG (lower panel, c, d) are shown in the above Gardner-Altman estimation plots. The groups are plotted on the left axes as a slopegraph: each paired set of observations is connected by a line. The paired Cohen's d is plotted on a floating axis on the right as a bootstrap sampling distribution. The Cohen's d is depicted as a dot; the 95% confidence interval is indicated by the ends of the vertical error bar.

Second Graders

Results for 41 children in three moments showed the SNR trend. It was not found significant effects of group factor for SNR in pre- to post-test (F = 6.03^{e-4}, p = .98, η^2p = .00) or in post- to follow-up test (F = 0.28, p = .60, η^2p = .00), with post-hoc differences in Pre- vs. Post-test and Post- vs. Follow-up (Table 2).

Table 2. Analysis of covariance (ANCOVA) results considering the group factor.

Variables	Control group (CG, n = 20)			Experimental group (EG, n = 21)			Group factor			ANCOVA CG vs EG
	Pre	Post	Fol	Pre	Post	Fol	F	p	$\eta^2 p$	
SNR	11.0 ± 3.70	11.0 ± 3.72	10.3 ± 2.93	11.1 ± 3.64	11.0 ± 3.78	9.73 ± 3.38	6.03^{e-4}	0.98	.00	a.
							0.28	0.60	.00	b.
nbLog	287 ± 212	288 ± 228	289 ± 231	298 ± 235	232 ± 162	265 ± 219	1.11	0.30	.03	a.
							0.11	0.74	.00	b.
SNR/nbLog	0.09 ± 0.12	0.18 ± 0.30	0.13 ± 0.21	0.09 ± 0.13	0.13 ± 0.23	0.14 ± 0.25	0.38	0.54	.01	a.
							0.10	0.76	.00	b.

Values in bold represent significant differences at p < 0.05.
a. Pre vs. Post-test; b. Post vs. follow-up-test.

In CG, from Pre- to Post-test, SNR values were the same (0.0873 [−1.3, 1.95]; with trivial ES) (Fig. 5a) as with the EG (−0.0183 [−0.847, 0.752]; with trivial ES) (Fig. 5c), denoting no changes with intervention. Again, both groups showed similar decrease trend from post- to follow-up test, with a higher ES in EG (−0.359 [−0.942, 0.203]) (Fig. 5d) than CG (−0.236 [−0.841, 0.327]) (Fig. 5b).

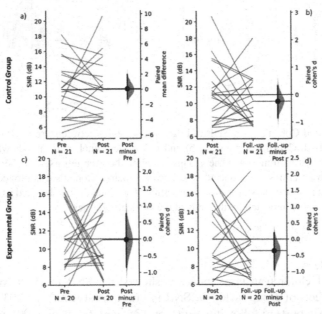

Fig. 5. The paired Cohen's d for SNR (second graders) between Pre vs. Post and Post vs. Follow-up for both CG (upper panel, a, b) and EG (lower panel, c, d) are shown in the above Gardner-Altman estimation plots. The groups are plotted on the left axes as a slopegraph: each paired set of observations is connected by a line. The paired Cohen's d is plotted on a floating axis on the right as a bootstrap sampling distribution. The Cohen's d is depicted as a dot; the 95% confidence interval is indicated by the ends of the vertical error bar.

Again, in nbLog parameter it was not found significant effects of group factor for SNR in pre- to post-test (F = 1.11, p = .30, η^2p = .03) or in post- to follow-up test (F = 0.11, p = .74, η^2p = .00). Children from CG did not show any changes from pre- to post-test (0.00476 [−0.292, 0.355]) (Fig. 6a) neither from post- to follow-up test (0.00187 [−0.642, 0.659]) (Fig. 6b). In contrast, EG had a decreased from pre- to post-test (0.328 [−0.992, 0.237]; with small ES) (Fig. 6c) and an increase post- to follow-up test (0.172 [−0.499, 0.787]; with small ES) (Fig. 6d).

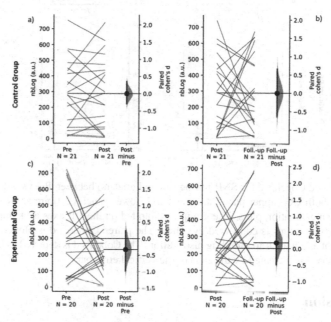

Fig. 6. The paired Cohen's d for nbLog (second graders) between Pre vs. Post and Post vs. Follow-up for both CG (upper panel, a, b) and EG (lower panel, c, d) are shown in the above Gardner-Altman estimation plots. The groups are plotted on the left axes as a slopegraph: each paired set of observations is connected by a line. The paired Cohen's d is plotted on a floating axis on the right as a bootstrap sampling distribution. The Cohen's d is depicted as a dot; the 95% confidence interval is indicated by the ends of the vertical error bar.

As expected, the SNR/nbLog outcomes promoted similar results to the ones observed in SNR. Non-significant effects of group factor (F = 0.38, p = .54, η^2p = .01) for the post-test neither for follow-up (F = 0.10, p = .76, η^2p = .00). An increase was identified from Pre- to Post-test in CG (0.371 [−0.163, 0.747]; with small ES) (Fig. 7a) and in EG (0.192 [−0.523, 0.7]; with small ES) (Fig. 7c). A decrease was observed from post-to follow-up test in both groups, with a bigger magnitude in CG (−0.212 [−0.704, 0.45]) (Fig. 6b) than in EG (−0.212 [−0.704, 0.45] (Fig. 7d).

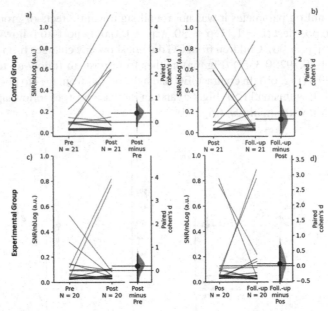

Fig. 7. The paired Cohen's d for SNR/nbLog (second graders) between Pre vs. Post and Post vs. Follow-up for both CG (upper panel, a, b) and EG (lower panel, c, d) are shown in the above Gardner-Altman estimation plots. The groups are plotted on the left axes as a slopegraph: each paired set of observations is connected by a line. The paired Cohen's d is plotted on a floating axis on the right as a bootstrap sampling distribution. The Cohen's d is depicted as a dot; the 95% confidence interval is indicated by the ends of the vertical error bar.

4   Discussion

4.1   Preschoolers

SNR values from pre- to post-test increased in CG but had a small increase in EG. When considering post- to follow-up test, both groups have the growing trend with similar effect sizes. We can conclude that the fine movement quality improved [42] with intervention, meaning a better quality of speed signal reconstruction [40, 42]. When considering nbLog values it was observed an increase in CG and a decrease in EG from pre- to post-test which means that EG needed less lognormals to reconstruct the pen stroke signal and movements were more fluid, after intervention. From post- to follow-up test there was a decrease in this parameter values, with more expression in EG, meaning that this group kept fluidity improvements in fine motor movement along six months [42, 43]. Finally, SNR/nbLog can be seen as a global indicator of handwriter performance [41]. Considering that EG had better results from pre- to post-test, it can be concluded that intervention improved handwriting performance, i.e., better quality of motor control. From post- to follow-up test, although CG had a bigger increase than EG, it can be considered more consistent in this last one considering the smaller CI.

4.2 Second Graders

Both groups showed similar trends in all assessment moments in SNR parameter: no changes values from pre- to post- test, and a decrease from post- to follow-up test, with a higher magnitude in EG. This indicates that intervention did not have any effect in fine motor quality assessed through children's copies and, after six months, got worse. In nbLog parameter, CG did not show any changes, in any assessment moment. EG improved their fine motor movement but did not keep this improvement after the end of intervention program. Again, in SNR/nbLog both groups were observed same trend with better handwriter performance after intervention and less retention of these gains after 6 months. The lack of maintenance of the improvements gained with the intervention or even worsening of the results, can be due to the handwriting automatization process that children with this age are passing through [14, 24, 25].

5 Conclusion

This study started from the hypothesis that children receiving intervention would show substantial improvement in handwriting performance revealed by SNR, nbLog and SNR/nbLog. In general, graphomotor intervention had positive effects in fine motor control and, consequently in Graphic Skills performance. This exploratory study was limited by its sample sizes and by the fact that there were no participants with handwriting difficulties. Considering the relevance of the analysis done in the present study, it is recommended that in the future, child Graphic Skills assessment use complementary information with traditional features [42] using process and product approaches [35].

Acknowledgements. This study was partly supported by Grant SFRH/BD/145069/2019 from Foundation for Science and Technology (FCT) to Helena Coradinho. The authors would like to sincerely thank Professor Bruno Gonçalves for his support in statistical analysis.

References

1. Puranik, C.S., Lonigan, C.J.: From Scribbles to scrabble: preschool children's developing knowledge of written language. Read Writ. **24**(5), 567–589 (2011)
2. Marr, D., Cermak, S., Cohn, E., Henderson, S.: Fine motor activities in head start and kindergarten classrooms. Am. J. Occup. Ther. **57**(5), 550–557 (2003)
3. Lifshitz, N., Har-Zvi, S.: A comparison between students who receive and who do not receive a writing readiness interventions on handwriting quality, speed and positive reactions. Early Child. Educ. J. **43**(1), 47–55 (2014)
4. Van Hartingsveldt, M.J., Cup, E.H.C., Hendriks, J.C.M., de Vries, L., de Groot, I.J.M., Nijhuis-van der Sanden, M.W.G.: Predictive validity of kindergarten assessments on handwriting readiness. Res. Dev. Disabil. **36**, 114–124 (2015)
5. Schneck, C., Amundson, S.: Prewriting and handwriting skills. In: Case-Smith, J., O'Brien, J. (eds.) Occupational Therapy for Children, pp. 555–580. Mosby Elsevier, Missouri (2010)
6. Beery, K.E.: The Developmental Test of Visual-Motor Integration. 3rd Rev. Modern Curriculum Press, Cleveland (1989)

7. Daly, C.J., Kelley, G.T., Krauss, A.: Relationship between visual-motor integration and handwriting skills of children in kindergarten: a modified replication study. Am. J. Occup. Ther. **57**(4), 459–462 (2003)
8. Marr, D., Windsor, M.M., Cermak, S.: Handwriting readiness: locatives and visuomotor skills in the kindergarten year. Early Child. Res. Pract. **3**(1), 1–16 (2001)
9. Weil, M., Amundson, S.: Relationship between visuomotor and handwriting skills of children in Kindergarten. Am. J. Occup. Ther. **48**(11), 982–988 (1994)
10. Van Hartingsveldt, M.J., de Groot, I.J.M., Aarts, P.B.M., Nijhuis-van der Sanden, M.W.G.: Standardized tests of handwriting readiness: a systematic review of the literature. Dev. Med. Child Neurol. **53**(6), 506–515 (2011)
11. Dinehart, L.H.: Handwriting in early childhood education: current research and future implications. J. Early Child. Lit. **15**(1), 97–118 (2015)
12. Denton, P.L., Cope, S., Moser, C.: The effects of sensorimotor-based intervention versus therapeutic practice on improving handwriting performance in 6- to 11-year-old children. Am. J. Occup. Ther. **60**(1), 16–27 (2006)
13. Alhusaini, A.A., Melam, G.R., Buragadda, S.: Short-term sensorimotor-based intervention for handwriting performance in elementary school children. Pediatr. Int. **58**(11), 1118–1123 (2016)
14. Feder, K.P., Majnemer, A.: Handwriting development, competency, and intervention. Dev. Med. Child Neurol. **49**(4), 312–317 (2007)
15. Soppelsa, R., Albaret, J.M.: Caractéristiques de la dysgraphie ou du trouble de l'apprentissage de la graphomotricité (TAG) au collège. ANAE - Approche Neuropsychologique des Apprentissages chez l'Enfant **26**(128), 53–58 (2014)
16. Mäki, H.S., Voeten, M.J.M., Vauras, M.M.S., Poskiparta, E.H.: Predicting writing skill development with word recognition and preschool readiness skills. Read. Writ. **14**(7–8), 643–672 (2001)
17. Singpun, P., Sriphetcharawut, S.: Effectiveness of the protocol for enhancing handwriting readiness skills of preschoolers aged 4–6 years. J. Assoc. Med. Sci. **52**(1), 73–78 (2019)
18. Biotteau, M., Danna, J., Baudou, É., Puyjarinet, F., Velay, J.L., Albaret, J.M., et al.: Developmental coordination disorder and dysgraphia: signs and symptoms, diagnosis, and rehabilitation. Neuropsychiatr. Dis. Treat. **15**, 1873–1885 (2019)
19. McCloskey, M., Rapp, B.: Developmental dysgraphia: an overview and framework for research. Cogn. Neuropsychol. **34**(3–4), 65–82 (2017)
20. McMaster, E., Roberts, T.: Handwriting in 2015: a main occupation for primary school–aged children in the classroom? J. Occup. Ther. Sch. Early Interv. **9**(1), 38–50 (2016)
21. Lachaux-Parker, C.: Troubles de l'écriture et psychomotricité. Revue Francophone d'Orthoptie. **5**(4), 143–147 (2012)
22. Volman, M.J.M., Van Schendel, B.M., Jongmans, M.J.: Handwriting difficulties in primary school children: a search for underlying mechanisms. Am. J. Occup. Ther. **60**(4), 451–460 (2006)
23. Klein, S., Guiltner, V., Sollereder, P., Cui, Y.: Relationships between fine-motor, visual-motor, and visual perception scores and handwriting legibility and speed. Phys. Occup. Ther. Pediatr. **31**(1), 103–114 (2011)
24. Overvelde, A., Hulstijn, W.: Research in developmental disabilities handwriting development in grade 2 and grade 3 primary school children with normal, at risk, or dysgraphic characteristics. Res. Dev. Disabil. **32**, 540–548 (2011)
25. Van Hoorn, J.F., Maathuis, C.G.B., Hadders-Algra, M.: Neural correlates of paediatric dysgraphia. Dev. Med. Child Neurol. **55**(4), 65–68 (2013)
26. Donica, D.K., Francsis, E.: Exploring content validity of shore handwriting screening and newly developed score sheet with pre-kindergarten students. Open J. Occup. Ther. **3**(3), 6 (2015)

27. Kadar, M., Wan Yunus, F., Tan, E., Chai, S.C., Razaob@Razab, N.A., Mohamat Kasim, D.H.: A systematic review of occupational therapy intervention for handwriting skills in 4–6-year-old children. Aust. Occup. Ther. J. **67**(1), 3–12 (2020)
28. Taverna, L., Tremolada, M., Dozza, L., Scaratti, R.Z., Ulrike, D., Lallo, C., et al.: Who benefits from an intervention program on foundational skills for handwriting addressed to kindergarten children and first graders? Int. J. Environ. Res. Public Health **17**(6), 2166 (2020)
29. Pfeiffer, B., Rai, G., Murray, T., Brusilovskiy, E.: Effectiveness of the size matters handwriting program. OTJR Occup. Particip. Health **35**(2), 110–119 (2015)
30. Sheedy, A.J., Brent, J., Dally, K., Ray, K., Lane, A.E.: Handwriting readiness among digital native kindergarten students. Phys. Occup. Ther. Pediatr. **41**, 655–669 (2021)
31. Hoy, M., Egan, M., Feder, K., Hoy, M.M., Egan, M.Y., Feder, K.P.: A systematic review of interventions to improve handwriting. Can. J. Occup. Ther. **78**(1), 13–25 (2011)
32. Albaret, J.-M., Santamaria, M.: Utilisation des digitaliseurs dans l'étude des caractéristiques motrices de l'écriture. Evol. Psychomotrices **8**(33), 115–119 (1996)
33. Albaret, J.-M., Soppelsa, R., Danna, J., Kaiser, M.-L.: Évaluation de l'écriture. Em: Albaret, J.-M., Kaiser, M.-L., Soppelsa, R. (eds.) Troubles de l'écriture chez l'enfant: Des modèles à l'intervention, pp. 135–153. De Boeck Supérieur, Bruxelles (2013)
34. Danna, J., Velay, J., Albaret, J.-M.: Dysgraphies. Em: Pinto, S., Sato, M. (eds.) Traité de neurolinguistique: du cerveau au langage, pp. 337–346. De Boeck Supérieur, Louvain-la-Neuve (2016)
35. Rosenblum, S., Livneh-Zirinski, M.: Handwriting process and product characteristics of children diagnosed with developmental coordination disorder. Hum. Mov. Sci. **27**(2), 200–214 (2008)
36. Rosenblum, S., Weiss, P.L., Parush, S.: Product and process evaluation of handwriting difficulties. Educ. Psychol. Rev. **15**(1), 41–81 (2003)
37. Rosenblum, S., Weiss, P.L., Parush, S.: Handwriting evaluation for developmental dysgraphia. Read. Writ.: Interdiscip. J. **17**, 433–458 (2004)
38. Soppelsa, R., Abizeid, C., Chéron, A., Laurent, A., Danna, J., Albaret, J.-M.: Dysgraphies et rééducation psychomotrice: Données actuelles. Em: Albaret, J.-M., Abizeid, C.-M., Soppelsa, R. (eds.) Les Entretiens de Bichat 2016, pp. 1–8. Europa Digital & Publishing, Toulouse (2016)
39. O'Reilly, C., Plamondon, R.: Development of a sigma-lognormal representation for on-line signatures. Pattern Recogn. **42**(12), 3324–3337 (2009)
40. Plamondon, R.: A kinematic theory of rapid human movements: part I: movement representation and generation. Biol. Cybern. **72**, 295–307 (1995)
41. Plamondon, R., O'Reilly, C., Rémi, C., Duval, R.: The lognormal handwriter: learning, performing, and declining. Front. Psychol. **4**, 945 (2013)
42. Duval, T., Rémi, C., Plamondon, R., Vaillant, J.: Combining sigma-lognormal modeling and classical features for analyzing graphomotor performances in kindergarten children. Hum. Mov. Sci. **43**, 183–200 (2015)
43. Faci, N., Nguyen, H., Laniel, P., Gauthier, B., Beaucham, M., Makagawa, M., et al.: Classifying the kinematics of fast pen strokes in children with ADHD using different machine learning models. In: The Lognormality Principles and its Applications in E-Security, E-Learning and E-Health, pp. 117–442. World Scientific Publishing (2021)
44. Faci, N., Bidias, S., Plamondon, R., Bergeron, N.: An interactive tablet-based system to run neuromuscular tests. In: The Lognormality Principles and its Applications in E-Security, E-Learning and E-Health, pp. 269–288. World Scientific Publishing (2021)
45. Charles, M., Soppelsa, R., Albaret, J.-M.: BHK: Échelle d'évaluation rapide de l'écriture chez l'enfant. ECPA, Paris (2004)
46. The Jamovi Project: Jamovi (2021). Disponível em: https://www.jamovi.org
47. Cumming, G.: Understanding the new statistics: effect sizes, confidence intervals, and meta-analysis. Routledge (2012)

48. Ho, J., Tumkaya, T., Aryal, S., Ho, J., Tumkaya, T., Aryal, S., et al.: Moving beyond P values: data analysis with estimation graphics. Nat. Methods **16**, 565–566 (2019)

49. Cohen, J.: The effect size. Statistical Power Analysis for the Behavioral Sciences. Routledge, pp. 77–83 (1988)

Copilotrace: A Platform to Process Graphomotor Tasks for Education and Graphonomics Research

Remi Celine[✉] and Nagau Jimmy

LAMIA, Université des Antilles, Pointe-à-Pitre, Guadeloupe
celine.remi@univ-antilles.fr

Abstract. Recent works highlight that a graphomotor analysis of the pupil's movements throughout his schooling for a maximum of writing and production situations could contribute to improving the support of the learning of handwriting well beyond the first years of school. However, to our knowledge, there is no tool to date that could constitute a shared and mobilizable help for all teachers from kindergarten to high school for such process. The Web-platform Copilotrace tries to answer this problem. After a review and a discussion of the uses of digital technology to assist teacher's practices of evaluation and monitoring of students' graphomotor skills, we present the architecture, and main functionalities of Copilotrace. These functionalities are centered on the contextualized acquisition, storage, and analysis of graphomotor tasks. Then, we illustrate the main contributions of the use of Copilotrace thanks to three research-actions of the EMagMa project.

Keywords: Graphomotor tasks · Web-platform · Online acquisition · Graphomotor analysis · Handwriting learning · Teaching · Graphonomics research · deltaPenlift

1 Introduction

Many works [1, 2] have highlighted that, in addition to the appreciation of the legibility, the visual conformity and the linguistical quality of the handwritten productions made by pupils, graphomotor analysis of their movements should produce meta-knowledge that should help teachers to improve their assistance to handwriting learning process from kindergarten up to high school (Fig. 1).

Therefore, even when teachers propose pedagogical activities that have as primary or exclusive goal the appreciation of meta-knowledge or meta-skills in areas such as knowledge of letters, handwriting, spelling, written production, space management, geometry, arithmetic calculation, etc.; the instructions they give to their students very frequently induce the production of what we have chosen to call graphomotor tasks.

A graphomotor task is the execution of a sequence of voluntary and controlled movements with the aim of producing traces by means of a writing implement (pen, pencil, finger…). School graphomotor tasks all have in common that they generate at least one

© Springer Nature Switzerland AG 2022
C. Carmona-Duarte et al. (Eds.): IGS 2021, LNCS 13424, pp. 129–143, 2022.
https://doi.org/10.1007/978-3-031-19745-1_10

Fig. 1. Examples of scholar handwritten productions. (a) a 4-year-old pupil's free-hand scribble and (b) a free-hand square produced at kindergarten by a 5-year-old pupil; (c) a word and (d) isolated cursive letters freely written by a pupil at elementary school; (e) a narrative text produced at middle school by a 11-year-old pupil.

visually persistent or non-persistent trajectory of either a pointing action, a dragging action, or a handwritten tracing action in a finite and oriented 2D space. The trajectory generated by a graphomotor task may, depending on the nature of the pedagogical activity, fall into at least one or more of the categories meaningful at school. Examples include line, straight line, curve, geometric shape, scribble, curvilinear scribble, figurative sketch, letter, alphanumeric symbol, cursive word...

Meetings with teachers from kindergarten to primary school within the Guadeloupe Academy led us to note two facts that are consistent with the observations made in France and Quebec [3]. First, very often, the teaching team can perceive and assess only the final visual rendering of the graphic objects pointed, dragged, or traced. Next, teachers rarely consider the other components of graphomotricity, although significant in all the schoolwork done by the pupil from nursery school onwards and throughout his schooling [4], as fundamental components that must be trained throughout school career. Thus, they assess these other components of pupils' graphomotor skills, as the motor dimension, and work on them only during the first schooling years. For example, in Guadeloupe, teachers try to work on these components only from kindergarten up to the beginning of the third year of primary school [5].

We argue that teachers should benefit of adequate tool for continuously assess, in the light of simple criteria and academic standards, the qualitative progression of their students' graphomotor abilities by analyzing their graphomotor tasks all along primary school period. However, to our knowledge there is currently no solution to help a teacher, within his usual practice, to conduct such analysis of students' graphomotor tasks.

In addition, although we have been able to note that researchers need data on the graphomotor behaviors of all-coming students during their learning, there is to our knowledge no solution that allows both: a non-intrusive and secure acquisition in real situations, i.e., in ordinary school environments as a reliable/controllable, fast and easy preparation of such data for research.

We have developed Copilotrace, a web-platform, which deals with such purposes. This paper aims to provide details about Copilotrace, and its previous uses as follows.

First, after a review of the literature dealing with the digital tools dedicated to graphomotor learning, we explain the choices we have made to design Copilotrace. Then, we describe the principles that underlie its architecture and functionalities. Next, we discuss three real uses of Copilotrace and conclude with perspectives.

2 Review of Uses of Digital Tools for Graphomotor Learning

Since the first developments of digital tools dedicated to graphomotor learning, the acquisition and processing apparatus have made enormous progress. The digitizer with its pen [6] used by software such as Scriptot [7], ComPET [8], MovAlyzeR [9] or MEDDRAW [10] at the start gradually gave way to embedded systems like Trazo with its tablet PC [11] or the Hello Kitty Digital Pen embedding Toutaki [12] in the early 2000s. Since then, more mobile, and elaborate devices like touch tablets have established themselves, due to the dazzling growth in their penetration of the consumer equipment market and their usage.

Although they have retained their shortcomings in terms of measurement uncertainty [13, 14], the models of touch tablet favored since 2010 by tools dedicated to graphomotor learning of handwriting have gained in lightness, autonomy and consequently in mobility compared to Tablet-PCs or to digitizers that cannot operate without computer. Though it is noticeably light and easy to manage, touch tablet, if its screen embeds electromagnetic technology rather than resistive or capacitive one, can also provide a qualitative experience of pen-oriented interaction thanks to electromagnetic resonance autonomous active styli.

Moreover, by natively embedding in their own OS powerful means of real-time computation, memorization, and network communication in addition to online visualization and recording solutions of the tracing or pointing movements used with the finger or the stylus on their surface, touch tablets have opened new application perspectives [15]. Thus, as far as the design of digital solutions for helping the learning of handwriting and graphomotor gestures is concerned, the Intuidoc team in partnership with the company Learn & GO have recently enriched existing solutions by developing Kaligo tool [16–18]. Kaligo is compatible with a wide range of touch tablets on different operating systems (Android, Apple, Chromebook). It is a software solution that stands out from its predecessors by the philosophy that underlies it. The principles that prevailed in its conception and that conditions its functioning and its uses at school [19] are, according to its designers:

- To provide a digital solution for the teacher and the children dedicated to the learning of the graphomotor gesture and the handwriting of the pupils,
- To enrich, using digital tools, the teaching of writing in accordance with the objectives set by the school programs,
- Adapt to the teacher's pedagogy while allowing for individualized learning paths and better monitoring of student progress,
- Formalize the solution of autonomous training for each student through a personal digital notebook accessible on a preconfigured tablet thanks to the School or Home QR codes created by the teacher for each of his students,
- Formalize the solution of pedagogical programming and monitoring of the effects of training via a web space Teacher,
- Encourage self-assessment with an automatic expertise of the writing based on a multifactorial analysis of the shape, the meaning, the order of the drawing, the pressure on pen and the respect of proportions from artificial intelligence engines,

- Systematize feedback on production via the display of an easy-to-understand indicator gauge that helps maintain the student's commitment to the task,
- Integrate remediation as a learning tool, i.e., offer the child the opportunity to redo the unsuccessful production as many times as necessary.

Several points limit the use of the pre-existing solutions we have studied. They are linked to their designers' conceptual and functional choices. Thus, some of these tools can exclusively work locally, others require a permanent connection with a remote server, while others require a specific type of hardware or a specific writing implement. Moreover, some tools impose the activities. This last choice constitutes a factor that limits the teacher in the design of his pedagogical sequences.

Finally, the constrained budgetary context in many scholar systems seems to also be a significant obstacle to the use of some of these solutions; for example, if a specific model of unsupported device already equip schools.

Lastly, the choice of equipment models is often heterogeneous from one school to another, and even within the same school. So, those who have chosen tablets without a pen, unless they have the necessary budget to buy pens compatible with the tablet models they own, cannot in this case exploit solutions that natively require a specific model of writing tool.

We think that a technologically open solution, i.e.: detached from the hardware, without limitation on the choice of models, writing tools, operating systems and exploitable pedagogical contents could: be more accessible to users who do not have access to pre-existing solutions for the reasons stated above; constitute a foundation for solutions that should offer a wider range of applications in terms of assistance to education and research. It is on this basis that we have designed Copilotrace platform.

3   Introduction of Copilotrace

Copilotrace is a digital platform that can offer pedagogical activities which induce graphomotor tasks specifically dedicated to the learning of efficient handwriting gestures and can assess pupils' levels of proficiency. Copilotrace can also assist other fields of learning or experimental studies concerned with the production of graphomotor tasks. Indeed, its conception principle is based on the constant and primordial concern to simultaneously make possible, at a lower cost and for the greatest number of users:

- the acquisition of relevant raw data on the graphomotor tasks,
- the contextualization and adaptative analysis of these data,
- the autonomous, transparent retrieval, aggregation, and storage of these data.

First, we have conceived Copilotrace as a progressive WEB application powered by web browsers, available on all operating systems (Windows, Android, macOS, IOS, chrome OS). This choice allows a quick installation on the equipment from an Internet address entered in the browser: https://copilotrace.univ-antilles.fr. Copilotrace also allows a use in white zone or, by small children from 3 to 5 years old, in accordance with the regulation recommendation relative to the limitation of continuous exposure to the waves generated by the wireless Internet. Copilotrace is based on five modules written in web technologies:

- A module to manage groups of users and users' graphomotor tasks (MUG),
- A module to collect raw data on trajectories (MCT),
- A module to design contextualized activities (MDC),
- A module to extract and export contextualized graphomotor data by query (MEQ),
- A module to store contextualized pedagogical activities (MSA).

The teacher, as an accompanist, can use the MUG to create user accounts with a writer profile and allocate an identification code or avatar for each pupil. The MUG help teacher to create group class, groups of need and to assign pupils to these groups. Before, the teacher must first create his own account with an accompanist profile.

The MCT is responsible for the online acquisition by various devices like tablets, smartphones, computers, iPad,.) and the analysis of raw data on the dragging, pointing and handwriting trajectories. The MCT collects at least the digital context and the raw data for each graphomotor task. The raw data acquired by the MCT consist in a sequence of dated position (t, X, Y) of the tip on the surface. Optionally, the MCT also acquires the pressure exerted on the tip of the writing tool. The digital context encapsulates meta-knowledge on the web-browser executing the MCT, the model of the material and the type of writing tool. Thanks to the MCT, Copilotrace can process trajectories made with finger or pen online for the adaptative analysis of graphomotor tasks.

The MDC allows the design of pedagogical activities (PA). This design process is based on the specification of a set of contextual elements like activity duration, number of repetitions, pedagogical supports, writing tools used, expected graphomotor states or procedures for problem solving, expression of consistency score… These contextual elements tune the PA complexity, the sequence of graphomotor tasks to perform and interaction with writer for their control.

The MCT uses meta-knowledge which encapsulate other contextual data, like expected graphomotor states and solving procedure, to parametrize the set of features estimated from the raw data recorded during a graphomotor task. If there are specifications of such contextual elements and of a consistency score, Copilotrace process the raw data online to compute the degree of spatio-graphical [20], procedural [21], temporal [22], or structural [23] consistency of the graphomotor task trajectory. Next, if a feedback flag is set on, Copilotrace can display this consistency score after the writer's graphomotor task. In such case, Copilotrace also suggests the next activity depending on the consistency score.

Lastly, for each graphomotor task done, the Copilotrace client aggregates the digital context and raw data collected by the MCT, the set of contextual elements previously specified with the MDC and the MUG. The client pushes those data on the Copilotrace data server when it detects an Internet access. Figure 2 synthesizes the profiles of users and several types of interactions with Copilotrace. Each bold use case shows a service according to the user profile: writer or accompanist. The italic use cases underline crucial internal automated functions of Copilotrace.

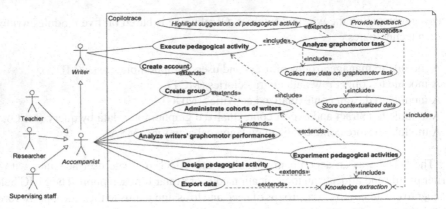

Fig. 2. A use case diagram that shows the two profiles for the users of Copilotrace and the goals of the interactions with the system for each of these two profiles.

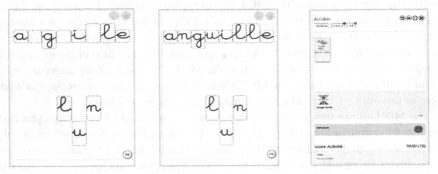

Fig. 3. Example of the word puzzle activity (left) with a writer's answer (middle); Copilotrace displays feedback, consistency score and a blue suggestion of next activity to perform (right). (Color figure online)

Figure 3 illustrates an example of use of Copilotrace by a writer to execute a stopgap pedagogical activity that induces pointing and dragging graphomotor tasks with the finger. It also illustrates feedback as suggestion of next pedagogical activity.

4 Examples of Use of Copilotrace

This is the Academic Region of Guadeloupe (ARG; http://www.ac-guadeloupe.fr/) that manages the French education system in Guadeloupe: an archipelagic territory composed of six islands. From 2010 until 2016, its evaluations revealed that:

1 The language and handwriting levels of ability are still below the levels targeted by School. This is true both at the end of kindergarten, during the transition to secondary school, and among the high rates of adolescents and young adults leaving the school system early.

2 The significant increase of Guadeloupe network coverage, of schools and family's equipment with tablets, smartphones and other tactile or pen-devices, did not sufficiently benefit either pupils' learnings or to question the effectiveness pedagogical practices.

At the same time, our team had highlighted that no existing project put the processing power of digital at the service of both development of students' handwriting proficiency and the evaluation of the effects of digital processing power on teachers' practices [24].

4.1 The EMagMa Project

Based on these observations, LAMIA and ARG designed EMagMa project. Its first objective was to determine if Copilotrace could be a suitable digital solution for tooling and assisting teachers on research-actions related to educational problems.

The first operational phase of experimentation of Copilotrace in real context of use started at the beginning of the school year 2017/2018 and involved one college, four elementary schools, and seven kindergartens into six research-actions. The longest one lasted two years. These research-actions involved a total of sixty-six teachers, four educational advisors in charge of digital education, four district inspectors and seventeen young assistants in civic services who have participated in the implementation of training or evaluation educational sequences on school time. Their protocols proposed various production contexts, materials, and conditions for the collection of the students' graphomotor tasks. 1582 students aged three up to fourteen, from twelve scholar grades, have participated to this first operational phase of EMagMa project.

Each following subsection will detail some benefits of the use of Copilotrace already denoted thanks to three of these research actions.

4.2 Copilotrace as a Data Collector for Graphonomics Research Purposes

At first, Copilotrace can constitute a new appreciable way to collect graphomotor data in unbiased realistic scholar situations for research-action purposes.

To illustrate this, let us take the case of the EMagMa research action on scribbling. This research has three objectives. The first is pedagogical. It is a question of determining how scribbling, this graphomotor activity which is non-linguistic and accessible to all children at an early age [25], can help to teach abilities that are useful in efficient scholar handwriting. The second objective is to determine if the sigma-lognormal analysis of scribbling activities [26] done on a touch tablet could help to evaluate a pupil's level of motor control. The last purpose is to assess if the criterion analysis [27] of the oldest student's scribbling sequences could reveal their capacity to simultaneously mobilize all the useful abilities to produce an efficient/proficient writing [28]. For the purposes of this research action, we have collected sequences of eight scribbles produced with a finger and a pen by more than nine hundred students, aged 3 to 11 years old, enrolled in classes at 12 school levels ranging from kindergarten to sixth grade, was conducted on a touch tablet thanks to Copilotrace during the two school years. For the study, students from sixth grade, aged 10 to 11 realized a set of scribbles on Wacom Intuos graphics tablets during the first school year, 2017/2018. Two researchers of the laboratory had to be continuously present all along 2 days to install the apparatus and to drive the acquisition of the scribbles on three digitizers.

The scribble collection had several interests. First, it helps to verify that the use of Copilotrace, because of its handiness both by the supervisors and the pupils from 3 years old, is adapted to the realization of important campaigns of secure collections of graphomotor productions useful for research purposes without the exclusive intervention of the researchers who are unknown from the pupils. Indeed, educational actors of the schools conducted several collections in an autonomous way during school time. Because the collection of data over two school years, some pupils produced the same types of graphomotor tasks four times, even though they had changed class or school. More than thirty pupils had moved from kindergarten to first grade in primary schools and others from fifth grade in primary school to sixth grade in middle schools that were also taking part in EMagMa project. Thanks to our conceptual choices on the MUG design: the module of management and follow-up of the cohort of writers, these school changes at the beginning of the school year were completely transparent and did not affect the analysis process of the data collected and aggregated with Copilotrace. Such a situation has no impact except that it shows that Copilotrace use offers the possibility of a longitudinal acquisition of graphomotor data without questioning the principle of anonymity of the research participants. Moreover, it allows easier access to the aggregated data that are related to all the productions of the students who changed school level. That is suitable in the context of longitudinal studies concerned by the study of the evolution of pupils' graphomotor performances [18]. Lastly, the collections made with Copilotrace produced a significant volume of contextualized data in a much shorter time than that required using digitizers. Finally, the comparative analysis of the traces collected on touch tablets thanks to Copilotrace and those acquired on digitizers allowed us to implement and to verify the interest, in terms of time saving for the researchers, of the functionality of aggregation of data resulting from heterogeneous material sources and of the functionality of extraction of data starting from requests. We present the first results of this action research in [29].

4.3   Copilotrace as a Testing Workbench for Criteria Issued from Graphonomics Research

Previously, we had seen that the deltaPenlift criterion, as a filter prior to Sigma-lognormal modeling, can help to measure the efficiency and procedural quality of pupils' cursive writing gestures [30]. As detailed by Eq. (1), the deltaPenlift criterion is equal to the difference between the number of pen-lifts done while writing a given word and the minimal number of pen-lifts expected according to the set of cursive rules taught at school.

$$\text{deltaPenlift} = (\text{number\_of\_penlifts\_done} - \text{number\_of\_expected\_penlifts}) \quad (1)$$

As part of EMagMa project, we conceived an experimentation with teachers to study sets of samples of various words handwritten on a touchpad. Our aim was to determine if the previous conclusions made on the deltaPenlift criterion in the case of the pupils' first name and the pseudo-word *tintin,* handwritten on a Wacom digitizer, remained valid in the case of handwriting of common words operated at school on a touch pad. Regular pupils of three types of schools from PS, which is the first kindergarten classrooms, up to sixth, which is the first class at the beginning of middle school, were volunteering to copy isolated cursive words on a touch pad driven by Copilotrace. We can notice that teachers had already labeled all the participants from sixth as poorest writers of their promotion while teachers of all the lowest scholar levels had not previously labeled their pupils according to their handwriting or graphomotor skills.

For this study, we explored the behavior of DeltaPenlift along all the four pedagogical periods when handwriting learning start in the French and Guadeloupean education system [31]. Table 1 synthesizes the definitions, duration, and of each of these four periods. The more advanced a pedagogical period is, which corresponds to the duration of exposure of students to work and a school use of the writing gesture more importantly, the greater is its number.

Table 1. Code, definition, and duration of each pedagogical period according to school.

School	Kindergarten	Primary school		Middle school
Period	1	2	3	4
Definition	Preparation for handwriting learning	Explicit teaching and intensive training to handwriting rules	Consolidation and automation of handwriting	First intensive uses of handwriting
Duration	3 years	1 year	3 years	1 year

We have chosen to consider only the legible samples for the usual and simple words *lunes* (i.e., moons) and *lundi* (i.e., Monday) produced by volunteer pupils from kindergarten up to the beginning of middle school. Table 2 gives the number of legible handwritten samples collected per period.

Table 2. Number of legible handwritten samples of *lunes* and *lundi* collected per period.

Period	1	2	3	4	All
lunes	34	74	25	35	168
lundi	18	69	20	36	143

According to the rules taught at school, the cursive movements necessary to write word *lunes* induce no pen lift while handwriting of the word *lundi* requires a minimum of two pen lifts. Whatever the word, the proportions in the compiled histograms (see Fig. 4) denote that: the higher the code of the pedagogical period, the more the proportion of legible samples handwritten by minimizing the number of pen lifts to better follow the rules of efficient cursive handwriting tends to increase. The performances seen for period 4, although they show greater variability, also confirm this trend, albeit to a lesser extent about the word *lunes*. The fact that the group of pupils for period 4 includes only poor writers may explain that.

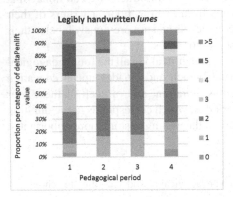
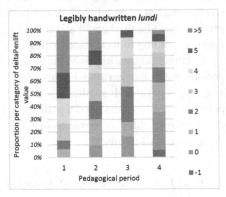

Fig. 4. Proportion of each category of deltaPenlift value observed on legible words for each pedagogical period for *lunes* (left histogram) and *lundi* (right histogram).

Finally, we can highlight two more general observations. They concern in the first place the area of relevance of the deltaPenlift criterion which extends over all pedagogical periods from the beginning of the preparation for the learning of writing from kindergarten until at least the entry into sixth grade. Secondly, these results confirm that there is still room for improvement in student performance. It is therefore appropriate to define how practices at school could involve pedagogical situations of adjustment and monitoring of the behavior of the deltaPenlift criterion.

This experimentation with usual words tends to show that deltaPenlift remains relevant, in more open contexts than in [30]. Moreover, deltaPenlift as computed by Copilotrace could help to resume and describe pupil's proficiency and procedural quality of cursive handwriting gestures. From these trends, we have designed an exercise dedicated to the handwriting of cursive words and random pseudo-words (see Fig. 5.a). It is based on a categorization of letters according to the cumulative cursive rules [30] that writers must activate when they do their cursive trajectories. For each word randomly proposed, Copilotrace automatically estimates the minimum number of expected pen lifts before computing the value of deltaPenlift thanks to Eq. 1. This process is based on a co-occurrence matrix that codes whether the cursive links of two following letters require a pen lift or not. Next, Copilotrace displays a consistency score computed with Eq. 2 and feedback which consists in a simple colored emotion icon (Fig. 5.b). Feedback that can be associated with the value of the consistency score (Fig. 5.c), indicates the degree of success of the procedure of realization of the expected graphomotor task. Copilotrace also provides proposals of activities to do. They appear in blue highlights like on Fig. 5b and 5c. In case illustrated by Fig. 5, Copilotrace estimates consistency score thanks to Eq. 2, where α is -1. The greater the difference between the number of pen lifts made during the writing of the word and the number of lifts in accordance with cursive rules, the closer the consistency score is to zero while a zero gap will result in a consistency score equal to 1.

$$Consistency\_score = e^{(\propto * |deltaPenlift|)} \qquad (2)$$

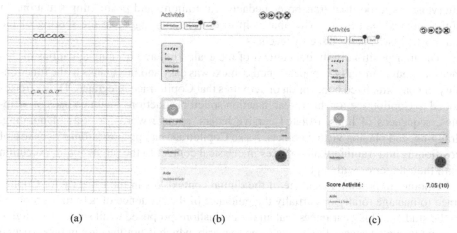

(a)   (b)   (c)

Fig. 5. (a) Example of an activity of cursive handwriting proposed in the Copilotrace platform with a scripter's answer into the dedicated zone. (b) Feedback provided by the system to the writer. (c) Feedback provided by the system with the addition of a score for more precision. (Color figure online)

4.4 Copilotrace: An Assistant to Experiment Pedagogical Approaches and Study Their Effects

The last example of research-action to illustrate the uses of Copilotrace is in progress. Its aims to evaluate the effects of Dorville's early learning method of scholar cursive handwriting (SCH) [32]. This method is based on a modular conception of SCH, the principle of complexity dissociation and techniques for a progressive construction of each component of this complex skill [27]. It proposes one independent sequence of exercises by component. The sequences consist in graphomotor activities of graduated complexity. Each sequence is supposed to help young writer to learn and automate, at his own pace, one component usually mobilized in conjunction with the other components of SCH. Dorville had conceived this method for a playful implementation from the age of three in a classical context with tangible manipulations of paper, pencil, and other objects. He had already presented this classical version of his method to teachers through many private and academic training plans. However, although this method was favorably appreciated by an increasing number of teachers who used it, its effects on handwriting performances had never been rigorously evaluated in scholar environment.

Therefore, we have initiated an EMagMa research-action with teachers of kindergarten and primary school for such purpose. This research-action is concerned with two contexts of use of Dorville's method: the classical one without digital assistance vs. a new context with digital assistance. We consider two usual pedagogical practices. The first one aims to do diagnostic assessments of the pupils' abilities for four components entitled: *Gym de la main, Puzzle, Espace* and *Parcours* [32]. The second pedagogical practice aims to train pupils from the beginning of kindergarten with various activities according to their initial diagnostic assessment. For this research-action Copilotrace intervenes as a tool that transposes pedagogical training and positioning situations in digital context and as a device that help to collect and aggregate the scoring of the diagnostic assessments done by teachers.

The transposition in digital context of the evaluation and training situations of this method thought initially in paper-pencil context was easy and fast thanks to the functionality of contextualized conception of activities that Copilotrace integrates. The exercises added to Copilotrace for this research action solicit productions on touch pads of scribbles, sequences of lines, isolated cursive letters, cursive words, actions of pointing, dragging, and placing virtual objects. As so Copilotrace can propose similar scenario of positioning and training than the ones in classical context to the pupils for an execution with their finger or with a pen.

Another important advantage of the digital context lies in the capacity for Copilotrace to manage totally or partially the guidance of the sequence of activities proposed to the student. This guarantees that all the evaluations proposed to all students in digital context take place according to the same scenario, which is not the case in paper-pencil context. Although Copilotrace can control it, the diagnostic assessment must, however, remain under the continuous attention of the teacher. This, so that the teacher can better devote himself to his roles of pedagogical guidance and mediator of the engagement in the digital context by basing his interactions with the pupils on the complementary information immediately computed and displayed by Copilotrace. In the classical context, the teacher's scoring task represents a time-consuming activity. Moreover, it represents a cognitive charge for the teacher who must drive it at least partly in competition with the mediation task with the student. As an illustration, it is interesting to note that only eighteen of the thirty-eight volunteer teachers had done the initial diagnostic assessments. This, while they were all trained beforehand in the use of assessment tools in a classic paper-context for each of the four components and they all stated that an initial assessment would be useful to help them better guide their actions to support the strengthening of their students' graphomotor skills. Teachers had systematically put forward lack of time to explain the non-realization of this initial assessment.

5   Conclusion

In this paper, first, we have introduced the concept of graphomotor task. Then, we showed how the exercise done by the student mobilize his graphomotor skills by soliciting the realization of graphomotor tasks. Next, from a review of the literature, we have underline that there was a broad consensus about the lack of tools to analyze and evaluate the quality of the student's graphomotor skill throughout his school curriculum in a maximum of handwriting situations. However, none of the existing solutions to support handwriting learning seemed suitable for this purpose for all the teaching community, from kindergarten up to middle school. To answer this problem, we have developed a new Progressive Web Application: Copilotrace. We explained the architecture and the functionalities of Copilotrace. These functionalities concern on-line acquisition of graphomotor tasks and their multifactorial analysis in context. Possibilities to aggregate and consider data coming from various contexts and models of touch and pen devices enrich Copilotrace. As so, Copilotrace is an open and flexible solution which can easily adapt to various contexts of use. To illustrate this point as well as the principal contributions of the use of Copilotrace, we provide details on three of the first research-actions initiated in real school environment within the framework of the project EMagMa.

The first research action, devoted to scribbling, allowed us to show that on the condition of registering the graphomotor analysis, whose benefit of a systematized practice is not any more to demonstrate, in a context of inter-cycle collaboration, when it is, moreover, multifactorial as the open character of Copilotrace authorizes it; then, the lessons on the evolution of the graphomotor behavior of the pupil produced by the graphomotor analysis can contribute much more than to enlighten and enrich the pedagogical practice of each teacher, cycle team or establishment. Indeed, beyond that, it can also help to develop a cooperative approach for the monitoring of the progression of graphomotor skills throughout all the student's school career.

Beyond the fact that the second and third research actions presented illustrate the simultaneous implementation of all the functionalities offered by Copilotrace, it is interesting to highlight that Copilotrace is not only a tool useful to enlighten and help teachers and students in their respective daily practices of teaching and learning. Copilotrace can also be useful for the researcher, either:

- the teacher who wishes, thanks to the practice of graphonomics, to question his practices, the effects of teaching methods and the causes of his students' progress,
- the researcher, teacher or not, who wishes to manage, capture, analyze and export multi-source and multimodal data aggregated on graphomotor tasks in context.

On this last part, in terms of perspectives, we will finish by indicating that we still have work to do within the EMagMa project to study the thousands of data collected and saved in a structured way thanks to Copilotrace. These data concern various graphomotor tasks acquired online and offline in quite different contexts.

The functions and flexible architecture of Copilotrace, a priori open it to teachers and researchers beyond Guadeloupe. With Copilotrace they can create collaborations to collect, constitute and share standardized large data banks useful to study contextualized graphomotor tasks, writers' behaviors, or handwriting teaching methods.

References

1. Vinter, A., Chartrel, E.: Effects of different types of learning on handwriting movements in young children. Learn. Instr. **20**(6), 476–486 (2010)
2. Labrecque, D., Morin, M.-F., Labrecque, N., Cantin, N., Barriault, L.: Le plaisir d'écrire: ça se prépare! Des pistes de réflexion et d'action pour le milieu scolaire. CTREQ, Québec. https://lectureecriture.ca/graphomotricite/. Accessed 12 Feb 2022

3. Morin, M.-F., Bara, F., Alamargot, D.: Apprentissage de la graphomotricité à l'école: Quelles acquisitions? Quelles pratiques? Quels outils? Sci. Paedagog. Exp. **54**(1–2), 47–84 (2017)
4. Bara, F., Morin, M.-F., Montésinos-Gelet, I., Lavoie, N.: Conceptions et pratiques en grapho-motricité chez des enseignants de primaire en France et au Québec. Revue française de pédagogie **176**, 41–56 (2011)
5. Morin, M.-F., Alamargot, D.: Les entraînements graphomoteurs: quelles pratiques, quels effets? A.N.A.E. **163**, 730–738 (2019)
6. Ward, J., Phillips, M.: Digitizer technology: performance characteristics and the effects on the user interface. IEEE Comput. Graph. Appl. **7**(4), 31–44 (1987)
7. Robert, J.M., Djeziri, S., Audet, M., Plamondon, R.: Scriptôt: pen-based software to support handwriting learning in primary schools, Technical report, EPTM (1999)
8. Rosenblum, S., Parush, S., Epstain, L., Weiss, P.L.: Process versus product evaluation of poor handwriting among children with developmental dysgraphia and ADHD. In: Teulings, H.L., Van Gemmert, A.W.A. (eds.) Proceedings of the 11th Conference of the International Graphonomics Society, Scottsdale, Arizona, USA, pp. 169–173 (2003)
9. Teulings, H.L., Romero, D.H.: Submovement analysis in learning cursive handwriting or block print. In: Teulings, H.L., Van Gemmert, A.W.A. (eds.) Proceedings of the 11th Conference of the International Graphonomics Society, Arizona, USA, pp. 107–110 (2003)
10. Glenat, S., Heutte, L., Paquet, T., Mellier, D.: Computer-based diagnosis of dyspraxia: the MEDDRAW project. In: Proceedings of the 12th Conference of the International Graphonomics Society, Zona, Salerno, Italy, pp. 49–53 (2005)
11. de Diego-Cottinelli, A., Barros, B.: TRAZO: a tool to acquire handwriting skills using tablet-PC devices. In: Proceedings of 9th International Conference Interact. Des. Child. IDC 2010, pp. 278–281. ACM (2010)
12. Conf'Lunch IRISA: http://videos.rennes.inria.fr/confLunch/yvan-ride/Evodia%20-%20Conf Lunch%20-TIC-Ecriture.pdf. Accessed 12 Feb 2022
13. Franke, K.: Capturing Reliable data for computer-based forensic handwriting analysis II: pen-position activations. In: Proceedings of 2009 10th International Conference on Document Analysis and Recognition, pp. 1310–1314. IEEE (2009)
14. Griechisch E., Ward J.-R., Hanczar G.: Anomalies in measuring speed and other dynamic properties with touchscreens and tablets. In: Proceedings of BIOSIG 2019, Lecture Notes in Informatics (LNI), Bonn, pp. 181–188 (2019)
15. Plamondon, R., Pirlo, G., Anquetil, É., Rémi, C., Teulings, H.-L., Nakagawa, M.: Personal digital bodyguards for e-security, e-learning and e-health: a prospective survey. Pattern Recogn. **81**, 633–659 (2018)
16. Simonnet, D., Anquetil, E., Bouillon, M.: Multi-criteria handwriting quality analysis with online fuzzy models. Pattern Recogn. **69**, 310–324 (2017)
17. Simonnet, D., Girard, N., Anquetil, E., Renault, M., Thomas, S.: Evaluation of children cursive handwritten words for e-education. PRL **121**, 133–139 (2019)
18. Bonneton-Botté N., Fleury S., Girard N., Le Magadou M., Cherbonnier A., et al.: Can tablet apps support the learning of handwriting? An investigation of learning outcomes in kinder-garten classroom. Comput. Educ. **151**, 38 (2020). https://doi.org/10.1016/j.compedu.2020.103831
19. Kaligo homepage. https://www.kaligo-apps.com/. Accessed 12 Feb 2022
20. Renau-Ferrer N., Rémi C.: Dominant points for spatio-graphic and procedural analysis of online drawings. In: Contreras-Vidal, P. (ed.) 15th International Conference of the Graphonomics Society – IGS, pp.140–143, Cancun, Mexico (2011)
21. Renau-Ferrer N., Rémi C.: Procedural analysis of a sketching activity: principles and appli-cations. In: Contreras-Vidal, P. (ed.) International Conference on Frontiers in Handwriting Recognition – ICFHR, pp. 461–466, Bari, Italy (2012)

22. Chartrel, E., Vinter, A.: The impact of spatio-temporal constraints on cursive letter handwriting in children. Learn. Instr. **18**(6), 537–547 (2008). https://doi.org/10.1016/J.LEARNINSTRUC.2007.11.003

23. Renau-Ferrer N., Rémi C.: A generic approach for recognition and structural modelisation of drawers' sketching gestures. In: The 2011 International Conference on Image Processing, Computer Vision, and Pattern Recognition, IPCV 2011, Las Vegas, USA, pp. 1-7 (2011)

24. Duval T., Remi C., Prevost L., Dorville A., Plamondon R.: Etude de la faisabilité e: l'évaluation de l'efficacité des mouvements de tracé du jeune apprenti-scripteur. In: IHM 2014 26e conférence sur l'Interaction Homme-Machine, Lille, France, pp.29–37 (2014)

25. Lurçat L.: L'activité graphique à l'école maternelle (4ème éd.). ESF editions. France, Paris: (1971 éd. 1988)

26. Rémi C., Vaillant J., Plamondon R., Prevost L, Duval T.: Exploring the kinematic dimensions of kindergarten children's scribbles. In: 17th Biennial Conference of the International Graphonomics Society, Pointe-à-Pitre, Guadeloupe, pp.79–82 (2015)

27. Dorville, A., Rémi, C.; BâtirlEcriture, un outil pour l'évaluation du savoir écrire de base. In: 20e colloque de l'ADMEE-Europe, Genève, Suisse, pp.1–7 (2008)

28. Rosenblum, S., Goldstand, S., Parush, S.: Relationships among biomechanical ergonomic factors, handwriting product quality, handwriting efficiency, and computerized handwriting process measures in children with and without handwriting difficulties. Am. J. Occup. Ther. **60**, 28–39 (2006)

29. Rémi, C., Nagau, J., Vaillant, J., Dorville, A., Plamondon, R.: Multimodal acquisition and analysis of children handwriting for the study of the efficiency of their handwriting movements: the @MaGma challenge. In: 16th International Conference on Frontiers in Handwriting Recognition, Niagara Falls, United States, pp.459–464 (2018)

30. Rémi, C., Nagau, J., Vaillant, J., Plamondon, R.: Could sigma-lognormal modeling help teachers to characterize the kinematic efficiency of pupils' cursive procedures of handwriting? In: Plamondon, R., Angelo, M., Ferrer, M.A. (eds.) The Lognormality Principle and its Applications in e-Security, e-Learning and e-Health, Series in Machine Perception and Artificial Intelligence, vol. 88, pp. 87–116. World Scientific (2020)

31. Dancel, B.: Apprendre à écrire, quelle histoire! Carrefours de l'éducation **S2**, 123–134 (2011). https://doi.org/10.3917/cdle.hs02.0123

32. Dorville, A., Baramble P.: Jeux d'écriture en famille: 4 séries de jeux: pour apprendre à lire dans la joie. @ comme @pprendre, Baie-Mahault, Guadeloupe (2015)

Novel Feature Extraction Methods to Detect Age from Handwriting

Najla AL-Qawasmeh[✉][iD], Muna Khayyat[iD], and Ching Y. Suen

Department of Computer Science and Software Engineering, Concordia University,
CENPARMI, Montreal, Canada
n_alqawa@encs.concordia.ca, munakhayyat@cenparmi.concordia.ca,
suen@cse.concordia.ca
http://www.concordia.ca/research/cenparmi.html

Abstract. Age detection from handwritten documents is a crucial research area in many disciplines such as forensic analysis and medical diagnosis. Furthermore, this task is challenging due to the high similarity and overlap between individuals' handwriting. The performance of the document recognition and analysis systems, depends on the extracted features from handwritten documents, which can be a challenging task as this depends on extracting the most relevant information from row text. In this paper, a set of age-related features suggested by a graphologist, to detect the age of the writers, have been proposed. These features include irregularity in slant, irregularity in pen pressure, irregularity in textlines, and the percentage of black and white pixels. Support Vector Machines (SVM) classifier has been used to train, validate and test the proposed approach on two different datasets: the FSHS and the Khatt dataset. The proposed method has achieved a classification rate of 71% when applied to FSHS dataset. Meanwhile, our method outperformed state-of-arts methods when applied to the Khatt dataset with a classification rate of 65.2%. Currently, these are the best rates in this field.

Keywords: Age detection · Machine learning · Image processing · Handwriting analysis

1 Introduction

Automated applications identifying personal information without involving the subject is becoming a crucial research area. Therefore, automatic age estimation or detection from handwritten documents is becoming an important research topic.

Age detection from handwriting is very essential in many applications, such as forensic studies and health diagnosis. In forensic studies, it helps limit investigation to a more targeted age group or category, which leads to improved results in writer identification and verification applications. Similarly, in health diagnosis, age estimation or detection helps determine whether the development

Supported by organization x.

in handwriting is commensurate with age development. For example, detecting significant handwriting degradation in a child's handwriting indicates an early pathological and neurodegenerative state. In addition, distinguishing the normal evolution of handwriting with age from abnormal change is potentially related to cognitive decline [1,2].

Age detection based on handwriting is a challenging and complex task for several reasons, for example the motor skills are not mastered before the age of 14. Moreover, the high similarity between people's writings made it harder to determine the right features to detect the writer's age, either manually or automatically.

These difficulties made the age detection systems an active research topic. Research in age detection can be done by visually inspecting a set of relevant features such as slant, spacing and letter size. Meanwhile, it can be performed automatically by extracting features from offline or online handwriting. Hence, the manual way of detecting age from handwriting suffers from many difficulties, such as being time-consuming, especially if there are many documents to be analysed. In addition, the process, is expensive, tedious and exhausting [3].

In this paper, we propose an age detection system based on extracting a set of new features to automatically detect the writer's age. These features are, the speed of writing which can be determined by extracting the irregularity in pen pressure and the irregularity in slant. The ratio of white to black pixels of the written document. In addition, the irregularity in text lines which have a good role in revealing the writer's age.

The rest of the paper is organized as follows: Sect. 2 is a literature review of some recent automatic handwriting age detection systems. Section 3 describes the proposed approach. Section 4 shows the experimental results obtained after applying the proposed method. Section 5 concludes the paper and suggests a future direction.

2 Literature Review

Few researchers in the literature have studied the problem of automatic age detection from handwriting. These studies vary in age groups to be detected and the extracted features proposed to detect age.

Basavaraja et al. [4] proposed a new method to estimate age from handwriting based on extracting disconnectedness features using Hu invariant. First, they explored the intersection points in the cany edge images. Then, they used K-means clustering to classify the handwritten documents of their dataset into four classes. Class–1 with ages ranging from 11–12 years, class–2 with ages ranging from 13–16 years, class–3 with ages ranging from 17–20 years and class–4 with ages ranging from 21–24 years. Each class has 100 images. However, for the two public datasets, IAM [5] and Khatt [6]. The images were divided into two classes. As a result, an accuracy rates of 66.25% has been achieved using the IAM dataset and 64.44% using the Khatt dataset.

Marzinotta et al. [2] provided a method to classify age and gender from online handwriting features available in the IRONOFF [7] dataset in French and

English languages. Their work is a two-layer schema. They used global features of handwritten words for a writer independent clustering in the first layer. However, the second layer was used to determine the stability across words for each writer by clustering the style variation at the previous level.

Bouadjenek et al. [3] introduced two gradient features to classify the writer's age, gender and handedness: the histogram of oriented gradients and gradient local binary patterns. They used the Support Vector Machine (SVM) [8] method to classify the documents. IAM and Khatt datasets were used to evaluate the system. IAM dataset was divided into two age classes based on age ranges: 25–34 years and 35–56 years. On the other hand, the khatt dataset was divided into three ranges that can be defined as "under 15 years", "16–25 years", and "26–50 years". They got a 70% accuracy rate when using the IAM dataset and a 55% accuracy rate when using Khatt dataset.

Almaadeed and Hassaine [9] developed a handwriting analysis system for age, gender, and nationality classification. They extracted a set of geometrical features combined using random forests and kernel discriminant analysis. They applied their system OUWI [10] dataset, and they got accuracies rates of 55.7% and 60.62% were achieved for age detection when all writers produced the same handwritten text and when each writer produced different handwritten text, respectively.

Marzinottto et al. [1] proposed an online age classification system based on a two-level clustering scheme. At the first level, writer independent word clusters are generated. On the other hand, the second level generates a bag of prototype words from each writer's words. Supervised learning then is used to categorise the handwritten documents in terms of age. A dataset sample acquired from Broca Hospital in Paris was used to conduct the experiments. The writer ages range between 60 and 85 years old. Their approach came out with the following findings: first, people above 65 years old present three handwritten patterns regarding the dynamic features, pen pressure and time on air. Second, people aged above 80 years have almost the same unique style with lower speed.

3   Methodologies

In this paper, we propose a machine learning-based age detection system, by automatically extracting a set of features recommended by a graphologist. The automatic handwriting analysis process consists of the following stages; image acquisition, preprocessing, feature extraction and classification. This section describes the proposed methodologies concerning the four mentioned stages. Figure 1 shows a diagram of our proposed age detection system.

3.1   Collecting Data and Image Acquisition

In the literature of handwriting analysis and recognition, several databases have been used to conduct research. These databases differ in terms of the language used, number of writers and the number of documents. We created our Arabic

Age Detection System

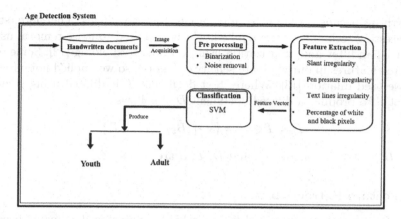

Fig. 1. Structure of the proposed system

handwritten dataset to train and evaluate the age detection proposed approach. The dataset was collected in Amman the capital city of Jordan. We called it free-style handwritten samples (FSHS) [11]. Each of the 2200 volunteers was asked to write a letter to someone the person love; this resulted in a large dataset that covers different handwritten styles. We also asked a portion of the volunteers to copy some paragraphs for future research purposes. The total number of samples is equal to 2700, written by 2200 writers. The writer's ages range from 15 to 75 years old, while 45% of the samples were written by males and 55% were written by females. Most of the writers are right-handed. To ensure the convenience of the writers, we did not put any conditions on the type of tool used for writing. However, we provided them with a white sheet of paper to write their letter on it. Volunteers were asked to fill up an information questionnaire, about their gender, age, handedness, and work position.

What is significant about our dataset is its size and the number of writers. The variety in age and the large number of writers accounted for the great diversity in the handwriting styles. The dataset was mainly written in Arabic, although some writers used the English language, the number did not exceed 15 samples. We digitized the handwritten samples with a resolution of 600 dpi. In total, the dataset contains 2700 digitized pages. Each page contains a minimum of five lines. Each line contains approximately ten words. The FSHS dataset can be used in many research areas related to human interaction, such as handwriting recognition if appropriately labelled, gender, and age detection.

3.2 Preprocessing

The preprocessing step is required to improve the quality of images before the feature extraction phase. In handwriting analysis systems, many preprocessing techniques can be applied to improve the quality of handwriting documents, such as binarization, noise removal, skew angle correction, thinning and skele-tonization. In our research, it is necessary to preserve the main features of the handwriting because it helps to differentiate the age ranges. Therefore, simple preprocessing techniques were applied, which is limited to noise removal using a 3×3 median filter and binarization using OTSU thresholding [12]. Some of the extracted features in our work are sensitive to noise, so we applied noise removal then we used dilation [13]. Where, text document T is dilated using structure element S to produce a dilated document D as follows:

$$D = T \oplus S = \{ z \mid [(\hat{B}_z) \cap T] \subseteq T \} \tag{1}$$

where $\hat{B} = \{c \mid c = -a, a \in S\}$, and D, T, S are sets in Z^2.

3.3   Feature Extraction

A set of features were extracted from Arabic handwritten documents based on the recommendations given by a psychologist and a graphologist. These features are Irregularity in pen pressure (IPP) with a vector of 200 features, Irregularity in slant (IS) with a feature vector of 100 features, Irregularity in text line (ITL) with a vector of 700 features, and the percentage of white and black pixels (PWB) with 4 features. We examined these features separately and combined by concatenating them. For example, one of the combinations is IPP (200 features) + IS (100 features). A full description of the proposed features is in the following section.

The proposed method explored a new age-related feature, the handwriting irregularity with its three factors slant, pen pressure, and text lines, indicating writing speed, where the youth writers have a slower writing style than the adult writers.

Slant Irregularity: Arabic writing is a horizontal cursive script whose words consist of sub-words or Pieces of Arabic Words, each consisting of one or more letters; this can be shown in Fig. 2, where each color corresponds to a single separated CC. Consequently, a connected component (CC) [14] Sub-word can be used to find the Irregularity in slant.

Fig. 2. Arabic text line

To find the irregularity in slant, we calculated the CCs of the binary images. Then, we applied the method of least square [15] to find the slant by locating the best fit line of each CC. Given a set of n points, the best fit can be found using Eq. 2 and to find the coefficients a and b, Eq. 3 and 4 were applied, respectively. While Eq. 5 was used to find the skew angle (α). The number of CCs used to find this feature was empirically set to 100 for FSHS dataset and 200 for Khatt dataset, with $size(CC) > 10$ pixels.

$$y = a + bx \tag{2}$$

$$b = \frac{n \sum_{i=1}^{n} x_i y_i - \sum_{i=1}^{n} y_i}{n \sum_{i=1}^{n} x_i^2 - (\sum_{i=1}^{n} x_i)^2} \tag{3}$$

$$a = \frac{\sum_{i=1}^{n} y_i - b \sum_{i=1}^{n} x_i}{n} \tag{4}$$

$$\alpha = \tan^{-1}(b) \tag{5}$$

Pen pressure irregularity: to find the irregularity in pen pressure, the grey-scale image was divided into uniform squares of size 100×100 pixels. The standard deviation (SD) and mean X' were calculated for each square separately, using Eqs. 6 and 7, respectively. The number of the segmented squares was empirically set to 200.

$$SD = \sqrt{\frac{1}{N-1} \times \sum_{i=1}^{n} \sum_{j=1}^{m} (X_{(i,j)} - X')^2} \tag{6}$$

$$X' = \frac{\sum_{i=1}^{n} \sum_{j=1}^{m} (X_{(i,j)})}{N} \tag{7}$$

where, X' is the mean value of the pixel intensities of the square, N is the number of pixels in a square $(n \times m)$, and $X_{(i,j)}$ is the intensity value of each pixel.

Text-line irregularity was measured by applying the horizontal projection profile after dilating the text in a given document. The horizontal projection profile f(y, p(y)) of the document is found for the first n rows of the document, which was experimentally chosen to be the first 850 pixels. The horizontal projection profile reflects the nature of the document and the distribution of the text lines. From f(y, p(y)) the algorithm considers the significant peaks and valleys.

Figure 3 shows the horizontal projection profile of two different documents. The horizontal projection profile in Fig. 3(a) shows that the lines are irregular and not well separated. In addition, there are no deep valleys in many parts of the profile, which indicates that the lines are skewed and close to each other. The profile of Fig. 3(b) shows that the lines in the documents are more regular and are nicely separated, since it has deep valleys and separated peaks.

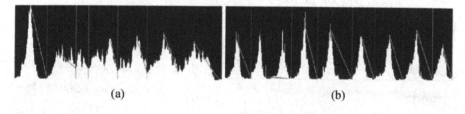

(a)   (b)

Fig. 3. Horizontal projection profile of two different documents

Percentage of black and white pixels in a handwritten document, this feature is an indication of the width of the handwriting. This process starts by cropping the image to a square with a width of m pixels. The size of the square was empirically chosen to be of size 250 × 250 pixels for the FSHS dataset, and 100 × 100 pixels for the khatt dataset. The ratio of the black pixels was calculated as follows: the number of black pixels in the cropped square was first calculated. Then the ratio between the number of black pixels and the size of the square was measured.

This feature consists of a vector of four values: the number of black pixels (BP), the number of white pixels (WP = mxm − BP), the percentage of black pixels (PBP = BP/(mxm)) and white pixels (PWP = WP/(mxm)) of the cropped square.

4   Experiments and Results

This section presents the experiments and the results obtained by the proposed system. The experimental setup is described in Sect. 4.1. Section 4.2 presents the Support Vector Machines (SVM) classifier to which the extracted features were fed so that the age group is predicted. Finally, the results are analyzed and discussed in Sect. 4.3.

4.1   Experimental Setup

FSHS dataset (Sect. 3.1) consists of 2700 handwritten samples. We used a subset of the FSHS dataset consisting of 2000 samples in our experiments. The images were divided into two main classes: youth adult class with ages ranging between 16 and 24 years old, and Mature adult class with ages ranging from 26 to 70. Where each class has 1000 samples. Figure 4(a) shows a document written by an adult youth writer with slant and text lines irregularity. While Fig. 4(b) shows mostly regular writing of a mature adult writer. To run the experiments and evaluate the proposed method, 70% of the documents were used for training, 15% for testing and 15% for validation. The SVM classifier was then used to train and test the proposed system.

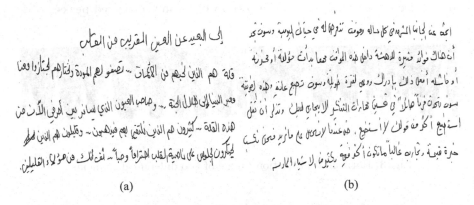

(a)   (b)

Fig. 4. Samples of handwritten documents from FSHS dataset

To benchmark the performance of the proposed method with other age detection methods, we applied our system to the public Khatt [6] dataset. That dataset contains Arabic handwritten documents with ground truth of gender, age, and handedness. It has three age ranges that can be defined as: "under 15 years old", "16 to 25 years old", and "26 to 50 years old". Each class contains 135 Samples. To evaluate our experiments, two classes were used, "16 to 25" and "26 to 50". Again, 70% of the dataset was used for training, 15% for testing and 15% for validation.

4.2 Classification

The proposed method was trained and tested using Support Vector Machines (SVM) [8]. We trained the classifier using all the features extracted from the training dataset. Meanwhile, we used a validation set to empirically determine the hyper-parameters. In our experiments, SVM was trained by a set of samples labelled with -1 and 1. Given a set of labeled training patterns $(v_1, y_1), (v_2, y_2) \ldots \ldots (v_n, y_n)$, where $y_i \in \{-1, 1\}$, $v_i \in V$, v is p-dimensional training vector and V is the feature vector space, SVM tends to solve the following optimization problem:

$$\min_{w,b,\xi} \frac{1}{2} \mathbf{w}^T \mathbf{w} + C \sum_{i=1}^{l} \xi_i \tag{8}$$

$$\text{subject to} \quad y_i(\mathbf{w}^T \phi(v_i) + b) \geq 1 - \xi_i, \qquad \xi \geq 0$$

The function ϕ maps the training vectors vi to a higher dimensional space, and C is a penalty strength of the error term. ξ are slack variables which help the model to avoid overfitting on the training data. The idea of constructing support vector machines comes from considering the general form of the dot-products:

$$\phi(u).\phi(v) = K(u, v) \tag{9}$$

where $K(u, v)$ is called the kernel function. In our experiments, we used Gaussian kernel function with a kernel scale of 59.5 and a box constraint level of 4.0557:

$$K(v_i, v_j) = exp(-\frac{\|v_i - v_j\|^2}{2\sigma^2}) \tag{10}$$

where v_i, v_j are the support vectors and testing data point respectively and $\sigma > 0$ is the kernel parameter. These parameters were empirically chosen by using the validation set, which helps to find the optimal hyper-parameters. For all the experiments, we used a Bayesian optimization algorithm with the expected improvement per second plus an acquisition function and the maximum number of iteration was set to 30. For example, the training of the combinations of all features (SI + PPI + TLI + PWB) on the FSHS dataset was stopped after 30 iterations, but the best point of hyper-parameters occurred in iteration 27; thus, the minimum error was equal to 0.3004.

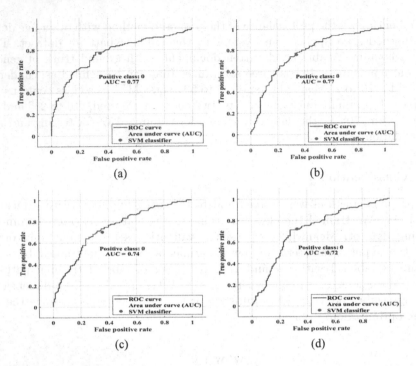

Fig. 5. Roc curves of the result of the proposed methods on FSHS dataset over the combinations of (a) all features, (b) SI + PPI + TLI feature, (c) SI + TLI + PWB features and (d) PPI + TLI + PWB features

4.3 Evaluation

Our experiment is a two-class classification problem where the outcomes are either youth adult writer or mature adult writer. The proposed method was evaluated using the evaluation metrics, accuracy, precision, and recall, which can be calculated as follows:

$$Accuracy = \frac{TP + TN}{TP + TN + FP + FN} \tag{11}$$

$$Recall = \frac{TP}{TP + FN} \tag{12}$$

$$Precision = \frac{TP}{TP + FP} \tag{13}$$

where, TP is true positives, TN is true negatives, FP is false positives and FN is false negatives.

The results of the proposed method on the FSHS dataset and the Khatt dataset are reported in Table 1 and Table 2, respectively. Table 1 shows the results of applying the proposed method on the FSHS dataset in terms of precision, recall and accuracy. It can be noticed that among the individual features, the best one is the TLI, with accuracy rates equaling 66.2%. On the other hand, when concatenating two features together. We found that the best performance is for two combinations, the first being SI + TLI and the second is TLI + PWB, where both groups have an accuracy rate of 64.3%. For the three features combination, (SI + PPI + TLI) has the highest accuracy of 70.7%. Finally, the all features combination gave the highest accuracy of 71%. The common feature among all the combinations with high performance is TLI, as this indicates the importance of this feature in detecting the writer's age from handwriting.

Table 1. The results of applying the proposed method on FSHS dataset

Extracted features				SVM				
SI	PPI	TLI	PWB	Accuracy 100%	Recall (100%)		Precision (100%)	
					Youth (adult)	Mature (adult)	Youth (adult)	Mature (adult)
✓	×	×	×	56.3	56.1	56.6	58	54.7
×	✓	×	×	53.8	54.4	53.4	49.2	58.5
×	×	✓	×	66.2	64.7	68.2	71.8	66.7
×	×	×	✓	55.7	63.4	53.5	27.5	83.9
✓	✓	×	×	55.3	55.3	55.3	55.3	55.3
✓	×	✓	×	64.3	62.4	67.2	73.5	55
✓	×	×	✓	56.7	56.8	56.5	55.3	58
✓	✓	✓	×	70.7	69.1	72.6	75.5	65.8
✓	✓	×	✓	60.7	60.8	60.5	61.6	59.7
✓	×	✓	✓	67.3	66.7	68.1	70.2	64.4
×	✓	✓	×	60.3	59.9	60.9	64.2	56.4
×	×	✓	✓	64.3	62.4	66.6	72	56.7
×	✓	✓	✓	69.7	68.8	70.6	72	67.3
✓	✓	✓	✓	71	68.9	73.7	76.7	65.3

Figure 5 Shows the roc curves of the feature combinations applied on the FSHS dataset and have the highest accuracy rates. The curves show the area under curves (AUC) for each combination which are: 0.77, 0.77, 0.74 and 0.72 for (a), (b), (c) and (d), respectively.

To compare the results of our work with other methods we applied our proposed method on the public Khatt dataset. Table 2 shows the accuracy rates of applying the proposed method on khatt dataset. The results show that the text lines irregularity (TLI) has the highest accuracy among the other individual features with an accuracy rate of 63.8%. While the combination of all features outperformed the state-of-the-art methods with an accuracy rate of 65.2%. This can be seen in Table 3.

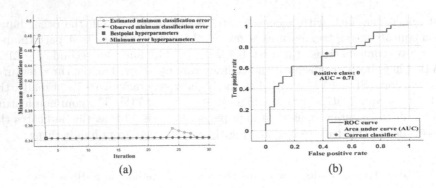

(a)   (b)

Fig. 6. The performance of the full combination on khatt dataset with respect to (a) the minimum classification error, (b) ROC curve

Table 2. The results of applying the proposed method on Khatt dataset

Extracted features	Accuracy 100%
Slant irregularity (SI)	62.3
Pen pressure irregularity (PPI)	53.6
Text-lines irregularity (TLI)	63.8
Percentage of black and white pixels (PWB)	59.4
SI + PPI + TLI + PWB	65.2

Figure 6(a) shows the performance of applying the proposed method with entire features combination on Khatt dataset and the minimum classification errors where the best point were obtained on iteration 3 with a minimum error of 0.34. While (b) shows the corresponding ROC curve with AUC equal 0.71.

Table 3. A comparison between the results of the proposed method and others.

Method	Extracted features	Classifier	Accuracy (100%)
Basavaraja et al.	Disconnectedness	K-means	64.44
Bouadjerek et al.	1. Histogram of oriented gradient	SVM	60.3
	2. Gradient local binary patterns		
Proposed method	1. Slant irregularity (SI)	SVM	65.2
	2. Pen pressure irregularity (PPI)		
	3. Text-lines irregularity (TLI)		
	4. Percentage of black and white pixels (PWB)		

Table 3 shows a comparison between the proposed method with other available methods. Accuracy, extracted features and the used classifier are presented in the table for better comparison. Similar to the available works on the khatt dataset, we adapted two age ranges, "16–25" and "26 and above". The proposed method outperformed the state-of-the-art an accuracy rate of 65.2 using a supervised classification method SVM similarly to work in [3]. On the other hand, the unsupervised classification method was used in [4] has achieved an accuracy rate of 64.44%.

In addition to performing the proposed method on the FSHS dataset and the Khatt dataset, we examined the ability of the proposed features to classify the age groups of handwritings written by only female writers and male writers. So the FSHS dataset was divided into two main subsets: female and male. Then the two age ranges were determined for each sub-set individually. To illustrate, the number of youth handwritten samples in the female subgroup were 465, and the number of mature adult handwritten samples were 435. At the same time, there were 435 samples of youth male writers and 465 for mature adult male writers.

Table 4 Shows the results obtained from applying the proposed system on female and male subsets separately. It can be noticed that the pen pressure irregularity can classify the age of the female writers better than male writers, where it gave an accuracy rate of only 54.5% for male writers compared to 63.6% accuracy rate for female writers. In contrast with the text line irregularity feature, which provided a classification rate of 69.5% in male handwriting while it gave an accuracy rate of 61.5% in female handwriting.

Table 4. The results of applying the proposed method on the female and male subsets of FSHS dataset

Extracted features	Accuracy (100%)	
	Female (subset)	Male (subset)
Slant irregularity (SI)	56.5	62.9
Pen pressure irregularity (PPI)	63.6	54.5
Text-lines irregularity (TLI)	66.7	64.7
Percentage of black and white pixels (PWB)	53.6	54.1
SI + PP1 + TLI + PWB	71.9	68

Figure 7(a) shows the ROC curve of all features combination SVM model applied on the male subset of the FSHS dataset where AUC equals 0.72. On the other hand, (b) shows all features combination SVM model performance concerning the minimum classification error. As the training was stopped on 30 iterations, the minimum classification error was 0.3 on iteration 26, where the performance becomes almost plateauing.

Figure 8(a) shows the ROC curve of all features combination SVM model applied on the female subset of the FSHS dataset where AUC equals 0.74. On the other hand, (b) shows the minimum classification error, which is equal to 0.253 on iteration 8.

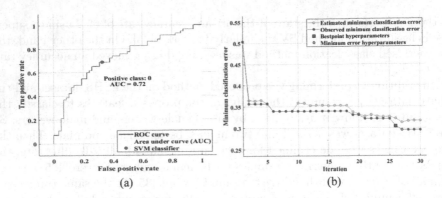

Fig. 7. The performance of all features SVM model on male subset of the FSHS dataset with respect to (a) ROC curve (b) the minimum classification error

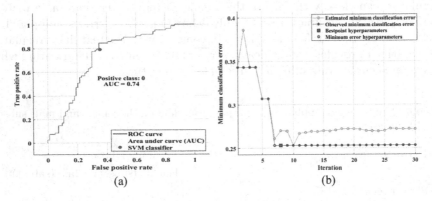

Fig. 8. The performance of all features SVM model on female subset of the FSHS dataset with respect to (a) ROC curve (b) the minimum classification error

5   Conclusion and Future Works

In this paper, we have shown that the automatic detection of age from hand-written documents using the computer without human intervention is a viable possibility. We implemented a set of highly discriminative age-related features recommended by a graphologist as well as a psychologist such as pen pressure irregularity, slant irregularity, text lines irregularity and the percentage of black and white pixels of a written document. We have also proposed powerful algorithms to extract them.

The experiments of the proposed method were divided into two steps. In the first step, the proposed method were applied on the FSHS dataset using different combinations of features, and we got an accuracy rate of 68.3% using the all feature combination. in the second step, and To compare the results of our proposed method with other available methods, we applied it to the public dataset Khatt. The full features' combination outperformed state-of-art works with an accuracy rate of 65.2.

Finally, The FSHS dataset was divided into male and female subsets. Then the proposed method was applied on both subsets individually. As a result, we got an accuracy rate of 71.9% using the female subset and 68% using the male subset.

For future work, we aim to explore more age-related features and apply deep learning to detect age from handwritten documents. Moreover, more languages can be explored for age detection.

References

1. Marzinotto, G., et al.: Age-related evolution patterns in online handwriting. Comput. Math. Methods Med. **2016** (2016)
2. Marzinotto, G., Rosales, J.C., El-Yacoubi, M.A., Garcia-Salicetti, S.: Age and gender characterization through a two layer clustering of online handwriting. In: Battiato, S., Blanc-Talon, J., Gallo, G., Philips, W., Popescu, D., Scheunders, P. (eds.) ACIVS 2015. LNCS, vol. 9386, pp. 428–439. Springer, Cham (2015). https://doi.org/10.1007/978-3-319-25903-1_37
3. Bouadjenek, N., Nemmour, H., Chibani, Y.: Age, gender and handedness prediction from handwriting using gradient features. In: 2015 13th International Conference on Document Analysis and Recognition (ICDAR), pp. 1116–1120. IEEE (2015)
4. Basavaraja, V., Shivakumara, P., Guru, D.S., Pal, U., Lu, T., Blumenstein, M.: Age estimation using disconnectedness features in handwriting. In: 2019 International Conference on Document Analysis and Recognition (ICDAR), pp. 1131–1136 (2019)
5. Marti, U.-V., Bunke, H.: The IAM-database: an English sentence database for offline handwriting recognition. Int. J. Doc. Anal. Recogn. **5**(1), 39–46 (2002). https://doi.org/10.1007/s100320200071
6. Mahmoud, S.A., et al.: KHATT: an open Arabic offline handwritten text database. Pattern Recogn. **47**(3), 1096–1112 (2014)
7. Viard-Gaudin, C., Lallican, P.M., Knerr, S., Binter, P.: The IRESTE on/off (IRONOFF) dual handwriting database. In: Proceedings of the Fifth International Conference on Document Analysis and Recognition, ICDAR 1999 (Cat. No. PR00318), pp. 455–458 (1999)
8. Hasseim, A., Sudirman, R., Khalid, P.I.: Handwriting classification based on support vector machine with cross validation. Engineering **05**, 84–87 (2013)
9. Al Maadeed, S., Hassaine, A.: Automatic prediction of age, gender, and nationality in offline handwriting. EURASIP J. Image Video Process. **2014**(1), 1–10 (2014)
10. Al-Maadeed, S., Ayouby, W., Hassaïne, A., Jaam, J.: QUWI: an Arabic and English handwriting dataset for offline writer identification. In: International Conference on Frontiers in Handwriting Recognition, pp. 746–751 (2012)
11. AL-Qawasmeh, N., Suen, C.Y.: Gender detection from handwritten documents using concept of transfer-learning. In: Lu, Y., Vincent, N., Yuen, P.C., Zheng, W.-S., Cheriet, F., Suen, C.Y. (eds.) ICPRAI 2020. LNCS, vol. 12068, pp. 3–13. Springer, Cham (2020). https://doi.org/10.1007/978-3-030-59830-3_1
12. Liu, D., Yu, J.: Otsu method and k-means. In: 2009 Ninth International Conference on Hybrid Intelligent Systems, vol. 1, pp. 344–349 (2009)

13. Khayyat, M., Lam, L., Suen, C.Y., Yin, F., Liu, C.-L.: Arabic handwritten text line extraction by applying an adaptive mask to morphological dilation. In: 10th IAPR International Workshop on Document Analysis Systems, DAS 2012, Gold Coast, Queenslands, Australia, pp. 100–104 (2012)
14. He, L., Chao, Y., Suzuki, K., Kesheng, W.: Fast connected-component labeling. Pattern Recogn. **42**(9), 1977–1987 (2009)
15. Chin, W., Harvey, A., Jennings, A.: Skew detection in handwritten scripts. In: TENCON 1997 Brisbane-Australia. Proceedings of IEEE TENCON 1997. IEEE Region 10 Annual Conference. Speech and Image Technologies for Computing and Telecommunications (Cat. No. 97CH36162), vol. 1, pp. 319–322. IEEE (1997)

Measuring the Big Five Factors from Handwriting Using Ensemble Learning Model AvgMlSC

Afnan Garoot[1]([⊠])[iD] and Ching Y. Suen[2][iD]

[1] Um Al-Qura University, Mecca, Saudi Arabia
ahgaroot@uqu.edu.sa
[2] Concordia University, Montreal, Canada
suen@cse.concordia.ca

Abstract. The Big Five Factors Model (BFFM) is the most widely accepted personality theory used by psychologists today. The theory states that personality can be described with five core factors which are Conscientiousness, Agreeableness, Emotional Stability, Openness to Experience, and Extraversion. In this work, we measure the five factors using handwriting analysis instead of answering a long questionnaire of personality test. Handwriting analysis is a study that merely needs a writing sample to assess personality traits of the writer. It started manually by interpreting the extracted features such as size of writing, slant, and space between words into personality traits based on graphological rules. In this work, we proposed an automated BFFM system called Averaging of SMOTE multi-label SVM-CNN (AvgMlSC). AvgMlSC constructs synthetic samples to handle imbalanced data using Synthetic Minority Oversampling Technique (SMOTE). It averages two learning-based classifiers i.e. Multi-label Support Vector Machine and Multi-label Convolutional Neural Network based on offline handwriting recognition to produce one optimal predictive model. The model was trained using 1066 handwriting samples written in English, French, Chinese, Arabic, and Spanish. The results reveal that our proposed model outperformed the overall performance of five traditional models i.e. Logistic Regression (LR), Naïve Bayes (NB), K-Neighbors (KN), Support Vector Machine (SVM), and Convolutional Neural Network (CNN) with 93% predictive accuracy, 0.94 AUC, and 90% F-Score.

Keywords: Big five factor model · Handwriting analysis · Computerized · Off-line handwriting · Learning model · Multi-label · Ensemble · SMOTE · SVM · CNN

1 Introduction

In the 1980s the BFFM began to receive wider scholarly attention. Today, it is a ubiquitous part of psychology research, and psychologists largely agree that personality can be grouped into the five basic traits of the BFFM.

© Springer Nature Switzerland AG 2022
C. Carmona-Duarte et al. (Eds.): IGS 2021, LNCS 13424, pp. 159–173, 2022.
https://doi.org/10.1007/978-3-031-19745-1_12

There are different versions of psychological tests with different number of scalable items, ranging between 10 and 300 items, used to measure the BFF. However, in this work, we will measure the BFF using a simple, thorough, and quick test named handwriting analysis which is also known as graphology. Handwriting analysis is a study that reveals personality traits such as emotional status, fears, honesty, and defenses from handwriting. It only requires a sample of handwriting to evaluate the character of the writer. Handwriting analysis has been applied widely in personality prediction, forensic evidence and disease analysis. Basically, it is done manually by: (1) extracting specific handwriting features from the sample such as slant, size of writing, and space between words, and then (2) interpreting the extracted features into personality traits based on graphological rules.

Manual handwriting analysis has a number of issues. It is a subjective, error prone task, and sometimes the same features of the same handwriting sample are extracted differently by different graphologists. Therefore, computerized handwriting analysis systems have been developed in order to help graphologists to extract and analyze handwriting features faster and more precisely using computers.

Early automated systems have deployed methods such as SVM, Artificial Neural Networks (ANN), and rule-based system separately. However, these methods are not tolerant to translation and distortion in the input image. In addition, they would have a large amount of input parameters which could add more noise during the training process. The current trend of computerized graphology shows that applying a combination of analysis methods and using big quantity of training data result in remarkable accuracy and have an impact on achieving better results [2,8]. Therefore, applying ensemble methods that deploy deep learning for designing an automated graphology system with a high accuracy rate is considered in this study.

2   Literature Review

2.1   The Big Five Factors Model (BFFM)

Each factor of the BFFM has a definition mentioned in [7]. Extraversion is characterized by excitability, sociability, talkativeness, assertiveness, and high amounts of emotional expressiveness. Agreeableness includes attributes such as trust, altruism, kindness, affection, and other prosocial behaviors. Conscientiousness includes high levels of thoughtfulness, good impulse control, and goal-directed behaviors. Emotional Stability refers to a person's ability to remain stable and balanced. Open to Experience features characteristics such as imagination and insight.

For measuring the BFFM, The IPIP-BFFM tests which are self-report tests used for measuring each factor using the international personality item pool-big five factor markers. They are questionnaires that contain sets of big five factor markers that vary in their length. The scale of each test composed of a number of items on a 5-point scale ranging from complete disagreement (1: Very false for me) to complete agreement (5: Very true for me).

2.2 Handwriting Analysis/Graphology

Graphology is considered as a modern form of psychology that reveals personality traits, including emotional outlay, fears, honesty, defences and others, from individual's handwriting but not identifying the writer's age, race, religion, or nationality. In other words, it is a technique used to evaluate and interpret the character of the writer from handwriting [6]. As it is mentioned in [11], there are two major schools of handwriting analysis which are Graphoanalysis and Gestalt graphology. Graphoanalysis is the most widely used in the United States. This is in which the graphoanalyst looks at the page as a collection of symbols where each symbol is evaluated independently from the whole [9]. However, Gestalt graphology is the school of handwriting study in Europe, particularly in Germany. It was developed alongside psychiatry and psychoanalysis. Gestalt graphology is always a combination of features related to form, movement and space that are used to establish a personality trait. In this work, we applied Gestalt graphology concept for analysing and labelling our handwriting samples used for training our computerized graphology system.

2.3 Related Works on Computerized Prediction of BFF

In 2017, Majumder et al. presented a method to extract personality traits from stream-of-consciousness essays using CNN [5]. They trained five different networks, all with the same architecture, for the five personality traits. Each network was a binary classifier that predicted the corresponding trait to be positive or negative. They used James Pennebaker and Laura King's stream-of-consciousness essay dataset. It contains 2,468 anonymous essays tagged with the authors' personality traits based on the Big Five factors. They evaluated the model performance by measuring the accuracy obtained with different configurations. The accuracy ranged between 50% to 62% across the five factors.

In 2018, Gavrilescu and Vizireanu proposed the non-invasive three-layer architecture based on neural networks that aims to determine the Big Five personality traits of an individual by analyzing off-line handwriting [3]. They used their own database that links the Big Five personality type with the handwriting features collected from 128 subjects containing both predefined and random texts. The main handwriting features used are the following: baseline, word slant, writing pressure, connecting strokes, space between lines, lowercase letter 't', and lowercase letter 'f'. They obtained the highest prediction accuracy for Openness to Experience, Extraversion, and Emotional Stability at 84%, while for Conscientiousness and Agreeableness, the prediction accuracy is around 77%.

In 2019, Akrami et al. created a model to extract Big Five personality traits from a text using machine learning techniques [1]. They created an extensive dataset by having experts annotate personality traits in a large number of texts from multiple on-line sources. From these annotated texts, they selected a sample and made further annotations ending up in a large low-reliability dataset and a small high-reliability dataset. The results show that the models based on the small high-reliability dataset performed better than models based on large low-reliability dataset.

In 2020, Salminen et al. combined automatic personality detection (APD) and data-driven personas (DDPs) to design personas with personality traits that could be automatically generated using numerical and textual social media data [10]. They developed a neural network with two major sub-architectures: a single dimensional convolutional neural network since there is a spatial structure in the input text, and a long short-term memory network since there is also a temporal correlation between the words in the input text. They used the F1 macro score for evaluating the model, F1 scores obtained for each BF trait using a dataset of 2,467 essays are as follows: (0.541, 0.529, 0.538, 0.553, and 0.484) for Extraversion, Openness to Experience, Conscientiousness, Agreeableness, and Emotional Stability, respectively.

3   Data Collection

3.1   Participants

The handwriting data used for our study is a private dataset were collected from two sources. The first is the paper-based survey that was approved by University Human Research Ethics Committee at Concordia University in Canada. The second is one graphologist who is a well-known professional and author of various publications. 192 handwriting samples were collected from the survey that has been responded by the participant in one laboratory room of Centre for Pattern Recognition and Machine Intelligence (CENPARMI) at Concordia university. However, the other 874 samples were collected by the graphologist for her business purposes. We ensured that these samples are collected under the same condition and environment followed in our survey. So, our handwriting dataset, named Handwriting for the Big Five Factors (HWBFF), consists of 1066 samples. 58.19% of the subjects are male while 18.71% are female and 23% are not informed. Their ages start from 18 years old in which 39.7% ranged between 18–35 and 48% ranged between 36 and 55 years old, see Fig. 1. An item of the survey asking about the country of origin of the respondents revealed that 61.86% of the participants were originally from Canada. The handwriting samples were written in different languages including English, French, Chinese, Arabic, and Spanish.

3.2   Labelling Dataset

The samples of HWBFF dataset were labelled by our graphologist. Each sample was annotated with the BFF measurement. For this, the handwriting features that reveal each BFF factor were specified firstly based on definitions and graphology rules. Table 1 shows the handwriting features corresponding to each

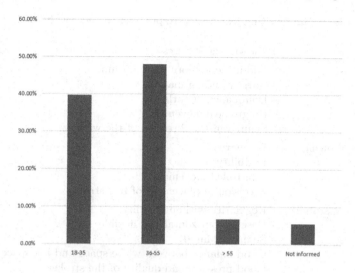

Fig. 1. Age distribution of the participants for handwriting samples

BFF factor. Then, each sample was evaluated by scaling manually each hand-writing feature of each factor. The scale of Extraversion, Emotional Stability, Agreeableness, and Open to Experience composed of 5 features on a 5-point scale where 1 = None or very low, 2 = Low, 3 = Average, 4 = High, and 5 = Very high. However, the scale of Conscientiousness factor composed of 4 features with the same 5-point scale. Once values are assigned for all the features in the scale for each factor, oho averaged the feature values to obtain a total scale score of measuring where (1 to 2) is low, 3 is average, (4 to 5) is high.

4 Data Distribution Analysis

In order to understand our dataset better and receive expected results, we need to do some analysis for data distribution in order to see whether our data is balanced or not. Having imbalanced data causes the machine learning classifier to be more biased towards the majority class and resulting in bad classification of the minority class. So, we aim to avoid the imbalanced data in order to get a high performance evaluation for our classifier. 1066 handwriting samples are included in our experiments. Figure 2 shows the distribution of the single-labels in the HWBFF dataset. It demonstrates that distribution of the single-labels for the big five factors is highly skewed, 85.55% of the dataset is occupied by medium agreeableness and while low emotional stability only holds 0.85% of the dataset.

Table 1. Handwriting features corresponding to each of the BFFM

Factor	Handwriting features
Extraversion	- Middle zone more than 2,5 mm - Narrow ending margin - Dominance of garlands - Progressive movement - Slanted in the direction of the writing
Conscientiousness	- Regularity - Legibility - Controlled movement - Precision of placement of free strokes
Emotional stability	- Regularity without rigidity - Baseline horizontal and flexible - Slightly slanted - Good balance between white space and ink space - Good pressure and quality of the stroke
Agreeableness	- Dominance of curves versus angles - Good space between letters, words, and lines - Letter width >5 mm - Round letters without loops and slightly open - Nourished stroke
Open to experience	- Good openness in loops - Good speed and movement - Slight angles in letters - Slanted in the direction of handwriting - Narrow ending margin

5   Data Digitization

Electronic conversion of handwriting samples were carried out using a process wherein a document is scanned in a color scale at the resolution of 600 dpi using HP Color LaserJet Enterprise M553 series scanner with feature of automatic document feeder.

6   Data Preprocessing

6.1   Data Augmentation

Our model included data augmentation in order to enlarge the training dataset. The augmented data are generated before training the classifier. We augmented our data using techniques that do not change or alter the handwriting features that the five factors are revealed from. Four augmentation techniques were used which are rescaling, height shifting wherein the image is shifted vertically, vertical flip, and brightness.

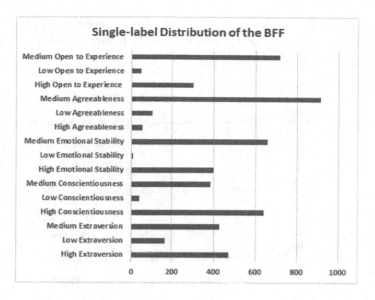

Fig. 2. Single-label distribution for the five factors jointly in HWBFF dataset

7 Model Architecture

The Big Five Factors test in psychology is formulated into a multi-label classification in computer science, since it predicts the measurement level (low, medium, or high) of the five factors simultaneously. Based on the analysis of data distribution, our HWBFF dataset is considered as an imbalanced dataset. Class imbalance fails to properly represent the distributive characteristics of the data and provide unsatisfying accuracy. Therefore, there is a need to handle our imbalanced dataset properly in order to get favorable results.

In this work, we proposed an ensemble method called Averaging of SMOTE Multi-label SVM-CNN (AvgMlSC). AvgMlSC constructs synthetic samples using Synthetic Minority Over-sampling Technique (SMOTE) to incorporate the borderline information and averaging the two classifiers i.e. Multi-label Support Vector Machine (MLSVM) and Multi-label Convolutional Neural Network (MLCNN) to produce one optimal predictive model. The following sections describe the proposed framework in detail.

7.1 Materials and Methods

Our multi-label classification problem is transformed firstly into five independent multi-class classification problems, one associated with each big five factor (Extraversion, Conscientiousness, Emotional Stability, Agreeableness, and Open to Experience). Then, each multi-class classification is transformed into three independent binary classification problems by fitting one binary classifier for each single class which is the measurement level (low, medium, and high) following (one-vs-all) scheme. So, at the end we have 15 binary classifiers, 3 classifiers for each big five factor, see Fig. 3.

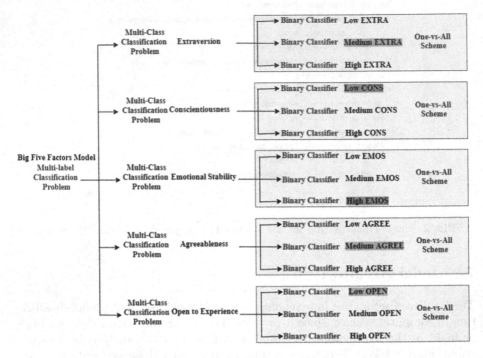

Fig. 3. Transforming multi-label BFF classification problem into five multi-class classification problems following (one-vs-all) scheme

The two classifiers (MLSVM and MLCNN) of the ensemble learning are trained and evaluated individually and sequentially. In each binary classifier inside each multi-class SVM and CNN, SMOTE which is an oversampling strategy is applied within 10-fold cross validation on each original single-label training set to construct synthetic samples from the minority classes. That means, before starting the oversampling process, Original Single-label Training Set is split into 10 folds. After that, the SMOTE is applied on each fold, then the resampled fold used for the training. After training, the model is evaluated using the validation set generated in the cross validation. The process of training and evaluation are repeated 10 times. At the end, the outputs of the five multi-class classifiers are joined together. Each model tested using unseen data and the predicted results of each classifier are averaged to produce one optimal output. The following subsections illustrate some basic knowledge and architecture of MLSVM, MLCNN, and the algorithm of SMOTE.

Synthetic Minority Over-Sampling Technique (SMOTE). SMOTE is an oversampling strategy that helps to overcome overfitting by focusing on the feature space rather than data space and interpolating synthetic samples along the line segments connecting seed samples and forcing the decision region of the minority class to become more general. Thus, in SMOTE, synthetic samples are not exact copies of the original ones. It oversamples the minority class by taking each minority class sample and introducing synthetic examples in the following way: Take the difference between the feature vector (sample) under consideration and its nearest neighbour. Multiply this difference by a random number between 0 and 1, and add it to the feature vector under consideration. Depending upon the amount of oversampling required, neighbours from the k nearest neighbours are randomly chosen and joined to the synthetic examples.

Multi-label Support Vector Machine (MLSVM). Support vector machine (SVM) is one of the popular classifiers in binary classification. In this work, we transformed our multi-label classification problem at the end into a set of independent binary classification problems by fitting one classifier per class. This mechanism named (one-vs-all) scheme which is a conceptually simple and computationally efficient solution for multi-label classification. Therefore, as a first classifier in our ensemble method, multi-label learning using support vector machine (MLSVM) for the binary classification problem associated with each class is conducted in this study.

Multi-label Convolutional Neural Network (MLCNN). The second classifier in our ensemble method is Multi-label Convolutional Neural Network (MLCNN). For this, we conduct multi-label learning under (one-vs-all) scheme by using Convolutional Neural Networks (CNNs) in order to transform our multi-label classification problem into a set of independent binary classification problems.

Figure 4 shows the architecture implemented in each binary CNN classifier for each single label. As we can see, the input of our MLCNN combines two types of data which are structured and unstructured data. Therefore, our MLCNN consists of two neural networks for inputs. The first one named ImageCNN which is a convolutional neural network used for unstructured data i.e. images of handwriting samples. The second network called FeatureFCNN which is a fully connected neural network used for structured data i.e. the values of handwriting features. Then, the outputs from the two networks are concatenated and passed to ClassifierFCNN which is a fully connected neural network that classifies the handwriting samples into one class.

Image Convolutional Neural Network (ImageCNN). To input the images of handwriting samples into MLCNN, we create a convolutional neural network that consists of one input layer which accepts a three dimensional color image of a fixed-size (512×512). Then, the input image is passed through 8 convolutional blocks. Each block consists of one convolution layer with filters of

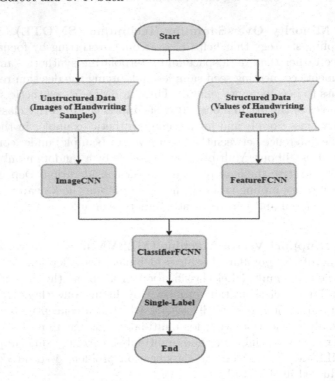

Fig. 4. The architecture of the binary CNN

(3 × 3) pixel window, one rectified linear unit (ReLU) activation function layer for reducing the effect of gradient vanishing during backpropagation, and one batch normalization layer, then the layers are followed by Max-pooling layer which is performed over a (2 × 2) pixel window. The number of filters in each block is: 16, 32, 64, 64, 64, 128, 256, and 512, respectively. Once the filtration process is applied on the input image, it is passed through a layer to be flattened out to two fully connected hidden layers. The first layer contains 16 nodes followed by (ReLU) activation function layer, batch normalization layer, and finally dropout with a rate of 0.5. The second hidden layer contains 4 nodes followed by (ReLU) activation function layer, the number of nodes in this layer should match the number of nodes coming out from FeatureFCNN. Max Pooling, Dropout and Batch Normalization layers are added to prevent overfitting and control the number of parameters in the network.

FeatureFCNN. In order to input the structured data into MLCNN, a sequential model named FeatureFCNN is created for accepting the values of 24 handwriting features selected by the graphologist based on graphological rules. FeatureFCNN is a fully connected neural network that consists of three layers. The first is the input layer which consists of the input shape as (None, 24). Then, the input features are passed through two fully connected hidden Layers. The first hidden layer contains 2 input vectors and 8 output vectors followed by rectified linear unit (ReLU) activation function and the second one contains 8 input vectors and 4 output vectors followed by rectified linear unit (ReLU) activation function.

ClassifierFCNN. The outputs of ImageCNN and FeatureFCNN are passed through Keras concatenation function to be concatenated and passed to the ClassifierFCNN which is a fully connected neural network that outputs multiple values. The ClassifierFCNN consists of two fully connected dense layers. The first one contains 4 nodes with (ReLU) activation function and the second layer contains one output class with sigmoid activation function.

Ensemble Method. Since our HWBFF dataset is imbalanced, an ensemble method is used to improve the performance of the overall system. Model averaging is used for this work. In averaging approach each ensemble member contributes an equal amount to the final prediction. In the case of predicting a class probability, the prediction can be calculated as the argmax of the summed probabilities for each class label. Argmax is an operation that finds the argument that gives the maximum value from a target function. Figure 5 shows the ensemble method for AvgMlSC.

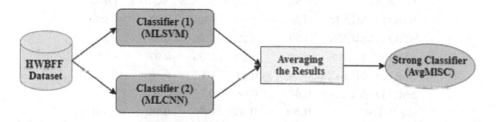

Fig. 5. Ensemble method for AvgMlSC

8   Experiments and Results

The training set was generated using approximately 90% of 1066 handwriting samples while the other 10% was used for testing.

8.1   A Comparative Analysis with the Baseline Classifiers

To establish the effectiveness of the proposed model, a comparative analysis with five popular baseline classifiers, i.e. Logistic Regression (LR), Naïve Bayes (NB), K-Neighbors (KN) Support Vector Machine (SVM), and Convolutional Neural Network (CNN) is presented in this section. For this, all classifiers have employed the same resampled HWBFF dataset for training and multi-label learning under

"one-vs-all" scheme with the same experimental protocol (10-fold cross validation) was considered. Tables 2, 3, and 4 present the overall average of predictive
accuracy, AUC, and F-Score, respectively, for the big five factors. For the predictive accuracy, the proposed model achieved the highest value for Extraversion, Conscientiousness, and Agreeableness. While for Emotional Stability LR
obtained the highest value. However, for Open to Experience, LR and AvgMLSC
were the best classifiers. For AUC, AvgMlSC obtained the highest numbers
for Extraversion, Conscientiousness, Agreeableness, and Open to Experience.
Whilst LR achieved the highest value for Emotional Stability. For the last measure which is F-Score, AvgMlSC produced the best result for Conscientiousness,
Agreeableness, and Open to Experience. However, KN was the best classifier for
Extraversion while LR was the best for Emotional Stability. Table 5 compares
the overall performance for the six classifiers in terms of the three measures. The
table and the figure reveal that the overall performance of AvgMlSC which is
our proposed ensemble learning is better than the individual learners with 93%
predictive accuracy, 0.94 AUC, and 90% F-Score.

Table 2. The average of predictive accuracy for each factor using the five baseline
classifiers and AvgMlSC

Classifier	EXTRA	CONS	EMOS	AGREE	OPEN
SMOTE-MLLR	0.79	0.86	**0.98**	0.97	0.96
SMOTE-MLNB	0.69	0.79	0.89	0.93	0.88
SMOTE-MLKN	0.82	0.88	0.95	0.97	0.95
SMOTE-MLSVM	0.76	0.84	0.97	0.96	0.94
SMOTE-MLCNN	0.66	0.68	0.77	0.96	0.85
AvgMLSC	**0.84**	**0.92**	0.96	**0.99**	**0.96**

Table 3. The average of AUC for each factor using the five baseline classifiers and
AvgMlSC

Classifier	EXTRA	CONS	EMOS	AGREE	OPEN
SMOTE-MLLR	0.74	0.82	**0.98**	0.83	0.91
SMOTE-MLNB	0.70	0.79	0.87	0.82	0.83
SMOTE-MLKN	0.80	0.80	0.79	0.64	0.82
SMOTE-MLSVM	0.71	0.79	0.97	0.54	0.86
SMOTE-MLCNN	0.73	0.74	0.78	0.87	0.75
AvgMLSC	**0.86**	**0.92**	0.97	**0.98**	**0.95**

Table 4. The average of F-Score for each factor using the five baseline classifiers and AvgMISC

Classifier	EXTRA	CONS	EMOS	AGREE	OPEN
SMOTE-MLLR	0.63	0.79	**0.98**	0.98	0.98
SMOTE-MLNB	0.61	0.69	0.66	0.69	0.75
SMOTE-MLKN	0.73	0.75	0.62	0.55	0.77
SMOTE-MLSVM	0.56	0.73	0.97	0.45	0.9
SMOTE-MLCNN	0.42	0.27	0.39	0.54	0.38
AvgMLSC	**0.68**	**0.9**	0.97	**0.99**	**0.97**

Table 5. The overall performance for the five baseline classifiers and AvgMISC

Classifier	Predictive accuracy	AUC	F-Score
SMOTE-MLLR	0.91	0.86	**0.88**
SMOTE-MLNB	0.84	0.80	0.68
SMOTE-MLKN	0.91	0.77	0.68
SMOTE-MLSVM	0.89	0.77	0.72
SMOTE-MLCNN	0.79	0.78	0.40
AvgMLSC	**0.93**	**0.94**	0.90

8.2   A Comparative Analysis with the State-of-the-Art

The results of two early computerized BFF model from the state-of-the-art have been chosen to be compared with the results of our proposed model. They have used the same form of data used in our model and the same performance measures to evaluate their proposed models.

The first work presented a method to extract personality traits from stream of-consciousness essays using a convolutional neural network (CNN) [5]. They trained five different networks, all with the same architecture, for the five personality traits. Each network was a binary classifier that predicted the corresponding trait to be positive or negative. They used James Pennebaker and Laura King's stream-of-consciousness essay dataset. It contains 2,468 anonymous essays tagged with the authors' personality traits based on the Big Five factors. They evaluated the model performance by measuring the predictive accuracy, see Table 6.

The second work combined automatic personality detection (APD) and data-driven personas (DDPs) to design personas with personality traits that could be automatically generated using numerical and textual social media data [10]. They developed a neural network with two major sub-architectures: a single dimensional convolutional neural network since there is a spatial structure in the input text, and a long short-term memory network since there is also a temporal correlation between the words in the input text. They used the F-score

Table 6. A comparison between AvgMlSC and Majumder et al. (2017)

	Predictive accuracy				
Automated BFF model	EXTRA	CONS	EMOS	AGREE	OPEN
Majumder et al. (2017)	58.09	57.30	59.38	56.71	62.68
AvgMlSC	**84.00**	**92.00**	**96.00**	**99.00**	**96.00**

for evaluating their model, F-score obtained for each BF trait using the same dataset used in the first work, see Table 7.

Table 7. A comparison between AvgMlSC and Salminen et al. (2020)

	F-Score				
Automated BFF model	EXTRA	CONS	EMOS	AGREE	OPEN
Salminen et al. (2020)	0.54	0.53	0.48	0.55	0.52
AvgMLSC	**0.68**	**0.90**	**0.97**	**0.99**	**0.97**

As can be observed from the two tables above, our proposed model achieved a remarkable improvement in accuracy and F-Score than the other two models.

9   Conclusion

This work introduced a robust yet simple framework named AvgMlSC to address imbalance problem in the big five factors classification. To the best of our knowledge, this is the first study to systematically investigate data imbalance issue in handwriting analysis in general and the big five factor classification in particular. AvgMlSC is based on ensemble learning that was employed along with SMOTE resample technique in order to handle the issue of imbalanced dataset. The prediction results of AvgMlSC were compared to five baseline classifiers and outperformed their results with 93% predictive accuracy, 0.94 AUC, and 90% F-Score. Moreover, it achieved higher values of accuracy and F-Score than the considered early computerized BFF models. So, the results show the potential of ensembling and SMOTE oversampling for predicting the measurement level of BFF using an imbalance handwriting analysis dataset. Moreover, it shows the potential of machine learning methods for predicting the measurement level of BFF using graphology data. Two assumptions can be considered as future work for researchers. First, adding features of signature and drawing to develop an automated graphology system for measuring the BFF. Second, developing an automated handwriting analysis system for measuring the BFF for a specific age group such as children or teenager.

References

1. Akrami, N., Fernquist, J., Isbister, T., Kaati, L., Pelzer, B.: Automatic extraction of personality from text: challenges and opportunities. In: Proceedings of the 2019 IEEE International Conference on Big Data (Big Data), pp. 3156–3164. IEEE (2019)
2. Djamal, E.C., Darmawati, R.: Recognition of human personality trait based on features of handwriting analysis using multi structural algorithm and artificial neural networks. In: Proceedings of the 2013 IEEE Conference on Control, Systems & Industrial Informatics (ICCSII), pp. 22–24 (2013)
3. Gavrilescu, M., Vizireanu, N.: Predicting the big five personality traits from handwriting. EURASIP J. Image Video Process. **2018**(1), 1–17 (2018). https://doi.org/10.1186/s13640-018-0297-3
4. Giraldo-Forero, A.F., Jaramillo-Garzón, J.A., Ruiz-Muñoz, J.F., Castellanos-Domínguez, C.G.: Managing imbalanced data sets in multi-label problems: a case study with the SMOTE algorithm. In: Ruiz-Shulcloper, J., Sanniti di Baja, G. (eds.) CIARP 2013. LNCS, vol. 8258, pp. 334–342. Springer, Heidelberg (2013). https://doi.org/10.1007/978-3-642-41822-8_42
5. Majumder, N., Poria, S., Gelbukh, A., Cambria, E.: Deep learning-based document modeling for personality detection from text. IEEE Intell. Syst. **32**(2), 74–79 (2017)
6. Ploog, H.: Handwriting Psychology: Personality Reflected in Handwriting. iUniverse (2013)
7. Power, R.A., Pluess, M.: Heritability estimates of the big five personality traits based on common genetic variants. Transl. Psychiatry **5**(7), e604–e604 (2015)
8. Raut, A.A., Bobade, A.M.: Prediction of human personality by handwriting analysis based on segmentation method using support vector machine. Int. J. Pure Appl. Res. Eng. Technol. (2014)
9. Roman, K.G.: Handwriting: a key to personality (1954)
10. Salminen, J., Rao, R.G., Jung, S., Chowdhury, S.A., Jansen, B.J.: Enriching social media personas with personality traits: a deep learning approach using the big five classes. In: Degen, H., Reinerman-Jones, L. (eds.) HCII 2020. LNCS, vol. 12217, pp. 101–120. Springer, Cham (2020). https://doi.org/10.1007/978-3-030-50334-5_7
11. Satow, R., Rector, J.: Using gestalt graphology to identify entrepreneurial leadership. Percept. Mot. Skills **81**(1), 263–270 (1995)

Recognition of Graphological Wartegg Hand-Drawings

Yunqi Xu$^{(\boxtimes)}$ and Ching Y. Suen

Centre for Pattern Recognition and Machine Intelligence (CENPARMI),
Gina Cody School of Engineering and Computer Science, Concordia University,
Montreal, QC H3G 1M8, Canada
{x_yunq,suen}@encs.concordia.ca

Abstract. Wartegg Test is a drawing completion task designed to reflect the personal characteristics of the testers. A complete Wartegg Test has eight 4 cm × 4 cm boxes with a printed hint in each of them. The tester will be required to use pencil to draw eight pictures in the boxes after they saw these printed hints. In recent years the trend of utilizing high-speed hardware and deep learning based model for object detection makes it possible to recognize hand-drawn objects from images. However, recognizing them is not an easy task, like other hand-drawn images, the Wartegg images are abstract and diverse. Also, Wartegg Test images are multi-object images, the number of objects in one image, their distribution and size are all unpredictable. These factors make the recognition task on Wartegg Test images more difficult. In this paper, we present a complete framework including PCC (Pearson's Correlation Coefficient) to extract lines and curves, SLIC for the selection of feature key points, DBSCAN for object cluster, and finally YoloV3-SPP model for detecting shapes and objects. Our system produced an accuracy of 87.9% for one object detection and 75% for multi-object detection which surpass the previous results by a wide margin.

Keywords: Wartegg test · Image processing · Object detection

1 Introduction

The Wartegg Test, also called Wartegg Zeichen Test, is a classic psychology test that can reflect personalities of a tester. A Wartegg Zeichen Test form is an A4 paper consisted of eight 4 cm × 4 cm squares in two rows with a simple printed sign in each square [15]. The tester will be required to draw anything in their mind in each square using a pencil. Recognizing testers' drawings inside those boxes correctly can help graphologists to detect the tester's thoughts and predict the tester's potential psychological problem [9]. In our experiment, we followed the above description to collect our Wartegg Zeichen Test forms and then scan

Supported by CENPARMI & NSERC.

C. Carmona-Duarte et al. (Eds.): IGS 2021, LNCS 13424, pp. 174–186, 2022.
https://doi.org/10.1007/978-3-031-19745-1_13

them into digital format, finally split one Wartegg Zeichen Test form into eight images.

In recent years, the huge amount of deep learning algorithms for object recognition make it possible to detect those hand-drawn pictures in Wartegg Test images using a computer. However, many problems become obstacles and make the detection of Wartegg Test image set very difficult. The challenges of recognition Wartegg Test images are the same as the other Hand-drawn images recognition tasks [16]. Firstly, these hand-drawn images are abstract, a complex object in real world can be present as a simple shape in hand-drawn images. Second, their colour context is lacking compared with the real images that was taken by camera. Third, they are diverse because different people have different draw style for the same object. However, the challenges of recognition of Wartegg Test are not just limited on these three aspects, Wartegg Test images are also unpredictable, not only the number of objects in each square, but also the size of an object. Usually, for training a detector, we need to input a huge amount of images to make sure the network is robust enought to achieve a high performance when testing it. But current open source hand-drawn image sets, such as QuickDraw [5], Sketchy [13] and Tu-Berlin [3] are all one object images with the same size and located in the center of the images. So, directly using these open source images as training images and testing on Wartegg Test images will not get a satisfactory result.

To make it possible to recognize Wartegg Test images using network, in this paper, we present a complete Wartegg Test image sets process, combine the PCC for the extraction of lines and curves, SLIC + DBSCAN for objects split, these methods solve the problem of different distribution of training image set and Wartegg Test image set and partly increase the robustness of the neural network. Finally, we used a transfer learning based approach to load the pre-trained ImageNet parameters into our YoloV3-SPP backbone network DarkNet53 to increase the converge speed of our network, and then train a YoloV3-SPP for shape detection.

The paper is structured as follows. Section 2 briefly introduces the previous work. Section 3 outlines the concepts of our methods, PCC, SLIC algorithm, DBSCAN algorithm and YoloV3-SPP. Section 4 describes the experimented details, and Sect. 5 for the conclusion and future work of our experiment.

2   Background

The begining of applying classification and recognition deep learning model to hand-drawn images can be retrospect from 2012. In this year, Tu-Berlin [3] presented their hand-drawn image set. After this, in 2016 Sketchy images have been presented [13] with 125 categories. In 2017, Google presented one of the largest sketch image set QuickDraw [5]. And in 2018, image sets SPG [8] and SketchSeg [14] were publised. Finally, in 2019, our Warteg Test image set [9] has been collected which contains 30 categories and more than 900 images. Accompanied with this image sets, some famous deep learning models also have been mentioned in the past ten years, such as Sketch-net [18], Deep visual sequential fusion net [6], SketchRNN [5] and Sketchmate [17]. Although these models achieve high performance, they are tested on Tu-Berlin and QuickDraw, some single object image sets. However, free hand-drawn images should be diverse, like our Wartegg Test image set which contains many images that have multiple objects in one image. So it is important to explore how to detect multiple objects using current open source image set.

3   Method

Some previous image processing methods are effective for specific image sets, but can not deal with a Wartegg Test image set, since many uncontrollable factors will influence the quality of the collected Wartegg Test image set as mentioned in Sect. 1. The motivation of our experiment is to unify the data distribution between training and testing image sets to increase the accuracy of the object detection task.

3.1   Image Processing

Image processing includes two parts. Firstly, using PCC (Pearson's Correlation Coefficient) [2] to extract lines and curves and remove slated noises caused by image format transformation. Secondly, utilizing the SLIC superpixel and DBSCAN cluster algorithm to extract every object in the image and delete meaningless parts.

PCC for Feature Selection. Donati [2] used PCC to extract the features of sketch images based on the relevance of the pixels in this image. Using this method, those pixels neither belong to lines nor curves can be deleted.

Firstly, define

$$kernel = Gaussian\_kernel(next\_odd(7 * \sigma_i, \sigma_i)) \tag{1}$$

where, $\sigma_i = C * \sigma_{i-1} = C^i * (w_{min}/b), i \in [1, \log_c(w_{max}/w_{min}) - 1]$, and w_{min} is the minimum line width, w_{max} is the maximum, C and b are constant, usually we will use 2 and 3 separately.

After generating the ith Gaussian kernels Using Eq. 1 we will use

$$PCC_{xy} = \frac{\sum_{j,k}(I_{xy}(j,k) - Avg(I_{xy}))(k_i(j,k) - Avg(k_i))}{\sqrt{\sum_{j,k}(I_{xy}(j,k) - Avg(I_{xy})^2 \sum_{j,k}(k_i(j,k) - Avg(k_i))^2}} \tag{2}$$

to calculate several PCC images, finally, we will use

$$MPCC = \begin{cases} maxPCC_{xy}, & | maxPCC_{xy} | > | minPCC_{xy} | \\ minPCC_{xy}, & otherwise \end{cases} \tag{3}$$

SLIC Algorithm for Superpixel Split. SLIC was mentioned by R.Achanta [1], which splits one image into many small sub patches (also called superpixels) based on their values and locations.

The algorithm of SLIC is presented in Algorithm 1:

Algorithm 1. SLIC algorithm

Input: k: number of superpixels ; m; $iterations$; $image\_width$; $image\_height$

Initialization:

$S = \sqrt{(image\_width * image\_height)/k}$; $centerset = C_k = (l_k, x_k, y_k)_{k=1...k}$;
update each $c_k.x_k$, $c_k.y_k$ to the lowest gradient in $[c_k.x_k - 1 : c_k.x_k + 1, c_k.y_k - 1 : c_k.y_k + 1]$
Set each pixel $p_i.cluster = None$, $p + i.distance = +\infty$, $i = 1$

1: **if** $i \leq$ iteration **then**
2:    **for** each cluster c_k in clusterset **do**
3:       **for** each point p_i in $[c_k.x - s : c_k.x + s ; c_k.y - s : c_k.y + s]$ **do**
4:          $D = \sqrt{(\sqrt{(p_i.l - c_k.l)^2}/m)^2 + (\sqrt{(p_i.x - c_k.x)^2 + (p_i.y - c_k.y)^2}/s)^2}$
5:          **if** $D < p_i.distance$ **then**
6:             $p_i.distance = D$
7:             $p_i.cluster = c_k$
8:    $i = i + 1$;

DBSCAN for Object Segmentation. DBSCAN was mentioned by M.Ester [4], which has been designed to discover clusters with arbitrary shape based on the density of dataset. The main idea of DBSCAN comes from the fact that the density inside a cluster is usually higher than the density outside a cluster, and different clusters may have different density. This idea is similar to our Wartegg Test image set, the density of lines and curves is usually higher in an object, e.g. Fig. 1.

    (a) Umbrella   (b) Rabbit   (c) Car

Fig. 1. Examples of Density distribution of Wartegg Test images

We will calculate the ratio of the number of pixels that have a value in a 5 * 5 window, and generate these density distribution images. The color in Fig. 1 which is close to white means the density score is high, on the other hand, when the color is black, it means the density score is approximately zero. These images agree with our conjecture, so we can utilize DBCANS to cluster objects in the same image.

After using Superpixel to split an image into numerous small sub-patches, for each patch, we keep those pixels at the center of the sub-patch located on the lines or curves. Based on previous tests, the remaining key points belong to the same object should be much closer, and for those points from different objects, they should have a different distribution. Also, points belonging to the noisy part should have a very low density.

The algorithm of DBSCAN is shown below:

Algorithm 2. DBSCAN algorithm

Input: *Eps, Minpts, Dataset*
Initialization: $clusterid = 0$; $\forall$ point p_i, $p_i \in$ dataset, p_i.cluster = None
1: **for** each point p_i in dataset **do**
2:     **if** p_i.cluster is None **then**
3:         clusterset = [$\exists\ p_j$, if dist$(p_i, p_j) \leq$ Eps]
4:         **if** clusterset.length < Minpts **then**
5:             p_i.cluster is Noise
6:         **else**
7:             **for** each point p_c in clusterset **do**
8:                 p_c.cluster = clusterid ; Remove p_i from clusterset
9:             **while** cluster is not Empty **do**
10:                 p_{new} = clusterset[0];*new_cluster* = [$\exists\ P'$, if dist$(p_{new}, p') \leq$ Eps]
11:                 **if** *new_clusterset*.length $\geq$ Minpts **then**
12:                     **for** each point p'_{new} in *new_clisterset* **do**
13:                         **if** p'_{new}.cluster is None **then**
14:                             clusterset.append(p'_{new}); p'_{new}.cluster = clusterid
15:                         **if** p'_{new}.cluster is Noise **then**
16:                             p'_{new}.cluster = clusterid
17:     clusterid += 1

3.2 YoloV3-SPP

The model we choose for the object detection task is YoloV3-SPP [19] which is the third version of the Yolo model with an SPP structure [7] that can improve the precision of the original YoloV3. Figure 2 presents the overall structure of YoloV3-SPP. It contains a backbone DarkNet53 [12] which is composed of many Residual blocks and a SPP structure, finally the output will be generated through three different feature maps for predicting different scales of an object. Compared with the first output directly follows the SPP structure and the Convolutional set (the first branch in Fig. 2), the second output and the last output comes from the concatenated (the green ball) result of a Residual × 8 block and a Upsample layer (the red box) accompany with a Convolutional set block.

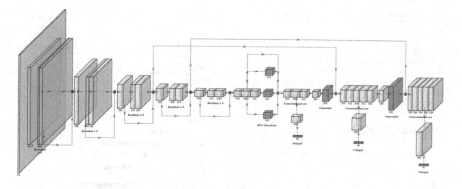

Fig. 2. The structure of YoloV3-SPP (Color figure online)

4   Experiment

Our experiment will follow the previous methods introduced in Sect. 3.1 to process our Wartegg Test image set. We will firstly introduce our training and test image sets in Sect. 4.1, and then discuss the pixel value augment in Sect. 4.2, describe the details of image processing result in Sect. 4.3, and finally analyze the object detection result in Sect. 4.4.

4.1   Introduction of Dataset

During our experiment, we used QuickDraw [5] as the training image set and our collected Wartegg Test image set as the testing input to validate the performance of the YoloV3-SPP model.

Testing Image Set. Our Wartegg Zeichen Test form are collected by Liu [9] in 2019. Firstly, we labeled all objects in each image, and then, merged together those categories that share the same pattern. For example, face, circle, cookie and tire, apple are circular patterns, they can be treated as the shape circle. Also, Parachute, hot air balloon and Umbrella all have a curved ceiling at the top and converging tail at the bottom.

Figure 3a shows the ratio between the area of an object and its image. For those images that have only one object, the area ratio is close to a normal distribution, the median value is around 0.4. On the other hand, for those images that have two, and multiple objects, there are more tiny objects in each image.

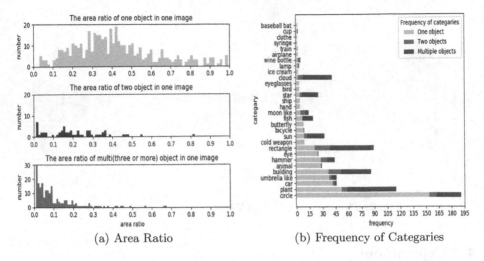

(a) Area Ratio   (b) Frequency of Categaries

Fig. 3. Examples of Density distribution of Wartegg Test images

After labeling and merging, we counted the frequency of each category as shown in Fig. 3b. Finally, we will select the top 11 classes frequently appeared in those images that contain only one object. The 11 classes are: circle, planet, car, umbrella, building, animal hammer, eye, rectangle, cold weapon and sun. Also, We have 439 images with a single object, 55 images have two objects and 93 images contain multiple objects.

QuickDraw Image Set. The QuickDraw image set [5] has been collected through the game "QuickDraw" developed by Google, which has very similar rules as "Drawize", instead drawing something and guessed by friend, Quick-Draw lets the tester draw an object based on a word hint, and the machine will guess what the tester has drawn. The QuickDraw image set contains more than 300 categories which is suitable for us to select the useful categories.

We generate the training image set based on the area distribution of Wartegg Test image set. There are 12000 images in our training image set, each image contains one object and we keep the area ratio of objects with the area of the image from 0.02 to 0.9 to cover most cases in the Wartegg Test image set. Also, the object can be randomly located in the image. Since QuickDraw was drawn by computer mouse or touch pad, electronic pencil, the width of its lines and curves is only one pixel, but the lines and curves of Wartegg Test image set are drawn by pencil, so their width varies from 4 to 8 pixels. Then, we will enlarge the width of lines and curves in QuickDraw to 6 pixels. Figure 4 shows how we generate training images with different scales and bold lines and curves of the training image set that make them suitable for the testing image set.

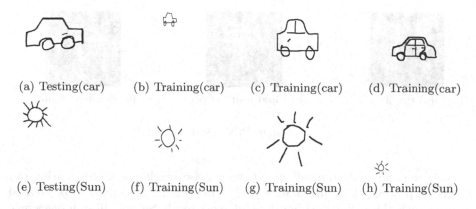

(a) Testing(car)   (b) Training(car)   (c) Training(car)   (d) Training(car)

(e) Testing(Sun)   (f) Training(Sun)   (g) Training(Sun)   (h) Training(Sun)

Fig. 4. Examples of testing and training images

4.2   Pixel Value Augment

The main purpose of Pixel Value Augment is to enlarge useful information and pretend such information has been deleted by applying PCC and following SLIC + DBSCAN algorithms.

As Fig. 5 shows, although the original Fig. 5a looks good, there are lots of noises in the image surrounding the lines and curves.

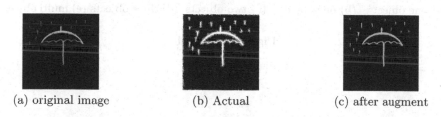

(a) original image   (b) Actual   (c) after augment

Fig. 5. Actual image with noise

By analyzing the Wartegg Test image set, the distribution of a line usually obeys the normal distribution. So for each line, if its width is greater than a width_threshold, we will enlarge its value, by normalization based on its smallest and highest values, in our experiment, the width_threshold is 4.

4.3   Image Processing Result

Before starting the processing steps, we will normalize the value of pixels between (0, 1), and then follow the steps described in Sect. 3.1 to extract lines and curves.

Figure 6a presents each filter step in the PCC process during our experiment. Figure 6b shows the result after PCC algorithm. Finally, Fig. 6c shows the denoised result. Compared with Fig. 5, those noises surrounding the lines and curves with unpredictable values are deleted.

| (a) Pcc 3 | (b) Final result of pcc | (c) denoised result |

Fig. 6. PCC result

However, not only the salt and pepper noise pixels are noises, during our detection process, those pixels with useless information also need to be treated as noise since this will impact our final inference result. So, we will split one whole image into many small superpixels (Fig. 7). Then, we kept those center points of a small pitches that located on strokes as our key points and use DBSCAN mentioned in Sect. 3.1 to classify these key points into multiple clusters.

(a) one object   (b) one object   (c) two objects (d) three objects (e) multi objects

Fig. 7. SLIC result

(a) one object   (b) one object   (c) two objects   (d) three objects (e) multi objects

Fig. 8. DBSCAN cluster result

Figure 8 shows the cluster result. Finally, based on the cluster result, we split each image into multiple images with only one object. Figure 9 shows the result. So, for an image which contains N objects, we will get N new images and one object per image in the end. For example, in Fig. 8d, we have three objects in the image: a house, a tree and a sun, after splitting, we will get Fig. 9e, Fig. 9f and Fig. 9g. By doing so, the Wartegg Test image set will have the same distribution as the training image set.

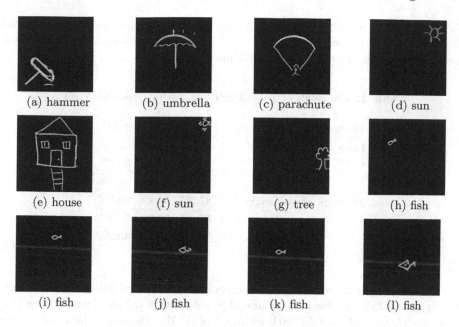

Fig. 9. Split result

4.4 YoloV3-SPP Object Detection

Note that the contour distributions of natural images and hand-drawn images are similar. In the training process, we use the transfer learning based approach that firstly loads the parameters of pre-trained DarkNet53 on ImageNet and fine-tune the last layer using the original QuickDraw images to make the backbone network learn the features of sketch images. The transfer learning can help us solve the problem of insufficient number of training images and increase the converging speed. In our experiment, loading the pre-trained parameters from well-trained DarkNet53 on the ImageNet, then fine-tune the last layer will spend less time, usually 5 epoches to converage, compared with directly training a DarkNet53 on QuickDraw images, which need around 15 epoches to let the network converage, and around 20 epoches to let the result of the network to be stable. Once the training process of DarkNet53 is completed, we load these parameters without the last fully Connected Layer of DarkNet53 into the YoloV3-SPP Network. Using our generated QuickDraw image set we train the YoloV3-SPP for the detection task.

During the testing process, We have three image sets, Image set 1 contains those images that the original images have only one object, Image set 2 contains those images which the original images have one or two object, and Image set 3 contains those images that the original images have one, two or multiple objects. We input each split Wartegg Test image into the trained YoloV3-SPP model to get the inference result. We will get the inference results for each image, then, we will merge those split images which belong to individual images together with their predicted bounding boxes. So, finally, we can calculate the performance of the YoloV3-SPP model. We will use the COCO image criterion to evaluate our result. The testing result is shown in Table 1.

Table 1. The result of YoloV3-SPP on Wartegg Test image set

Method	Image set	AP_{50}	AP_{75}	mAP
Ours	1	87.9%	76.3%	67.7%
	2	78.9%	66.8%	56.7%
	3	75.0%	57.1%	51.8%
Without ours	(Original) 1	81.2%	73.8%	62.5%
	(Original) 2	57.8%	56.2%	51.4%
	(Original) 3	52.6%	46.4%	43.9%

Table 1 shows that we got a much better result compared with previous result, which got 68.72% (IoU = 0.5) for one object detection [10], and we increase this score to 87.9% (IoU = 0.5) with an mAP of 67.7%. However, the result drops when testing on one and two objects, 78.9% for Iou = 0.5 and the mAP is 56.7%. The performance drops continuously for the detection task of one, two and multiple objects, i.e. 75.0% when IoU = 0.5 and 51.8% for mAP Score. By analyzing this phenomenon, the main reason is because with an increase in the object number, the area ratio of each object with its image size will decrease. On the other hand, for multiple object detection, there are more tiny objects in the testing image set compared with one object image set. As Fig. 3a shows, these tiny objects will lower the performance of the network. On the other hand, as a comparision, we also use the original images as the testing image set to verify the performance of the trained detector on original Wartegg Test image set. The result has decreased significantly, especially for image sets 2 and 3. These may be because in the training image set, each image has one object, but in our Wartegg test image set, an image contains an indeterminate number of objects, also if an image contains more than one object, the distance between two objects is short, the target area inside a bounding box may contain two objects, and one object could be treated as the interference part when another object is detected.

5   Conclusion and Future Work

In this paper, we present a complete framework of the Wartegg Test image set in object detection. Our method becomes a bridge between one object hand-drawn image set and multiple object detection task. Our method does not only simplify the multi-object detection task of Wartegg Test image set, but also improves the result of the performance of Wartegg Test image set in object detection. However, there still are some limitations of our approach, firstly, the DBSCAN cluster is not suitable for those objects tightly connected or overlapped together, the DBSCAN will treat them as one object which will not be recognized by YoloV3-SPP. Secondly, the parameters of DBSCAN are manually modified, although we have already classified images based on their object area and batch processing the images, we still need to modify the parameters several times. Finally, YoloV3-SPP may not be very suitable for tiny object detection [11], the next step may need to design part of the network which is suitable for both large and tiny objects to improve the performance.

References

1. Achanta, R., Shaji, A., Smith, K., Lucchi, A., Fua, P., Süsstrunk, S.: SLIC super-pixels compared to state-of-the-art superpixel methods. IEEE Trans. Pattern Anal. Mach. Intell. **34**(11), 2274–2282 (2012). https://doi.org/10.1109/TPAMI.2012.120
2. Donati, L., Cesano, S., Prati, A.: A complete hand-drawn sketch vectorization framework. Multimed. Tools Appl. **78**(14), 19083–19113 (2019). https://doi.org/10.1007/s11042-019-7311-3
3. Eitz, M., Hildebrand, K., Boubekeur, T., Alexa, M.: Sketch-based image retrieval: benchmark and bag-of-features descriptors. IEEE Trans. Vis. Comput. Graph. **17**(11), 1624–1636 (2011)
4. Ester, M., Kriegel, H.P., Sander, J., Xu, X., et al.: A density-based algorithm for discovering clusters in large spatial databases with noise. In: KDD, vol. 96, pp. 226–231 (1996)
5. Ha, D., Eck, D.: A neural representation of sketch drawings. In: International Conference on Learning Representations (2018)
6. He, J.Y., Wu, X., Jiang, Y.G., Zhao, B., Peng, Q.: Sketch recognition with deep visual-sequential fusion model. In: Proceedings of the 25th ACM International Conference on Multimedia, pp. 448–456 (2017)
7. He, K., Zhang, X., Ren, S., Sun, J.: Spatial pyramid pooling in deep convolutional networks for visual recognition. IEEE Trans. Pattern Anal. Mach. Intell. **37**(9), 1904–1916 (2015). https://doi.org/10.1109/TPAMI.2015.2389824
8. Li, K., et al.: Universal sketch perceptual grouping. In: Ferrari, V., Hebert, M., Sminchisescu, C., Weiss, Y. (eds.) ECCV 2018. LNCS, vol. 11212, pp. 593–609. Springer, Cham (2018). https://doi.org/10.1007/978-3-030-01237-3_36
9. Liu, L., Pettinati, G., Suen, C.Y.: Computer-aided Wartegg drawing completion test. In: Lu, Y., Vincent, N., Yuen, P.C., Zheng, W.-S., Cheriet, F., Suen, C.Y. (eds.) ICPRAI 2020. LNCS, vol. 12068, pp. 575–580. Springer, Cham (2020). https://doi.org/10.1007/978-3-030-59830-3_50
10. Ly, N.T., Liu, L., Suen, C.Y., Nakagawa, M.: Hand-drawn object detection for scoring Wartegg Zeichen test. In: Lu, Y., Vincent, N., Yuen, P.C., Zheng, W.-S., Cheriet, F., Suen, C.Y. (eds.) ICPRAI 2020. LNCS, vol. 12068, pp. 109–114. Springer, Cham (2020). https://doi.org/10.1007/978-3-030-59830-3_9
11. Nguyen, N.-D., Do, T., Ngo, T.D., Le, D.-D.: An evaluation of deep learning methods for small object detection. J. Electr. Comput. Eng. **2020**, 1–18 (2020). https://doi.org/10.1155/2020/3189691. Article ID 3189691
12. Redmon, J., Farhadi, A.: YOLOv3: an incremental improvement. arXiv (2018)
13. Sangkloy, P., Burnell, N., Ham, C., Hays, J.: The sketchy database: learning to retrieve badly drawn bunnies. ACM Trans. Graph. (TOG) **35**(4), 1–12 (2016)
14. Wang, F., et al.: Multi-column point-CNN for sketch segmentation. Neurocomputing **392**, 50–59 (2020)

15. Wartegg, E.: Gestaltung und charakter. ausdrucksdeutung zeichnerischer gestaltung und entwurf einer charakterologischen typologie (1939)
16. Xu, P., Hospedales, T.M., Yin, Q., Song, Y.-Z., Xiang, T., Wang, L.: Deep learning for free-hand sketch: a survey. IEEE Trans. Pattern Anal. Mach. Intell. 1. https://doi.org/10.1109/TPAMI.2022.3148853.
17. Xu, P., et al.: SketchMate: deep hashing for million-scale human sketch retrieval. In: Proceedings of the IEEE Conference on Computer Vision and Pattern Recognition, pp. 8090–8098 (2018)
18. Yu, Q., Yang, Y., Liu, F., Song, Y.Z., Xiang, T., Hospedales, T.M.: Sketch-a-net: a deep neural network that beats humans. Int. J. Comput. Vis. **122**(3), 411–425 (2017). https://doi.org/10.1007/s11263-016-0932-3
19. Zhang, P., Zhong, Y., Li, X.: SlimYOLOv3: narrower, faster and better for real-time UAV applications. In: Proceedings of the IEEE/CVF International Conference on Computer Vision (ICCV) Workshops, October 2019

Motor Control

iDeLog3D: Sigma-Lognormal Analysis of 3DHuman Movements

Miguel A. Ferrer[1]($\boxtimes$) (iD), Moises Diaz[1,2] (iD), Cristina Carmona-Duarte[1] (iD),
Jose Juan Quintana[1] (iD), and Réjean Plamondon[3] (iD)

[1] Universidad de Las Palmas de Gran Canaria, Las Palmas, Spain
{miguelangel.ferrer,moises.diaz,cristina.carmona,
josejuan.quintana}@ulpgc.es
[2] Universidad del Atlantico Medio, Las Palmas, Spain
[3] Ecole Polytechnique, Montreal, Canada
rejean.plamondon@polymtl.ca

Abstract. This paper proposes a 3D representation of human kinematics with the Kinematic Theory of Rapid Human Movements and its associated Sigma-Lognormal model. Based on the lognormality principle, a human movement is decomposed as a vector sum of temporally overlapped simple movements called strokes, described as two virtual target points linked by an arc of circumference and with the movement velocity having a lognormal shape. The paper extends the former 2D theory to the third dimension by linking the 3D virtual target points with planar circumferences covered with lognormal velocity profiles and reconstructing the 3D kinematics of the whole movement with temporally overlapping consecutive planes. Parameter optimization is accomplished jointly in the temporal and spatial domains. Moreover, the lognormal parameters used are numerically estimated, potentially providing a set of possible solutions that gain insights into the physical and biological meanings of the Sigma-Lognormal model parameters. We show that the 3D model, called iDeLog3D, achieves competitive results in analyzing the kinematics of multiple human movements recorded by various sensors at different sampling rates. The iDeLog3D is available to the scientific community following license agreements.

Keywords: Biometrics · Kinematic theory of rapid human movements · Analysis of human 3D movements · Modeling 3D human actions

1 Introduction

Many human-related computer vision problems can be approached by analyzing the kinematics of human movements [1]. Kinematics variables include linear and angular displacements, velocities, and accelerations. In addition, these data typically register the kinematics of anatomical landmarks such as the center of gravity of body segments, the centers of joint rotations, the end effectors of limb segments, key anatomical prominences, among others.

© Springer Nature Switzerland AG 2022
C. Carmona-Duarte et al. (Eds.): IGS 2021, LNCS 13424, pp. 189–202, 2022.
https://doi.org/10.1007/978-3-031-19745-1_14

Exploring human kinematics provides fundamental insight to understand the mechanisms that characterize natural human motion, the higher-level strategies of realizing complex tasks, and the interactions with the external environment. It might be helpful to develop tools for characterizing human motion changes due to disease, aging, or injury recovery. This can help understand how fine motor control is learned by elementary school children and provide quantitative and objective learning indexes. In addition, it can facilitate rehabilitation applications, including the design of prostheses and exoskeletons, workplace ergonomics, sports medicine, orthopedics, and physical therapy, which are of paramount importance for human welfare.

Lately, several acquisition devices and software development kits (SDKs) for capturing 3D kinematics have emerged in the market. On the one hand, some of them are based on an external device such as leap motion, Microsoft Kinect, Optitrack MOCAP, etc. On the other hand, wearable sensors such as neuronmocap suits and gloves or some smartwatches include inertial measurement units (IMU), which also allow to recover the trajectory.

Many theories have tried to approach the kinematics of human movement in general [2]. Among them, the Kinematic Theory of Rapid Human Movements [2–5] and its associated Delta-Lognormal [6] and Sigma-Lognormal [7] models have been extensively used to explain most of the fundamental phenomena covered by classical studies on human motor control and to study several factors involved in fine motricity.

Two different methods have been proposed to calculate the Sigma-Lognormal parameters: ScriptStudio [7], which optimizes the velocity, and iDeLog (iterative Decomposition in Lognormals) [8], which optimizes the velocity and the trajectory jointly.

These methods transform kinematic data into a sequence of circumference arcs between two virtual target points. Each arc is defined by starting and ending angles. An ending virtual target point is the starting virtual target point of the next circumference, and so on, up to the end of the movement. Similarly, each arc can be considered as having a starting and ending time, but the finishing time of an arc is not the same as the starting time of the next arc. Thus, the arcs are temporally overlapped. Each arc is covered with a lognormal velocity profile, and all the lognormal samples corresponding to the same time are summed to generate the trajectory.

Consequently, the space-time trajectory is transformed into a sequence of virtual target points, starting and ending angles, and lognormal parameters.

To the best of author knowledge, the Delta-Lognormal and Sigma-Lognormal models have been applied to the 2D spatiotemporal sequence for several applications. Even though a few attempts have been made to extract the Delta-Lognormal or Sigma-Lognormal parameters from 3D sequences, there is still room for improvements.

1.1 Related Works

ScriptStudio and iDeLog are two operational frameworks that computerize the kinematic theory of rapid movements. Some approaches have been developed to extend the Delta-Lognormal and Sigma-Lognormal models to 3D in the ScriptStudio framework.

The first attempts to mathematically extend the Delta-Lognormal and Sigma-Lognormal model to 3D movements were proposed in [9] and [10], respectively. Subsequently, an efficient and fully automatic 3D extension of the Delta-Lognormal model was proposed in [11, 12]. The authors assumed that a 3D short and fast hand stroke is a planar movement on a 3D coordinate plane. They, therefore, proposed to rotate the plane of the movement to the xy plane, after which they performed a 2D analysis, and finally, the result was rotated to the original plane of the movement.

A Sigma-Lognormal extension to 3D following the ScriptStudio framework was presented in [13, 14]. The authors assumed that each stroke acts similarly to a rotation around a pivot and the stroke can be described in spherical coordinates with the distance to the origin ρ, the azimuth φ and polar ϑ angles. The circular link between each pair of virtual target points is built by rotating the azimuth and polar angles along their pivot in a lognormal fashion. This procedure was evaluated with three datasets, and Signal-to-Noise Rate (SNR) between velocities of around 20 dBs were obtained. The quality of this procedure is also measured by comparing the recognition ratio of the original and reconstructed databases with similar performances (Table 1).

Table 1. Related works on kinematic theory of rapid movements in 3D.

Papers	Model	Method[*]	Main characteristic	Evaluation
Leduc et al. 2001 [9], Djioua et al. 2007 [10]	DL		Seven delta-lognormal parameters plus two 2D curvatures and two angular plane orientations	Velocity
Chidami et al. 2018 [11], 2020 [12]	DL	SS	Parameter extraction in a bidimensional plane and 3D rotation	Velocity
Schindler et al. 2018 [13], Fischer et al. 2020 [14]	SL	SS	A natural extension to 3D by adding a third coordinate and polar angle	Velocity and classification
This work, 2022	SL	iDeLog	Linking 3D virtual target points through planar circumferences with 3D synthesis	Velocity, trajectory and recognition

[*]DL stands for Delta-Lognormal. SL stands for Sigma-Lognormal. SS stands for ScriptStudio

1.2 Our Contribution

This paper adds the third dimension to the equations of iDeLog [8] by establishing a new mathematical basis for analyzing 3D human-like kinematics called iDeLog3D. The mathematical analysis lead to solve a set of equations to calculate the Sigma-Lognormal parameters. We highlight that it does not have a single solution. From a neuromotor perspective, choosing which possible solutions to the equations are the most appropriate remains a challenge. In this context, iDeLog3D produces not only a new solution to the Sigma-Lognormal equations, but also, a new set of viable solutions. All in all, the main contributions of the present paper can be summarized as follows:

- A new and robust framework to develop the Kinematic Theory of Rapid Human Movement into 3D based on planar links, while maintaining the biological background of the Kinematic Theory of Rapid Human Movements.
- A pool of solutions to the Sigma-Lognormal equations. With similar mathematical performances, all these practical solutions might allow new biological analyses.

These contributions are expected to provide new insights into understanding complex and lengthy human kinematics. Finally, we publicly make available the iDeLog3D to facilitate the repeatability of the experiments following free license agreements ay www. gpds.ulpgc.es.

The remainder of the paper is organized as follows: Sect. 2 briefly reviews the Sigma-Lognormal model. Section 3 establishes the mathematical framework for analyzing 3D human movement kinematics. Experimental validation of the proposed analysis is reported in Sect. 4. Section 5 concludes the article by summarizing its key contributions.

2   3D Sigma-Lognormal Equations

The Kinematic Theory of Rapid Human Movements [4] and its associated Sigma-Lognormal model provide a velocity $\vec{v_o}(t)$ modeling regardless of the dimension of the movement. It was formulated in [7] in 2D and in [13, 14] in 3D in the ScriptStudio framework. For the tridimensional case, namely, ScriptStudio3D in this work, let $\left[x_o(t), y_o(t), z_o(t)\right]^T$ be the trajectory of a 3D human movement whose vectorial velocity and module are defined by:

$$\vec{v_o}(t) = \begin{bmatrix} v_{ox}(t) \\ v_{oy}(t) \\ v_{oz}(t) \end{bmatrix} = \begin{bmatrix} dx_o(t)/dt \\ dy_o(t)/dt \\ dz_o(t)/dt \end{bmatrix} \tag{1}$$

$$v_o(t) = \left| \vec{v_o}(t) \right| = \sqrt{v_{ox}^2(t) + v_{oy}^2(t) + v_{oz}^2(t)} \tag{2}$$

The velocity $\vec{v_o}(t)$ is decomposed as a sum of temporally overlapped strokes. Each stroke is a spatiotemporal trajectory between two virtual target points with a lognormal velocity profile [14]. Thus, the velocity is modeled as a sum of N lognormals as:

$$\vec{v_r}(t) = \sum_{j=1}^{N} D_j \begin{bmatrix} \sin(\varphi_j(t))\cos(\vartheta_j(t)) \\ \sin(\varphi_j(t))\sin(\vartheta_j(t)) \\ \cos(\varphi_j(t)) \end{bmatrix} v_j(t) \tag{3}$$

where

$$v_j(t) = \frac{1}{\sigma_j \sqrt{2\pi}(t - t_0)} exp \left\{ -\frac{\left[\ln(t - t_0) - \mu_j\right]^2}{2\sigma_j^2} \right\} \tag{4}$$

is the lognormal velocity at the jth stroke, t is the basis of time, t_0 is the time of stroke occurrence, D_j is the amplitude of the input commands, μ_j is the stroke time delay on a logarithmic time scale and σ_j is the stroke response time.

The similarity between the original velocity $v_o(t)$ and the reconstructed velocity $v_r(t)$ is calculated through the Signal-to-Noise Ratio SNR_v [8].

Regarding the trajectory, $\varphi_j(t)$ and $\vartheta_j(t)$ are the azimuth and polar angular sweep of the arc between the two virtual target points corresponding to the jth stroke. They are defined as [14]:

$$\varphi_j(t) = \varphi_{sj} + \left(\varphi_{ej} - \varphi_{sj}\right) \int_0^t v_j(\tau)d\tau$$

$$\vartheta_j(t) = \vartheta_{sj} + \left(\vartheta_{ej} - \vartheta_{sj}\right) \int_0^t v_j(\tau)d\tau \tag{5}$$

Once the Sigma-Lognormal parameters, $\left\{D_j, t_{0j}, \mu_j, \sigma_j^2, \vartheta_{sj}, \vartheta_{ej}, \varphi_{sj}, \varphi_{ej}\right\}_{j=1}^N$ are obtained, the velocity $\overrightarrow{v_o}(t)$ can be reconstructed as $\overrightarrow{v_r}(t)$ following (3), and the trajectory recovered as:

$$\overrightarrow{s_r}(t) = \begin{bmatrix} x_r(t) \\ y_r(t) \\ z_r(t) \end{bmatrix} = \int_0^t \overrightarrow{v_r}(\tau)d\tau \tag{6}$$

The reconstruction quality of the trajectory is determined through the Signal-to-Noise Ratio SNR_t between the 8-connected original and reconstructed trajectories [8].

3   iDeLog3D

The above procedure determines the Sigma-Lognormal parameters from the velocity, which produces a first-order error resulting from the trajectory obtained by the integration of the velocity (6). Indeed, this is a shortcoming for lengthy and complex spatio-temporal trajectories. This paper addresses this challenge by developing the iDeLog3D, which jointly optimizes the spatial and temporal Sigma-Lognormal parameters. Thus, the trajectory and velocity errors are balanced. Furthermore, as an additional conceptual difference with the ScriptStudio3D, the iDeLog3D links the 3D virtual target points through planar circumferences instead of sweeping the azimuth and polar angles. Moreover, because the iDeLog3D determines the Sigma-Lognormal parameters numerically instead of analytically, as in the ScripStudio3D, it is possible to work out alternative solutions.

In short, the iDeLog3D works as follows: Firstly, it segments a spatiotemporal trajectory into strokes; secondly, for each stroke $j = 1, \ldots, N$ it estimates the spatial parameters (the starting and ending virtual target points, azimuth and polar angles of the curve: $tp_{j-1}, tp_j, \vartheta_{sj}, \vartheta_{ej}, \varphi_{sj}$ and φ_{ej}, respectively); thirdly, it calculates the temporal parameters, i.e., the lognormal parameters D_j, t_{0j}, μ_j and σ_j^2. After this first solution, the computational method iteratively optimizes the target point location and the velocity function parameters to improve the 3D spatiotemporal trajectory representation.

3.1 Stroke Segmentation

The ScriptStudio3D [14] segments the strokes by adjusting a lognormal to the highest velocity peak. Next, such lognormal is subtracted from the velocity. The procedure is repeated on the remaining velocity iteratively until a defined quality is reached in the adjustment. As a result, a single peak is defined by as many lognormal functions as needed to improve the SNR performance.

A completely different strategy is used in iDeLog3D for the joint spatiotemporal segmentation. We segment the strokes by estimating the piece of the trajectory between velocity minima. A proficiency velocity minima detection helps us find only a single lognormal per peak, which is supposed to have a closer biological meaning [8]. Let the time of the velocity minima be $t_{minj} = 0, \ldots, N$, where N is the number of strokes, $t_{min0} = 0$, and $t_{minN} = T$ is the temporal length of the 3D human movement. In this case, the velocity peak, which corresponds to stroke j, was defined as:

$$v_{oj}(t) = \begin{cases} \left| \vec{v_o}(t) \right| & t_{minj-1} \leq t \leq t_{minj} \\ 0 & \text{otherwise} \end{cases}, 1 < j < N \tag{7}$$

where $v_o(t)$ is the velocity of the human movement. In the trajectory, the velocity minima are expected to correspond to salient points $sp_j, j = 0, \ldots, N$, with sp_0 being the first sample, and sp_N, the last. Note that $t_{\min j} \cdot f_m$ is the index of the sample sp_j, with f_m being the sampling frequency.

3.2 Temporal Parameters for Stroke

The temporal parameters are those related to the velocity, i.e., the lognormal parameters t_{0j}, D_j, μ_j and σ_j^2 for each stroke $v_{oj}(t)$. In the case of ScriptStudio3D [14], these parameters are obtained analytically by solving the system of equations that best fit the lognormal to three selected points of $v_{oj}(t)$. In iDeLog3D, following [8], t_{0j} is defined in advance and D_j, μ_j and σ_j^2 are later obtained numerically.

Lognormal Timing. First, t_{0j} is defined as $t_{0j} = t_{min,j-1} - \Delta t_j$. This procedure leaves the work of approaching the shape of $v_{oj}(t)$ to the lognormal parameters μ_j and σ_j^2. It could thus be stated that Δt simulates the time between the neuron firing and the muscle reaction, while μ_j and σ_j^2 describe the muscle response to the firing [15]. Note that different values of Δt_j will provide a different solution for μ_j and σ_j^2, and with all of them having a similar SNR_v. It should be mentioned that D_j is also necessary to approach $v_{oj}(t)$, but D_j barely depends on Δt. Therefore, this procedure can provide different solutions for further biological analysis. By default, we use $\Delta t_j = 0.5s \forall j$, which is a human averaged reaction time [16]. In practice, a constant Δt_j produces similar values of μ_j and σ_j^2 for most of the strokes, which is reasonable, since the μ_j and σ_j^2 responses approximate the impulsive response of the end effector that carries out the whole movement. This is another difference between iDeLog3D and ScriptStudio3D.

Lognormal Shape. Regarding the estimation of the D_j, μ_j and σ_j^2 lognormal parameters, to approach the velocity peak $v_{oj}(t)$, iDeLog3D calculates them numerically through a nonlinear least-squares minimization of the function:

$$\int_{t=t_{min,j-1}}^{t_{min,j}} \left| D_j v_j\left(t; t_{0j}, \mu_j, \sigma_j^2\right) - v_{oj}(t) \right|^2 dt \tag{8}$$

The minimization is performed using a Levenberg-Marquardt algorithm (LMA), which is chosen to solve a generic curve-fitting problem in many software applications.

This procedure has several limitations as the peak is cropped between $t_{min,j-1}$ and $t_{min,j}$ (8). It causes narrow and sharp peaks. To alleviate this drawback, the integration interval of (8) is empirically widened $(t_{min,j} - t_{min,j-1})/3$ on each side to improve the adjustment of the velocity peak $v_{oj}(t)$.

3.3 Spatial Parameters for Stroke

The Kinematic Theory of Rapid Human Movements represents the trajectory, which relies on the virtual target points and the curves between them. The ScriptStudio3D defines such curves through the integration of the vectorial velocity. In iDeLog3D, the initial virtual target points and the curves between them are estimated geometrically.

Virtual Target Points. Each stroke aims to reach the virtual target points. These are not reached since the next simple movement starts before the previous one ends. Consequently, a virtual target point $tp_j, j = 1, ..N$ is assigned to each salient point sp_j and is estimated through the triangle defined by the vertices sp_{j-1}, sp_j and sp_{j+1}. Specifically, tp_j is located on the median of the vertex sp_j at a distance dtp_j outwards from the vertex sp_j defined as $dtp_j = Dtp_j sin(\chi_j/2)$, where Dtp_j the distance between the vertex sp_j and the midpoint of the opposite side and χ_j is the angle of the vertex sp_j. In this way, the closer the angle of the vertex sp_j, the further tp_j from sp_j.

Trajectory Between Virtual Target Points. Two approaches were identified for defining the trajectory of a simple movement between two virtual target points. The first one assumes that the simple movements are planar, i.e., executed in a 2D plane [11]. Consequently, the ensuing temporal overlapping of curves in different 2D planes builds up a full 3D trajectory. The second one, used by the ScripStudio3D in [13], sweeps the azimuth and polar angle from the starting to the end values independently, as defined in (5). Both propositions are valid from a mathematical perspective.

Alternatively, the iDeLog3D opts for modeling each simple movement with a planar curve. It mainly shows that it is possible to approach free 3D human-like movements linking overlapped planar curves [9].

To estimate the 2D plane of the jth stroke or simple movement, three points are required, namely, tp_{j-1}, tp_j and the middle point mp_j of the trajectory between the salient points sp_{j-1} and sp_j. From these three points, an orthonormal base of the plane $\vec{r}_j$ and $\vec{s}_j$ is calculated from the vectors $mp_j - tp_{j-1}$ and $mp_j - tp_j$, through the Gram-Schmidt process. Thus, the parametric equation of the plane of stroke j is defined as $P_j \equiv tp_{j-1} + \lambda \vec{r}_j + \mu \vec{s}_j$.

Once we define the plane P_j, the points mp_j, sp_{j-1} and sp_j are projected onto P_j, employing basic geometrical operations giving as results pmp_j, psp_{j-1} and psp_j. The circumference traversing these three projected points is obtained. The slopes of this circumference in the points psp_{j-1} and psp_j represent the start θ_{sj} and end θ_{ej} angles, respectively. Finally, the link between tp_{j-1} and tp_j is the circumference $\left(r_{cj}(t), s_{cj}(t)\right)$ on the plane P_j that traverses tp_{j-1} with angle θ_{sj} and tp_j with angle θ_{ej}. This procedure is illustrated in Fig. 1. The coordinates $\left(r_{cj}(t), s_{cj}(t)\right)$ of this circumference traveled at a speed $D_j v_j(t; t_{0j}, \mu_j, \sigma_j^2)$ are converted to 3D to get the recovery trajectory as follows:

$$(x_r(t), y_r(t), z_r(t)) = \sum_{j=1}^{N} \left(x_j(t), y_j(t), z_j(t)\right) \tag{9}$$

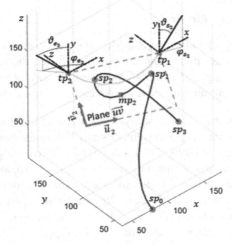

Fig. 1. Trajectory between virtual target points

3.4 Fine-Tuning Refinement

As a result of the above procedure, an initial estimate of the parameters of the 3D Sigma-Lognormal model, $t_{0j}, D_j, \mu_j, \sigma_j, tp_j, \vartheta_{sj}, \vartheta_{ej}, \varphi_{sj}$ and $\varphi_{ej}, j = 1, \ldots, N$, are obtained. Then, the iDeLog3D method initiates a fine-tuning algorithm to optimize the position of the virtual target points tp_j. Furthermore, it improves both the reconstructed trajectory and velocity profiles jointly. Similarly to [8], the improvement is carried out using an iterative Least Mean Square (LMS) algorithm applied stroke by stroke in the same order as the original movement.

Examples of the reconstruction of different real human movements are shown in Fig. 2.

4 Experiments

Experiments assess the similarity of original and reconstructed spatio-temporal sequences with iDeLog3D. They were conducted to validate the applicability of spatio-temporal sequences in different computer vision applications in 3D. To this aim, we analyze, the accuracy of the human kinematics modeling in terms of SNR_v and SNR_t as the performance in gesture recognition and signature verification benchmarks.

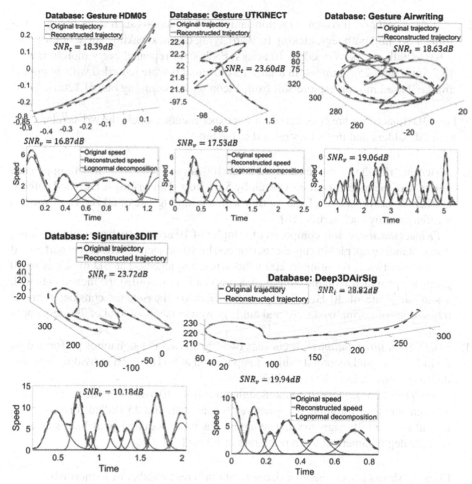

Fig. 2. Example of original and reconstructed specimens by iDeLog3D

4.1 Databases

Five publicly available databases were used in the experiments: three corpora of gestures for classification and two corpora of signatures for verification experiments. The three gesture databases were chosen to compare our results with the previous works [13, 14]. The databases selected comprise different sensors and gestures for studying the ability of the iDeLog3D algorithm to tackle different scenarios. Sensors included are motion capture suits based on a video, gloves based on inertial measure units (IMUs), Kinect, and leap motion devices. The sampling frequency also varies from 30 Hz up to 125 Hz. Furthermore, the databases include short movements such as grab something to more complex ones such as 3D handwriting in the air.

Specifically, five databases used were:

1. *HDM05 database.* It contains motion samples of 11 actions such as grabbing something aloft, hop both legs, kicking forward, lying down, sneaking, squat or throwing a basketball, etc. performed by 10 actors. Each actor repeated every motion from 2 to 7 times with 250 samples, in total. The movements were recorded with an optical marker-based motion capture suit from Vicon with a sampling rate of 120 Hz [17].

   Four 3D trajectories are considered for our experiments, namely the wrists relative to the shoulders and the ankles related to the hips.

2. *Airwriting database.* The dataset includes 100 short words written with uppercase letters with the index finger into the air by 5 subjects. The writing is recorded without markers or gloves using a Leap motion with a sampling rate of 60 Hz. Each word is written once by each writer [18].

3. *UTKinect database.* It is composed of samples of 10 actions such as walking, sitting down, standing up, picking up, etc. performed by 10 subjects. Each subject performed each action twice, resulting in 200 valid action sequences. The 3D locations of 20 joints are provided with the dataset. A Kinect camera recorded the movements with a sampling rate of 30 Hz. Similar to the HDM05 dataset, we consider four 3D trajectories of normalized wrist and ankle movements with a total of 796 sequences [19].

4. *3DIIT Signatures database.* It consists of 1600 air-written signatures performed by 80 individuals and recorded using a Leap motion at 60 Hz. Each individual repeated their signature at least 20 times [20].

5. *Deep3DSigAir database.* It contains signatures from 40 users. For each user, include 10 signatures for training, 10 signatures for the test, and 25 skilled forgeries with a total of 1800 3D signatures. The signatures were acquired with Intel's creative senz3D depth camera at a sampling rate of 60 Hz [21].

Figure 2 shows a specimen per dataset with different number of lognormals.

4.2 Accuracy of Human Kinematics Analysis

We aim to measure the similarity between original and reconstructed specimens. We propose three analyses for this purpose: the accuracy of the human kinematics modeling measured in terms of SNR_v and SNR_t; the recognition accuracy in gesture classification experiment and the Equal Error Rate (EER) for signature verification. It is worth highlighting that iDeLog3D takes around three seconds for parameter extraction and recosntruction on an i7 2.90 GHz microprocessor computer from a one-second signal.

Analysis in Terms of SNR. For SNR, a real movement was analyzed and reconstructed by iDeLog3D. In this case, the SNR_v and SNR_t quantify the ability of iDeLog3D to reconstruct 3D kinematics in different environments accurately.

Table 2 shows such averaged values next to their standard deviations for HDM05, Airwriting, UTKinect, 3D signature IIT, and Deep3DAirSig. It also contains the SNRs reported in [14] as a baseline for similar experiments with Scriptstudio3D.

The results show SNR_t and SNR_v reconstruction accuracy over 15 dB. According to [7], this threshold is acceptable to consider a movement human-like for recognition purposes. These results are consistent for both gesture and airwriting, thanks to the joint trajectory and velocity optimization used. It highlights the ability of the iDeLog3D to handle spatiotemporal sequences of different lengths and complexity obtained from multiple sensors and sampling frequencies.

Table 2. Reconstruction accuracy of the 3DKTT with HDM05, Airwriting, UTKinect, AirWriting, 3D signatures IIT, and Deep3DAirSig databases.

Database	SNR_t	SNR_v	SNR_v [15]
HDM05	$25.73_{5.73}$ dB	$19.60_{2.69}$ dB	$18.52_{4.09}$ dB
Airwriting	$22.99_{4.89}$ dB	$17.97_{1.49}$ dB	$12.52_{2.02}$ dB
UTKinect	$21.97_{6.46}$ dB	$18.62_{3.72}$ dB	$20.21_{4.40}$ dB
Signatures3DIIT	$23.15_{3.69}$ dB	$19.23_{3.01}$ dB	
Deep3DAirSig	$23.36_{4.43}$ dB	$15.03_{2.46}$ dB	

Analysis in Terms of Recognition and Verification Performances. This section measures the accuracy of the iDeLog3D analysis from the perspective of movement recognition and verification. Thus, classification and verification experiments for gestures and signatures were respectively conducted. If the reconstruction is accurate, similar performances should be achieved for the original and iDeLog3D reconstructed databases.

To allow a comparison, the classifier used for gesture recognition was the dynamic time warping (DTW), as in [13, 14]. The performance is given in accuracy and cumulative matching curves (CMC).

Similarly, the signature verification experiments were carried out with a DTW [8]. We consider the two typical scenarios of random and skilled forgeries to estimate whether a signature is genuine or a forgery [22]. Moreover, the performance is given in terms of EER and DET plots.

Remarkable similarities between the real and reconstructed data were found. For example, the reconstructed Signature3DIIT and the reconstructed Deep3DAirSig databases, in the case of random and skilled forgeries, show a very close performance with their original counterpart, as it is shown in Fig. 3. The performance of the Deep3DAirSig database is significantly better than that of the Signature3DIIT database. It is worth pointing out that our purpose is to achieve similar performances regarding the original specimens rather than improving the recognition or verification results. For this reason, sometimes the EER of the reconstructed signatures may be lower than the real one, as the case of the Signature3DIIT database, or viceversa, as the case of the Deep3DAirSig database. The results of similar experiments conducted in [14] with ScriptStudio3D are provided as a baseline in the caption of Fig. 3.

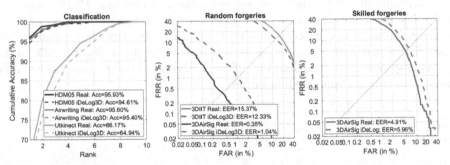

Fig. 3. Results of classification and verification experiments. Left, classification results from the experiment with real and reconstructed by iDeLog3D of HDM05, Airwriting, and UTKinect databases for gesture recognition*. Center: Results of the verification experiments in the randon forgeries scenario carried out with Signature3DIIT and Deep3DAirSig real and iDeLog3D reconstructed databases. Right: Results of the verification experiments in the skilled forgeries scenario carried out with Deep3DAirSig real and iDeLog3D reconstructed databases. *As baseline, the classification accuracies reported in [18] were HDM05 Real: Acc = 96.4%, HDM05 reconstructed: Acc = 96.1%, Airwriting Real: Acc = 99.0%, Airwriting reconstructed: Acc = 98.2%, UTkinect Real: Acc = 94.0% and UTkinect reconstructed: Acc = 92.0%.

5 Conclusions

This paper proposes a new algorithm called iDeLog3D to analyze 3D human kinematics. Following the Kinematic Theory of Rapid Human Movements principles and its associated Sigma-Lognormal model, iDeLog3D decomposes 3D spatiotemporal sequences as a sum of temporally overlapping planar circumferences traveled with a lognormal speed profile.

Experiments show that the iDeLog3D can represent real 3D human kinematics obtained with different sensors and sampling frequencies with an SNR over 15 dB in velocity and trajectory. Furthermore, databases reconstructed with the iDeLog3D parameters perform similarly to the original databases.

The iDeLog3D is made publicly available for interested readers as supplementary material at www.gpds.ulpgc.es. Furthermore, this computational model may be helpful in many applications such as human-computer interfaces, medicine, education, games, etc. We thus hope that this paper's models and tools will help the research community develop 3D human-like kinematics.

Acknowledgments. This study was funded by the Spanish government's MIMECO PID2019-109099RB-C41 research project and European Union FEDER program/funds, the CajaCanaria and la Caixa bank grant 2019SP19, and NSERC grant RGPIN-2015-06409. C. Carmona-Duarte was supported by a Viera y Clavijo grant from ULPGC.

References

1. Winter, D.A.: Biomechanics and Motor Control of Human Movement. Wiley, Hoboken (2009)
2. Plamondon, R., O'Reilly, C., Galbally, J., Almaksour, A., Anquetil, É.: Recent developments in the study of rapid human movements with the kinematic theory: Applications to handwriting and signature synthesis. Pattern Recognit. Lett. **35**(1), 225–235 (2014). https://doi.org/10.1016/j.patrec.2012.06.004
3. Plamondon, R.: A kinematic theory of rapid human movements: part i. movement representation and generation. Biol. Cybern. **72**(4), 295–307 (1995). https://doi.org/10.1007/BF0020 2785
4. Plamondon, R.: A kinematic theory of rapid human movements: part III. Kinetic outcomes. Biol. Cybern. **78**(2), 133–145 (1998). https://doi.org/10.1007/s004220050420
5. Plamondon, R.: A kinematic theory of rapid human movements. part iv: a formal mathematical proof and new insights. Biol. Cybern. **89**(2), 126–138 (2003). https://doi.org/10.1007/s00422-003-0407-9
6. Plamondon, R., Guerfali, W.: The generation of handwriting with delta-lognormal synergies. Biol. Cybern. **78**, 119–132 (1998). https://doi.org/10.1007/s004220050419
7. O'Reilly, C., Plamondon, R.: Development of a Sigma-Lognormal representation for on-line signatures. Pattern Recognit. **42**(12), 3324–3337 (2009). https://doi.org/10.1016/j.pat cog.2008.10.017
8. Ferrer, M.A., Diaz, M., Carmona-Duarte, C., Plamondon, R.: iDeLog: iterative dual spatial and kinematic extraction of sigma-lognormal parameters. IEEE Trans. Pattern Anal. Mach. Intell. **42**(1), 114–125 (2020). https://doi.org/10.1109/TPAMI.2018.2879312
9. Leduc, N., Plamondon, R.: A new approach to the study of human movements: the three-dimensional delta-lognormal model. In: 10th International Conference on Graphonomics Society, pp. 98–102 (2001)
10. Djioua, M., Plamondon, R., Della Cioppa, A.: Contributions à la généralisation, à la compréhension et à l'utilisation de la théorie cinématique dans l'analyse et la synthèse du mouvement humain, Dissertation for Doctoral Degree. Montréal: Ecole Polytechnique de Montréal (2007)
11. Chidami, S., Archambault-Caron, M., Plamondon, R.: The delta-lognormal model in 2.5D. In: International Conference on Pattern Recognition and Artificial Intelligence, pp. 743–747 (2018)
12. Chidami, S., Archambault-Caron, M., Plamondon, R.: Applying the delta-lognormal model to simple 3D hand movements. In: The Lognormality Principle and Its Applications in e-security, e-learning and e-health, vol. 88, pp. 403–406. World Scientific (2020). ISBN: 978-081-122-682-2
13. Schindler, R., Bouillon, M., Rejean, P., Fischer, A.: Extending the sigma-lognormal model of the kinematic theory to three dimensions. In: International Conference on Pattern Recognition and Artificial Intelligence, pp. 748–752 (2018)

14. Fischer, A., Schindler, R., Bouillon, M., Plamondon, R.: Modeling 3D movements with the kinematic theory of rapid human movements. In: Plamondon, R., Marcelli, A., Ferrer, M.A. (eds.) The Lognormality Principle and Its Applications in e-security, e-learning and e-health, Series in Machine Perception Artificial Intelligence, vol. 88, pp. 327–342. World Scientific (2020). ISBN 978-081-122-682-2
15. Plamondon, R.: The lognormality principle: a personalized survey. In: The Lognormality Principle and Its Applications in e-security, e-learning and e-health, vol. 2020, pp. 1–40. World Scientific (2021). ISBN 978-081-122-682-2
16. Kandel, E.R., Schwartz, J.H., Jessell, T.M.: Principles of Neural Science, vol. 4 (2013)
17. Müller, M., et al.: Documentation Mocap Database HDM05, Technical report, No. CG-2007-2, ISSN 1610-8892, Univ. Bonn (2007)
18. Chen, M., AlRegib, G., Juang, B.-H.: Air-writing recognition—part ii: detection and recognition of writing activity in continuous stream of motion data. IEEE Trans. Hum.-Mach. Syst. **46**(3), 436–444 (2016). https://doi.org/10.1109/THMS.2015.2492599
19. Xia, L., Chen, C.-C., Aggarwal, J.K.: View invariant human action recognition using histograms of 3D joints. In: 2012 IEEE Computer Society Conference on Computer Vision and Pattern Recognition Workshops, pp. 20–27 (2012). https://doi.org/10.1109/CVPRW.2012.6239233
20. Behera, S.K., Dogra, D.P., Roy, P.P.: Analysis of 3D signatures recorded using leap motion sensor. Multimedia Tools Appl. **77**(11), 14029–14054 (2017). https://doi.org/10.1007/s11 042-017-5011-4
21. Malik, J., Elhayek, A., Guha, S., Ahmed, S., Gillani, A., Stricker, D.: DeepAirSig: end-to-end deep learning based in-air signature verification. IEEE Access **8**, 195832–195843 (2020). https://doi.org/10.1109/ACCESS.2020.3033848

Should We Look at Curvature or Velocity to Extract a Motor Program?

Antonio Parziale[1,2](✉) [ID] and Angelo Marcelli[1,2] [ID]

[1] DIEM, University of Salerno, Via Giovanni Paolo II 132, 84084 Fisciano, SA, Italy
{anparziale,amarcelli}@unisa.it
[2] AI3S Unit, CINI National Laboratory of Artificial Intelligence and Intelligent Systems, University of Salerno, Fisciano, SA, Italy

Abstract. Experimental studies led by Lashley and Raibert in the early phase of human movement science highlighted the phenomenon of motor equivalence, according to which complex movements are represented in the brain abstractly, in a way that is independent of the effector used for the execution of the movement. This abstract representation is known as motor program and it defines the temporal sequence of target points the effector has to move towards to accomplish the desired movement. We present and compare two algorithms for the extraction of motor programs from handwriting samples. One algorithm considers that log-normal velocity profiles are an invariant characteristic of reaching movements and it identifies the position of the target points by analysing the velocity profile of samples. The other algorithm seeks target points by identifying the trajectory points corresponding to maximum curvature variations because experimental studies have shown that the activity of the primary motor cortex encodes the direction of the movement. We have compared the performance of the two algorithms in terms of the number of virtual target points extracted by handwriting samples generated by 32 subjects with their dominant and non-dominant hands. The results have shown that the two algorithms show a similar performance over ∼55% of samples but the extraction of motor programs by analysing the curvature variations is more robust to noise and unmodeled motor variability.

Keywords: Motor equivalence · Motor program extraction · Handwriting representation

1 Introduction

The analysis of movement, as the analysis of gait or handwriting, is the core of many tools used for biometric [6,7,17,18,24] and diagnostic [2–4,20] purposes. That is because complex movements are the result of a learning process that is individual and neurodegenerative disorders, like Parkinson's and Alzheimer's disease, affect motor skill learning, execution and retention.

© Springer Nature Switzerland AG 2022
C. Carmona-Duarte et al. (Eds.): IGS 2021, LNCS 13424, pp. 203–216, 2022.
https://doi.org/10.1007/978-3-031-19745-1_15

Being able to infer the representations of movements acquired by learning and stored in the brain is of paramount importance because it allows to distinctively identify a person or to monitor the onset and the progression of neurodegenerative diseases.

The phenomenon named *motor equivalence* suggests that *"actions are encoded in the central nervous system in terms that are more abstract than commands to specific muscles"* [35]. This abstract representation is known as *motor program*, which has been also defined as *"a central representation of a sequence of motor actions"* [28]. Therefore, a motor program is an effector-independent representation of the movement that is made up of a sequence of target points that have to be reached in order to execute the desired movement. To a motor program may correspond more than one effector-dependent representation of the movement, each of which encodes the motor commands that will be delivered to the specific neuromuscular system recruited for the execution of the movement [14,25].

Different algorithms have been proposed for extracting the motor program from a trajectory, i.e. to identify within a handwriting movement the elementary movements, from here on named strokes, it is made up of [8,12,13,16,19]. Because variations in the writing conditions and in the psychophysical state of a subject influence the execution of a complex movement, we can observe differences in the motor programs extracted from different executions of the same trajectory. Differences can be observed in the number of extracted strokes, in the parameter values used for representing strokes and in the x-y position of target points.

We present and compare two algorithms for the extraction of motor programs from handwriting samples; one defines the position and the number of the target points from the analysis of the velocity profile, while the other finds the target points by looking at the variation of curvature along the trajectory. Because, by definition, a motor program is independent of the variability affecting different executions of the same drawing or word, we compared the two algorithms in terms of the number of strokes extracted from each sample. The desired outcome is the extraction of the same motor program from any repetition of the same learned movement.

The remaining of the paper is structured as follows: Sect. 2 describes the two algorithms and the theoretical framework within which they were conceived, Sect. 3 describes data collection and the experimental procedure, and it reports the results that are then discussed in Sect. 4. Eventually, Sect. 5 concludes the work by discussing further investigations of this preliminary work.

2   Method

2.1   Theoretical Overview

The repetition of a complex movement over time has the effect of creating a compact representation of the movement that, in the final stages of learning, is stored in the brain as a succession of target points that have to be reached.

The execution of a learned movement, i.e. the realization of a motor program, results from the interaction between brain areas, spinal cord networks, muscles and the proprioceptive receptors [21,27]. In a nutshell, to initiate the movement, the brain sends commands to recruit the muscles and to set the forces they have to exert on the bones they are connected to, while, during execution, the spinal cord modulates such commands depending on the information received by the proprioceptive receptors in order to keep the execution as close as possible to the learned one. The effects of those modulations are therefore the source of the observed variability, and they should not be considered as the results of commands stored in the motor plan.

The active role of the spinal cord in the control of movements became clear with studies on spinal cord plasticity and spinal stretch reflexes. Studies have shown that spinal cord plasticity contributes to the acquisition of motor skills, and to compensation for the peripheral and central changes caused by ageing, disease, and trauma [36]. More recently, it has been proved that spinal feedback pathway is able to integrate proprioceptive inputs from multiple muscles to produce efficient corrective responses that take advantage of musculoskeletal redundancy [34].

Thus, after a movement has been learned, i.e. when the subject executing the movement is no longer conscious of the elementary movements it is composed of, the variability observed in repeated executions may be ascribed to the neuromuscular system executing the movement. Extracting the motor program by observing the execution of a complex movement requires to be able to identify those corrective movements introduced on the fly by spinal cord networks.

In the next subsection, we introduce two algorithms for the extraction of motor programs, MPE and CMMPE. Both the algorithms adopt the lognormal representation of handwriting movements derived from the kinematic theory of rapid human movement [22]. Therefore, each elementary movement is characterized by a lognormal velocity profile and it is described in terms of command generation time, magnitude and direction of motion, response time and time delay of the neuromuscular system [23]. The two algorithms were designed starting from different but complementary findings in the field of motor control and, therefore, they differ in the way they seek movements embedded in the motor program.

MPE seeks for strokes by looking at the velocity profile of a sample. This choice follows from the experimental evidence that reaching movements show some stereotypical properties like a roughly straight path and, more importantly, a velocity profile with a dominant slightly asymmetric peak [15,23]. Therefore, MPE identifies strokes in a sample by positioning lognormal functions at the more significant peaks of the velocity profile.

CMMPE seeks for strokes by looking at the curvature variation along the trajectory of samples. Experimental studies have shown that neural activity in the primary motor cortex is related to movement direction that is uniquely predicted by the action of a population of motor cortical neurons [9]. Therefore, CMMPE seeks for strokes by detecting the points of the trajectory where there is the maximum variation of curvature because at those points the change of direction in the movement is evident and significant and, therefore, it is more plausible that it is the effect of a central command than of a corrective movement.

2.2 Motor Program Extraction

MPE. The Motor Program Extractor algorithm, hereinafter MPE, analyzes velocity profiles to recover the sequence of virtual target points the motor commands issued by the brain intended to reach. The fundamental idea behind this algorithm is that both the brain and spinal cord contribute to the final movement by generating elementary movements with a lognormal velocity profile. Movements commanded by brain areas are those encoded in the motor program, while the spinal cord contributes with fast corrective movements by integrating commands from brain areas and proprioceptive signals. Movements introduced by the spinal cord are generated when the ongoing movement is going far from the intended/planned movement. MPE extracts the motor program from one handwriting sample by detecting and discarding the corrective movements introduced by the spinal cord.

MPE adopts the same iterative procedure proposed by the RX0 algorithm [16] to extract elementary movements by the analysis of the velocity profile and models each elementary movement with the Sigma-Lognormal model [23]. At each iteration, the velocity profile of a handwriting sample is analyzed searching for peaks. A movement generated by the spinal cord should correspond to either a velocity peak whose amplitude is much smaller than the amplitudes of the velocity peaks related to movements encoded in the motor plan, or whose duration is shorter than the duration of the movements defined by the motor plan. Therefore, the amplitude and the duration of each peak are compared with two thresholds, denoted by V_{th} and T_{th}, respectively, and peaks whose amplitude or duration are lower than the respective threshold are ignored. A detailed description of the algorithm and its validation on a data set different by the one adopted in this paper is available at [19].

CMMPE. The Curvature Multiscale Motor Program Extractor, hereinafter CMMPE, analyzes curvature profiles to estimate the position of the virtual target points the motor commands issued by the brain intended to reach. The fundamental idea behind this algorithm is that the amount of time superimposition between two consecutive elementary movements regulates the smoothness, and therefore the curvature, of the trajectory. If the second elementary movement starts when the first one is ended, the virtual target is visible in the actual trajectory, while it disappears when the second movement starts before the end of the previous movement. The region of the trajectory where the maximum curvature variation is measurable defines the region external to the trajectory where the virtual target point may be located, as shown in Fig. 1.

CMMPE detects the points corresponding to the maximum curvature variation, from here on segmentation points, by exploiting an algorithm based on the

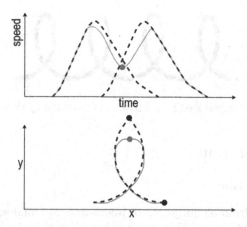

Fig. 1. Example of segmentation point (red dot) in a trace composed of two time-superimposed strokes (grey line). The dashed black line represents the strokes if no superimposition was applied, and the black dots are the virtual targets. (Color figure online)

concept of saliency introduced for modelling visual attention shift [5]. Following this approach, the trajectory represents the scene the system is looking at, and its curvature represents the feature whose saliency is estimated. Curvature is computed at different resolutions and then values at each scale are combined in order to estimate a saliency map S_{MAP}. Thus, the algorithm carries out a saliency-based multiscale analysis of the curvature profile and the values of the saliency map higher than a threshold S_{th} correspond to the segmentation points. The detection of segmentation points is much more invariant with respect to locally prominent but globally non-significant changes of curvature, which means it is able to filter the local variation of curvature introduced by corrective movements. The threshold S_{th} depends on the parameters w and α as defined by Eq. 1:

$$S_{th} = \text{average}(\text{moving\_mean}(S_{MAP}, w)) * \alpha \tag{1}$$

where w defines the length of the moving mean, while α modulates the mean saliency.

CMMPE assumes that a virtual target point is located along the line perpendicular to the tangent to the trajectory at the segmentation point. Even this algorithm models each elementary movement with the Sigma-Lognormal model but, differently from MPE and other algorithms proposed in the literature, it first analyses the trajectory to locate the position of a target point and then it computes the lognormal velocity profile related to the elementary movement that reaches the target point.

Fig. 2. Trajectory reproduced by each subject involved in the experimentation.

3   Experimentation

3.1   Data Collection

We collected data from 32 subjects, 18 males and 14 females, whose age ranges in the interval 13–63 years with a mean value of 34.40 and a standard deviation of 15.58. Participants volunteered to take part in the experiment and expressed their written informed consent to participate. We administered a questionnaire to each subject in order to define their level of education, health conditions and whether they use routinely drugs or other substances that are known to affect motor control.

Each subject wrote the handwriting pattern "llll", whose template is shown in Fig. 2, 10 times with his/her dominant hand and then 10 times with his/her non-dominant hand. This pattern has been adopted in many experiments on handwriting generation modelling [29,30,32] because it is reasonable to assume that its motor program has been already learned by the subjects involved in the experiments and it is complex enough to evaluate how motor variability and motor noise affect the execution of a planned motor program.

We collected samples drawn with both hands to verify our hypothesis that the number and the position of target points are less stable among different repetitions when movements are executed with non-dominant hands. That is because each subject will try to execute the trajectory by the non-dominant hand by reaching the sequence of target points encoded in the learned motor program even though the sequence of motor commands to control the new effector is not yet learned. As a consequence, a stronger intervention of spinal and supraspinal neural networks will be triggered and a greater variability among the samples, as well as among the extracted motor programs, will be evident.

Overall, we collected 320 handwriting samples drawn with dominant hands and as many samples drawn with the non-dominant hands. The handwriting samples were collected by using an ink-and-paper WACOM Bamboo Folio digitizing tablet with 200 Hz sampling rate. We developed a custom application to acquire and store each sample.

We adopted an ink-and-paper digitizing tablet to avoid unexpected proprioceptive feedback and the following corrective movements that may arise by using a stylus-and-screen digitizing tablet. In fact, it has been shown that handwriting is influenced by the lower friction of tablet surfaces in a way that subjects are required to additionally control handwriting movements [10].

3.2 Experimental Procedure

The experimentation aims at comparing the two algorithms in terms of the number of strokes, i.e. the number of virtual target points, extracted from the handwriting samples. This is because the handwriting samples produced by each subject should be the execution of the same motor program and, therefore, they should be made up of the same number of strokes.

Both MPE and CMMPE require to set a couple of parameters, (V_{th}, T_{th}) and (w, α), respectively. V_{th} and T_{th} define the amplitude and duration of a corrective movement generated by the spinal cord networks. w and α regulate the minimum variation of curvature that is considered as the effect of a new motor command issued by the brain instead of a corrective movement introduced by the spinal cord. In both cases, the parameters define the boundary between corrective and planned movements.

Studies in literature have shown that activity-dependent plasticity occurs in the spinal cord as well as in the brain [31, 36] and that spinal cord plasticity is important in the acquisition of motor behaviours throughout life [37]. For example, it has been shown that athletic training, such as that undertaken by ballet dancers, gradually alters spinal reflexes [37, 38]. Therefore, it is plausible to assume that the extent of corrective movements introduced by the spinal cord varies subject by subject.

Therefore, both for MPE and CMMPE, we tuned the parameters per each subject to characterize their personal spinal cord activity. In particular, starting from the assumption that executions of the pattern "llll" with the dominant hand are the actuation of the same motor program, we set the parameters at values that produced the minimal variation in terms of the number of extracted strokes from the ten repetitions. For both algorithms, we adopted a grid search approach to set the parameter values. For MPE, V_{th} was varied between 10% to 60% of the maximum velocity peak measured in the sample under analysis, T_{th} was varied between 20 ms and 90 ms because voluntary movements toward a target are usually executed in a time range that varies between ~350 ms and ~1200 ms, depending on the subject [33]. For CMMPE, w was varied between 1 and 5 and α between 0.6 and 1 with a step of 0.2. These two ranges were defined by a preliminary analysis carried out on another data set [18, 19].

Given a subject, the parameter values tuned on the samples drawn with the dominant hand are used to extract strokes from the ten samples executed with the non-dominant hand.

3.3 Results

Table 1 reports the mean number of strokes extracted by the two algorithms on the samples drawn with the dominant or non-dominant hand by the 32 subjects.

Figure 3 shows the distributions of the handwriting samples drawn with the dominant hand per number of strokes. We applied a two-sided Wilcoxon signed rank test to verify the null hypothesis that the difference between the distribution obtained with MPE and the one obtained with CMMPE has zero median. The

Table 1. Mean number of strokes (±standard deviation) per algorithm and per end-effector

	MPE	CMMPE
Dominant Hand	8.38 ± 0.62	8.03 ± 0.90
Non-dominant Hand	9.53 ± 1.75	9.10 ± 1.60

null hypothesis was rejected ($p\text{-}value = 2.43 * 10^{-10}$) and a right-tailed Wilcoxon signed rank test rejected the null hypothesis ($p\text{-}value = 1.23 * 10^{-10}$) in favour of the alternative hypothesis that the difference distribution has a median greater than 0, i.e. MPE extracts more strokes than CMMPE. Figure 4 shows that when the same sample is elaborated by the two algorithms the same number of strokes were extracted 221 times out of 320 ($\sim$69%). For 58 out of 320 samples ($\sim$18%) the motor programs extracted by MPE and CMMPE differ for one stroke.

Figure 5 shows the distributions of the handwriting samples drawn with non-dominant hands per number of strokes. We applied a two-sided Wilcoxon signed rank test to verify the null hypothesis that the difference between the distribution obtained with MPE and the one obtained with CMMPE has zero median. The null hypothesis was rejected ($p\text{-}value = 1.85 * 10^{-07}$) and a right-tailed Wilcoxon signed rank test rejected the null hypothesis ($p\text{-}value = 9.31 * 10^{-08}$) in favour of the alternative hypothesis that the difference distribution has a median greater than 0, i.e. MPE extracts more strokes than CMMPE also in this case. Figure 6 shows that when the same sample is elaborated by the two algorithms the same number of strokes were extracted 130 out of 320 times ($\sim$41%). For 110 out of 320 samples ($\sim$34%) the motor programs extracted by MPE and CMMPE differ for one stroke.

Eventually, we compared the distributions of strokes extracted by MPE and CMMPE subject by subject. Each distribution was computed over all the samples drawn by each subject, therefore including the samples drawn by the two end-effectors. We performed 32 two-sided Wilcoxon signed rank test at the 5% significance level and for 12 subjects the null hypothesis that the difference between the distribution obtained with MPE and the one obtained with CMMPE had zero median was rejected.

4   Discussions

Table 1, Fig. 3 and Fig. 5 show that motor programs extracted from samples drawn with non-dominant hands are made up of a greater number of strokes with respect to the motor programs extracted by the sample drawn by dominant hands. Moreover, there is a greater variability in the number of strokes extracted from the samples written with the non-dominant effector. Even though motor equivalence suggests that samples generated by both the effectors are the executions of the same motor program, we postulate that the greater variability we observed in the motor program extracted by samples written with non-dominant hands is an effect of motor learning.

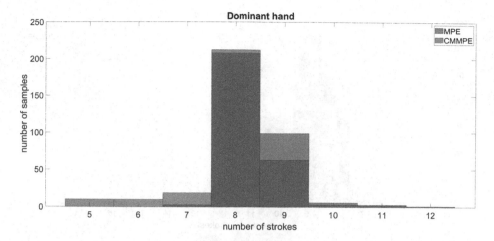

Fig. 3. Distribution of samples written with dominant hands per number of strokes.

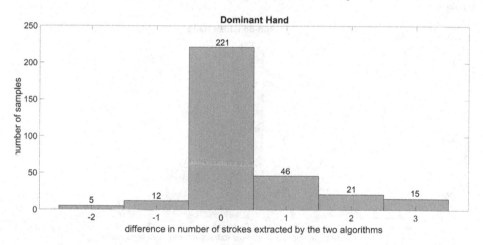

Fig. 4. Distribution of samples written with dominant hands per difference of strokes between MPE and CMMPE. The difference is computed with respect to the strokes extracted by CMMPE.

Subjects were not familiar with writing with their non-dominant effector and we hypothesize a motor learning process was triggered when they drew the desired trajectory with the new group of muscles. By limiting the maximum number of repetitions of the motor task with the non-dominant hand, we set the learning time equal to all the subjects even though different subjects may need a different time to learn a new motor task. In fact, it is known that the rate of motor learning is an individual feature and part of motor variability is an expression of the individual way each subject explores the motor command space [11]. It follows that, in the case of samples drawn by non-dominant hands,

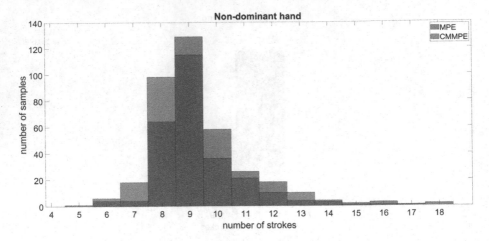

Fig. 5. Distribution of samples written with non-dominant hands per number of strokes.

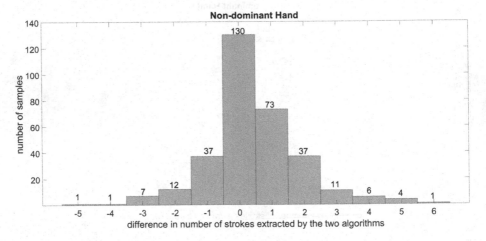

Fig. 6. Distribution of samples written with non-dominant hands per difference of strokes between MPE and CMMPE. The difference is computed with respect to the strokes extracted by CMMPE.

the correction of the ongoing movements was introduced only in part by the spinal cord but more significantly by supraspinal areas like the cerebellum, whose corrective actions differ from the ones executed by the spinal cord for latency, intensity and duration [1,26].

In order to take into account the individuality of learning and execution processes, both the algorithms were adjusted to each subject in a way that the variability in the number of strokes extracted from the samples drawn by the dominant hand was minimized. We analysed the selected parameters in order to verify if some values were more frequent than others.

For MPE, the most frequent couple of parameters, which was assigned to 14 out of 32 subjects, was ($V_{th} = 10\% * v_{peak}, T_{th} = 20\,\text{ms}$). The threshold $T_{th} = 20$ ms was selected for 30 out of 32 subjects while $T_{th} = 70\,\text{ms}$ and $T_{th} = 80$ ms were selected for the remaining 2 subjects. Values equal to or lower than $30\% * v_{peak}$ were assigned to V_{th} for 18 subjects. Overall, this analysis confirms that corrective movements are characterized by a short duration and a small amplitude for the majority of the subjects.

For CMMPE, the most frequent couple of parameters, which was assigned to 12 out of 32 subjects, was ($w = 3, \alpha = 0.6$). The parameter value $\alpha = 0.6$ was selected for 31 out of 32 subjects while $\alpha = 0.8$ was selected for the remaining subject. When $\alpha = 0.6$, a value equal to or lower than 4 was assigned to the parameter w for 22 subjects. Overall, this analysis suggests that the parameter α is roughly independent of the subject's motor skills.

Eventually, the statistical analysis presented in the previous section shows that CMMPE extracts fewer strokes than MPE, independently of the end-effector used to draw the samples. Nevertheless, the two algorithms extracted the same number of strokes from ∼55% of samples (221 drawn with dominant hands and 130 with non-dominant ones) and they had a similar behaviour over the samples produced by 20 subjects. Overall, these results suggest that both the algorithms are modelling the same phenomena, i.e. the introduction of corrective movements to keep the ongoing movement close to the desired one, from a different perspective, and that CMMPE is more robust than MPE to noise or non-modelled motor variability that is an expression of the intervention of supraspinal centres.

These findings are in line with the results obtained by the algorithm IDeLog [8], which is used for the detection of the strokes that allow a high-fidelity reproduction of handwriting samples in terms of velocity and trajectory profiles. So, differently from MPE and CMMPE, it captures also small variations in velocity and trajectory because the aim is to perfectly reproduce a single sample rather than to find the general model behind many repetitions of the same movement. IDeLog was able to improve the reconstruction of a sample by analysing the velocity profile in search of target points and then exploiting the information about the curvature and the location of segmentation points in order to move the target points and improve the trajectory reconstruction.

5   Conclusions

We have proposed and compared two algorithms, MPE and CMMPE, that extract the motor program from the analysis of handwriting samples. Both the algorithms discriminate between movements that are embedded in the motor program stored in the brain and other movements that are generated in reaction to proprioceptive feedback. MPE discriminates between the two classes of movements by analysing the velocity profile of a sample and looking for peaks that correspond to corrective movements introduced by the spinal cord, while CMMPE detects the movements encoded in the motor program by observing the curvature profile with a multiscale approach.

By keeping in mind the experimental studies of Lashley and Raibert that led to the discovery of the motor equivalence phenomenon, we asked the participants to draw a trajectory with their dominant and non-dominant hands. Both the algorithms showed a greater variability in the number of extracted strokes when they analysed the samples written with non-dominant hands. This greater variability could be explained by taking into account that subjects were writing with their non-dominant hand for the first time and therefore our experiment triggered the cerebellar mechanisms devoted to learning a new motor skill. These considerations suggest organising data collection in different sessions so that in the last session the learning mechanism is off.

The experimental results have shown that both the approaches are able to extract the same number of strokes from different executions of the same drawing performed by a subject. Moreover, the number of strokes extracted by MPE is equal to the number of strokes extracted by CMMPE for ~55% of the handwriting samples. CMMPE is resulted to be more robust to noise or non-modelled motor variability caused by the motor learning process triggered during the experimental session with non-dominant hands.

Our future investigations will be aimed at evaluating as the performance of each algorithm varies as the learning process progresses. We will set up a new data collection campaign organized in different sessions spanned over a longer period of time so that we will be able to capture the acquisition in the long term memory of the motor commands used to execute a motor plan with the non-dominant hand. Eventually, we plan to combine in a new algorithm the two approaches adopted by MPE and CMMPE so that the curvature will be analyzed to detect the position of the target points and the velocity will be analyzed to infer the parameters of the velocity profile of each elementary movement between two target points.

References

1. Alstermark, B., Isa, T.: Circuits for skilled reaching and grasping. Annu. Rev. Neurosci. **35**, 559–578 (2012)
2. Chen, S., Lach, J., Lo, B., Yang, G.Z.: Toward pervasive gait analysis with wearable sensors: a systematic review. IEEE J. Biomed. Health Inform. **20**(6), 1521–1537 (2016)
3. Cilia, N.D., De Gregorio, G., De Stefano, C., Fontanella, F., Marcelli, A., Parziale, A.: Diagnosing alzheimer's disease from on-line handwriting: a novel dataset and performance benchmarking. Eng. Appl. Artif. Intell. **111**, 104822 (2022). https://doi.org/10.1016/j.engappai.2022.104822
4. De Stefano, C., Fontanella, F., Impedovo, D., Pirlo, G., di Freca, A.S.: Handwriting analysis to support neurodegenerative diseases diagnosis: a review. Pattern Recogn. Lett. **121**, 37–45 (2019)
5. De Stefano, C., Guadagno, G., Marcelli, A.: A saliency-based segmentation method for online cursive handwriting. Int. J. Pattern Recognit. Artif. Intell. **18**(07), 1139–1156 (2004)

6. Diaz, M., Ferrer, M.A., Parziale, A., Marcelli, A.: Recovering western on-line signatures from image-based specimens. In: 2017 14th IAPR International Conference on Document Analysis and Recognition (ICDAR), vol. 1, pp. 1204–1209. IEEE (2017)
7. Faundez-Zanuy, M., Fierrez, J., Ferrer, M.A., Diaz, M., Tolosana, R., Plamondon, R.: Handwriting biometrics: applications and future trends in e-security and e-health. Cogn. Comput. **12**(5), 940–953 (2020). https://doi.org/10.1007/s12559-020-09755-z
8. Ferrer, M.A., Diaz, M., Carmona-Duarte, C., Plamondon, R.: iDeLog: iterative dual spatial and kinematic extraction of sigma-lognormal parameters. IEEE Trans. Pattern Anal. Mach. Intell. **42**(1), 114–125 (2018)
9. Georgopoulos, A.P., Schwartz, A.B., Kettner, R.E.: Neuronal population coding of movement direction. Science **233**(4771), 1416–1419 (1986)
10. Gerth, S., et al.: Is handwriting performance affected by the writing surface? comparing preschoolers', second graders', and adults' writing performance on a tablet vs. paper. Front. Psychol. **7**, 1308 (2016)
11. Herzfeld, D.J., Shadmehr, R.: Motor variability is not noise, but grist for the learning mill. Nat. Neurosci. **17**(2), 149–150 (2014)
12. Huang, J., Zhang, Z.: A novel sigma-lognormal parameter extractor for online signatures. In: Lladós, J., Lopresti, D., Uchida, S. (eds.) ICDAR 2021. LNCS, vol. 12823, pp. 459–473. Springer, Cham (2021). https://doi.org/10.1007/978-3-030-86334-0_30
13. Liu, M., Guo, X., Wang, G.: Stroke parameters identification algorithm in handwriting movements analysis by synthesis. IEEE J. Biomed. Health Inform. **19**(1), 317–324 (2014)
14. Marcelli, A., Parziale, A., Senatore, R.: Some observations on handwriting from a motor learning perspective. In: AFHA, vol. 1022, pp. 6–10. Citeseer (2013)
15. Morasso, P.: Spatial control of arm movements. Exp. Brain Res. **42**(2), 223–227 (1981). https://doi.org/10.1007/BF00236911
16. O'Reilly, C., Plamondon, R.: Development of a sigma-lognormal representation for on-line signatures. Pattern Recogn. **42**(12), 3324–3337 (2009)
17. Parziale, A., Carmona-Duarte, C., Ferrer, M.A., Marcelli, A.: 2D vs 3D online writer identification: a comparative study. In: Lladós, J., Lopresti, D., Uchida, S. (eds.) ICDAR 2021. LNCS, vol. 12823, pp. 307–321. Springer, Cham (2021). https://doi.org/10.1007/978-3-030-86334-0_20
18. Parziale, A., Diaz, M., Ferrer, M.A., Marcelli, A.: SM-DTW: stability modulated dynamic time warping for signature verification. Pattern Recogn. Lett. **121**, 113–122 (2019)
19. Parziale, A., Parisi, R., Marcelli, A.: Extracting the motor program of handwriting from its lognormal representation. In: The Lognormality Principle and its Applications in E-security, E-learning And E-health, pp. 289–308. World Scientific (2021)
20. Parziale, A., Senatore, R., Della Cioppa, A., Marcelli, A.: Cartesian genetic programming for diagnosis of Parkinson disease through handwriting analysis: performance vs. interpretability issues. Artif. Intell. Med. **111**, 101984 (2021)
21. Parziale, A., Senatore, R., Marcelli, A.: Exploring speed-accuracy tradeoff in reaching movements: a neurocomputational model. Neural Comput. Appl. **32**(17), 13377–13403 (2020). https://doi.org/10.1007/s00521-019-04690-z
22. Plamondon, R.: A kinematic theory of rapid human movements: part i. movement representation and generation. Biol. Cybern. **72**(4), 295–307 (1995)
23. Plamondon, R., Djioua, M.: A multi-level representation paradigm for handwriting stroke generation. Hum. Mov. Sci. **25**(4–5), 586–607 (2006)

24. Prakash, C., Kumar, R., Mittal, N.: Recent developments in human gait research: parameters, approaches, applications, machine learning techniques, datasets and challenges. Artif. Intell. Rev. **49**(1), 1–40 (2018). https://doi.org/10.1007/s10462-016-9514-6
25. Raibert, M.H.: Motor control and learning by the state space model. Ph.D. thesis, Massachusetts Institute of Technology (1977)
26. Reschechtko, S., Pruszynski, J.A.: Stretch reflexes. Curr. Biol. **30**(18), R1025–R1030 (2020)
27. Senatore, R., Marcelli, A.: A neural scheme for procedural motor learning of handwriting. In: 2012 International Conference on Frontiers in Handwriting Recognition, pp. 659–664. IEEE (2012)
28. Summers, J.J., Anson, J.G.: Current status of the motor program: revisited. Hum. Mov. Sci. **28**(5), 566–577 (2009)
29. Tucha, O., et al.: Kinematic analysis of dopaminergic effects on skilled handwriting movements in Parkinson's disease. J. Neural Transm. **113**(5), 609–623 (2006). https://doi.org/10.1007/s00702-005-0346-9
30. Ünlü, A., Brause, R., Krakow, K.: Handwriting analysis for diagnosis and prognosis of Parkinson's disease. In: Maglaveras, N., Chouvarda, I., Koutkias, V., Brause, R. (eds.) ISBMDA 2006. LNCS, vol. 4345, pp. 441–450. Springer, Heidelberg (2006). https://doi.org/10.1007/11946465_40
31. Vahdat, S., Lungu, O., Cohen-Adad, J., Marchand-Pauvert, V., Benali, H., Doyon, J.: Simultaneous brain-cervical cord FMRI reveals intrinsic spinal cord plasticity during motor sequence learning. PLoS Biol. **13**(6), e1002186 (2015)
32. Van Gemmert, A.W., Teulings, H.L., Stelmach, G.E.: Parkinsonian patients reduce their stroke size with increased processing demands. Brain Cogn. **47**(3), 504–512 (2001)
33. Wang, C., Xiao, Y., Burdet, E., Gordon, J., Schweighofer, N.: The duration of reaching movement is longer than predicted by minimum variance. J. Neurophysiol. **116**(5), 2342–2345 (2016)
34. Weiler, J., Gribble, P.L., Pruszynski, J.A.: Spinal stretch reflexes support efficient hand control. Nat. Neurosci. **22**(4), 529–533 (2019)
35. Wing, A.M.: Motor control: mechanisms of motor equivalence in handwriting. Curr. Biol. **10**(6), R245–R248 (2000)
36. Wolpaw, J.R.: The education and re-education of the spinal cord. Prog. Brain Res. **157**, 261–399 (2006)
37. Wolpaw, J.R.: The negotiated equilibrium model of spinal cord function. J. Physiol. **596**(16), 3469–3491 (2018)
38. Wolpaw, J.R., Tennissen, A.M.: Activity-dependent spinal cord plasticity in health and disease. Annu. Rev. Neurosci. **24**(1), 807–843 (2001)

The RPM3D Project: 3D Kinematics for Remote Patient Monitoring

Alicia Fornés[1], Asma Bensalah[1], Cristina Carmona-Duarte[2],
Jialuo Chen[1], Miguel A. Ferrer[2], Andreas Fischer[3]([✉]), Josep Lladós[1],
Cristina Martín[4,5], Eloy Opisso[4,5], Réjean Plamondon[4,5],
Anna Scius-Bertrand[3], and Josep Maria Tormos[4,5]

[1] Computer Vision Center, Computer Science Department,
Universitat Autònoma de Barcelona, Barcelona, Spain
{aformes,abensalah,jchen,josep}@cvc.uab.es
[2] Universidad de Las Palmas de Gran Canaria, Municipality of Las Palmas, Spain
{cristina.carmona,miguelangel.ferrer}@ulpgc.es
[3] Institute of Complex Systems, University of Applied Sciences and Arts Western
Switzerland, Fribourg, Switzerland
andreas.fischer@unifr.ch, Anna.Scius-Bertrand@hefr.ch
[4] Institut Guttmann, Neurorehabilitation Institute,
Camí de Can s/n, 08916 Badalona, Spain
{cmartin, eopisso, jmtormos}@guttmann.com
[5] Département de Génie Électrique, Polytechnique Montréal, Montréal, Canada
rejean.plamondon@polymtl.ca

Abstract. This project explores the feasibility of remote patient monitoring based on the analysis of 3D movements captured with smartwatches. We base our analysis on the Kinematic Theory of Rapid Human Movement. We have validated our research in a real case scenario for stroke rehabilitation at the Guttmann Institute (https://www.guttmann.com/en/) (neurorehabilitation hospital), showing promising results. Our work could have a great impact in remote healthcare applications, improving the medical efficiency and reducing the healthcare costs. Future steps include more clinical validation, developing multimodal analysis architectures (analysing data from sensors, images, audio, etc.), and exploring the application of our technology to monitor other neurodegenerative diseases.

Keywords: Healthcare applications · Kinematic Theory of Rapid Human Movements · Human activity recognition · Stroke rehabilitation · 3D kinematics

---

Supported by the ATTRACT project funded by the EC under Grant Agreement 777222.

1   Introduction

Stroke, defined as the lack of blood flow or bleeding in the brain [1], is the second leading cause of death in Europe. Moreover, experts estimate that strokes will rise dramatically in the next 20 years due to an ageing population[1]. Moreover, 60% of the survivors have different degrees of disability, with a socio-economic impact of the first magnitude for the patient [2,3], their environment, the health system and the society in general [4,5]. Therefore, in addition to stroke prevention, it is crucial to find personalized and suitable treatments during stroke rehabilitation, the most important phase of stroke survivors.

The Kinematic Theory of Rapid Human Movement [6–8] provides a mathematical description of the movements made by individuals, reflecting the behaviour of their neuromuscular system. It has demonstrated a great potential for analysing fingers, hand, eye, head, trunk and arm movements as well as speech. According to the lognormal principle, the motor learning process and its deterioration with aging can be followed, allowing to monitor neuromuscular diseases in terms of the alteration of the ideal parameters. O'Reilly et al. [9] showed that brain stroke risk factors can be associated with the deterioration of many cognitive and psychomotor characteristics. The psychomotor tests demonstrated that the features extracted from the kinematic motion analysis of handwriting were successfully correlated with risk factors (e.g. obesity, diabetes, hypertension, etc.).

However, the use of the Kinematic Theory in monitoring rehabilitation processes is a challenge: it requires to collect and to analyse the movement data using robust, efficient and task oriented lognormal parameter extraction algorithms. These constraints must be removed to develop a universal tool for brain stroke treatments and rehabilitation. Stroke patients, especially in early stages of the recovery treatment, cannot write using a stylus on a tablet device, so most of the analysis of their motor skills improvement is based on simple hands or arms movements.

Recently, inertial and magnetic sensors, including accelerometers, gyroscopes and magnetometers, have been incorporated into wearables, such as smartbands, to assess, among others, the biomechanics of sports performance. These devices are increasingly popular, which make us propose the hand/arm movements as a source to extract the lognormal patterns. Moreover, these devices are not intrusive, so they could be used for continuous remote patient monitoring (RPM) in the rehabilitation stages and during the routine daily life of patients, improving the medical efficiency and reducing the healthcare costs.

For the above mentioned reasons, we aim to explore the use of the Kinematic Theory of Rapid Human Movements for analysing continuous 3D movements captured with smartwatches (a worldwide affordable and non-intrusive technology), and thus, to provide an objective estimator of the improvement of the patients' motor abilities in stroke rehabilitation.

---

[1] The Burden of Stroke in Europe: http://www.strokeeurope.eu/.

This paper describes the RPM3D project[2] [10], which aims to make a step forward towards the removal of such constraints to develop a universal tool for monitoring rehabilitation processes. Indeed, such a tool can have a great impact in remote health care tasks in general. The integration of an analytic tool in a consumer and affordable technology such as smartwatches (instead of high-end clinical devices) could be used for continuous remote patient monitoring in the rehabilitation stages of different neuromuscular diseases, improving the medical efficiency and reducing the healthcare costs.

The overview of our approach is shown in Fig. 1. The main project results are the following:

- We have developed a smartwatch application to record data from the inertial sensors of smartwatches (concretely, the Apple Watch).
- We have proposed a model to segment and classify the relevant gestures in continuous 3D movements for their posterior analysis.
- We have adapted the parameter extraction algorithms of the kinematic model to these relevant 3D movements captured with the smartwatch.
- We have defined the experimental protocol and validated our research in a real case scenario for stroke rehabilitation at the Guttmann Institute (neurorehabilitation hospital).

The innovation potential of this project is the provision of a new tool to obtain significant measures of the human movement of patients of brain strokes in the rehabilitation phase using wearable devices such as smartwatches. Conveniently calibrated, this tool can be seen as a *thermometer* of the human neuromotor system, and with the appropriate interpretation (according to the correlation with the clinical indicators), medical doctors will be able to make decisions on the rehabilitation prescription and treatment of patients.

The rest of the paper is organized as follows. In Sect. 2, we overview the state of the art. Next, in Sect. 3, we describe the application protocol and the capturing of data from the smartwatches. Section 4 is devoted to the recognition of movements, whereas Sect. 5 describes the kinematic analysis performed. Section 6 is devoted to the conclusions and future work.

2   State of the Art

Assessing the physical condition in rehabilitation scenarios is challenging because it involves Human Activity Recognition (HAR) [11] and kinematic analysis.

HAR methods must deal with intraclass variability and interclass similarities [12,13]. Also, the detection of target (relevant) movements is difficult due to the diversity of non-target movements. In continuous time series data, the challenge is to detect and segment those subsequences (target movements) so that they can be properly analysed by the kinematic model. This is especially difficult when the movements are non-repetitive and that is why a major part of

---

[2] http://dag.cvc.uab.es/patientmonitoring/.

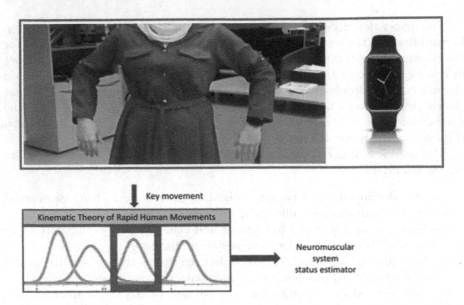

Fig. 1. Overview of the pipeline.

activity recognition works deal only with repetitive(periodic) movements such as: walking [14], stair ascent or descent [15], running, sport exercises [16].

HAR is about seeking high-level knowledge that describes human activities, ergo HAR benefited broadly from deep learning since this latter one can provide automatic feature extraction [17–19].

At the same time, traditional machine learning like Support Vector Machines (SVMs) [20,21], K-Nearest-Neighbours (KNNs) [22,23] still provide an efficient accurate solution for HAR tasks due to the fact that they perform better in few data problems which is the case of most HAR tasks that suffer from data scarce.

As mentioned in the introduction, the Kinematic Theory of Rapid Human Movement [24] has demonstrated a great potential for monitoring neuromuscular diseases, but it requires robust algorithms to estimate the model parameters with an excellent precision for a meaningful neuromuscular analysis. So far, most algorithms (Idelog [25] and Robust XZERO [26,27]) have mainly focused on 1D and 2D movements in a controlled scenario, e.g. pen movements on a tablet computer. This constraint makes the approach unrealistic for stroke rehabilitation. Stroke patients have severe mobility limitations, especially in early stages, so the analysis of their motor skills improvement is based on simple hands or arms movements. Thus, the recently proposed 3D algorithm [28] must be adapted to continuous movements in unconstrained scenarios (closer to real use cases). Finally, the hardware is an extra difficulty, because the smartwatch could be less accurate than clinical devices.

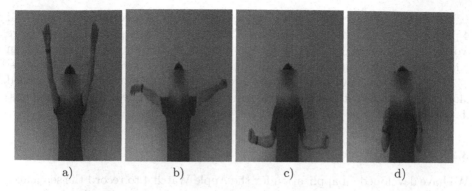

Fig. 2. Target movements. a) Movement 1; b) Movement 2; c) Movement 3; d) Movement 4.

In summary, the challenges are the following:

- The use of sensors from consumer devices instead of clinical devices, which can decrease the quality of the data for the application of the kinematic model.
- The extraction of the model parameters from the continuous 3D movement sequences for their posterior analysis.
- The accurate detection, segmentation and analysis of the target movements in uncontrolled scenarios.

3   Application Protocol and Data Capturing

Next, we describe the application protocol and the recorded movements.

3.1   Application Protocol

We have designed an upper-limb assessment pipeline inspired by the Fugl-Meyer Assessment scale, an index to assess the sensorimotor impairment in stroke patients. Concretely, we have defined four target (non-repetitive) movements (see Fig. 2), based on the following joint movements:

1. Shoulder extension/flexion
2. Shoulder adduction/abduction
3. External/internal shoulder rotation
4. Elbow flexion/extension

We have recorded these movements in two scenarios:

- L1 is a constrained scenario which consists in performing the same target movement in a sequence, but alternating the arm (left, right or both).
- L2 is an unconstrained scenario, where target movements appear inside longer sequences that include non-target movements (e.g. common daily life activities like eating, pouring water into a glass, brushing your teeth, scratching the ear, etc.).

As a proof of concept, we have recorded data from 25 healthy individuals and 4 patients from Guttmann Institute. Out of the 25 healthy individuals, 48% are women and 52% are men. While for the patient population, there is one woman and 3 men. Healthy and patient individuals' age range between 20 and 60 years.

The users wear two watches, one in each wrist. Patients data was recorded along four sessions with an interval of one to two weeks, while healthy individuals' data was recorded in one session.

3.2   Data Capturing

We have developed an application for the Apple Watch 4 to record the sequences of movements, as shown in Fig. 1. The user-generated acceleration (without gravity) for all three axes of the device, unbiased gyroscope (rotation rate), magnetometer, altitude (Euler angles) and temporal information data have been recorded in the watch's internal memory 100 Hz sampling rate.

The two watches are synchronised thanks to an audio signal. Afterwards, the data is transmitted to the mobile phone and the cloud service. Finally, the signal is **preprocessed** to minimize the sensor drift, which often leads to inaccurate measures and larger accumulated error.

4   Human Activity Recognition

We have used the Euler angles and the linear acceleration. To detect the target movements in the unconstrained scenario L2, we explored two segmentation options:

1. Segmenting the complete sequence using non-overlapping sliding windows (namely action recognition).
2. Picking the positive peaks in the signal as candidates to be relevant movements (namely gesture spotting).

We have also explored two classification methods. First, SVMs, a machine learning approach typically used in HAR, together with the following feature vector set: the mean, the minimum, the maximum and the standard variation of the window. Second, Convolutional Neural Networks (CNN), a deep learning model in which the input is the linear acceleration signal instead of a feature vector set. More details can be found at [29].

As shown in Table 1, action recognition is preferable. In healthy individuals, the SVM classifier obtains better results (84% in L1 and 61% in L2) than the CNN one (65% in L1 and 59% in L2) because the CNN is a data hungry method. Concerning gesture classification, the results by the two classifiers are similar. In patients, the accuracy in the unhealthy body part decreases (56% in L1 and 41% in L2) in comparison with their healthy side (84,5% in L1 and 61% in L2), because these movements are less accurate due to their loss of motor function.

Table 1. HAR classification and spotting results

Scenario	Healthy individuals				Patients	
	Action recognition		Gesture spotting		Action recognition	Gesture spotting
	SVM	CNN	SVM	CNN	SVM	SVM
L1	84%	65%	55%	60%	56%	41%
L2	61%	59%	51%	53%	41%	35%

5 Kinematic Analysis

The Kinematic Theory of Rapid Human Movements describes the resulting speed of a neuromuscular system action as a lognormal function [6–8]. To analyse the 3D movements captured by smartwatches, we utilize a recently proposed 3D extension of the Sigma-Lognormal model [28] to decompose observed 3D movements into sequences of elementary movements with lognormal speed. There are several model parameters that can be analysed with a view to the patients' motor abilities.

Here, we focus on the signal-to-noise-ratio (SNR) between the observed trajectory of the smartwatch and the reconstructed trajectory using the analytical model. A high SNR indicates a high model quality, i.e. a good representation of the 3D movement. Furthermore, healthy subjects tend to achieve a higher SNR than patients with motor control problems [24].

Table 2. Kinematic analysis mean standard deviation

	Healthy individuals	Patients
Samples	649	126
Duration [s]	4.1 ± 1.0	4.9 ± 0.8
Number of lognormals	17.3 ± 4.7	17.6 ± 4.5
SNR [dB]	22.2 ± 2.8	21.3 ± 2.1

Table 2 and Fig. 3 present the first results of our kinematic analysis, comparing 649 movements from 25 healthy individuals with 126 movements from 4 patients. In both cases an excellent SNR is achieved, indicating that the 3D Sigma-Lognormal model is suitable for analysing the smartwatch movements. Furthermore, we observe that the patients needed more time to execute the movements, more lognormals were needed to model the patients' movements, and a lower SNR was achieved. The difference in SNR is statistically significant (Mann-Whitney U test, $p < 0.0001$). These observations are consistent with the lognormality principle [28] and encourage a more detailed kinematic analysis of the patients' motor abilities based on the Kinematic Theory.

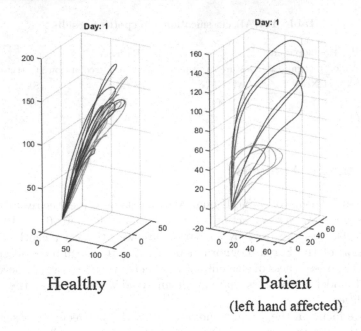

Healthy   Patient
                          (left hand affected)

Fig. 3. Kinematic analysis results.

6   Conclusion and Future Steps

In this paper, we have presented the RPM3D project, which aims to ease the monitoring of patients during the neurorehabilitation stages.

In the future, we plan to focus on the continuous and remote monitoring of the patients' neuromotor status. Concretely:

- We will to perform more clinical validation through an exhaustive analysis of the correspondence between the kinematic analysis and the clinicians' estimations. We will also continue the comparative analysis between healthy users and patients.
- We will explore the use of other lower-cost wearables (e.g. smarbands) and also, the possibility to combine the sensor data with video images or speech. Also, we would like to recognize functional (purposeful) movements to determine the degree of integration of the affected side of the body in the patients' daily life actions.
- We will explore the adaptation of our approach for monitoring patients suffering from Multiple Sclerosis or Parkinson diseases, the ageing effects in elderly people, the effects of medication in clinical trials, etc.

Acknowledgement. This work has been partially supported by the Spanish project RTI2018-095645-B-C21, the CERCA Program/Generalitat de Catalunya and the FI fellowship AGAUR 2020 FI-SDUR 00497 (with the support of the Secretaria d'Universitats i Recerca of the Generalitat de Catalunya and the Fons Social Europeu).

References

1. Coupland, A.P., Thapar, A., Qureshi, M.I., Jenkins, H., Davies, A.H.: The definition of stroke. J. Roy. Soc. Med. **110**(1), 9–12 (2017)
2. Majersik, J., Woo, D.: The enormous financial impact of stroke disability. Neurology **94**(9), 377–378 (2020). 2 cites
3. Rajsic, S., et al.: Economic burden of stroke: a systematic review on post-stroke care. Eur. J. Health Econ. **20**(1), 107–134 (2018). https://doi.org/10.1007/s10198-018-0984-0
4. Bartoli, F., Di Brita, C., Crocamo, C., Clerici, M., Carrà, G.: Early post-stroke depression and mortality: meta-analysis and meta-regression. Front. Psychiatry **9**, 530 (2018)
5. Hussein, A., Idris, I., Abbasher, M., Abbashar, H., Mohamed Ahmed Abbasher, K.: Post stroke depression. J. Neurol. Sci. **405**, 70 (2019). Abstracts from the World Congress of Neurology (WCN 2019)
6. Plamondon, R.: A kinematic theory of rapid human movements: part I. Movement representation and generation. Biol. Cybern. **72**(4), 295–307 (1995). https://doi.org/10.1007/BF00202785
7. Plamondon, R.: A kinematic theory of rapid human movements: part II. Movement time and control. Biol. Cybern. **72**(4), 309–320 (1995). https://doi.org/10.1007/BF00202786
8. Plamondon, R.: A kinematic theory of rapid human movements: part III. Kinetic outcomes. Biol. Cybern. **78**(2), 133–145 (1998). https://doi.org/10.1007/s004220050420
9. O'Reilly, C., Plamondon, R., Lebrun, L.-H.: Linking brain stroke risk factors to human movement features for the development of preventive tools. Front. Aging Neurosci. **6**, 150 (2014)
10. Fornés, A., et al.: Exploring the 3D kinematics for brain stroke rehabilitation. In: Plamondon, R., Marcelli, A., Ferrer, M.Á. (eds.) The Lognormality Principle and Its Applications in e-Security, e-Learning and e-Health, pp. 349–352. World Scientific Publishing (2020)
11. Mahbub, U., Ahad, M.A.R.: Advances in human action, activity and gesture recognition. Pattern Recogn. Lett. **155**, 186–190 (2022)
12. Akila, K., Chitrakala, S.: An efficient method to resolve intraclass variability using highly refined hog description model for human action recognition. Concurr. Comput. Pract. Exp. **31**(12), e4856 (2018)
13. Alharbi, F., Ouarbya, L., Ward, J.A.: Comparing sampling strategies for tackling imbalanced data in human activity recognition. Sensors **22**(4), 1373–1373 (2022)
14. Nan, Y., Lovell, N., Wang, K., Delbaere, K., van Schooten, K.: Deep learning for activity recognition in older people using a pocket-worn smartphone. Sensors **20**, 7195 (2020)
15. Semwal, V.B., Gupta, A., Lalwani, P.: An optimized hybrid deep learning model using ensemble learning approach for human walking activities recognition. J. Supercomput. **77**(11), 12256–12279 (2021). https://doi.org/10.1007/s11227-021-03768-7. 10 cites
16. Margarito, J., Helaoui, R., Bianchi, A.M., Sartor, F., Bonomi, A.G.: User-independent recognition of sports activities from a single wrist-worn accelerometer: a template-matching-based approach. IEEE Trans. Biomed. Eng. **63**(4), 788–796 (2016)

17. Straczkiewicz, M., James, P., Onnela, J.: A systematic review of smartphone-based human activity recognition methods for health research. NPJ Digit. Med. **4**(1), 1–15 (2021). 6 cites
18. Hernández, N., Lundström, J., Favela, J., McChesney, I., Arnrich, B.: Literature review on transfer learning for human activity recognition using mobile and wearable devices with environmental technology. SN Comput. Sci. **1** (2020). https://doi.org/10.1007/s42979-020-0070-4. 21 cites
19. Wu, L.-F., Wang, Q., Jian, M., Qiao, Yu., Zhao, B.-X.: A comprehensive review of group activity recognition in videos. Int. J. Autom. Comput. **18**(3), 334–350 (2021). https://doi.org/10.1007/s11633-020-1258-8. 8 cites
20. Chen, Z., Zhu, Q., Soh, Y.C., Zhang, L.: Robust human activity recognition using smartphone sensors via CT-PCA and online SVM. IEEE Trans. Ind. Inform. **13**, 3070–3080 (2017)
21. Chathuramali, K.G.M., Rodrigo, R.: Faster human activity recognition with SVM. In: International Conference on Advances in ICT for Emerging Regions (ICTer2012), pp. 197–203 (2012)
22. Liu, Z., Li, S., Hao, J., Jingfeng, H., Pan, M.: An efficient and fast model reduced kernel KNN for human activity recognition. J. Adv. Transp. **1–9**, 2021 (2021)
23. Ferreira, P.J.S., Cardoso, J.M.P., Mendes-Moreira, J.: kNN prototyping schemes for embedded human activity recognition with online learning. Computers **9**, 96 (2020)
24. Plamondon, R., O'Reilly, C., Rémi, C., Duval, T.: The lognormal handwriter: learning, performing, and declining. Front. Psychol. **4**, 945 (2013)
25. Ferrer, M.A., Diaz, M., Carmona-Duarte, C., Plamondon, R.: iDeLog: iterative dual spatial and kinematic extraction of sigma-lognormal parameters. IEEE Trans. Pattern Anal. Mach. Intell. **42**(1), 114–125 (2020)
26. O'Reilly, C., Plamondon, R.: Development of a sigma-lognormal representation for on-line signatures. Pattern Recogn. **42**(12), 3324–3337 (2009). New Frontiers in Handwriting Recognition
27. Djioua, M., Plamondon, R.: A new algorithm and system for the extraction of delta-lognormal parameters (2008)
28. Fischer, A., Schindler, R., Bouillon, M., Plamondon, R.: Modeling 3D movements with the kinematic theory of rapid human movements, pp. 327–342 (2021)
29. Bensalah, A., Chen, J., Fornés, A., Carmona-Duarte, C., Lladós, J., Ferrer, M.Á.: Towards stroke patients' upper-limb automatic motor assessment using smartwatches. In: Del Bimbo, A., et al. (eds.) ICPR 2021. LNCS, vol. 12661, pp. 476–489. Springer, Cham (2021). https://doi.org/10.1007/978-3-030-68763-2_36

Age Reduces Motor Asymmetry in a Graphic Task

Deborah M. Watson[1], Zhujun Pan[1(✉)] (iD), Qun Fang[1,2], Arend Van Gemmert[3] (iD), and Christopher Aiken[4] (iD)

[1] Mississippi State University, Starkville, Mississippi State, MS 39762, USA
zp147@msstate.edu
[2] Qingdao University, Qingdao 266071, SD, China
[3] Louisiana State University, Baton Rouge, LA 70803, USA
[4] New Mexico State University, Las Cruces, NM 88003, USA

Abstract. The purpose of the present study was to compare motor asymmetry between older and younger adults performing a graphic task. Thirty-four right-handed older and 38 younger adults drew continuous cursive "l" loops on a digitizer tablet using their right and left hand, respectively, aimed to assess age-related hand asymmetry differences in the performance of movements. Primary dependent variables were mean velocity, peak velocity, stroke size, and the ratio of the duration to decelerate to the duration of the overall movement time (RDP). A 2-way mixed-design ANOVA with age-group as the between factor (young and old) and hand (left and right) as the within factor was conducted. The results showed a significant age-by-hand interaction for mean velocity ($p = .012$) and peak velocity ($p < .001$), supporting decreased asymmetry when aging after young adulthood. Further analysis revealed a greater decline in the dominant (right) hand compared to the non-dominant (left) hand which seems to be the origin of observed reductions in motor asymmetry across the lifespan.

Keywords: Aging · Motor asymmetry · Graphics task

1 Introduction

The National Institutes of Health [15] reports the world's population of persons aged 80 and above is anticipated to triple in the years 2015 through 2050. With an increasing "oldest old" population, it is of imminent importance to assist this population aging healthy. Evidence has pointed to decreased physical and cognitive abilities associated with natural aging. Milanović et al. [12] reported a 1–2% loss of muscle strength in the upper extremities of the elderly population. Physical declines, such as loss of muscle mass, have a connection with deficits in function and loss of independence for older adults [20]. The declines of some functions become steeper when growing older (e.g., walking, see [7]). Functional deficits due to physical deterioration are further exacerbated by cognitive decline underpinning additional reductions of function. Some cognitive processes that decline with age include decision-making, problem-solving, planning

© Springer Nature Switzerland AG 2022
C. Carmona-Duarte et al. (Eds.): IGS 2021, LNCS 13424, pp. 227–239, 2022.
https://doi.org/10.1007/978-3-031-19745-1_17

and sequencing of responses, and multitasking [13]. Learning and memory retrieval has also been shown to decline with age [10].

Changes in motor control when an individual ages can be influenced by changes in the cortex. Cortical Structures and functions change due to aging, thus it impacts motor control and ultimately motor performance [21]. Seidler et al. [21] reported that areas of the prefrontal cortex and basal ganglia, which areas are important for motor control, are substantially affected by the aging process. Older adults need to recruit more neuronal resources to perform even simple motor tasks [11]. Mattay et al. [11] revealed through button press tasks that some areas of the cortex were more active in older adults than younger adults, in particular the contralateral sensorimotor cortex, lateral premotor area, supplementary motor area, and ipsilateral cerebellum, showed higher activation levels. The study also discovered active brain areas in older adults that did not show similar activation levels in younger adults during the motor task; more specifically the contralateral cerebellum, ipsilateral sensorimotor cortex, and putamen (left greater than right) showed higher activation levels in older adults. This study also reported additional neuronal resources were utilized by older adults in the contralateral hemisphere as well as the ipsilateral hemisphere. The significant neuroimaging findings comparing younger and older adults provided evidence that hemispheric activation patterns required to perform a motor task differ between older and younger adults.

Research exploring age related changes in motor performance uncovered patterns that can help explain the different movement control mechanisms in younger and older adults. Francis and Spirduso [8] found that older adults performed slower in tasks such as the Minnesota Rate of Manipulation, Purdue Pegboard, Steadiness Tester, triangle tracing, and a tapping test using a stylus. Rosenblum et al. [19] investigated executive function and handwriting, and found differences in handwriting performance with increased age, such as increased letter size. Walton [23] also observed a reduction in handwriting quality with aging, and an inequality of movement execution as evidenced by a combination of slower movements and inconsistent pressure. Several reasons for these observed differences exist because handwriting is a combination of motor and cognitive processes while it requires feedback from visual and proprioceptive systems [5]. Given the requirements for handwriting do include cognitive, motor, and perceptual components, this task and other graphic tasks, such as drawing, tracing, and pointing, are useful motor skills for investigating the effects of aging on movement control.

Patterns that might explain motor function differences between young and older adults have been identified, such as right-hand advantage. Right hand advantage (it is assumed that the dominant hand is the right hand which is more common within the general population) is a theory describing the superiority of right (dominant) hand performance compared to the left (non-dominant) hand performance. This is primarily evident in younger adults' proficiency in motor tasks with the right hand and the relatively inferior ability to perform motor tasks with the left hand. The motor performance between younger adults' left and right upper extremities is more asymmetrical than the more symmetrical motor performance of older adults. For example, the observable handwriting difference in younger adults' reveals the dominant hand performs more clear, smooth and refined movement compared to their nondominant hand, indicating asymmetric motor behavior. Participants in a study by Raw et al. [18] performed a tracing task with both hands and found the younger group clearly exhibited asymmetries between the hands, while the older group did not exhibit those differences between hands. Francis and Spirduso [8] found differences between younger and older adults' performance in tapping and Purdue Pegboard tasks with their right hand due to the peak performance level of this practiced hand. In relation to younger adults, older adults exhibit slower movement execution. This study reports that younger adults outperformed older adults in some tasks because the right hand of the younger adult is at a greater performance level compared to the older adult's right hand.

Teixeira [22] also provided support for the explanation that aging is accompanied with increases in symmetry of motor behavior patterns. Younger adults' right hand outperforms their own left hand. Conversely, the older adult's performance between hands (left hand versus right hand) is more symmetrical. There is a performance difference between the older adult's left hand and the younger adults' left hand. Similarly, there is a difference in performance between the younger adults' right hand and the older adults' right hand. When comparing the difference in the left-hand performance of older and younger adults, to the difference in right-hand performance between older and younger adults, the performance of the right hand appears to have been reduced to a greater extent in older adults than performance of the left hand.

As mentioned left and right-hand performance differs in both older and younger populations. The difference between left and right hands is notably greater in younger adults than in older adults. Although some changes due to aging may be task-specific [8], it has not yet been thoroughly investigated as to which components of each task contribute to observed age-related declines in motor asymmetry. For example, the study of Francis and Spirduso [8] recognized significant age-by-hand interactions in 2 out of the 5 motor tasks performed by participants, suggesting task complexity contributed to the age-related pattern of findings. Moreover, the Purdue Pegboard task showed changes in asymmetry between older and younger adults, possibly due to the complex nature of this task, requiring speed and preciseness. The tracing task, requiring speed and precision, also indicated age-related differences in performance asymmetry. In contrast, the Tapping task, Steadiness Tester, and Minnesota Rate of Manipulation did not display age-related differences. Thus, the increased complexity of the task may play a role in revealing significant asymmetries.

Research on cognitive changes with age has utilized neuroimaging techniques to develop theories to explain some of the changes in activation patterns during cognitive tasks [6, 16] and motor tasks [4, 25]. Cabeza [2] investigated changes in cognitive activation patterns for older adults and introduced a model to describe cognitive activity during cognitive tasks associated with aging called Hemispheric Asymmetry Reduction in Older Adults (HAROLD). Davis et al. [6] proposed another cortical activation pattern theory to describe other notable age-related cortical changes associated with aging. Age-related reduction in occipital activity coupled with increased frontal activity is the foundation for a posterior-anterior shift in aging (PASA). Although PASA and HAROLD are theories more commonly used, other theories have been proposed in the literature to understand age-related cortical changes. Hill et al. [9] conducted a review of existing literature utilizing neuroimaging techniques to explore both motor and hemispheric asymmetries related to aging. Older individuals were found to activate additional neuronal resources in order to perform at higher performance levels during cognitive tasks [3]. The overactivation phenomena may be caused by one of two contrasting models; compensation or dedifferentiation. The compensation model suggests that the overactivation, which may occur in areas such as the premotor cortex, primary motor cortex, or prefrontal cortex, would result in increased motor performance of the non-dominant hand [14], whereas overactivation from dedifferentiation may result in reduced performance of the dominant hand[1]; i.e., both resulting in a reduction of hand performance asymmetry.

Exploration of cognitive changes associated with the aging brain has uncovered patterns supporting greater cortical hemispheric asymmetry in younger adults compared to older adults (i.e., older adults exhibit more symmetrical brain activation patterns). HAROLD model was proposed to explain this age-related change of cortical activation patterns in cognitive processing and it offers an insight into the potential of compensatory neural activity being responsible for similar motor performance of older and younger adults performing the same motor task. In a study conducted by Pryzbyla et al. [17], participants engaged in an aiming task, using both the dominant (right) and non-dominant (left) hand. Results indicated significant motor asymmetries in younger adults, whereas older adults did not exhibit asymmetry. This endeavor broadened the applicability of the HAROLD construct to observed motor behavior. Wang et al. [24] also found evidence of motor asymmetry reductions in older adults exploring the transfer between the limbs of a motor task requiring adaptation to distorted feedback. The findings of latter study provides additional support for the notion of reduced cortical lateralization for motor control. These motor studies utilized the HAROLD model to explain the reduced asymmetry signifying the plausibility of applicability of the HAROLD model to the motor behavior domain.

In the present study, a graphic test was conducted to investigate several kinematic variables: mean velocity, peak velocity, stroke size, and the ratio of deceleration phase. The goal of this research was to increase our understanding of age-related changes of asymmetries in motor performance. An added secondary aim of this study was to determine whether age-related motor asymmetry changes fit the hemispheric activation models predicting hemispheric activation asymmetry changes developed using cognitive tasks.

2   Method

2.1   Participants

Participants in this study included 34 right-hand dominant older adults (77.8 ± 2.7 years, 24 female) and 38 right-hand dominant younger adults (21.3 ± 3.2, 24 female). All participants self-reported normal or corrected-to-normal vision via questionnaire. Inclusion criteria for the older participants included: age 60 years or over, right-hand dominant, a score of >21(Average above 25) on the Mini-Mental State Examination (MMSE), no recent surgeries, and no limiting cardiovascular or respiratory conditions. Inclusion criteria for younger adults included healthy adults absent of neurological pathology, hearing, and vision difficulties. Participants signed informed consent forms and the project was approved by the Institutional Review Board of Mississippi State University.

2.2 Instruments and Procedure

Edinburgh Handedness Inventory (Oldfield 1971) was used at the start of the study to determine participants' handedness before performing the graphics test. Participants were allowed practice trials to familiarize themselves with all conditions. To investigate the kinematics of hand movements similar to handwriting, participants completed a graphic test utilizing a WACOM Intuos3 12 × 19 digitizer tablet (see Fig. 1). The digitizer tablet recorded the x- and y-positions of the tip of the pen with a sampling frequency of 200 Hz and a spatial resolution of 0.001 cm. In the graphic test, participants drew cursive "l" loops in three sizes [small (1 cm), medium (3 cm), and large (5 cm)] and at two speeds requirement [comfortable or maximum speed (max)]. For each loop size, two lines were provided for participants to visualize loop requirements. These lines were available during the drawing (see Fig. 1). Instruction for speed was provided visually and verbally before each trial. Each of these six conditions was performed 4 times with each hand, totaling 24 trials (4 trials × 6 conditions) per hand.

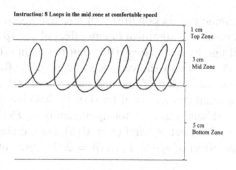

Fig. 1. Cursive l loops

Four kinematic measures assessed from this test included one movement outcome measure (stroke size) and three-movement production measures [mean velocity, peak velocity, and the ratio of the duration of the deceleration phase to the total movement time (RDP)]. Mean values for each participant's different conditions were found by taking the average from all trials for that specific condition. The mean velocity measure was used to describe the average velocity per stroke whereas peak velocity was used to describe the maximum velocity for each stroke. RDP is a function of the total movement time in relation to the duration from the point where peak velocity was reached to the ending point (deceleration phase). For each stroke, there is a duration of time spent in acceleration and a duration of time spent in deceleration. If the time spent in acceleration and deceleration phases were equal, then the resultant RDP would be .50. An RDP of 50% is likely to be the most efficient profile for this variable. However, if the RDP is greater than 50% then a larger proportion of the movement time was spent decelerating the tip of the pen, indicating decreased efficiency in motor control. By reducing speed of the movement, efficiency is sacrificed for increased task accuracy.

$$RDP = \frac{time\ of\ deceleration\ phase}{movement\ time} \times 100\%$$

3 Statistical Analysis

Analysis was conducted utilizing IBM SPSS 24 software. A two-way mixed-design ANOVA was conducted to examine the effects of aging and used the hand on motor performance. Age (young and old) was the between-group factor, and hand (left and right) was the within-group factor. The dependent variables were mean velocity, peak velocity, RDP, and stroke size. Results with P values below 0.05 were identified as statistical significance.

4 Results

4.1 Pooled Effects

The overall effects combine the six conditions of size and speed requirements. *Mean velocity* was identified to show a significant main effect of age ($p < .001$) and showed an interaction effect of age by hand ($p = .012$), but the main effect of hand was not significant ($p = .165$). *Peak velocity* showed a significant main effect of age ($p < .001$), hand ($p < .001$) and the interaction of age and hand ($p < .001$). For *stroke size*, the overall effect showed a significant effect of hand ($p < .001$) but not for age ($p = .99$). The interaction of age and hand was also not significant ($p = .891$). *RDP* overall effect indicated a significant main effect of hand ($p = .016$), but the main effect of age ($p = .264$) and the interaction effect of age by hand ($p = .221$) were not significant.

4.2 Mean Velocity

Mean velocity indicated that the drawing of older adults is slower than younger adults. Specifically, average velocities of older adults left (13.78 cm/s) and right (13.03 cm/s) hands were significantly slower ($p < .001$) than younger adults' average velocities (left

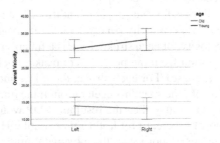

Fig. 2. Overall velocity

= 30.50 cm/s, right = 33.06 cm/s). The significant interaction between age and hand for mean velocity ($p = .012$) indicated a change in performance difference between the hands in older adults compared to this difference in younger adults. This interaction effect, illustrated in Fig. 2, is evidence of a reduction of motor asymmetry as people age from young adulthood to older ages. The significant results from mean velocity provide evidence of reduced asymmetry in older adults caused predominantly by a greater reduction of movement speed in the right hand.

When investigating the size and speed conditions (i.e., 3 size × 2 speed requirements), the dependent variable, **_mean velocity_**, revealed significant effects when maximum speed was required. In this condition the small size requirement [age ($p < .001$), hand ($p = .025$), age by hand ($p = .044$)] and large size requirement [age ($p < .001$), hand ($p = .309$), age by hand ($p = .023$)] showed significant effects on mean velocity. Mean velocities of these small and large size conditions in the maximum speed condition are represented in the figures below (Fig. 3A and Fig. 3B).

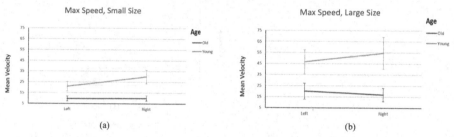

Fig. 3. (A) Specific condition; max speed, small size (B) specific condition; max speed, large size

4.3 Peak Velocity

Peak velocity also indicated slower handwriting/drawing of older adults compared to younger adults ($p < .001$). Older adults' left (21.13 cm/s) and right (23.47 cm/s) hands were slower than younger adults' (left = 33.06 cm/s, right = 45.62 cm/s). The significant interaction between age and hand ($p < .001$) revealed a change in hand difference in older adults compared to the hand difference in younger adults. This interaction effect,

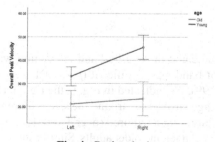

Fig. 4. Peak velocity

illustrated in Fig. 4, is evidence of a reduction of motor asymmetry as people age from younger to older adulthood. The significant results from peak velocity provide evidence that reduced asymmetry in older adults is predominantly caused by a greater reduction of movement speed in the right hand.

When investigating size and speed conditions, the dependent variable, *peak velocity*, revealed significant findings in the specific condition of max speed with medium size [age ($p = .001$), hand ($p = .001$), age by hand ($p < .001$)], and some significant findings in max speed with large size [age ($p = .004$), hand ($p = .612$), age by hand ($p < .001$)]. Significant results were also discovered in the conditions comfortable speed combined with small size [age ($p = .001$), hand ($p = .026$), age by hand ($p = .003$)] and large size [age ($p = .006$), hand ($p = .001$), age by hand ($p = .021$)]. Peak velocities of these four specific conditions are represented in the figures below (Fig. 5A through Fig. 5D).

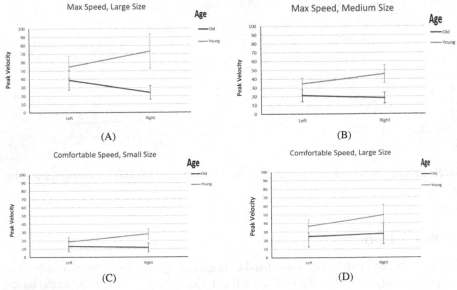

Fig. 5. (A) Specific condition; max speed, large size. (B) specific condition; max speed, medium size. (C) specific condition; comfortable speed, small size. (D) specific condition; comfortable speed, large size

4.4   Stroke Size

Results for stroke size indicated the age-by-hand interaction was not significant ($p = .891$). The main effect of hand was significant ($p < .001$), but the main effect of age was not significant ($p = .99$). As indicated in Fig. 6, the right hand could fulfill the size requirement with an average stroke size around the size requirement of 3 cm, while the left hand tended to draw larger than required (over 3 cm). However, the hand difference was comparable between younger and older adults. Similar stroke sizes between younger and older adults were found when comparing younger adults' left hand (3.33 cm) to older adults' left hand (3.34 cm), and similar stroke sizes between younger adults' right hands (2.94 cm) and older adults' right hands (2.92 cm).

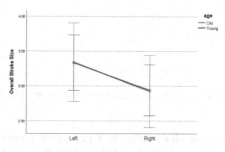

Fig. 6. Stroke size

Interestingly, the investigation into specific conditions of stroke size indicated significant age by hand interaction in *max speed with small size* ($p = .034$), even though the main effects were non-significant, age ($p = .861$), hand ($p = .054$). Upon closer inspection of the specific conditions, in the stroke size variable of max speed and small size (1 cm), both young and older adults drew larger than required when the task required drawing at maximum speed. However, young adults reveal a difference between left (2.48 cm) and right (1.82 cm) hands, whereas older adults show similar performance between the left (2.075 cm) and right (2.11 cm) hands (Fig. 7). When attempting to draw the small size parameter (1 cm) at max speeds, both older and younger adults' left and right hands drew larger than the provided criterion. This could result from the difficult nature of attempting to control movement at high velocities; Both age groups exhibited poor movement control with high speeds.

Young adults drew the closest to the size required when using their right hand (1.82 cm). Interestingly, young adults drew the largest loops with their left hand (2.48 cm), even when comparing stroke sizes to older adults' left (2.075 cm) and right (2.11 cm) hands. Results indicate, that when drawing small sizes with max speed, young adults exhibited good motor control with the right hand, but poorer motor control with the left hand. As for older adults, left and right hands exhibited more similar stroke sizes, displaying a more symmetrical performance than younger adults. A significant interaction was not found in other specific conditions of stroke size.

4.5 Ratio of Deceleration Phase

Finally, results for RDP, as visually depicted in Fig. 8, did not reveal a statistically significant age-by-hand interaction effect ($p = .221$). The main effect of hand yielded statistically significant results ($p = .016$), however, the main effect of age ($p = .264$) and all specific conditions yielded no significant results.

An RDP of 50% indicates maximum efficiency for this variable. The results for young adults' RDP with the right hand (.50) revealed maximum efficiency, exhibiting proportionally equal acceleration and deceleration phases. Left hands of younger adults (.54) and older adults (.52) yielded results greater than 50% RDP, indicating more time

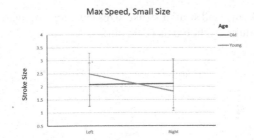

Fig. 7. Specific condition; max speed, small size

was spent in the deceleration phase than the acceleration phase while drawing loops. Younger and older adults drawing with their left hand exhibited reduced efficiency (above 50%) and relied on feedback systems for controlling motor movement. Thus, increased movement times during the deceleration phase were required for improved motor control. Conversely, older adults' RDP for the right hand (.47) was below 50% RDP, indicating more time was spent in the acceleration phase. A score below 50% indicated older adults relied more on feedforward mechanisms of movement control, such as pre-programming, and less on feedback to modify actions and produce appropriate movements.

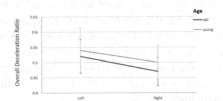

Fig. 8. Ratio of deceleration phase

5 Discussion

The primary aim of this study was to investigate the changes in motor asymmetry as people age. The movement parameters, stroke size, mean velocity, peak velocity, and RDP were examined as participants drew a series of continuous loops (i.e., cursive connected l's). The present study has three major findings. First, age-related reduction of motor asymmetry was identified in average velocity and peak velocity. These results indicate a relationship between motor symmetry and age exists which supports the notion of an age-related motor asymmetry reduction. Secondly, reduced asymmetry in older adults seems predominantly caused by a greater performance reduction in the right (dominant) hand, indicating the role of age-related elimination of the dominant-hand advantage in motor performance. Lastly, since the age-related reduction of asymmetry in stroke size was primarily observed in the condition requiring the smallest size while writing at maximum speed, it is reasonable to hypothesize that increased task difficulty is an important component of age-related reductions of asymmetric execution of motor tasks performed using the dominant and non-dominant hand.

As proposed with the HAROLD, and other cognitive models, age-related changes in brain structure and function necessitate the system to utilize compensation or dedifferentiation by employing more symmetrical brain activation patterns, and/or the recruitment of more neuronal resources to perform the same task as younger adults [2, 3, 6, 9]. The possibility exists for the motor control system to similarly require a compensation pattern, utilizing more symmetrical cortical activation, in order for the motor system to compensate for age-related changes that occur on the physiological and neural levels. The suggestion of cognitive changes such as reduced lateralization of brain activation may be an underlying cause of reduced motor asymmetry when aging [17], and findings in this study support the extension of HAROLD to the area of motor behavior. As the contralateral hemisphere reduces activation and its related assistance with motor performance, the ipsilateral hemisphere increases in activation to help accomplish the motor task. The result of the increased bilateral cortical activation is more symmetrical performance of unimanual motor tasks when performance of either hand is compared. In the same vein, Wang et al. [24] predicted an increase in motor performance symmetry in older adults when a motor task requiring visuomotor adaptation was being transferred from the left to the right hand or vice versa. The symmetrical transfer of task performance between the hands adds to evidence suggesting that reductions of hemispheric lateralization of cortical areas controlling motor function are the origin of these observed age-related reductions in asymmetry of performance levels between the hands. Moreover, these findings support the notion of increased symmetrical cortical activation of bilateral hemispheres causing more symmetry in motor behavior when we age.

A separate question still is unanswered; are age-related changes in motor asymmetry and asymmetric changes in the cognitive domain related. Park and Reuter-Lorenz [16] suggested reduced hemispherical asymmetry as a sign of compensation and a way for the cortex to adapt to structural and functional declines naturally occurring with aging. Similarly, motor behavior patterns of reduced motor asymmetry with aging are perhaps a compensatory technique implemented by the human body to help adjust for declines of structures and functions required to perform motor skills. More research is required to explore the specific association between components of cognitive and motor behavior changes. The continued study of brain activation patterns during a combination of cognitive and motor tasks is imperative to add knowledge to this area of age-related changes and compensatory strategies counteracting motor skill decline. Neuroimaging techniques combined with (dual) motor tasks would be needed to concretely extend our models of cognitive compensation patterns from the cognitive domain to the area of motor behavior. Research may reveal patterns that resemble the already uncovered cognitive activation patterns or uncover new cortical activation patterns. Perhaps further undiscovered cognitive-motor patterns will be uncovered propelling theories of motor changes associated with aging forward. Combining neuroimaging components to this area of study is crucial to discover whether younger and older adults show similarities and/or differences in cortical activation patterns when performing motor and cognitive tasks and whether age-related activation pattern changes are associated with age-related asymmetry changes of task performance.

The investigation of compensatory activation patterns related to motor behavior changes with age should aim to prevent motor skill decline and more broadly, functional decline. Thorough discovery of motor performance patterns, cognition, brain activation patterns, and compensatory techniques, will provide insights into the decline of functional motor performance associated with aging. This knowledge will provide the potential to build new interventions, and/or adding treatment options to existing ones, in order to maintain and/or prevent loss of motor function in older adults.

References

1. Bernard, J.A., Seidler, R.D.: Evidence for motor cortex dedifferentiation in older adults. Neurobiol. Aging **33**(9), 1890–1899 (2012)
2. Cabeza, R.: Hemispheric asymmetry reduction in older adults: the HAROLD model. Psychol. Aging **17**(1), 85–100 (2002)
3. Cabeza, R., Anderson, N.D., Locantore, J.K., McIntosh, A.R.: Aging gracefully: compensatory brain activity in high-performing older adults. Neuroimage **17**(3), 1394–1402 (2002)
4. Carp, J., Park, J., Hebrank, A., Park, D.C., Polk, T.A.: Age-related neural dedifferentiation in the motor system. PloS ONE **6**(12) (2011)
5. Danna, J., Velay, J.: Basic and supplementary sensory feedback in handwriting. Front. Psychol. **6**(169), 1–11 (2015)
6. Davis, S.W., Dennis, N.A., Daselaar, S.M., Fleck, M.S., Cabeza, R.: Que PASA? The posterior-anterior shift in aging. Cereb. Cortex **18**(5), 1201–1209 (2008)
7. Ferrucci, L., Cooper, R., Shardell, M., Simonsick, E.M., Schrack, J.A., Kuh, D.: Age-related change in mobility: perspectives from life course epidemiology and geroscience. J. Gerontol. Ser. A Biol. Sci. Med. Sci. **71**(9), 1184–1194 (2016)
8. Francis, K.L., Spirduso, W.W.: Age differences in the expression of manual asymmetry. Exp. Aging Res. **26**, 169–180 (2000)
9. Hill, C.H., Van Gemmert, A.W.A., Fang, Q., Hou, L., Wang, J., Pan, Z.: Asymmetry in the aging brain: a narrative review of cortical activation patterns and implications for motor function. Laterality **25**(4), 413–429 (2020)
10. Lezak, M.D., Howieson, D.B., Bigler, E.D., Tranel, D.: Neuropsychological Assessment, 5th edn. Oxford University Press, New York (2012)
11. Mattay, V.S., et al.: Neurophysiological correlates of age-related changes in human motor function. Neurology **58**, 630–635 (2002)
12. Milanović, Z., Pantelić, S., Trajković, N., Sporiš, G., Kostić, R., James, N.: Age-related decrease in physical activity and functional fitness among elderly men and women. Clin. Interv. Aging **8**, 549–556 (2013)
13. Murman, D.L.: The impact of age on cognition. Semin. Hear. **36**(3), 111–121 (2015)
14. Naccarato, M., Calautti, C., Jones, P.S., Day, D.J., Carpenter, T.A., Baron, J.-C.: Does healthy aging affect the hemispheric activation balance during paced index-to-thumb opposition task? An fMRI study. Neuroimage **32**(3), 1250–1256 (2006)
15. National institutes of health. The world's older population grows dramatically. https://www.nih.gov/news-events/news-releases/worlds-older-population-grows-dramatically. Accessed 27 Jan 2022
16. Park, D.C., Reuter-Lorenz, P.: The adaptive brain: aging and neurocognitive scaffolding. Annu. Rev. Psychol. **60**, 173–196 (2009)
17. Przybyla, A., Haaland, K.Y., Bagesterio, L.B., Sainburg, R.L.: Motor asymmetry reduction in older adults. Neurosci. Lett. **489**, 99–104 (2011)

18. Raw, F.K., Wilkie, R.M., Culmer, P.R., Mon-Williams, M.: Reduced motor asymmetry in older adults when manually tracing paths. Exp. Brain Res. **217**, 35–41 (2012). https://doi.org/10.1007/s00221-011-2971-x
19. Rosendblum, S., Engel-Yeger, B., Fogel, Y.: Age-related changes in executive control and their relationships with activity performance in handwriting. Hum. Mov. Sci. **32**, 363–376 (2013)
20. Santilli, V., Bernetti, A., Mangone, M., Paoloni, M.: Clinical definition of sarcopenia. Clin. Cases Miner. Bone Metab. **11**(3), 177–180 (2014)
21. Seidler, R.D., et al.: Motor control and aging: links to age-related brain structural, functional, and biomechanical effects. Neurosci. Biobehav. Rev. **34**(5), 721–733 (2010)
22. Teixeira, L.A.: Categories of manual asymmetry and their variation with advancing age. Cortex **44**(6), 707–716 (2008)
23. Walton, J.: Handwriting changes due to aging and Parkinson's syndrome. Forensic Sci. Int. **88**(3), 197–214 (1997)
24. Wang, J., Przybyla, A., Wuebbenhorst, K., Sainburg, R.L.: Aging reduces asymmetries in interlimb transfer of visuomotor adaptation. Exp. Brain Res. **210**(2), 283–290 (2012). https://doi.org/10.1007/s00221-011-2631-1
25. Ward, N.S., Frackowiak, R.S.: Age-related changes in the neural correlates of motor performance. Brain **126**(4), 873–888 (2003)

Motor Movement Data Collection from Older People with Tablets and Digital Pen-Based Input Devices

Gergely Hanczár[1,2] (ID), Erika Griechisch[1,2](✉) (ID), Ákos Molnár[1],
and Gábor Tóth[2]

[1] Cursor Insight Ltd., 20-22, Wenlock Road, London N1 7GU, UK
{gergely,erika,amolnar}@cursorinsight.com
[2] Patient Record Ltd., Gárdonyi utca 2/C, Bátaszék 7140, Hungary
gabor.toth@patient-record.com
https://cursorinsight.com, https://patient-record.com

Abstract. Our study's aim is two-fold. Firstly, to assess the technical capabilities of digital tablets with digital pen inputs to establish their suitability as data collection equipment for use in screening for Mild Cognitive Impairment (MCI). Secondly, to test such equipments' usability in clinical settings by test subjects who are over 65 years of age and would be the typical participants in such screening tests. Before we started to analyze the fine motor movement of older people in order to diagnose the motor movement-based symptoms of Alzheimer's disease and MCI, we had to gain experience in data collection in this age group. Our goal was to check the quality of the data collected with different devices from older people. First, data was collected using our standard measurement protocol and also we collected real-life handwritten signatures. The collected "in vitro" and "in vivo" data were analyzed. In the second part of the research, we asked older people to solve different writing and drawing tasks on certain digital devices that are able to collect data about their hand motor movement. We found that every device had pros and cons. Overall, the data we collected with them were good quality and provided a good basis for further research. We have also established that the use of such tablet devices to collect data did not pose any usability challenges for participants.

Keywords: Data quality · Tablets · Handwritten signature · Drawing · Handwriting · MCI · Alzheimer's disease · Neurodegenerative diseases · Dementia

1 Introduction

Recent studies [4,5,10] suggest that identification of impairment of visuomotor (VM) abilities in the earliest stages of MCI could open the door for wide-scale early detection of dementia. Our aim is to confirm that equipment readily available today provides the means to collect data of the highest quality and sampling

© Springer Nature Switzerland AG 2022
C. Carmona-Duarte et al. (Eds.): IGS 2021, LNCS 13424, pp. 240–251, 2022.
https://doi.org/10.1007/978-3-031-19745-1_18

rate as possible, especially while collecting and quantifying hand motor movement data. Furthermore, we worked with the hypothesis that these equipment, used in everyday clinical settings, would pose no discernable problem for participants over the age of 65.

Unfortunately, data quality of the different tablets and how to test them is a rarely studied area; only some articles and studies can be found about it [3, 7, 9, 12]. We may also note here that pressure is considered an important feature when we analyze fine motor movement, for example in signatures [2, 6, 8, 11].

To establish the validity of using digital tablet devices for MCI and Alzheimer's disease screening, we tested the quality of our devices' data collection capabilities by using a standardized measurement protocol developed by our team. This protocol consists of sampling rate estimations; linear and circular accuracy tests; pressure level checks and pressure homogeneity tests; and tilt level (azimuth and altitude) tests. The most important findings from the device data quality testing are summarized below.

The other key question was how these tablets perform in real life when older people use them to complete specific cognitive tests. We chose two main different types of devices. One of them included a paper, a pen, and a tablet which was placed under the paper and collected the data. The other type included a digital pen and a tablet as closely resembling writing on paper as technologically possible. The most important outcomes of the pilot data collection are summarized after the standardized measurement protocol section results.

2 Standardized Measurement Protocol

We developed a unique software to collect data from tablet devices in order to gain insight into the granularity and sensitivity of the hand movement data captured by the devices.

The software displays a background image with a filled gray circle indicating the corner of the origin; unfilled circles help during drawing lines and also assist pressure measurement acquisition. Figure 1 shows this background image. The software also displays on the devices' screen the last reported values of each property that the device can capture. Our software collects the following properties:

- timestamp (in milliseconds);
- x and y-coordinate (in pixel);
- pressure for each device (p);
- altitude (α) and azimuth (θ) angles for Wacom MobileStudio Pro
- tiltX and tiltY for reMarkable tablets.

The following subsections describe the measurement process in detail.

2.1 Lines

Lines were drawn with a regular ruler at a slow pace holding the pen tilted at roughly 60°. To minimize sliding around the edges, the lines' start- and endpoints were away from the screen's edge. The lines took up around 80 to 90% of the width or height of the screen's surface. Horizontal, vertical, main diagonal and subdiagonal lines were drawn. Two diagonals were drawn from one corner to the opposite: subdiagonal from the bottom-left corner to top-right, the main diagonal from the top-left corner to bottom-right. See Fig. 2 for an illustration of line placements.

2.2 [HV]MinAndMax Lines

MinAndMax lines were drawn to cover the full range of the x and y coordinates. Two MinAndMax lines were recorded: a HMinAndMax and a VMinAndMAX where H and V abbreviate horizontal and vertical.

Each measurement consists of 4 half-lines drawn slowly using a ruler. The starting and ending points of the lines were drawn as illustrated on the left image of Fig. 3. For HMinAndMax: starting from the red rectangle with number 1 and moving towards the right along the ruler until the edge of the active area. The second half-line started at the green rectangle with 2 and moved towards the left side until the edge of the active area. The 3rd and 4th lines were similar to the 1st and 2nd. The only difference is they were closer to the bottom of the screen. VMinAndMax was drawn similarly in vertical directions, see illustration on the right image in Fig. 3.

2.3 Increasing Pressure

The pen tip was held on the instrument with as little pressure as possible at the start of the measurement. The pen was pressed slowly harder and harder until the maximum pressure value p was reached. The actual p value was continuously checked during the measurement as the data collector software continuously showed the actual p value on the screen. The path of the pen was not strictly defined. However, a spiral drawing was recommended. To estimate what is the minimum and maximum gram the device can distinguish, a digital scale was placed under the device.

2.4 PressurePoints

Different weights were applied using the turntable settings given in detail in our previous research [2], and the pen tip was placed perpendicular to the surface. The platter of the turntable was manually pushed to the left, then to the right, and released until it stopped. This was repeated at several different points on the surface.

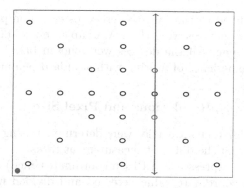

Fig. 1. Background pattern image of the data collector software

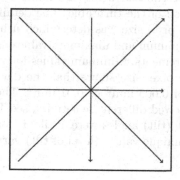

Fig. 2. Illustration of horizontal, vertical, main diagonal and subdiagonal linear measurements

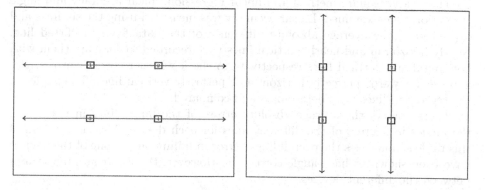

Fig. 3. Illustration of HMinAndMax (left) and VMinAndMax (right) measurements

3   Standardized Measurement Protocol Results

The protocol was used to test three different devices. The first one was the Wacom MobileStudio Pro 13 with an inking pen. To use this device, a sheet of writing paper was fixed to the tablet's screen using a non-permanent adhesive spray. The other two devices were the reMarkable and reMarkable2, both were used with a digital pen. All the devices were chosen based on their ability to closely mimic the experience of writing with standard pen and paper.

3.1   Ranges, Levels, Resolutions and Pixel Size

The ranges of the different properties were determined using the data extracted by our software during the different measurement tasks.

The resolution is expressed in LPI (in coordinates/inch) and was calculated using the maximal coordinate value detected and divided with the real width $(\max(x))$ and height $(\max(y))$ of the active area of the device's screen (in inches). The sampling rate was estimated using the number of data points within a whole circle and the speed of the turntable. The details of the findings can be found in Table 1. Sensor pixel size was determined using the actual size of the device in mm and the minimum and maximum values using particularly the two [HV]MinAndMax measurements. Minimum values for x and y were both 0. The estimation of the sensor pixel size shows that the devices have a square pixel with width and height of 0.005 mm^2 or 0.01 mm^2. The pressure level changed from 256 to 8192 and showed different sensitivity, see Table 2.

Azimuth and altitude (tilt) angles were available for all devices. The ranges and also the number of unique values (level of tilt) vary among the devices, see Table 3.

3.2   Linear Accuracy and Angle Correction

Using the least square method and linear regression, linear accuracy and angle correction were examined. Linear accuracy was measured using the six lines and expressed as the average absolute difference of the data from the fitted line. Nearly horizontal and nearly vertical lines were recorded to compare them with horizontal and vertical lines respectively to check whether correction of angles is present towards perfectly horizontal or perfectly vertical lines. The angles of the regression lines were determined and compared.

Table 4 shows the average absolute errors of the linear lines in pixels and the angles in degrees of the different lines for each device. The last column of this table summarizes the overall linear error in millimeters. None of the devices have been shown to have angle correction. However, the linear accuracy varies between the different devices.

3.3   Force (Pressure) Properties

Homogeneity and gram-p relationship were examined. The pressure homogeneity was analyzed using the PressurePoints measurements. A constant line was fitted to the data and the error was measured as the average distance from this line. The gram-p relationship was examined using the constant value determined as

Table 1. The estimated sampling rate, coordinate range, resolution and pixel size.

Device	Sampling rate (Hz)	max(x)	max(y)	LPI (x/y)	Pixel size (mm^2)
reMarkable	200	20968	15726	2560/2578	0.01 × 0.01
reMarkable2	540	20966	15725	2557/2559	0.01 × 0.01
Wacom MS Pro	194	59552	33848	5134/5207	0.005 × 0.005

Table 2. Pressure p and mass ranges; uv means the number of unique values.

Device	p range	uv. p (level)	Gram range
reMarkable	0–4095	3900 (4096)	9–180
reMarkable2	0–4095	3949 (4096)	N/A–150
Wacom MS Pro	0–836	835 (1024?)	15–620

Table 3. Tilt ranges; tilt difference and number of unique levels. α denotes azimuth or tiltX, θ denotes altitude or tiltY. diff means the difference between consecutive property values, uv means unique values.

Device	α range	α diff	α uv	θ range	θ diff	θ uv
reMarkable	−6300–6300	100	95	−5800–5800	100	87
reMarkable2	−6300–6300	100	89	−6300–6300	100	89
Wacom MS Pro	250–900	10	66	0–3580	10	336

Table 4. Linear accuracy in pixels and angle of the regression line in degrees. H means horizontal line, NH = nearly horizontal, V = vertical, NV = nearly vertical, MD = main diagonal, SD = sub diagonal. The last column shows linear accuracy in mm.

Device	LineH	LineNH	LineV	LineNV	LineMD	LineSD	Result (mm)
reMarkable error	3.15	4.66	3.08	1.39	7.32	7.47	0.01–0.08
reMarkable angle	−0.05	0.57	89.99	91.21	36.78	−36.72	
reMarkable2 error	14.40	14.26	12.11	8.35	21.39	8.93	0.08–0.21
reMarkable2 angle	0.16	1.80	90.13	91.49	37.08	−36.76	
W MS Pro error	5.88	6.22	8.55	10.95	9.11	18.36	0.02–0.09
W MS Pro angle	0.07	0.39	89.99	91.10	29.50	−29.47	

the best fit of the PressurePoints measurement. The result of such a relationship is a graph with mass in grams on the x-axis and the pressure on the y-axis. The PressurePoints measurement was repeated with 3–5 different masses in the gram range the device could distinguish. These relationship graphs usually showed linear and logarithmic relationships.

4   Data Collection Pilot

In the second part of our study we tested the collected data quality not only in our laboratory but also in real life collecting signatures and data while people from all age group and especially older people were using the devices. In this section, we have divided our research into two parts.

4.1   Signature

Our database has information about more than 500 individuals' motor movement data because earlier we made several kinds of research in this field. In one of our pilots, we also collected signatures with the Wacom MobileStudio Pro 13 and the reMarkable tablet. 24 different people gave their handwritten signature 20 times and all of their hand motor movement data were collected. We used these data in this research as well.

4.2   Drawing and Writing

The whole dataset was collected using a reMarkable2 and a Wacom MobileStudio Pro 13 with an inking pen from 16 people from age 36 to 82. See Table 5 about the distribution of age (in years) and biological gender. Before we started the data collection, we tested the data collection procedure on 3 different people.

Table 5. Distribution of age and biological gender of drawing and writing tasks

Age group	Gender		Total
	Female	Male	
<45	1	3	4
45–64	1	4	5
65–74	2	2	4
≥75	3	0	3
Total	7	9	16

Every participant had to perform seven different tasks with dominant on one of the devices. In Task 1 the patient was asked to write the letter "l" altogether ten times in cursive. In Task 2 the participant wrote a sentence in cursive made up of seven words. Task 3 had two different parts. In Part A the participant drew a spiral along a visible line. In Part B the participant drew a spiral between two printed lines. Task 4 also has two different parts. In Part A the participant drew a square along a visible line. In Part B the participant drew a square with his or her free hand. Finally, in Task 5, the participant had to perform Trail Making test B [1] to connect letters and numbers in alphabetical and growing order (A-1, B-2, C-3, ...). See Fig. 4 which describes each task in Hungarian.

5 Data Collection Pilot Outcomes

Pressure distributions in Fig. 5 visualize the data from a pilot when 24 signers contributed signatures and these two devices were among the used devices in the data collection.

The reMarkable tablet clearly does not have the full range to distinguish the pressure properly for signature data. The Wacom MobileStudio Pro has a large frequency value at the end of its sensitivity range, which means for stronger pressure some data is lost. The distribution seems much more reliable for the Wacom device.

Pressure distributions in Fig. 6 shows the data from the research when we collected the data from the older people while they were writing and drawing

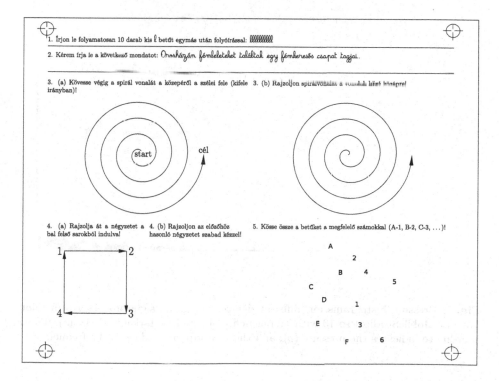

Fig. 4. Drawing, writing and Trail Making test B tasks (in Hungarian)

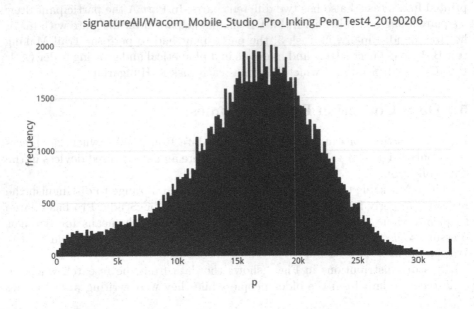

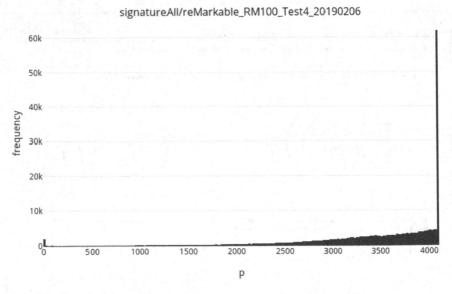

Fig. 5. Pressure histograms for different devices using the signature data of a pilot: Wacom MobileStudio Pro 13 with inking pen (top) and reMarkable (bottom). The x coordinate indicates the pressure (p), and the y coordinate indicates the frequency.

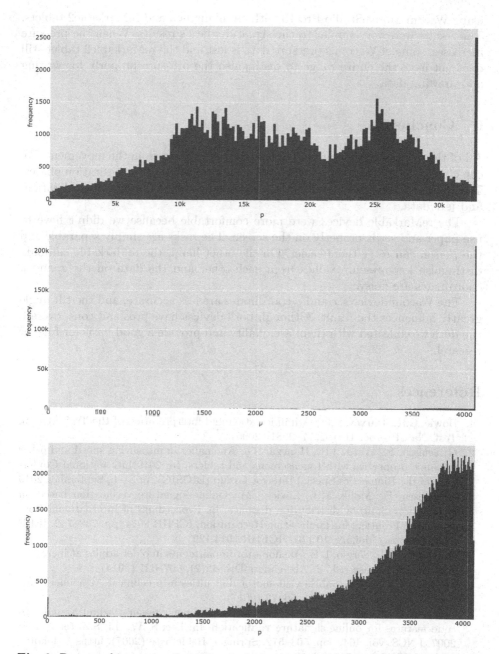

Fig. 6. Pressure histograms for different devices using the data collected from study subjects in all age range. Devices: Wacom MobileStudio Pro 13 with inking pen (top) and reMarkable2 (middle). The bottom plot shows a distribution from reMarkable2 pressure frequencies excluding the largest p value (4095). The x coordinate indicates the pressure (p), and the y coordinate indicates the frequency.

using Wacom MobileStudio Pro 13 with an inking pen and reMarkable2 tablets. The results were very similar to the signature data's results. When the pressure increases, some of Wacom's pressure data is lost and the reMarkable2 tablet still does not have the entire range to distinguish the pressure properly for writing and drawing data.

6   Conclusion

All of the devices provide quality and well-detailed data from the movement. We can clearly see the stoppages of the person's movement and the hesitation phases. The temporal and spatial resolutions are good as well as the speed, acceleration, and jerk data.

The reMarkable devices were more comfortable because we didn't have to use paper and set it properly on the screen. The tasks are simply separable and the person can retry them easier. On the other hand, the reMarkable can only distinguish low-pressure values from each other and the data on the x and y coordinates are noisy.

The Wacom device's x and y coordinates are less accurate, and the tilt angle greatly influences the result. Although both devices have pros and cons, overall, the data we collected with them are quality and provide a good basis for further research.

References

1. Bowie, C.R., Harvey, P.D.: Administration and interpretation of the Trail Making Test. Nat. Protoc. **1**(5), 2277–2281 (2006)
2. Griechisch, E., Ward, J.R., Hanczár, G.: Anomalies in measuring speed and other dynamic properties with touchscreens and tablets. In: 2019 International Conference of the Biometrics Special Interest Group (BIOSIG), pp. 1–6, September 2019
3. Griechisch, E., Malik, M.I., Liwicki, M.: Online signature verification based on Kolmogorov-Smirnov distribution distance. In: Proceedings of International Conference on Frontiers in Handwriting Recognition, ICFHR 2014, pp. 738–742. IEEE (2014). https://doi.org/10.1109/ICFHR.2014.129
4. Hawkins, K.M., Sergio, L.E.: Visuomotor impairments in older adults at increased Alzheimer's disease risk. J. Alzheimers Dis. **42**(2), 607–621 (2014)
5. Mollica, M.A., et al.: Subtle visuomotor difficulties in preclinical Alzheimer's disease. J. Neuropsychol. **11**(1), 56–73 (2017)
6. Muramatsu, D., Matsumoto, T.: Effectiveness of pen pressure, azimuth, and altitude features for online signature verification. In: Lee, S.-W., Li, S.Z. (eds.) ICB 2007. LNCS, vol. 4642, pp. 503–512. Springer, Heidelberg (2007). https://doi.org/10.1007/978-3-540-74549-5_53
7. NeuroScript: testing the accuracy of pen tablets. www.tinyurl.com/tablet-test-neuroscript. Accessed 25 Apr 2022
8. Okawa, M., Yoshida, K.: Offline writer verification based on forensic expertise: analyzing multiple characters by combining the shape and advanced pen pressure information. J. Jpn. Soc. Forensic Sci. Technol. **22**(2), 61–75 (2017)

9. Phillips, M.: Several simple tests can help you choose the correct digitizer. Comput. Technol. Rev. **7**(1) (1987)

10. Tippett, W.J., Sergio, L.E.: Visuomotor integration is impaired in early stage Alzheimer's disease. Brain Res. **1102**(1), 92–102 (2006). https://doi. org/10.1016/j.brainres.2006.04.049. www.sciencedirect.com/science/article/pii/ S0006899306010936

11. Tolosana, R., Vera-Rodriguez, R., Fierrez, J., Ortega-Garcia, J.: Feature-based dynamic signature verification under forensic scenarios. In: 3rd International Workshop on Biometrics and Forensics (IWBF 2015), pp. 1–6 (2015). https://doi.org/ 10.1109/IWBF.2015.7110241

12. Ward, J.R., Phillips, M.J.: Digitizer technology: performance characteristics and the effects on the user interface. IEEE Comput. Graph. Appl. **7**(4), 31–44 (1987). https://doi.org/10.1109/MCG.1987.276869

Handwriting for Neurodegenerative Disorders

Prodromal Diagnosis of Lewy Body Diseases Based on the Assessment of Graphomotor and Handwriting Difficulties

Zoltan Galaz[1]([envelope]) [iD], Jiri Mekyska[1] [iD], Jan Mucha[1] [iD], Vojtech Zvoncak[1] [iD], Zdenek Smekal[1] [iD], Marcos Faundez-Zanuy[2] [iD], Lubos Brabenec[3] [iD], Ivona Moravkova[3,4,5] [iD], and Irena Rektorova[3,4] [iD]

[1] Department of Telecommunications, Faculty of Electrical Engineering and Communication, Brno University of Technology, Brno, Czech Republic
xgalaz00@gmail.com
[2] Escola Superior Politecnica, Tecnocampus, Mataro, Barcelona, Spain
[3] Applied Neuroscience Research Group, Central European Institute of Technology – CEITEC, Masaryk University, Brno, Czech Republic
[4] First Department of Neurology, Faculty of Medicine and St. Anne's University Hospital, Masaryk University, Brno, Czech Republic
[5] Faculty of Medicine, Masaryk University, Brno, Czech Republic

Abstract. To this date, studies focusing on the prodromal diagnosis of Lewy body diseases (LBDs) based on quantitative analysis of graphomotor and handwriting difficulties are missing. In this work, we enrolled 18 subjects diagnosed with possible or probable mild cognitive impairment with Lewy bodies (MCI-LB), 7 subjects having more than 50% probability of developing Parkinson's disease (PD), 21 subjects with both possible/probable MCI-LB and probability of PD > 50%, and 37 age- and gender-matched healthy controls (HC). Each participant performed three tasks: Archimedean spiral drawing (to quantify graphomotor difficulties), sentence writing task (to quantify handwriting difficulties), and pentagon copying test (to quantify cognitive decline). Next, we parameterized the acquired data by various temporal, kinematic, dynamic, spatial, and task-specific features. And finally, we trained classification models for each task separately as well as a model for their combination to estimate the predictive power of the features for the identification of LBDs. Using this approach we were able to identify prodromal LBDs with 74% accuracy and showed the promising potential of computerized objective and non-invasive diagnosis of LBDs based on the assessment of graphomotor and handwriting difficulties.

The original version of this chapter was revised: an acknowledgment has been inserted. The correction to this chapter is available at
https://doi.org/10.1007/978-3-031-19745-1_27

Keywords: Lewy body diseases · Online handwriting · Graphomotor difficulties · Handwriting difficulties · Machine learning · Prodromal diagnosis

1   Introduction

Lewy body diseases (LBDs) is a term describing a group of neurodegenerative disorders characterized by a pathophysiological process of α-synuclein accumulation in specific brain regions leading to the formation of Lewy bodies and Lewy neurites resulting in cell death. LBDs consists of two major clinical entities: Parkinson's disease (PD) and dementia with Lewy bodies (DLB) [29,38]. Although the phenotypes and temporal evolution of motor and cognitive symptoms of these two diseases vary, they share many clinical and pathophysiological features and are therefore referred to as LBDs spectrum. Together with Alzheimer's disease (AD), LBDs comprise the major part of all cases of neurodegenerative disorders.

It is known that LBDs do not start suddenly. At the time the clinical symptoms occur, the neurodegenerative process has reached a severe degree in which most of the targeted neurons have already been damaged. Before the clinical diagnosis based on the presence of typical clinical symptoms becomes possible, there is a long period of the underlying neurodegenerative process with subtle or nonspecific symptoms [18,29] such as sleep disturbances, mood changes, smell loss, constipation, etc. This period of LBDs is called the prodromal stage.

One of the early markers of PD is PD dysgraphia (micrographia and other alterations in handwriting, e.g. kinematic and dynamic) [21,32,33]. Similarly, some manifestations of dysgraphia have been observed in the prodromal DLB as well [23]. Although modern approaches to the analysis of graphomotor and handwriting difficulties (utilising digitising tablets) were proved to work well during e.g. diagnosis of the clinical stage of PD [9,11,35], assessment of cognition in PD patients [4], or discrimination of AD and mild cognitive impairment (MCI) [15], to the best of our knowledge, no studies employed this technology (with high potential) in the prodromal diagnosis of LBDs in a larger scale.

Identification of the early stages of LBDs is crucial for the development of disease-modifying treatment since the neurodegeneration may be possibly stopped or treated before the pathological cascades start. Therefore, the goal of this study is to explore whether the computerised assessment of graphomotor and handwriting difficulties could support the prodromal diagnosis of LBDs, more specifically, we aim to:

1. identify which task significantly discriminates LBD patients and age- and gender-matched healthy controls (HC),
2. identify what conventional online handwriting features have good discrimination power.

2   Materials and Methods

2.1   Dataset

We enrolled 39 subjects (19 females, 20 males, age = 69.53 ± 6.61) diagnosed
with possible or probable MCI (based on the scores of the MoCA – Montreal
Cognitive Assessment [25] and based on the CCB – Complex Cognitive Battery,
see the explanation below) who were simultaneously diagnosed with possible or
probable MCI-LB (i.e. mild cognitive impairment with Lewy bodies) based on
the criteria published by McKeith et al. [22]. In this group, 21 subjects also
had more than 50% probability of developing PD (calculated following the MDS
criteria published in [18]). In addition, we enrolled 7 subjects (2 females, 5 males,
age = 66.41 ± 4.32) without possible/probable MCI-LB, but still with more than
50% probability of developing PD. Finally, we enrolled 37 HC (26 females, 11
males, age = 67.60 ± 5.61). In the experiments, we stratified the subjects into
two groups, HC vs. LBD (i.e. people with a high risk of developing PD or DLB).

CCB was used to evaluate four cognitive domains: 1) memory (The Brief
Visuospatial memory test–revised [2], Philadelphia Verbal Learning Test [3]);
2) attention (Wechsler Adult Intelligence Scale-III: Letter-Number Sequencing,
Digit Symbol Substitution [37]); 3) executive functions (Semantic and phonemic
verbal fluency [30], Picture arrangement test [37]); and 4) visuospatial functions
(Judgment of Line Orientation [36]). The cognitive domain z-scores were computed as the average z-scores of the tests included in the particular domain.

The participants were asked to perform a set of three tasks:

1. Archimedean spiral (spiral) – we consider this task as a graphomotor one, i.e.
   it is a building block of some letter shapes; in addition, it is a golden standard
   in PD dysgraphia diagnosis [35]
2. sentence "Tramvaj dnes už nepojede" (translation: "A tram will not go
   today.") writing (sentence) – this handwriting task was used e.g. in the
   PaHaW database [11]
3. pentagon copying test (pentagons) – it is a task frequently used for quantification of cognitive decline [4]

All participants were right-handed and had Czech as their native language.
They all signed an informed consent form that was approved by the local ethics
committee.

2.2   Feature Extraction

The participants were asked to perform the tasks (using the Wacom Ink pen)
on an A4 paper that was laid down and fixed to a digitizing tablet Wacom
Intuos 4 M (sampling frequency $f_s = 130\,\mathrm{Hz}$). Before the acquisition, they had
some time to get familiar with the hardware. The recorded time series (x and
y position; timestamp; a binary variable, being 0 for in-air movement and 1 for
on-surface movement, respectively; pressure exert on the tablet's surface during

writing; pen tilt; azimuth) were consequently parameterised utilising the following set of features (we selected the set based on available reviews and based on our experience [9,11,35]):

1. temporal – duration of writing, ratio of the on-surface/in-air duration, duration of strokes, and ratio of the on-surface/in-air stroke duration
2. kinematic – velocity, and acceleration
3. dynamic – pressure, tilt, and azimuth
4. spatial – width, height, and length of the whole product, as well as its particular strokes, i.e. stroke width, height, and length
5. spiral-specific – degree of spiral drawing severity [31], mean drawing speed of spiral [31], second-order smoothness of spiral [31], spiral precision index [5], spiral tightness [31], variability of spiral width [31], and first-order zero-crossing rate of spiral [31]
6. other – number of interruptions (pen elevations), number of pen stops [27], tempo (number of strokes normalised by duration), number of on-surface intra-stroke intersections, relative number of on-surface intra-stroke intersections, number of on-surface inter-stroke intersections, and relative number of on-surface inter-stroke intersections, Shannon entropy [4], number of changes in the velocity profile, relative number of changes in the velocity profile

Most of the features were extracted using the recently released Python library handwriting-features (v 1.0.1) [14], the rest of them were coded in Matlab. Some features (mainly spatial, temporal and kinematic) were extracted from both on-surface and in-air movements. In addition, kinematic features were also analysed in horizontal and vertical projection. Features represented by vectors were consequently transformed to a scalar value using median, non-parametric coefficient of variation (nCV; interquartile range of feature divided by its median), slope and 95th percentile (95p).

2.3   Statistical Analysis and Machine Learning

To compare the distribution of features between the HC and LBD subjects, we conducted Mann-Whitney U-test with the significance level of 0.05. Moreover, to assess the strength of a relationship between the features and the subject's clinical status (HC/LBD), we computed Spearman's correlation coefficient (ρ) with the significance level of 0.05. Finally, during this exploratory step, we calculated Spearman's correlation with the domains of CCB and the overall score of MDS–Unified Parkinson's Disease Rating Scale (MDS–UPDRS), part III (motor part) [16].

To identify the presence of graphomotor or handwriting difficulties, we built binary classification models using an ensemble extreme gradient boosting algorithm known as XGBoost [6] (with 100 estimators). This algorithm was chosen due to its robustness to outliers, ability to find complex interactions among features as well as the possibility of ranking their importance. To build models with an optimal set of hyperparameters, we conducted 1000 iteration of randomized search strategy via stratified 5-fold cross-validation with 10 repetitions aiming to optimize balanced accuracy score (BACC; described in more detail along with other evaluation scores below). The following set of hyperparameters were optimized: the learning rate [0.001, 0.01, 0.1, 0.2, 0.3], γ [0, 0.05, 0.10, 0.15, 0.20, 0.25, 0.5], the maximum tree depth [6, 8, 10, 12, 15], the fraction of observations to be randomly sampled for each tree (subsample ratio) [0.5, 0.6, 0.7, 0.8, 0.9, 1.0], the subsample ratio for the columns at each level [0.4, 0.5, 0.6, 0.7, 0.8, 0.9, 1.0], the subsample ratio for the columns when constructing each tree [0.4, 0.5, 0.6, 0.7, 0.8, 0.9, 1.0], the minimum sum of the weights of all observations required in a child node [0.5, 1.0, 3.0, 5.0, 7.0, 10.0], and the balance between positive and negative weights [1, 2, 3, 4].

The classification test performance was determined using the following classification metrics: Matthew's correlation coefficient (MCC), balanced accuracy (BACC), sensitivity (SEN) also known as recall (REC), specificity (SPE), precision (PRE) and F1 score (F1). These metrics are defined as follows:

$$\mathrm{MCC} = \frac{TP \times TN + FP \times FN}{\sqrt{N}}, \tag{1}$$

$$\mathrm{BACC} = \frac{1}{2}\left(\frac{TP}{TP+FN}\frac{TN}{TN+FP}\right), \tag{2}$$

$$\mathrm{SPE} = \frac{TN}{TN+FP}, \tag{3}$$

$$\mathrm{PRE} = \frac{TP}{TP+FP}, \tag{4}$$

$$\mathrm{REC} = \frac{TP}{TP+FN}, \tag{5}$$

$$\mathrm{F1} = 2\frac{PRE \times REC}{PRE+REC} \tag{6}$$

where $N = (TP+FP) \times (TP+FN) \times (TN+FP) \times (TN+FN)$, TP (true positive) and FP (false positive) represent the number of correctly identified LBD subjects and the number of subjects incorrectly identified as having LBDs, respectively. Similarly, TN (true negative) and FN (false negative) represent the number of correctly identified HC and the number of subjects with LBDs incorrectly identified as being healthy.

To further optimize the trained classification models, we fine-tuned the models' decision thresholds via the receiver operating characteristics (ROC) curve. Using the fine-tuned decision thresholds, we evaluated the classification performance of the models using the leave-one-out cross-validation. The ROC curves were plotted using the probabilities of the predicted labels obtained via the cross-validation procedure that was employed during the final evaluation of the fine-tuned models.

And finally, to evaluate the statistical significance of the prediction performance obtained by the built classification models, a non-parametric statistical method named permutation test was employed [7, 28]. For this purpose, we applied 1 000 permutations with the significance level of 0.05. To estimate the performance of the models on the permuted data, we used the same classification setup as employed during the training phase [26].

3   Results

The results of the exploratory data analysis are summarized in Table 1 (sorted based on the p-value for the Mann-Whitney U-test). The following features were found as the most distinguishing ones in terms of the differentiation between HC and subjects with LBD (the top 4 features are listed; *, **, and *** denote the p-values for both the Mann-Whitney U-test and Spearman's correlation coefficient being bellow the significance level of 0.05, 0.01, and 0.001, respectively; if both p-values are bellow a different significance level, the weaker statistical significance is selected): a) spiral – nCV of acceleration (on-surface) $\rho = -0.2438^*$, variability of spiral width $\rho = 0.2439^*$, median of azimuth $\rho = 0.2378^*$, and spiral precision index $\rho = 0.2367^*$; b) sentence – number of pen stops $\rho = 0.3460^{**}$, slope of duration of stroke (in-air) $\rho = 0.2823^{**}$, median of vertical velocity (on-surface) $\rho = -0.2438^*$, and median of vertical acceleration (on-surface) $\rho = 0.2317^*$; and c) pentagons – width of writing (on-surface) $\rho = -0.3045^{**}$, median of length of stroke (on-surface) $\rho = -0.2894^{**}$, nCV of length of stroke (on-surface) $\rho = 0.2489^*$, and median of duration of stroke (on-surface) $\rho = -0.2327^*$.

Table 1. Results of the exploratory analysis.

Feature	p(U)	ρ	p(ρ)
Spiral			
nCV of acceleration (s)	0.0138	−0.2438	0.0263
Variability of spiral width	0.0138	0.2439	0.0263
Median of azimuth	0.0158	0.2378	0.0304
Spiral precision index	0.0162	0.2367	0.0312
nCV of duration of stroke (s)	0.0438	−0.1892	0.0867
Sentence			
Number of pen stops	0.0009	0.3460	0.0014
Slope of duration of stroke (a)	0.0054	0.2823	0.0097
Median of vertical velocity (s)	0.0138	−0.2438	0.0263
Median of vertical acceleration (s)	0.0182	0.2317	0.0351
Rel. total number of intra-stroke intersections	0.0232	−0.2206	0.0451
Pentagons			
Width of writing (s)	0.0030	−0.3045	0.0051
Median of length of stroke (s)	0.0045	−0.2894	0.0080
nCV of length of stroke (s)	0.0123	0.2489	0.0233
Median of duration of stroke (s)	0.0178	−0.2327	0.0343
Median of horizontal acceleration (s)	0.0182	0.2317	0.0351

p(U) – p-value of Mann-Whitney U-test; ρ – Spearman's correlation coefficient; p(ρ) – p-value of ρ; (s) – on-surface movement; (a) – in-air movement.

Next, Table 2 presents the results of the correlation analysis (*, and ** denote the p-values for Spearman's correlation coefficient being below the significance level of 0.05 and 0.01, respectively) between the features summarized in Table 1 and the following clinical information: a) MDS–UPDRS, and b) CCB domains.

Table 2. Results of the correlation analysis.

Feature	ρ (UPDRS)	ρ (V)	ρ (A)	ρ (E)
Spiral				
nCV of acceleration (s)	−0.3411*	−0.0013	0.1130	0.1899
Variability of spiral width	0.1653	−0.3973**	−0.2981*	−0.1666
Median of azimuth	0.0442	−0.3656*	−0.1029	−0.0490
Spiral precision index	0.0606	−0.0942	−0.3987**	−0.2126
nCV of duration of stroke (s)	−0.1089	−0.1344	−0.1618	−0.0469
Sentence				
Num. of pen stops	−0.1018	−0.1181	0.1012	−0.1956
Slope of duration of stroke (a)	0.2620	−0.1928	−0.0513	−0.1025
Median of vertical velocity (s)	0.0314	0.1106	0.0025	0.1794
Median of vertical acceleration (s)	−0.2641	−0.0301	0.3246*	0.0193
Rel. total num. of intra-stroke intersections	0.0477	0.1647	0.1143	0.0962
Pentagons				
Width of writing (s)	−0.3448*	0.2947*	0.1351	0.1362
Median of length of stroke (s)	−0.1545	0.1607	0.0501	0.1511
nCV of length of stroke (s)	0.3065*	−0.2435	−0.1126	−0.1155
Median of duration of stroke (s)	−0.0348	0.0080	−0.0085	−0.0269
Median of horizontal acceleration (s)	0.3215*	−0.0226	−0.1632	−0.2060

ρ – Spearman's correlation coefficient (* denotes p-value < 0.05 and ** denotes p-value < 0.01); UPDRS – MDS–Unified Parkinson's Disease Rating Scale, part III (motor part) [16]; V – visuospatial domain of CCB; A – attention domain of CCB; E – executive functions domain of CCB; (s) – on-surface movement; (a) – in-air movement.

To visualize the difference in the distribution of the top 4 features summarized above for HC and subjects with LBD, the box-violin plots are presented in Figs. 1, 2 and 3. The Fig. 1 shows the distribution of the features for the spiral drawing, the Fig. 2 shows the distribution of the features for the sentence writing, and the Fig. 3 is dedicated to the distribution of the features for the pentagon copying test.

The results of the classification analysis are summarized in Table 3. We trained 4 models in total: 3 models dedicated to each task separately and a model combining all of the tasks. The following results were achieved (where * and ** denote p-value of the permutation test bellow < 0.05 and < 0.01, respectively): a) spiral – BACC = 0.6848**, SEN = 0.8696, SPE = 0.5000; b) sentence – BACC = 0.7283**, SEN = 0.9783, SPE = 0.4783 c) pentagons – BACC = 0.6848**, SEN = 0.9348, SPE = 0.4348; and d) all tasks combined –

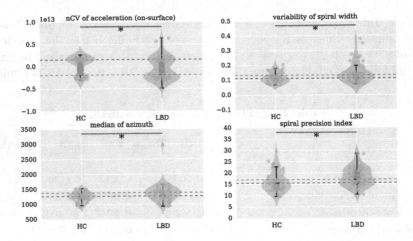

Fig. 1. Distribution of the top 4 most discriminating features (spiral drawing).

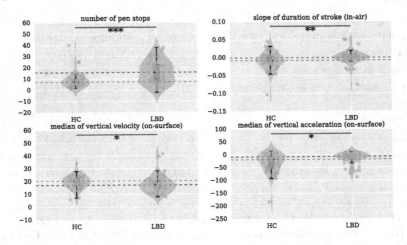

Fig. 2. Distribution of the top 4 most discriminating features (sentence writing).

BACC = 0.7391**, SEN = 0.8043, SPE = 0.6739. The ROC curves of the trained models are shown in Fig. 4.

4   Discussion

As mentioned in the methodology, the Archimedean spiral is considered as a gold standard, especially in the assessment of graphomotor difficulties in PD patients [5,8,31], nevertheless, it has been utilised during the quantitative analysis of Huntington's disease, essential tremor, or brachial dystonia as well [13]. Concerning the spiral features with the highest discrimination power (as identified by the Mann-Whitney U-test), we observed that the LBD group was associated with a lower range in on-surface acceleration, which we suppose is caused

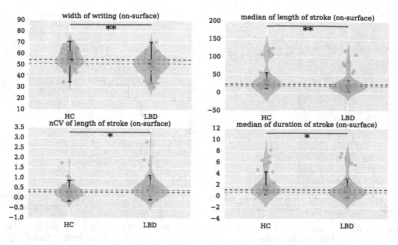

Fig. 3. Distribution of the top 4 most discriminating features (pentagons copying test).

Table 3. Results of the classification analysis.

Task	MCC	BACC	SEN	SPE	PRE	F1	threshold	p
Spiral	0.3977	0.6848	0.8696	0.5000	0.6349	0.7339	0.26	**
Sentence	0.5271	0.7283	0.9783	0.4783	0.6522	0.7826	0.36	**
Pentagons	0.4267	0.6848	0.9348	0.4348	0.6232	0.7478	0.13	**
All tasks combined	0.4824	0.7391	0.8043	0.6739	0.7115	0.7551	0.48	**

MCC – Matthew's correlation coefficient; BACC – balanced accuracy; SEN – sensitivity; SPE – specificity, PRE precision; F1 – F1 score; p – p-values computed by the permutation test (1 000 permutations, * denotes p-value < 0.05 and ** denotes p-value < 0.01); threshold – fine-tuned decision threshold.

by rigidity. This assumption is supported by the fact that the measure significantly correlates ($\rho = -0.3$, $p < 0.05$) with the overall score of MDS–UPDRS III. Next, the LBD group was not able to keep small variability of loop-to-loop spiral width index, which is in line with findings reported in [31]. We also observed a significant correlation between this feature and the visuospatial ($\rho = -0.4$, $p < 0.01$) and the attention ($\rho = -0.3$, $p < 0.05$) domain of CCB. On the other hand, the LBD group had generally higher values of the spiral precision index than the HC one, which is against our initial assumptions (also the correlation with the attention domain of CCB is surprisingly negative; $\rho = -0.4$, $p < 0.01$). Finally, the last significant correlation with the clinical status was identified in the median of azimuth, which was higher in the LBD group (in addition we observed a negative correlation with the visuospatial domain of CCB; $\rho = -0.4$, $p < 0.05$).

Regarding the classification analysis, based on the spiral features, we were able to discriminate the LBD and HC groups with 68% balanced accuracy (area under the curve (AUC) = 71%), which is the worst result when compared to other

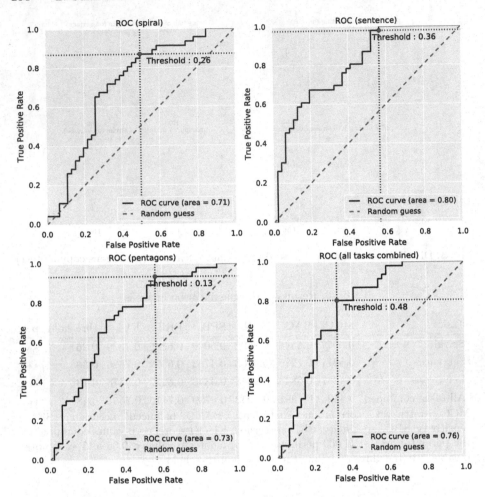

Fig. 4. Receiver operating characteristic curves for the trained models.

tasks and which supports our previous findings that even though the spiral is considered as a gold standard the sentence copy task accents the manifestations of dysgraphia much better [11].

Regarding the sentence, the most discriminative feature extracted from this task is the number of pen stops (i.e. a pen is in contact with the paper and does not vary its position for at least 30 ms [8]), which was higher in the LBD group. This parameter has been mainly employed in the diagnosis of developmental dysgraphia in children population [27], however, in one study, Danna et al. observed that this measure (but extracted from the spiral) was significantly different between PD patients in the OFF state and HC [8]. Initially, we assumed that the feature could be theoretically linked with cognitive deficits, but we did not observe any significant correlation with the visuospatial, attention, or executive functions domain of CCB. The second most significant feature was the slope of the duration of in-air strokes. The positive correlation coefficient suggests that the LBD subjects were associated with progressing fatigue [1,12,17]. Next, in the LBD group, we observed lower on-surface vertical velocity (this is in line with e.g. [21,35]), but increased on-surface vertical acceleration. This could be probably explained by the slow and less smooth handwriting. In terms of projection, the reason why these deficits dominate in the vertical movement could be explained by the fact that the finger system (which is mainly involved in the vertical movement) is more affected by muscular fatigue than the wrist system (which controls horizontal movement) [20]. The vertical movement requires coordinated movement and finer flexions/extensions of more joints (interphalangeal and metacarpophalangeal), thus it is more complex than ulnar abductions of the wrist [10,34] and could more accent the rigidity and bradykinesia. In addition, this manifestation could be associated with the progressive/consistent vertical micrographia, i.e., progressive/consistent reduction in letter amplitude [33].

In terms of classification, by modelling features extracted from the sentence, we were able to differentiate both groups with 73% balanced accuracy (AUC = 80%). In comparison with the state of the art in supportive LBD or PD diagnosis [9,19,35], it is not a competitive result, but on the other hand, we would like to highlight that we deal with results evaluating diagnosis of LBDs in the prodromal state that has not been targeted by other research teams yet.

Concerning the last (cognitive) task, all the top 5 discriminative features were extracted from the on-surface movement. In our recent article [4] we proved that in-air entropy-based parameters could be used to identify early cognitive deficits in PD without major cognitive impairment and that they correlate with the level of attention. In the current study, these in-air measures were not significant, but on the other hand, their on-surface variants (i.e. median of Shannon entropy calculated from the global/vertical movement) had the p-values of the Mann-Whitney U-test < 0.05, moreover, they significantly correlated with the visuospatial domain of CCB (e.g. $\rho = -0.3$, $p < 0.05$). The top 5 parameters consist of the width of the product, which was smaller in the LBD group. It slightly correlates with the lower median of the length of strokes ($\rho = 0.3$) and lower median of the duration of strokes ($\rho = 0.2$) and probably means that the subjects in the LBD group made the overlapped pentagons smaller. In addition, since the non-parametric coefficient of variation of the length of strokes was higher, we assume that the LBD subjects were not able to keep a stable length of strokes (nevertheless, based on the scoring published in [24], this is assumed as a very small deviation). Regarding the width, we also observed a negative correlation ($\rho = -0.3$, $p < 0.05$) with the overall score of MDS–UPDRS III.

The classification based on the pentagon copying test provided 68% balanced accuracy (AUC = 0.73%), which is slightly better than in the case of the spiral, but not as high as in the case of the sentence.

And finally, a machine learning model based on the whole set of features (tasks) enabled us to improve the accuracy to 74% (AUC = 76%). This shows that the combination of the graphomotor, handwriting and cognitive deficits can be used to achieve reasonable performance in the prodromal diagnosis of LBDs.

5 Conclusion

This study has several limitations. Our dataset has a small sample size and the HC and LBD groups are imbalanced, therefore to get better results in terms of their generalisation, a bigger database must be analysed. Next, due to the small sample size, we fused subjects with a high risk of developing PD or MCI-LB into one LBD group. Nevertheless, subjects with MCI-LB in its prodromal stage are associated mainly with cognitive (executive or visuospatial) decline, while subjects with prodromal PD experience mainly motor deficits. In other words, we suppose that further stratification of these participants into two groups could increase the classification accuracy (we hypothesise that MCI-LB would be more pronounced in the pentagon copying task and PD in the handwriting one). Finally, although we tried a correction of multiple comparisons during the statistical analysis, almost no significant features appeared after this adjustment. To sum up, concerning the limitations mentioned above, the study should be considered as a pilot one.

In conclusion, despite the limitations, to the best of our knowledge, it is the first work exploring the impact of computerised analysis of a graphomotor, cognitive, and handwriting task on the prodromal diagnosis of these neurodegenerative disorders. It bridges the knowledge gap in the field of LBDs, and provides baseline results for future studies focusing on the prodromal diagnosis of LBDs via a computerized and objective analysis of graphomotor and handwriting difficulties.

Acknowledgment. This work was supported by grant no. NU20-04-00294 (Diagnostics of Lewy body diseases in prodromal stage based on multimodal data analysis) of the Czech Ministry of Health and by Spanish grant of the Ministerio de Ciencia e Innovación no. PID2020-113242RB-I00 and by EU grant Next Generation EU (project no. LX22NPO5107 (MEYS)).

References

1. Aouraghe, I., Alae, A., Ghizlane, K., Mrabti, M., Aboulem, G., Faouzi, B.: A novel approach combining temporal and spectral features of Arabic online handwriting for Parkinson's disease prediction. J. Neurosci. Methods **339**, 108727 (2020)
2. Benedict, H.: Brief Visual Memory Test-Revised: Professional Manual. Psychological Assessment Resources, Odessa (1997)
3. Bezdicek, O., et al.: Development, validity, and normative data study for the 12-word Philadelphia Verbal Learning Test [czP (r) VLT-12] among older and very old Czech adults. Clin. Neuropsychol. **28**(7), 1162–1181 (2014)
4. Brabenec, L., Klobusiakova, P., Mekyska, J., Rektorova, I.: Shannon entropy: a novel parameter for quantifying pentagon copying performance in non-demented Parkinson's disease patients. Parkinsonism Relat. Disord. **94**, 45–48 (2022)
5. Cascarano, G.D., et al.: Biometric handwriting analysis to support Parkinson's disease assessment and grading. BMC Med. Inform. Decis. Mak. **19**(9), 1–11 (2019). https://doi.org/10.1186/s12911-019-0989-3

6. Chen, T., Guestrin, C.: XGBoost. In: Proceedings of the 22nd ACM SIGKDD International Conference on Knowledge Discovery and Data Mining - KDD 2016. ACM Press (2016). https://doi.org/10.1145/2939672.2939785

7. Combrisson, E., Jerbi, K.: Exceeding chance level by chance: the caveat of theoretical chance levels in brain signal classification and statistical assessment of decoding accuracy. J. Neurosci. Methods **250**, 126–136 (2015). https://doi.org/10.1016/j.jneumeth.2015.01.010

8. Danna, J., et al.: Digitalized spiral drawing in Parkinson's disease: a tool for evaluating beyond the written trace. Hum. Mov. Sci. **65**, 80–88 (2019)

9. De Stefano, C., Fontanella, F., Impedovo, D., Pirlo, G., di Freca, A.S.: Handwriting analysis to support neurodegenerative diseases diagnosis: a review. Pattern Recogn. Lett. **121**, 37–45 (2019)

10. Dounskaia, N., Van Gemmert, A., Stelmach, G.: Interjoint coordination during handwriting-like movements. Exp. Brain Res. **135**(1), 127–140 (2000). https://doi.org/10.1007/s002210000495

11. Drotár, P., Mekyska, J., Rektorová, I., Masarová, L., Smékal, Z., Faundez-Zanuy, M.: Evaluation of handwriting kinematics and pressure for differential diagnosis of Parkinson's disease. Artif. Intell. Med. **67**, 39–46 (2016)

12. Drotár, P., Mekyska, J., Smékal, Z., Rektorová, I., Masarová, L., Faundez-Zanuy, M.: Prediction potential of different handwriting tasks for diagnosis of Parkinson's. In: 2013 E-Health and Bioengineering Conference (EHB), pp. 1–4. IEEE (2013)

13. Faundez-Zanuy, M., Mekyska, J., Impedovo, D.: Online handwriting, signature and touch dynamics: tasks and potential applications in the field of security and health. Cogn. Comput. **13**(5), 1406–1421 (2021). https://doi.org/10.1007/s12559-021-09938-2

14. Galaz, Z., Mucha, J., Zvoncak, V., Mekyska, J.: Handwriting features (2022). www.github.com/BDALab/handwriting-features

15. Garre-Olmo, J., Faundez-Zanuy, M., López-de Ipiña, K., Calvó-Perxas, L., Turró-Garriga, O.: Kinematic and pressure features of handwriting and drawing: preliminary results between patients with mild cognitive impairment, Alzheimer disease and healthy controls. Curr. Alzheimer Res. **14**(9), 960–968 (2017)

16. Goetz, C.G., et al.: Movement disorder society-sponsored revision of the unified Parkinson's disease rating scale (MDS-UPDRS): scale presentation and clinimetric testing results. Mov. Disord. Off. J. Mov. Disord. Soc. **23**(15), 2129–2170 (2008)

17. Harralson, H.H., Teulings, H.L., Farley, B.G.: Handwriting variability in movement disorder patients and effects of fatigue. In: Proceedings of the Fourteenth Biennial Conference of the International Graphonomics Society, pp. 103–107 (2009)

18. Heinzel, S., et al.: Update of the MDS research criteria for prodromal Parkinson's disease. Mov. Disord. **34**(10), 1464–1470 (2019)

19. Impedovo, D., Pirlo, G.: Dynamic handwriting analysis for the assessment of neurodegenerative diseases: a pattern recognition perspective. IEEE Rev. Biomed. Eng. **12**, 209–220 (2018)

20. Kushki, A., Schwellnus, H., Ilyas, F., Chau, T.: Changes in kinetics and kinematics of handwriting during a prolonged writing task in children with and without dysgraphia. Res. Dev. Disabil. **32**(3), 1058–1064 (2011)

21. Letanneux, A., Danna, J., Velay, J.L., Viallet, F., Pinto, S.: From micrographia to Parkinson's disease dysgraphia. Mov. Disord. **29**(12), 1467–1475 (2014)

22. McKeith, I.G., et al.: Research criteria for the diagnosis of prodromal dementia with Lewy bodies. Neurology **94**(17), 743–755 (2020)

23. Monvoisin-Joly, T., Furcieri, E., Chabran, E., Blanc, F.: Writing in prodromal and mild dementia with Lewy bodies: an exploratory and preliminary study. Geriatrie et Psychologie Neuropsychiatrie du Vieillissement **19**(3), 341–351 (2021)
24. Nagaratnam, N., Nagaratnam, K., O'Mara, D.: Intersecting pentagon copying and clock drawing test in mild and moderate Alzheimer's disease. J. Clin. Gerontol. Geriatr. **5**(2), 47–52 (2014)
25. Nasreddine, Z.S., et al.: The Montreal Cognitive Assessment, MoCA: a brief screening tool for mild cognitive impairment. J. Am. Geriatr. Soc. **53**(4), 695–699 (2005)
26. Ojala, M., Garriga, G.: Permutation tests for studying classifier performance. In: ICDM 2009: Ninth IEEE International Conference on Data Mining 2009, pp. 908–913, December 2009. https://doi.org/10.1109/ICDM.2009.108
27. Paz-Villagrán, V., Danna, J., Velay, J.L.: Lifts and stops in proficient and dysgraphic handwriting. Hum. Mov. Sci. **33**, 381–394 (2014)
28. Phipson, B., Smyth, G.K.: Permutation P-values should never be zero: calculating exact P-values when permutations are randomly drawn. Stat. Appl. Genet. Mol. Biol. **9**(1) (2010). https://doi.org/10.2202/1544-6115.1585
29. Postuma, R.B., et al.: MDS clinical diagnostic criteria for Parkinson's disease. Mov. Disord. **30**(12), 1591–1601 (2015)
30. Preiss, M., et al.: Test verbální fluence-vodítka pro všeobecnou dospělou populaci. Psychiatrie **6**(2), 74–77 (2002)
31. San Luciano, M., et al.: Digitized spiral drawing: a possible biomarker for early Parkinson's disease. PLoS ONE **11**(10), e0162799 (2016)
32. Saunders-Pullman, R., et al.: Validity of spiral analysis in early Parkinson's disease. Mov. Disord. Off. J. Mov. Disord. Soc. **23**(4), 531–537 (2008)
33. Thomas, M., Lenka, A., Kumar Pal, P.: Handwriting analysis in Parkinson's disease: current status and future directions. Mov. Disord. Clin. Pract. **4**(6), 806–818 (2017)
34. Van Galen, G.P.: Handwriting: issues for a psychomotor theory. Hum. Mov. Sci. **10**(2–3), 165–191 (1991)
35. Vessio, G.: Dynamic handwriting analysis for neurodegenerative disease assessment: a literary review. Appl. Sci. **9**(21), 4666 (2019)
36. Warrington, E.K., James, M.: The visual object and space perception battery (1991)
37. Wechsler, D., et al.: WAIS-III WMS-III Technical Manual. Psychological Corporation, San Antonio (1997)
38. Yamada, M., et al.: Diagnostic criteria for dementia with Lewy bodies: updates and future directions. J. Mov. Disord. **13**(1), 1 (2020)

Generation of Synthetic Drawing Samples to Diagnose Parkinson's Disease

Gennaro Gemito[1] , Angelo Marcelli[1,2] , and Antonio Parziale[1,2][(✉)]

[1] DIEM, University of Salerno, Via Giovanni Paolo II 132, 84084 Fisciano, SA, Italy
gemito.gen@gmail.com, {amarcelli,anparziale}@unisa.it
[2] AI3S Unit, CINI National Laboratory of Artificial Intelligence and Intelligent Systems, University of Salerno, Fisciano, SA, Italy

Abstract. The state-of-the-art artificial intelligence tools for automatic diagnosis of Parkinson's disease from handwriting require a lot of training samples from both healthy subjects and patients to exhibit impressive performance. Publicly available datasets include very few samples drawn by a small number of individuals and that limits the use of deep learning architectures. In this paper, we evaluate if the performance of a Convolutional Neural Network that recognizes the handwriting of Parkinson's disease patients can be improved by adding synthetic samples to the training set. In the experimentation, we synthetically generated dynamic signals of spirals and meanders through the use of a Recurrent Neural Network. The performance of the system was evaluated on the NewHandPD dataset and the results showed that the use of synthetic samples increases the recognition accuracy of the convolutional neural network.

Keywords: Data augmentation · Handwriting synthesis · Parkinson's disease · Handwriting analysis · CNN · RNN

1 Introduction

Parkinson's disease (PD) is a neurodegenerative disorder that affects dopaminergic neurons in the Basal Ganglia, whose death causes several motor and cognitive symptoms. PD patients show impaired ability in controlling movements and disruption in the execution of everyday skills, due to postural instability, the onset of tremors, stiffness and bradykinesia [10, 14, 23, 24].

There is no cure for the disease and the decline can only be somehow managed during its progression. This creates a critical need for improving the procedures and the tools for diagnosing them as early as possible.

The analysis of handwritten production has brought many insights for uncovering the processes occurring during both physiological and pathological conditions [3, 28, 29] and providing a non-invasive method for evaluating the stage of the disease [22].

C. Carmona-Duarte et al. (Eds.): IGS 2021, LNCS 13424, pp. 269–284, 2022.
https://doi.org/10.1007/978-3-031-19745-1_20

The main advantage of diagnostic systems based on handwriting analysis with respect to other diagnostic procedures is that collecting handwriting samples is cheap and tests are easy to administer. Therefore, different artificial intelligence based approaches for the automatic identification of Parkinson's and Alzheimer's disease motor symptoms have been proposed, together with a variety of motor tasks administered to healthy individuals and patients [16,20].

The desire of applying top-performing and most recent deep learning techniques to this application domain has highlighted the lack of a huge collection of handwriting samples. All the publicly available datasets include samples drawn by a reduced number of subjects and are, in some cases, unbalanced. Collecting data from patients is, in general, more complex than collecting data from healthy subjects mainly for two reasons: the need of reaching patients at their living places and the participation of specialized medical personnel during the administration of the diagnostic test.

To overcome the difficulty in collecting data from patients, in a very recent paper we have proposed to adopt machine learning tools based on *one-class* classification algorithms, i.e. algorithms capable of solving a two-class classification problem by learning the distinctive characteristics of only one class [17]. We have shown that is possible to reach state-of-the-art performance by training the Negative Selection Algorithm only with samples drawn by healthy subjects.

To overcome the more general problem of the scarcity of data and, therefore, to improve the performance of classifiers and to avoid overfitting of models, some papers investigated the usefulness of data augmentation and transfer learning to improve the classification performance [11,15,25]. The alterations introduced by data augmentation methods generate new samples that may not correspond to credible real samples. So, in this paper, we propose to increase the size of datasets by exploiting algorithms that are able to generate synthetic handwriting samples. To the best of our knowledge, that is the first time that these algorithms are applied to the application domain of diagnosis of neurodegenerative diseases. In particular, we evaluated the performance of the generator of synthetic samples based on a Recurrent Neural Network proposed by Alex Graves in [7].

The paper is organised as it follows. In Sect. 2, we review the previous works on synthetic handwriting generation and data augmentation and we show that there are different algorithms to generate synthetic handwriting but, up to now, they have not yet used to diagnose PD from handwriting. In Sect. 3, we briefly introduce the real data used in the experimentation, while in Sect. 4 we present the approach adopted to generate synthetic drawing samples. Section 5 introduces the CNN used as classifier and the approach adopted to convert signals to 2D images. Section 6 discusses the system that combines the synthetic generator of drawing samples and the classifier in order to select the best synthetic samples that will be used to train the final system. Sections 7 and 8 discuss the setup adopted to perform the experiments and the results we obtained. Eventually, Sect. 9 briefly discusses the results and Sect. 10 concludes the work.

2 Related Works

Many algorithms have been proposed in the literature for the generation of synthetic handwriting and they can be grouped in two different families: template-based approaches [4,5,9] and learning-based approaches [7,12,13]. The main difference between these two methodologies is that template-based approaches generate synthetic samples by perturbing real samples while learning-based approaches train neural networks to build a high-dimensional interpolation between training examples that will be used to generate synthetic samples.

Synthesis of handwriting samples has been applied to improve the performance of automatic systems for writer and signature verification [5,21] and for handwriting recognition [1,9,12].

In the field of handwriting analysis for the diagnosis of neurodegenerative disorders, as Parkinson's and Alzheimer's disease, classical approaches of data augmentation have been recently implemented to boost the performance of deep learning networks. Classical approaches of data augmentation are those that have been applied in the more general field of computer vision and they include geometrical distortions and noise addition to real samples.

Rotations, flipping and contours were adopted in [15] to increase by a factor of 13 the cardinality of the dataset that was used to train the convolutional neural network AlexNet. In [11] the authors observed that rotation and thresholding had a negative impact on performance while illumination showed significantly better performance in comparison.

Data augmentation methods as jittering, scaling, time-warping, and averaging were applied directly to time series to increase the cardinality of the dataset used to train a CNN-BLSTM network [25]. The results showed that the combination of CNN-BLSTM and data augmentation was not effective when a single task was considered, but it increased the accuracy of 7.15% when the classification outputs per each task were combined.

3 Dataset of Real Sample

In this study, we used the NewHandPD dataset [19], a public dataset that includes handwritten data produced by 31 PD patients and 35 healthy subjects. The healthy group includes 18 male and 17 female individuals with ages ranging from 14 to 79 years old (average age of 44.05 ± 14.88 years), while the patient group includes 21 male and 10 female individuals with ages ranging from 38 to 78 years old (average age of 57.83 ± 7.85 years).

Each individual drew 12 samples: 4 spirals, 4 meanders, 2 circled movements, and 2 diadochokinesis. The dynamics of each sample were recorded by means of a Biometric Smart Pen (BiSP), while an image of the sample was available only for spirals, meanders and circles. A BiSP records 6 signals from as many sensors: voice signal $m(t)$, fingergrip $gr(t)$, axial pressure of ink refill $p(t)$, tilt and acceleration in X direction $a_x(t)$, tilt and acceleration in Y direction $a_y(t)$, tilt and acceleration in Z direction $a_z(t)$.

In this study only the signals acquired with BiSP were taken into account while the images were not used. Moreover, we used only signals related to spirals and meanders, which are the classical motor tasks adopted to diagnose Parkinson's disease [30].

4 Generation of Synthetic Samples

4.1 The Method

The system we realized to generate synthetic drawing samples is based on the approach proposed by Alex Graves [7], which exploits Long Short-term Memory recurrent neural networks to generate complex sequences by predicting one data point at a time. The main idea behind the approach proposed by Graves is that RNN can be trained on real data sequences one step at a time so that the network can predict which point follows another one. Predicting the trajectory one point at a time has the advantage of increasing the diversity among the samples generated by the network.

It's worth noting that the network isn't trained to predict the next location of the pen, but to generate a probability distribution of what happens at the next instant of time, including whether the pen gets lifted up. In particular, a Gaussian mixture distribution is generated to predict the pen offset from the previous location while a Bernoulli distribution predicts if the pen stays on the paper or not.

This prediction is realized through the use of a *mixture density network* [2], which uses the outputs of a neural network to parameterise a mixture distribution. The combination of mixture density and RNN has the effect that the output distribution is conditioned not only on the current input, but on the history of previous inputs too.

In the original implementation proposed by Graves, each input vector x_t to the network is made-up of a real-valued pair $\{x_t^1, x_t^2\}$, which defines the pen offset from the previous input, and a binary x_t^3 that has value 1 if the vector ends a stroke. Each output vector y_t consists of the end-of-stroke probability e_t, a two-dimensional vector of means μ^j, a two-dimensional vector of standard deviation σ^j, correlations ρ^j and mixture weights π^j, which are scalars, for the M mixture components. The outputs of the network are transformed so that they satisfy the bounds related to the quantity they represent (for example, the real value used as correlation is bound between -1 and 1 with a hyperbolic tangent). Overall, the total number of outputs is equal to $(1 + M * 6)$.

The probability density $Pr(x_{t+1}|y_t)$ of the next input x_{t+1} given the output vector y_t is defined as follows:

$$Pr(x_{t+1}|y_t) = \sum_{j=1}^{M} \pi_t^j \mathcal{N}(x_{t+1}|\mu_t^j, \sigma_t^j, \rho_t^j) \begin{cases} e_t & \text{if } x_{t+1}^3 = 1 \\ 1 - e_t & \text{otherwise} \end{cases} \tag{1}$$

The probability given by the network to the input sequence x is

$$Pr(x) = \prod_{t=1}^{T} Pr(x_{t+1}|y_t) \tag{2}$$

and the sequence loss $L(x)$ used to train the network is the negative logarithm of $Pr(x)$

$$L(x) = -\sum_{t=1}^{T} log(Pr(x_{t+1}|y_t)) \tag{3}$$

Once trained the RNN network is able to generate synthetic time sequences of a given length. As initial input, a vector of zeros is passed to the network and the end-of-stroke signal is turned on, signalling to the network that the next point it produces will be the start of a new stroke, rather than a continuation of an existing one. A zero state is also passed into the network for the initialization. After that, the network outputs the parameters of the probability distributions from which we randomly sample a set of values that represent a point of the synthetic sample. Afterwards, we repeat the loop and feed in the sampled point and network state back in as inputs, to get another probability distribution to sample from for the next point, and we repeat until we get the desired number of points.

4.2   The Implementation

The method described before was proposed to generate synthetic handwritten text, which consists of sequences of characters and then of words, and therefore, in the original implementation, the term end-of-stroke referred to the end of a pen-down.

Instead, in this paper, we want to synthesize drawing samples that are usually executed in a single pen-down. We know by handwriting generation theory that a pen-down is a superimposition of elementary movements, so, in our implementation, the end of a stroke corresponds to the end of an elementary movement.

The real samples were segmented in elementary movements by looking at the zero crossings of the tangential velocity along the y-axis [26]. Because the samples in NewHandPD include only the acceleration along the three axes, we needed to integrate these signals to detect the start and the end of elementary movements. Accelerations were filtered before integration, as suggested in another paper that used a smartpen similar to the one used for collecting NewHandPD data [27]. We filtered the acceleration signals between 0.5 Hz and 12 Hz with a 4th order Butterworth filter to remove the DC component related to slow oscillations and gravity and the frequencies beyond the range of relevant tremor components.

Given the time series available for each real sample, the inputs of the network were the acceleration along x and y instead of x and y as in Graves' paper.

As with regards to the architecture of the network, we used a 2-layer stacked basic-LSTM network (no peephole connections) with 256 nodes in each layer. The number M of mixture components was set equal to 20, as in the original

Graves' paper. Overall, the network outputs 121 real values used to infer the probability distribution.

In our experiments, we adopted the implementation made available by David Ha at [8]. This implementation adopts mini-batches to fast the learning process. Mini-batches require to be the same length to be efficient and therefore time series were divided in sequences of length SL. Afterward, continuous portions of SL points were randomly sampled from the training sample and included in the mini-batches. Eventually, a dropout layer was included for each of the output layers of the LSTM to regularise training and reduce the overfitting.

5   Classification Stage

5.1   From Signal to Image

Let K be the total number of time series available for each handwriting sample and k the time series selected for the generation of the 2D image. Let n be the number of points of each time series.

The selected k time series of a handwriting sample are rearranged into a $(\sqrt{n \times k}, \sqrt{n \times k})$ square matrix Im that, in turn, is resized into a 64×64 image using the Lanczos resampling method. When $n \times k$ is not a square number, time series are truncated just enough to guarantee that Im has two natural numbers as dimensions.

Im is built by concatenating n arrays of k elements. In particular, the i-th array is made up of the value at time t_i of each time series. The arrays are horizontally concatenated so that the rows of Im are filled one by one. It is worth noting that the values of the time series are scaled in the range $[0, 255]$ so that each value can be represented by a grayscale pixel.

This approach for the generation of a 2D image from the time series of a sample is similar to the ones proposed in [19,25] but differs in the way Im is filled. In particular, the approaches in the literature concatenate the arrays so that the columns of the matrix, instead of rows, are filled one by one. Figure 1 shows an example of an image generated by following the approach described in this subsection.

5.2   Convolutional Neural Network

The 2D images representing the time series of handwriting samples are classified by a Convolutional Neural Network (CNN) whose architecture is taken from the neural network CIFAR-10 presented in [18]. The network has been fully implemented from scratch using the Python *TensorFlow2.0* library. Figure 2 shows a top-level view of the entire architecture and the hyper-parameters related to each layer.

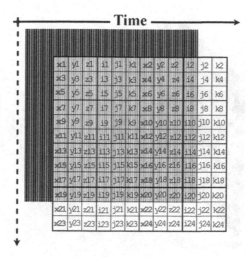

Fig. 1. An example of a grayscale 2D image obtained by $k = K = 6$ time series

6   Validation of Synthetic Data

The solution adopted in this work to assess the output of the RNN draws inspiration from the operation of Generative Adversarial Networks, or GANs [6]. GANs learn how to generate new data by adopting an architecture with two agents: a *Generator Model*, which generates a new example, and a *Discriminator Model*, which decides if the generated example is real or synthetic. Both the *Generator* and the *Discriminator* are Neural Networks: the Generator output is connected directly to the Discriminator input so, through backpropagation, the Discriminator's classification provides signals that the Generator uses to update its weights.

The main difference between standard GAN models and the approach proposed here is that the Generator doesn't learn from Discriminator's feedback since the two models are independent of each other. In fact, while in the GANs the two agents are connected through backpropagation so that the output of the Discriminator updates the weights of the Generator, in this work *Generator* and *Discriminator* are two separate subsystems: the RNN described in Sect. 4 generates synthetic data and, in a separate moment, these data are validated by the classifier described in Sect. 5 and trained on real data. So, the synthetic samples correctly classified by the CNN will be used to increase the dimension of the training set while the others will be discarded. Figure 3 shows the system implemented to validate synthetic samples.

It is worth noting that in our system the Discriminator consists of 5 CNNs and it classifies samples by a majority vote algorithm. The dataset of real samples is shuffled 5 times and each time a CNN is trained with 35% of the data.

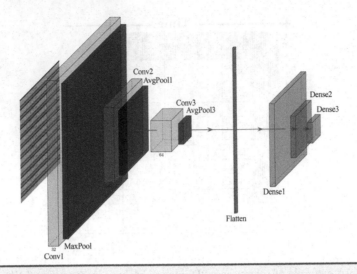

Fig. 2. Top-level view of the CNN used as classifier and hyper-parameters of each layer. The image was realized with Plotneuralnet.

7 Experimental Setup

7.1 Time Series Selection

We performed a preliminary experiment to verify if representing each sample with two time series instead of six could affect the performance of the classifier. In particular, we compared the performance of the network when the following two sets of time series were considered:

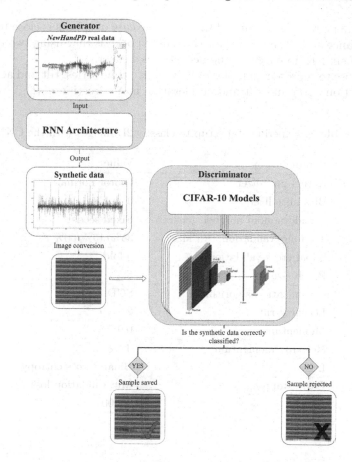

Fig. 3. The approach adopted to validate synthetic samples

- $\{m(t_i), gr(t_i), p(t_i), a_x(t_i), a_y(t_i), a_z(t_i)\}$;
- $\{a_x(t_i), a_y(t_i)\}$

Table 1 resumes all the choices we did to configure the experiment and the learning process of the convolutional neural network. Those values were selected after a fine-tuning process aimed at avoiding overfitting and maximizing the performance of the network on the validation set. The partition of the data in training, validation and test sets was made by guaranteeing that all the samples drawn by an individual were included in only one of the sets. We trained two different CNNs, one devoted to discriminating between PD and healthy subjects by looking at spirals and the other by looking at meanders.

Table 2 shows the results obtained by the two CNNs when images are generated by one of the two sets of time series. For each drawing task, we evaluated if the difference between the classification accuracies was statistically significant or not by performing a Wilcoxon test, with a level of significance $\alpha = 0.05$. As shown in the table, differences are not statistically significant, both for spirals and meanders, but the p-value obtained in the case of spirals is close to the level of significance and the evidence for the null hypothesis that using two time series instead of six has no effect on the accuracy is weaker.

We chose to represent samples only with two time series, tilt and acceleration in X direction $a_x(t)$ and tilt and acceleration in Y direction $a_y(t)$.

Table 1. Experimental setup to classify 2D images with the CNN

Parameter	Value
Kernel initializer	Glorot normal
Bias initializer	0
Pseudorandom number generators	Fixed seeds
Training/validation/test size	35%/15%/50%
k-fold cross validation	5-fold
Batch size	5
Optimization algorithm	SGD
Learning rate	2×10^{-5}
Momentum	0.9
Nesterov momentum	True
Loss	Binary cross entropy
Early stopping	Min validation loss
Epochs	10000

Table 2. Performance of the CNN when two different sets of time series are considered. The last column reports the p-value of the Wilcoxon statistical test. 2 time series: $\{a_x(t_i), a_y(t_i)\}$, 6 time series: $\{m(t_i), gr(t_i), p(t_i), a_x(t_i), a_y(t_i), a_z(t_i)\}$.

Task	Accuracy (%)		p-value
	2 time series	6 time series	
Spirals	70.75 ± 3.22	77.01 ± 3.25	0.07961
Meanders	74.42 ± 7.81	74.72 ± 2.62	0.89274

7.2   Generation and Validation of Synthetic Samples

We trained 4 different RNNs, which were implemented according to the architecture described in Sect. 4: the first synthesized spiral drawn by healthy subjects, the second synthesized spiral drawn by PD patients, the third and the fourth synthesized meanders drawn by healthy and PD patients, respectively.

Table 3 reports the hyper-parameter values used for these networks, which were fine-tuned with the aim of minimizing the loss on the validation set.

Once the 4 networks were trained, each of them generated SS valid samples. The validity of a sample was verified with the system that combines the synthetic generator and the classifier, as described in Sect. 6. We evaluated seven conditions with $SS = [100, 300, 500, 600, 800, 1000, 1500]$.

The length of each sample (the number of its points) generated by one of the RNNs was chosen so that the distribution of synthetic samples per number of points was similar to the distribution of real samples per number of points.

Table 3. RNN hyper-parameters to generate synthetic samples

Parameter	Value
RNN hidden state	256
Number of stacked cells (layers)	2
Cell type	LSTM
Sequence length SL	512
Number of epochs	300
Learning rate	0.005
Number of mixture M	20
Dropout keep probability	0.8
Training/validation set	70%/30% of total samples
Loss function	Log likelihood loss

7.3   Data Augmentation and Classification

Two CNNs were trained with both real and synthetic samples to diagnose Parkinson's disease: one processed spirals, the other one meanders. The two CNNs were trained using the hyper-parameters reported in Table 1, the same ones we used to train the network with only real samples.

The $2 * SS$ synthetic spirals (SS per class) and the $2 * SS$ synthetic meanders were added to the 50% of real samples used in the training phase, which were split between training and validation sets. Synthetic samples were not included in the test set.

The performance was measured by averaging on 5 training of the CNNs. Every time, the real dataset was shuffled and 50% of subjects were kept apart as test set. So, the samples drawn by an individual were included in the training or in the test set but never in both of them.

8   Results

Figure 4 shows how the accuracy of the system varies as the number of synthetic samples varies from 0 to 1500, both for spirals and meanders. Figure 4a shows

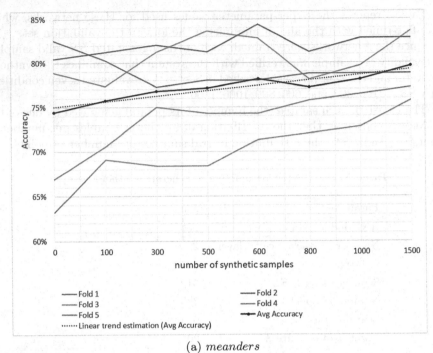

(a) *meanders*

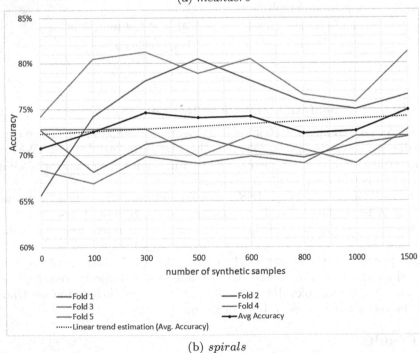

(b) *spirals*

Fig. 4. Accuracy vs number of synthetic samples for meanders and spirals

Table 4. Accuracy (Acc.), Sensitivity (Sens.) and Specificity (Spec.) of the CNN when it is trained without or with synthetic samples.

	No synthetic samples			1500 synthetic samples		
	Acc. (%)	Sens. (%)	Spec. (%)	Acc. (%)	Sens. (%)	Spec. (%)
Spirals	70.75 ± 3.22	68.69 ± 5.19	72.62 ± 3.17	74.93 ± 3.58	74.08 ± 5.54	76.09 ± 3.26
Meanders	74.42 ± 7.81	75.60 ± 6.22	73.54 ± 8.10	79.63 ± 3.09	78.77 ± 4.28	80.32 ± 6.78

an evident increasing linear trend of the average accuracy as the number of synthetic meanders in the training set increases. Moreover, the increase in the number of synthetic meanders reduces the differences in the performance of the system when it is trained with a different set of data. Figure 4b shows that these comments are still valid for spirals even though less evident.

Table 4 reports the results obtained when the CNN described in Sect. 5 was trained only with real samples or with the addition of 1500 synthetic samples (15% of which were used as validation).

The use of synthetic spirals had the effect of increasing accuracy, sensitivity and specificity of 4.18%, 5.39% and 3.47%, respectively. The use of synthetic meanders had the effect of increasing accuracy, sensitivity and specificity of 5.21%, 3.17% and 6.78%, respectively. Moreover, the standard deviation of the system trained with real and synthetic samples is lower than the variability of the system trained with real data only. In particular, the standard deviation of the accuracy is more than halved when synthetic samples are used.

9   Discussion

The RNN used to generate synthetic samples does not directly output the next location of the pentip but the parameters of mixture distributions that are sampled to predict the next point of the trajectory. Sampling one point at a time from probability distributions favours the diversity between real and synthetic samples. A preliminary analysis confirmed that the synthetic samples differ from the ones in the test set although the entire real dataset was used to train and validate the RNN. Nevertheless, this aspect will be further investigated in future works by keeping the test set apart from the data used to train the generator network.

The difference in performance when the system is trained with meanders instead of spirals could be ascribed to the selection of time series. In fact, as we can see in Table 2, the use of two time series instead of six has no effect on meanders but lower the accuracy when spirals are evaluated, even though it is not statistically significant. This aspect needs to be investigated in the future by increasing the number of experiments.

10 Conclusions

Publicly available datasets are made-up of samples handwritten by small numbers of subjects. This aspect limits the use of top-performing deep learning algorithms that need a huge amount of data to correctly classify samples. To solve this problem, we have proposed to use algorithms for handwriting synthesis to increase the size of the training set.

Preliminary results have confirmed that the addition of synthetic samples to the training set increases the performance of a basic convolution neural network and reduce the variability of performance as the training set varies.

In our future investigations, we will aim at performing a systematic investigation that will take into account different neural network architectures as well as samples corresponding to other motor tasks, as for example words and sentences. Moreover, we plan to combine template-based and learning-based methods to increase the diversity of synthetic samples. Eventually, we will exploit a correlation analysis between basic handwriting features and the clinical state of participants in order to evaluate if it is possible to generate synthetic samples that denote different stages of PD, from early to severe stages.

References

1. Bhattacharya, U., Plamondon, R., Dutta Chowdhury, S., Goyal, P., Parui, S.K.: A sigma-lognormal model-based approach to generating large synthetic online handwriting sample databases. Int. J. Doc. Anal. Recogn. (IJDAR) **20**(3), 155–171 (2017). https://doi.org/10.1007/s10032-017-0287-5
2. Bishop, C.: Mixture density networks. Technical report NCRG/94/004, Aston University, January 1994. https://www.microsoft.com/en-us/research/publication/mixturedensity-networks/
3. Broderick, M.P., Van Gemmert, A.W., Shill, H.A., Stelmach, G.E.: Hypometria and bradykinesia during drawing movements in individuals with Parkinson's disease. Exp. Brain Res. **197**(3), 223–233 (2009). https://doi.org/10.1007/s00221-009-1925-z
4. Carmona-Duarte, C., Ferrer, M.A., Parziale, A., Marcelli, A.: Temporal evolution in synthetic handwriting. Pattern Recogn. **68**, 233–244 (2017)
5. Diaz, M., Ferrer, M.A., Eskander, G.S., Sabourin, R.: Generation of duplicated offline signature images for verification systems. IEEE Trans. Pattern Anal. Mach. Intell. **39**(5), 951–964 (2016)
6. Goodfellow, I.J., et al.: Generative adversarial networks (2014)
7. Graves, A.: Generating sequences with recurrent neural networks (2013). https://doi.org/10.48550/ARXIV.1308.0850. https://arxiv.org/abs/1308.0850
8. Ha, D.: Write RNN TensorFlow (2018). https://github.com/hardmaru/writernntensorow.git
9. Haines, T.S., Mac Aodha, O., Brostow, G.J.: My text in your handwriting. ACM Trans. Graph. (TOG) **35**(3), 1–18 (2016)
10. Jankovic, J.: Parkinson's disease: clinical features and diagnosis. J. Neurol. Neurosurg. Psychiatry **79**(4), 368–376 (2008)

11. Kamran, I., Naz, S., Razzak, I., Imran, M.: Handwriting dynamics assessment using deep neural network for early identification of Parkinson's disease. Future Gener. Comput. Syst. **117**, 234–244 (2021)
12. Kang, L., Riba, P., Wang, Y., Rusiñol, M., Fornés, A., Villegas, M.: GANwriting: content-conditioned generation of styled handwritten word images. In: Vedaldi, A., Bischof, H., Brox, T., Frahm, J.-M. (eds.) ECCV 2020. LNCS, vol. 12368, pp. 273–289. Springer, Cham (2020). https://doi.org/10.1007/978-3-030-58592-1_17
13. Kumar, K.M., Kandala, H., Reddy, N.S.: Synthesizing and imitating handwriting using deep recurrent neural networks and mixture density networks. In: 2018 9th International Conference on Computing, Communication and Networking Technologies (ICCCNT), pp. 1–6. IEEE (2018)
14. Marsden, C.: Slowness of movement in Parkinson's disease. Mov. Disord. Off. J. Mov. Disord. Soc. **4**(S1), S26–S37 (1989)
15. Naseer, A., Rani, M., Naz, S., Razzak, M.I., Imran, M., Xu, G.: Refining Parkinson's neurological disorder identification through deep transfer learning. Neural Comput. Appl. **32**(3), 839–854 (2020). https://doi.org/10.1007/s00521-019-04069-0
16. Parziale, A., Senatore, R., Della Cioppa, A., Marcelli, A.: Cartesian genetic programming for diagnosis of Parkinson disease through handwriting analysis: performance vs. interpretability issues. Artif. Intell. Med. **111**, 101984 (2021)
17. Parziale, A., Della Cioppa, A., Marcelli, A.: Investigating one-class classifiers to diagnose Alzheimer's disease from handwriting. In: Sclaroff, S., Distante, C., Leo, M., Farinella, G.M., Tombari, F. (eds.) ICIAP 2022. LNCS, vol. 13231, pp. 111–123. Springer International Publishing, Cham (2022). https://doi.org/10.1007/978-3-031-06427-2_10
18. Pereira, C.R., et al.: A new computer vision-based approach to aid the diagnosis of Parkinson's disease. Comput. Methods Programs Biomed. **136**, 79–88 (2016)
19. Pereira, C.R., Weber, S.A.T., Hook, C., Rosa, G.H., Papa, J.P.: Deep learning-aided Parkinson's disease diagnosis from handwritten dynamics. In: Proceedings of the Conference on Graphics, Patterns and Images, pp. 340–346. IEEE (2016)
20. Pereira, C.R., Pereira, D.R., Weber, S.A., Hook, C., de Albuquerque, V.H.C., Papa, J.P.: A survey on computer-assisted Parkinson's disease diagnosis. Artif. Intell. Med. **95**, 48–63 (2019)
21. Pignelli, F., Costa, Y.M.G., Oliveira, L.S., Bertolini, D.: Data augmentation for writer identification using a cognitive inspired model. In: Lladós, J., Lopresti, D., Uchida, S. (eds.) ICDAR 2021. LNCS, vol. 12824, pp. 251–266. Springer, Cham (2021). https://doi.org/10.1007/978-3-030-86337-1_17
22. Senatore, R., Marcelli, A.: A paradigm for emulating the early learning stage of handwriting: performance comparison between healthy controls and Parkinson's disease patients in drawing loop shapes. Hum. Mov. Sci. **65**, 89–101 (2019)
23. Sheridan, M., Flowers, K., Hurrell, J.: Programming and execution of movement in Parkinson's disease. Brain **110**(5), 1247–1271 (1987)
24. Stelmach, G.E., Teasdale, N., Phillips, J., Worringham, C.J.: Force production characteristics in Parkinson's disease. Exp. Brain Res. **76**(1), 165–172 (1989). https://doi.org/10.1007/BF00253633
25. Taleb, C., Likforman-Sulem, L., Mokbel, C., Khachab, M.: Detection of Parkinson's disease from handwriting using deep learning: a comparative study. Evol. Intell. (2020). https://doi.org/10.1007/s12065-020-00470-0
26. Teulings, H.L.: Handwriting movement control. In: Heuer, H., Keele, S.W. (eds.) Motor Skills, Handbook of Perception and Action, vol. 2, pp. 561–613. Academic Press (1996). https://doi.org/10.1016/S1874-5822(06)80013-7

27. Toffoli, S., et al.: A smart ink pen for spiral drawing analysis in patients with Parkinson's disease. In: 2021 43rd Annual International Conference of the IEEE Engineering in Medicine Biology Society (EMBC), pp. 6475–6478 (2021)
28. Tucha, O., et al.: Kinematic analysis of dopaminergic effects on skilled handwriting movements in Parkinson's disease. J. Neural Transm. **113**(5), 609–623 (2006). https://doi.org/10.1007/s00702-005-0346-9
29. Van Gemmert, A., Adler, C., Stelmach, G.: Parkinson's disease patients undershoot target size in handwriting and similar tasks. J. Neurol. Neurosurg. Psychiatry **74**(11), 1502–1508 (2003)
30. Vessio, G.: Dynamic handwriting analysis for neurodegenerative disease assessment: a literary review. Appl. Sci. **9**(21), 4666 (2019)

Early Dementia Identification: On the Use of Random Handwriting Strokes

Vincenzo Gattulli[1], Donato Impedovo[1], Giuseppe Pirlo[1],
and Gianfranco Semeraro[1,2(✉)]

[1] Department of Computer Science, University of Studies of Bari "Aldo Moro", Via Edoardo Orabona, 4, 70125 Bari, BA, Italy
donato.impedovo@uniba.it
[2] University School for Advanced Studies IUSS Pavia, Palazzo del Broletto, Piazza Della Vittoria, 15, 27100 Pavia, PV, Italy
gianfranco.semeraro@iusspavia.it

Abstract. Timely diagnosis plays a crucial role for the treatment of neurodegenerative diseases. In particular, Dementia Identification in early stages is important to help patients have a better quality of life and to help clinicians to find a pathway of treatments to slow the effects. To the aim, a wide set of different handwriting tasks is here considered, and Shallow and Deep Learning methodologies are compared. Furthermore, Random Hybrid Stroke (RHS) are adopted to represent the handwriting time series. This solution outperforms the classical Deep Learning methodology and it is compared to a state-of-art shallow learning approach. Finally, a decision-level fusion for the results is adopted.

Keywords: Neurodegenerative disease · Handwriting · Kinematic theory · Velocity-based features · Hand-Uniba · Random hybrid stroke · Bidirectional LSTM

1 Introduction

Neurodegenerative diseases are a diverse group of diseases affecting the central nervous system, united by a chronic and selective process of cell death of neurons. Depending on the type of disease, the deterioration process may involve a range of symptoms affecting the individual's memory, cognitive, functional, and motor skills. *Alzheimer's disease (AD)* and *Parkinson's disease (PD)* are the most common neurodegenerative disorders characterized by a progressive decline in cognitive, functional, and behavioral areas of the brain [1, 2]. Unfortunately, there are no cures for these diseases. However, an early diagnosis is crucial for the prospect of appropriate medical treatment.

Non-invasive behavioral biometric techniques traditionally used for security purposes can also be used effectively in the medical field by showing good accuracies in binary (healthy/diseased) classification [3, 4]. Indeed, as an integral part of neurological testing, handwriting appears to be a complex activity involving cognitive, functional, and perceptual-motor components whose changes may be an effective biomarker for the

C. Carmona-Duarte et al. (Eds.): IGS 2021, LNCS 13424, pp. 285–300, 2022.
https://doi.org/10.1007/978-3-031-19745-1_21

assessment of degenerative dementia [5]. So, changes in handwriting are linked to neurodegenerative diseases because it involves cognitive, kinesthetic, and perceptual-motor tasks [1, 2]. In the field of medical and computer science research, behavioral biometrics are used for the assessment of Dementia that results in diseases such as PD and AD [6–9].

Alzheimer's disease is the most common form of degenerative Dementia, progressively crippling and occurs mainly in the presenile age (over 65 years). The most frequent initial symptom is difficulty in remembering recent events. With advancing age, the following symptoms may occur aphasia, disorientation, sudden mood changes, depression, inability to take care of oneself, behavioral problems [3]. Parkinson's disease, on the other hand, has more obvious movement-related symptoms, including tremors, rigidity, slowness of movement, and difficulty walking. Later, cognitive, and behavioral problems may occur, with Dementia sometimes appearing in the advanced stages, except in cases of early Dementia with Lewy bodies, which are associated with a more severe prognosis. Parkinson's disease is more common in the elderly [4].

In this work, a subset of the "*HAND-UNIBA dataset,*" is adopted. It includes individuals, divided between healthy and dementia diseased [10]. In this way, the classification considered in this work is binary. More specifically distinguishing individuals who are healthy from individuals who are in the very early stages of dementia is difficult. To the best of authors' knowledge this is one of the first attempts since many other works also considered patient in advanced disease stages.

Moreover, the large majority of works have tried to understand which features could be better than others for discrimination aims. Even if some general conclusion can be stated, the set of relevant features is user and task dependent, moreover it is also dependent from the specific task execution. In this direction, this work adopts a random sampling of handwritings coupled with Deep Learning techniques. Results are compared to standard state of art approaches.

This study aims to build a system that could help the sustainability of the health care looking the third Sustainable Development Goals (SDGs). The SDGs are goals to reach found, approved and accepted by the UN. Specifically, the third one about "*Ensure healthy lives and promote well-being for all at all ages*". So, achieving an affordable, safe, quality and effective health treatment it's the first aspect that this study is covering with the presentation of a lower costs, non-invasive system. Furthermore, the cut of the costs in diagnosis could lead in financial investment in health system following the target 3.c of the third SDGs. It is specified that each SDGs is composed by a different number of target and each target is composed by one or more indicators to measure the improvement in the target direction.

In this study, we consider the task of early dementia identification using Shallow Learning and Deep Learning approaches (Sect. 2). After this we show the experimental protocol (Sect. 3) and the dataset properties (Sect. 4). Then we compare the results with related discussion (Sect. 5) and the consequent conclusion (Sect. 6).

2   Related Works

Scientific research has moved towards predictive models that can detect subtle changes in handwriting behavior. The techniques illustrated in this work will support clinicians in preventing neurodegenerative diseases through online sub-tasks in handwriting [10, 11].

Online writing is a methodology studied and implemented in scientific research, which is why this work will consider this methodology. As illustrated in many state-of-the-art works [10, 11] the capture tool is a digital tablet with a pen. This device captures spatial and temporal data and saves it in storage memory. Often, after data acquisition phase, there is a feature extraction phase in order to perform classification in the field of Shallow Learning [1, 11]. Different authors have used different types of classifiers of the Shallow Learning's approaches (SVM, K-NN, Random Forest). Other used approaches are that of the field of Deep Learning [11, 12].

As far as Shallow Learning approaches are concerned, Impedovo D. et al. [1] used different features on five other datasets called EMOTHAW [13], PaHaw [12], Parkinson-HW [14], ISUNIBA [15], NewHandPH [16]. EMOTHAW [13] was the first public available dataset which relates emotional states to handwriting and drawing. This dataset includes samples of 129 participants whose emotional states, namely anxiety, depression, and stress, are assessed by the Depression–Anxiety–Stress Scales (DASS) questionnaire. Seven tasks are recorded through a digitizing tablet. PaHaw [12] is composed by 37 medicated PD patients and 38 age- and sex- matched controls. The handwriting samples were collected during seven tasks such as writing a syllable, word, or sentence. ParkinsonHW [14] is composed by 25 PD patients and 15 control subjects that performs handwriting drawing task using a graphics tablet. ISUNIBA [15] is composed by 50 patients affected by Alzheimer diseased patients. Each patient supplied 10 of his/her handwriting words in two different sessions (5 for each session). NewHandPH [16] is the extended version of HandPD [17] dataset which is composed by images extracted from handwriting exams. The novelty in this new version is the adding of signals extracted from the smart pen. The new version comprises 35 individuals, 14 diseased patients and 21 healthy patients, which performs online handwriting drawing tasks such as spirals and meanders drawings. The features used are button state, position, pressure, azimuth, altitude, displacement, speed, and acceleration. The results obtained contain accuracies ranging from 79.4% to 93.3%.

Zhang X. et al. [18] have work on the use of the Recurrent Neural Network (RNN) to perform online writer identification independent from the executed task [18]. They also used a Bi-Directional Long Short-Term Memory (BiLSTM) in combination with a newer data augmentation technique called Random Hybrid Stroke (RHS) [18]. RHS are here adopted based on the intuition that there could be an underlining dementia pattern in handwriting which is independent from the specific written text.

The use of RNN to identify the writer was explored also from different works as Doetsch P. et al. [19] that studied BiLSTMs with Attention Mechanisms [20] for online handwriting recognition, obtaining actual results on the RIMES handwriting recognition task [19]. Furthermore, the use of BiLSTM, despite the Multi-Level LSTM, was encouraged by Puigcerver J. [21] explored the use of BiLSTM compared to the use of Multi-Level LSTM showing that BiLSTM has better or equivalent results than the other ones and allowing a faster network training.

In this work it was used the same classifier as in [18] with and without the RHS technique. Furthermore, it was used the same protocol for the Shallow Learning as in [11]. The complete description is in the next section.

3   Methods

3.1   Shallow Learning

Following the protocol related to the Shallow Learning in [11], each of the data sequencies was elaborated by a Features Extraction module. In this module the extracted features are Distance-Based Features, Velocity-Based Features, Kinematic-Based Features, features related to the application of Discrete Cosine Transform and Discrete Fourier Transform and related to the velocity aspect. Every feature is a time-series, thus statistical functions such a mean, median, standard deviation 1st and 99th percentile was applied to obtain synthetic description of that time-series. Interested readers can find details here omitted for the sake of readability in our previous work [11].

For each writing task, the Random Forest [22] was used to select features [11]. The number of selected features is approximately in the range from 400 to 500. Obviously, that number and the specific set of features change for each task thus demonstrating once more that the dementia affects handwriting in different ways based on the specific writing task. Table 1 shows some of the common selected features.

Table 1. Common features on each task

Common features name	Description
ACCx_ia [99 per]	Acceleration in x
GL_FD_ACC_seventh_ia [99 per]	Grunwald-Letnikov Acceleration fractional derivatives alpha = 0.7 in-air
GL_FD_JERKy_sixth_os [mean]	Grunwald-Letnikov JERKy fractional derivatives alpha = 0.6 on-surface
GL_FD_JERKx_eighth_os [99 per]	Grunwald-Letnikov JERKx fractional derivatives alpha = 0.8 on-surface
GL_FD_ACC_first [1–99 per]	Grunwald-Letnikov Acceleration fractional derivatives alpha = 0.1
GL_FD_DISx_fifth [stan. Dev.]	Grunwald-Letnikov Displacement x fractional derivatives alpha = 0.5
GL_FD_ACC_fifth_os [median]	Grunwald-Letnikov Acceleration fractional derivatives alpha = 0.5 on-surface
GL_FD_VEL_seventh_os [1 per]	Grunwald-Letnikov Velocity fractional derivatives alpha = 0.7 on-surface

(*continued*)

Table 1. (*continued*)

Common features name	Description
GL_FD_JERK_third_os [99 per]	Grunwald-Letnikov JERK fractional derivatives alpha = 0.3 on-surface
VELx_os [1–99 per]	Velocity in x on-surface
ACCx_os [stan. Dev.]	Acceleration in x on-surface
GL_FD_DISx_seventh [mean]	Grunwald-Letnikov Displacement x fractional derivatives alpha = 0.7
GL_FD_VEL_eighth [mean]	Grunwald-Letnikov Velocity fractional derivatives alpha = 0.8
GL_FD_VEL_ninth_os [1 per]	Grunwald-Letnikov Velocity fractional derivatives alpha = 0.9 on-surface

The Random Forest [22] is also used as a classifier, taking selected features from the previous model as input, with the purpose of disambiguating the diseased class from the healthy class. For the next sections, experiments performed with this approach are referred as "*RF*".

3.2 Deep Learning

BiLSTM with Self-Attention [20] with and without Random Hybrid Stroke (RHS) [18] has been adopted.

The RHS [18] technique makes it possible to perform classification on data that are independent of the task in which they are sampled. The RHS [18] technique requires that the data points' sequences are time series composed by X and Y coordinates and the pen status (a binary value that indicates that the pen is touching the device or not, respectively 0 and 1). So, the data-points sequence S will be of the following form:

$$S = [[x_1, y_1, p_1], [x_2, y_2, p_2], \ldots, [x_n, y_n, p_n]] \tag{1}$$

where p_i is the features related to the pen-status and its values will be 0 for the pen-up and 1 for the pen-down and n is the number of the points. Subsequently, the sequence S is transformed to obtain information related to the strokes rather than information related to the points. In this phase, strokes are defined as the segment between two points. Furthermore, the transformation distinguishes the strokes in real and imaginary ones. The imaginary ones are which one that occurs when, between two points, there is -at least- a point with button status as pen-up. It is specified that to avoid misunderstanding by the term "imaginary" that the points with button status as pen-up are sampled by the device and they are the effective pen position in air. Furthermore, imaginary stroke was chosen because of in the study of the effectiveness of imaginary stroke in [18] that point of those real and imaginary strokes are better than only the real one. Meanwhile the real ones are which one that occur between points with button status as pen-down (Figure 1 shows an example of real and imaginary stroke).

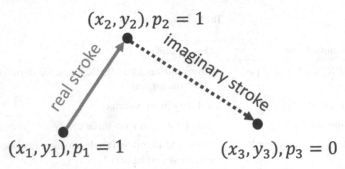

$(x_2, y_2), p_2 = 1$

real stroke

imaginary stroke

$(x_1, y_1), p_1 = 1$ $(x_3, y_3), p_3 = 0$

Fig. 1. Example of real and imaginary stroke [18].

The sequence S is as follows:

$$\Delta S = \begin{bmatrix} [x_2 - x_1, y_2 - y_1, p_2 \times p_1], \dots \\ [x_i - x_{i-1}, y_i - y_{i-1}, p_i \times p_{i-1}], \dots \\ [x_n - x_{n-1}, y_n - y_{n-1}, p_n \times p_{n-1}] \end{bmatrix} \tag{2}$$

After this transformation, an N number of random sub-sequences were sampled which are the "Random Hybrid Stroke" (RHS). This technique is adopted in the contest of writer's identification when shorts sequences of handwriting text are available and a writer could haven't enough training data. Moreover, these techniques make the task of identification independent from the text extrapolating subsequences from the text that lead the model such as RNN to learn features related to writer rather than related to the task. In our case, we are attempting to learn a disease pattern independently from the specific task execution. So, this random sampling is performed taking multiple short continuous subsequences from ΔS. Each of the sub-sequences will be in the following form:

$$RHS = [\dots, [\Delta x_i, \Delta y_i, \tilde{p}_i], \dots] \tag{3}$$

where $\Delta x_i = x_i - x_{i-1}$, $\Delta y_i = y_i - y_{i-1}$, and $\tilde{p}_i = p_i \times p_{i-1}$.

Once obtained a number N of RHS for each patient, such RHS are given to a model following the protocol described in [18]. Clearly, our experiments aim to label the patients as diseased or healthy rather than identifies the patients. So, the label described in dataset subsection are One-Hot Encoded. To simplify the reading of the results, the original label was the indices of the position of the 1 in the one-hot encoded label. As in [18], after the model gives N results for the N RHS, the results are averaged to obtain a final vector where, applying the argmax gives us the classification of the patients. To achieve this a SoftMax Activation function was used in the last layer. Figure 2 shows the model used by this work.

Deep Learning with RHS, was initially tested with 1000 RHS of length 100 samples, as experimented in the paper [18]. However different setup showed different results, 90 RHS of length 30 was used in this paper. For this experiment the reference acronym is set to "**RHS**".

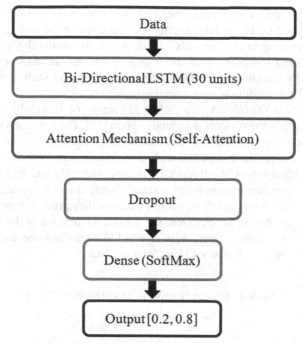

Fig. 2. Deep learning model structure

It was tested the same model described above (Fig. 2) but using the raw data sequencies. Because of the obviously difference in terms of data sequencies' length between patients, the sequencies was Zero Padded at task level considering as length to achieve the max length of all the sequencies. Then, all the padded data sequencies was given to the same model as in Fig. 2. This experiment is referenced with the acronym "**NORHS**". This was a required test to inspect potentialities of RHS.

The number of LSTM Units was chosen by a comparison of different setups, as for the choose of the number and the length of the RHS.

4 Data

The dataset here adopted is called "Balanced-Hand" and name stands for "Balanced HAND-UNIBA". "HAND-UNIBA" [10] originally contains handwriting data from 97 patients (diseased patients) with four different level of dementia assessed by a group of medics, it also contains (at this date) 56 healthy persons (healthy patients). Table 2 shows the described division.

Each patient had to perform several tasks that includes cognitive and functional tests. The tasks recorded were of the category: *Mental Status Assessment of Older Adults (Mini-COG), Mini Mental State Examination (MMSE), Attentional Matrix, Trail making* test and some *other test*. The full description is in Table 3.

For each user, and for each performed task, the x and y coordinates were recorded, the pressure applied by the patients during the execution of the task in range between 0 and 1, the timestamp in milliseconds, the azimuth-x and azimuth-y of the pen in the range between 0 and 1 and the button status (pen-up and pen-down). For the use of RHS technique, x and y coordinates and Button State were used for each of the experiments that are described in the following subsection.

The original "*HAND-UNIBA*" is unbalanced because of the number of patients with dementia is more than the patients without dementia [10]. Thus, patients with the second and third level of dementia are clearly diseased and their classification through handwriting is meaningless since the disease is already evident and overt. With this small prologue, the balanced method report is introduced. Patients with mild and first-stage dementia were selected, incorporating these terms into the generic class (*diseased*). These patients are more difficult to distinguish from healthy because they present dementia symptoms or very early stages. As can be seen from the Table 2 the number of diseased patients is 49. In this way, 49 healthy patients were selected to have the same number of healthy patients. This is how the "*Balanced-Hand*" dataset was built.

Table 2. Classes division of "HAND-UNIBA" [10]

Class	N° Patients
Healthy patients	56
Mild	17
First	32
Second	32
Third	16

Table 3. Task and their description

Abbreviation	Description	User request	Category
CDT	Clock drawing test	Draw a clock with numbers in it, then draw the clock hands at 11.10 a.m	Mini-COG
SW	Sentence drawing test	Think and then write a sentence	MMSE
IPC	Pentagons drawing test	Copy the shape of this design	
M1	First matrix test	Mark all the numbers "5" in the matrix, without correcting the barriers already made	Trail

(*continued*)

Table 3. (*continued*)

Abbreviation	Description	User request	Category
M2	Second matrix test	Mark all the numbers "2" and "6" in the matrix, without correcting the barriers already made	
M3	Third matrix test	Mark all the numbers "1", "4" and "9" in the matrix, without correcting the barriers already made	
TMT1	First trail-making test	Connect the circles following the order of the numbers. For example, 1–2-3, and so on. Perform the exercise as quickly as possible and never lift the pen. In case of error, correct immediately	
TMT2	Second trail-making test	Connect the circles alternately following the order of the numbers and the order of the letters of the alphabet. For example, 1-A-2-B-3-C, and so on. Perform the exercise as quickly as possible and never lift the pen. In case of error, correct immediately	
TMTT1	Trail test 1	Connect the circles following the order of the numbers. For example, 1-2-3, and so on. Perform the exercise as quickly as possible and never lift the pen. In case of error, correct immediately	
TMTT2	Trail test 2	Connect the circles alternately following the order of the numbers and the order of the letters of the alphabet. For example, 1-A-2-B-3-C, and so on. Perform the exercise as quickly as possible and never lift the pen. In case of error, correct immediately	

(*continued*)

Table 3. (*continued*)

Abbreviation	Description	User request	Category
H	Writing the word test	Write the word "Ciao" in italics, resting your wrist on the tablet	Additional tests
VP	Connecting two vertical points tests	Link the vertical points with a straight line four times by going back and forth	
HP	Connecting two horizontal points tests	Link the horizontal points with a straight line four times by going back and forth	
SC	Square copy task	Copy the square drawing shown	
S1	First signature acquisition	Sign your signature here	
S2	Second signature acquisition	Sign your signature here	
CS	Spiral copying test	Copy the shape of this design	
TS	Retrace spiral test	Retrace the shape of this design	
CHK	Bank check copying task	Look at the fields on the completed check and copy them back to the blank check below	
LE	Write "le" repetitions	Write a sequence of "L" and "E" in italics, for example "LELELELE"	
MOM	Writing the word test	Write the word "MAMMA" in italics inside the three boxes, from top to bottom	
W	Writing the word test	Write the word "FINESTRA" in italics	
DS	Listen and write sentence	Listen and write in italics what you will hear. (The sentence "Oggi è una bella giornata" will be dictated)	

After the balancing of the dataset in terms of the distribution of the patients between the two class (to obtain a 50% of healthy patients and 50% of diseased patients), it's important to exploit that, for some tasks there were less than 50 points. For this reason, that patients haven't been considered during the training and test phases for that specific task. This policy of exclusion was the same for all the experiments, so all the experiments are comparable at task-level. We mean that all the experiments are performed with the same raw data. The situation is summarized in Table 5 including the final size of the dataset.

The dataset couldn't be shared with the research community because of the presence of sensible data by the patients.

5 Results

Experiments share the same dataset, the same type of encoding patient's label and the same methodology of train/test phases: the Leave-One Out (LOO). The LOO methodology consists of training and testing the model N times and each times using N-1 samples as training data and 1 sample as test data. Assuming that N is the number of patients. For the experiments described above, from the training data one patient at time is excluded and then used it as test data. After all the experiments, the results were used to calculate the evaluation metrics. Related to the encoding phases, the diseased patients were considered as positive class, so they had the label "1", and the healthy patients were considered as negative class, with the label "0". The practical meaning is that the reported F1-Scores are referencing the diseased class. These values are important because they are a balanced evaluation of the two base metrics needed for the calculus of F1-Scores: Precision and Recall. In this way obtained values in the range [0, 1] that it's an important information about the quality of the model to recognize the diseased patients. F1-Score is defined as follow:

$$F_1 = 2 \frac{precision \times recall}{precision + recall} \qquad (4)$$

So, the precision and recall are defined as:

$$precision = \frac{TP}{TP + FP} \qquad (5)$$

$$recall = \frac{TP}{TP + FN} \qquad (6)$$

where TP is the number of True Positive, diseased patients classified as diseased, FP is the number of False Positive, healthy patients classified as diseased, and FN is the number of False Negative, diseased patients classified as healthy.

Table 4 presents the F1-Scores for each task and for each algorithm used in the experiments. The first three columns contain the results of their homonymous experiments, the fourth column contain the acronym of the considered task, the fifth column summarize which experiment has the best result for that task and the last column contains the task's category looking Table 3.

Furthermore, Table 5 contains the information about the quantity of data available for each task regarding the total number the patients (98 patients) and how much diseased patients was an-available due to the fact that some patients did not perform the task.

The "**NORHS**" reach the best result only with the "le" task which is a very simple task composed by the repetition of a similar pattern: "l" and the "e" in italics have the same movement on a different scale during the handwriting. The approach has very

Table 4. Results obtained from the previous experiments

NORHS	RF	RHS	Task	Best technique	Category task
0,3571	0,6237	**0,6383**	cdt	RHS	Mini-CGO
0,5556	**0,7273**	0,6972	chk	RF	Additional tests
0,1867	**0,6316**	0,6168	cs	RF	Additional tests
0,4211	0,6517	**0,6545**	ds	RHS	Additional tests
0,3218	**0,6392**	0,5376	h	RF	Additional tests
0,3291	**0,6593**	0,56	hp	RF	Additional tests
0,381	**0,6882**	0,5517	ipc	RF	MMSE
0,6721	0,6526	0,5631	le	NORHS	Additional tests
0,5849	0,6316	**0,6972**	m1	RHS	Matrix
0,5098	0,7253	**0,7818**	m2	RHS	Matrix
0,338	**0,76596**	0,75	m3	RF	Matrix
0,5217	**0,6667**	0,5714	mom	RF	Additional tests
0,4348	0,6136	**0,6725**	s1	RHS	Additional tests
0,5287	**0,6526**	0,6061	s2	RF	Additional tests
0,5641	**0,6531**	0,6372	sc	RF	Additional tests
0,4578	0,6222	**0,6552**	sw	RHS	MMSE
0,4146	**0,7640**	0,6218	tmt1	RF	TRAIL
0,4839	**0,6462**	0,5714	tmt2	RF	TRAIL
0,3768	**0,8041**	0,5057	tmtt1	RF	TRAIL
0,1538	**0,7027**	0,5652	tmtt2	RF	TRAIL
0,411	**0,6739**	0,6237	ts	RF	Additional tests
0,5275	**0,6598**	0,5102	vp	RF	Additional tests
0,3846	0,622	**0,6942**	w	RHS	Additional tests

instable performance on different tasks thus showing that the use of a "black box" deep learning approach merely fails when the classification task is not sustained by the presence of handwriting from severe diseased patients. "**RHS**" reaches the best results on tasks "cdt", "ds", "m1", "m2", "s1", "sw" and "w". Meanwhile, "**RF**" reaches the best results on all the other tasks. Both the RHS and RF systems have a stable behavior among the different tasks.

It's important highlight that the "**RF**" covers all the tasks of the TRAIL category (in the Table 3 there are all the task with their category). Furthermore, "**RF**" reaches the best result around on the totality of tasks of the Additional Test category. Similarly, the "**RHS**" reach the bests results on Mini-COG and the first two tasks of MATRIX category. The highest F1 score is achieved adopting "**RF**" on the trail test 2 (i.e., "Connect the circles alternately following the order of the numbers and the order of the letters of

Table 5. The differences in quantity of data available for each task

Task	Best technique	Patients performing the task (ratio)	Patients performing the task (final size)	Diseased people not performing the task
cdt	RHS	98,98%	97	1,02%
chk	RF	**100,00%**	98	0,00%
cs	RF	98,98%	97	1,02%
ds	RHS	**100,00%**	98	0,00%
h	RF	**100,00%**	98	0,00%
hp	RF	**100,00%**	98	0,00%
ipc	RF	98,98%	97	1,02%
le	NORHS	98,98%	97	1,02%
m1	RHS	**100,00%**	98	0,00%
m2	RHS	**100,00%**	98	0,00%
m3	RF	**100,00%**	98	0,00%
mom	RF	**100,00%**	98	0,00%
s1	RHS	98,98%	97	1,02%
s2	RF	98,98%	97	1,02%
sc	RF	**100,00%**	98	0,00%
sw	RHS	**100,00%**	98	0,00%
tmt1	RF	97,96%	96	2,04%
tmt2	RF	83,67%	82	**16,33%**
tmtt1	RF	98,98%	97	1,02%
tmtt2	RF	90,82%	89	9,18%
ts	RF	98,98%	97	1,02%
vp	RF	**100,00%**	98	0,00%
w	RHS	**100,00%**	98	0,00%

the alphabet. For example, 1-A-2-B-3-C, and so on. Perform the exercise as quickly as possible and never lift the pen. In case of error, correct immediately").

At this stage it is difficult to draw some consistent conclusion and more research is needed.

More experiments are going to be performed. In the following a first is briefly described. It deals with task-based "**RHS**" results and their combination. In particular, it has been investigated the case in which the classification of each patient is performed independently for each task adopting the "RHS" system as previously discussed. Then, the resulting decision (0 or 1) is used to build a single feature vector. In this way, a table was obtained as in the example in Table 6.

The new matrix of data was containing some *"NaN"* values because some patients had not performed some tasks. Then, columns with *"NaN"* values were removed resulting in a matrix full of values, considering all values of a patient as a single vector to perform decision-level fusion.

Table 6. Example of the obtained features for decision level fusion

Id	Ground truth	Task1	Task2	Task3	Task4	Task5	...	TaskN
1234	0	0	0	1	0	1	...	0
5678	1	1	0	0	1	1	...	1

The AdaBoost classifier with 100 decision tree estimators was used and the training and testing phase in LOO. The result is summarized in the next table Table 7.

Table 7. Result from the decision-level fusion

RHS decision-level fusion	Ada-Boost
F1-Score	0.7238

This test has shown that decision-level fusion using all the decision from **"RHS"**, for each of the task the was performed by all the patients, reach an F1-Score that is the third, in a rank, compared with the other F1-Score.

6   Conclusion

This work has shown the possibility to identify dementia from handwriting considering data of patients at the very early stages of the disease. To the aim, RHS has been adopted to cope with high variability of results obtained with deep learning techniques. RHS also represents a possibility to open the research within a task independent disease recognition. Although the use of RHS significantly improve F1-Score if compared to the use of raw coordinates, a standard random forest approach built upon a massive set of features still represent the best performing approach on the majority of tasks.

Conflicts of Interest.   The authors declare no conflict of interest.

References

1. Impedovo, D., Pirlo, G.: Dynamic handwriting analysis for the assessment of neurodegenerative diseases: a pattern recognition perspective. IEEE Rev. Biomed. Eng. **12**, 209–220 (2018). https://doi.org/10.1109/RBME.2018.2840679

2. de Stefano, C., Fontanella, F., Impedovo, D., Pirlo, G., Scotto di Freca, A.: Handwriting analysis to support neurodegenerative diseases diagnosis: a review. Pattern Recogn. Lett. **121**, 37–45 (2019). https://doi.org/10.1016/J.PATREC.2018.05.013

3. Ström, F., Koker, R.: A parallel neural network approach to prediction of Parkinson's disease. Expert Syst. Appl. **38**, 12470–12474 (2011). https://doi.org/10.1016/J.ESWA.2011.04.028

4. Faundez-Zanuy, M., Mekyska, J., Impedovo, D.: Online handwriting, signature and touch dynamics: tasks and potential applications in the field of security and health. Cogn. Comput. **13**, 1406–1421 (2021). https://doi.org/10.1007/S12559-021-09938-2/TABLES/1

5. Impedovo, D., Pirlo, G., Vessio, G., Angelillo, M.T.: A Handwriting-based protocol for assessing neurodegenerative dementia. Cogn. Comput. **11**(4), 576–586 (2019). https://doi.org/10.1007/s12559-019-09642-2

6. Cilia, N.D., De Stefano, C., Fontanella, F., Molinara, M., Scotto Di Freca, A.: Using handwriting features to characterize cognitive impairment. In: Ricci, E., Rota Bulò, S., Snoek, C., Lanz, O., Messelodi, S., Sebe, N. (eds.) Image Analysis and Processing – ICIAP 2019. LNCS, vol. 11752, pp. 683–693. Springer, Cham (2019). https://doi.org/10.1007/978-3-030-30645-8_62

7. Kahindo, C., El-Yacoubi, M.A., Garcia-Salicetti, S., Rigaud, A.-S., Cristancho-Lacroix, V.: Characterizing early-stage alzheimer through spatiotemporal dynamics of handwriting; characterizing early-stage alzheimer through spatiotemporal dynamics of handwriting. IEEE Sig. Process. Lett. **25** (2018). https://doi.org/10.1109/LSP.2018.2794500

8. Cilia, N.D.: Handwriting analysis to support Alzheimer disease diagnosis: a preliminary study. In: Vento, M., Percannella, G. (eds.) Computer Analysis of Images and Patterns, vol. 11679, pp. 143–151. Springer, Cham (2019). https://doi.org/10.1007/978-3-030-29891-3_13

9. Cilia, N.D., de Stefano, C., Fontanella, F., di Freca, A.S.: An experimental protocol to support cognitive impairment diagnosis by using handwriting analysis. Procedia Comput. Sci. **141**, 466–471 (2018). https://doi.org/10.1016/J.PROCS.2018.10.141

10. Dentamaro, V., Impedovo, D., Pirlo, G.: An analysis of tasks and features for neurodegenerative disease assessment by handwriting. In: Del Bimbo, A., et al. (eds.) ICPR 2021. LNCS, vol. 12661, pp. 536–545. Springer, Cham (2021). https://doi.org/10.1007/978-3-030-68763-2_41

11. Dentamaro, V., Giglio, P., Impedovo, D., Pirlo, G.: Benchmarking of shallow learning and deep learning techniques with transfer learning for neurodegenerative disease assessment through handwriting. In: Barney Smith, E.H., Pal, U. (eds.) ICDAR 2021. LNCS, vol. 12917, pp. 7–20. Springer, Cham (2021). https://doi.org/10.1007/978-3-030-86159-9_1

12. Drotár, P., Mekyska, J., Rektorová, I., Masarová, L., Smékal, Z., Faundez-Zanuy, M.: Decision support framework for Parkinson's disease based on novel handwriting markers. IEEE Trans. Neural Syst. Rehabil. Eng. **23**, 508–516 (2015). https://doi.org/10.1109/TNSRE.2014.2359997

13. Likforman-Sulem, L., Esposito, A., Faundez-Zanuy, M., Clemencon, S., Cordasco, G.: EMOTHAW: a novel database for emotional state recognition from handwriting and drawing. IEEE Trans. Hum.-Mach. Syst. **47**, 273–284 (2017). https://doi.org/10.1109/THMS.2016.2635441

14. Improved Spiral Test Using Digitized Graphics Tablet for Monitoring Parkinson's Disease. https://www.researchgate.net/publication/291814924_Improved_Spiral_Test_Using_Digitized_Graphics_Tablet_for_Monitoring_Parkinson's_Disease. Accessed 13 Feb 2022

15. Impedovo, D., et al.: Writing Generation Model for Health Care neuromuscular System. 7° Convegno Nazionale di Viticoltura, Piacenza, 9–11 luglio 2018, p. 43 (2013)

16. Pereira, C.R., Weber, S.A.T., Hook, C., Rosa, G.H., Papa, J.P.: Deep learning-aided parkinson's disease diagnosis from handwritten dynamics, pp. 340–346 (2016). https://doi.org/10.1109/SIBGRAPI.2016.054

17. Pereira, C.R., et al.: A step towards the automated diagnosis of Parkinson's disease: analyzing handwriting movements. In: 2015 IEEE 28th International Symposium on Computer-Based Medical Systems, pp. 171–176 (2015). https://doi.org/10.1109/CBMS.2015.34
18. Zhang, X.Y., Xie, G.S., Liu, C.L., Bengio, Y.: End-to-end online writer identification with recurrent neural network. IEEE Trans. Hum.-Mach. Syst. **47**, 285–292 (2017). https://doi.org/10.1109/THMS.2016.2634921
19. Doetsch, P., Zeyer, A., Ney, H.: Bidirectional decoder networks for attention-based end-to-end offline handwriting recognition (2016)
20. Vaswani, A., et al.: Attention is all you need. CoRR. abs/1706.03762 https://arxiv.org/abs/1706.03762 (2017)
21. Puigcerver, J.: Are multidimensional recurrent layers really necessary for handwritten text recognition? In: Proceedings of the International Conference on Document Analysis and Recognition, ICDAR, vol. 1, pp. 67–72 (2017). https://doi.org/10.1109/ICDAR.2017.20
22. Breiman, L.: Random forests (2001)

Spectral Analysis of Handwriting Kinetic Tremor in Elderly Parkinsonian Patients

Serena Starita[1]($\boxtimes$), Katerina Iscra[1], Monica Guerra[2], Lorenzo Pascazio[2], and Agostino Accardo[1]

[1] Department of Engineering and Architecture, University of Trieste, Via Valerio 10, 34127 Trieste, Italy
serena.starita@phd.units.it

[2] Geriatric Unit, Department of Medicine, Surgery and Health Sciences, Trieste University Hospital – ASUGI Piazza dell'Ospitale 2, 34129 Trieste, Italy

Abstract. Tremor is one of the motor impairments of Parkinson's disease (PD) and manifests as different types, i.e. rest, kinetic and postural. To date, kinetic tremor in PD is barely examined and there is no agreed methodology to test and analyse it. In this exploratory and preliminary study, we aimed at characterizing handwriting-related kinetic tremor in PD during Archimedes' Spiral and over-lapped Circles drawing execution using a digitizing tablet. To achieve this, we integrated classical kinematic analysis with spectral analysis to establish the set of parameters better suited to discriminate PD patients from healthy controls. 15 PD patients and 11 elderly healthy control subjects were enrolled in the trial.

The results reveal that there are significant differences between PD patients and control subjects, especially at the level of spectral features. PD tremor produces higher Spectral Power and a clear peak in the band of involuntary movements, while Spectral Power of enhanced physiological tremor in controls is lower and randomly distributed over the frequencies. We conclude that spectral analysis and features extracted from the band of involuntary movements can be used to char-acterize parkinsonian handwriting kinetic tremor. The findings support the theory that the kinetic tremor in PD patients can be distinguished from the involuntary movement of the elderly caused by physiological age-related deterioration of the neuromuscular system's functional capacity.

Keywords: Parkinson's disease · Spectral analysis · Handwriting-related kinetic tremor · Physiological tremor

1 Introduction

Parkinson's Disease (PD) is a progressive neurodegenerative disorder characterized by motor impairments and manifested as muscular rigidity, resistance to passive move-ments, smaller amplitude of movements (hypokinesia), lower frequency of movement (bradykinesia), delay in movement initiation (akinesia) and rest tremor [1]. Generally, PD is diagnosed by a clinical examination of patient's signs, symptoms, and health his-tory. During the last years, research on PD has focused on the analysis of movements

© Springer Nature Switzerland AG 2022
C. Carmona-Duarte et al. (Eds.): IGS 2021, LNCS 13424, pp. 301–307, 2022.
https://doi.org/10.1007/978-3-031-19745-1_22

during the execution of specific handwriting tasks utilizing digitizing tablets that seem to represent a convenient method to evaluate upper limb motor dysfunctions. This non-invasive and low-cost approach offers a solution to quantify handwriting impairments, to identify biomarkers and has the potential to develop into a diagnostic tool to support clinicians [2].

Kinematic analysis is the most used approach to characterize handwriting impairments in PD and is applied to two task categories: drawing tasks of simple geometrical figures and writing tasks. The most widespread drawing task is the reproduction of a spiral because it is easy to perform and well tolerated by patients [3]. To characterize writing abnormalities, repetitive l-loops and patients' mother-tongue sentences are rather used. These tasks allow portraying anomalies concerning not only the typical parkinsonian micrographia but also other complex alterations involving velocity, acceleration, pressure, and fluency, comprehensively defined as PD dysgraphia [4]. PD subjects show lower pressure, lower velocity and acceleration, smaller movements, longer in-air movements, and an overall loss of fluency [5].

Rest tremor is one of the cardinal criteria for PD diagnosis but clinical research states that parkinsonian tremor can manifest also in other forms, i.e. kinetic tremor and postural tremor [6]. Since each patient can manifest none, one or more tremor types, it leads to the great variability of tremor clinical appearance. Even if there is no complete consensus about tremor types definitions and corresponding frequency ranges [7], the classification in rest, postural and kinetic tremor is well accepted as well as the associated frequency ranges of 4–6 Hz for rest tremor and 4–9 Hz for postural and kinetic tremors [8]. Spectral analysis of velocity and acceleration signals is a tool to analyse tremor. However, only a few studies have focused on that approach to analyse handwriting kinetic tremor in PD, reporting conflicting results. A study estimated spectral power of velocity and acceleration signals in two specific frequency bands, associated with voluntary movement execution or with involuntary tremor; the results did not show any statistically significant difference between healthy subjects and PD patients [9]. Another study used the same approach and found a higher power in the 4–6 Hz band for PD patients compared to controls [10]. Handwriting-related kinetic tremor can occur also in healthy subjects, especially in the elderly. In this case, tremor is physiological and due to a natural decline in the functional capacity of the neuromuscular system with aging. Physiological kinetic tremor (4–10 Hz) associated to digitized drawings of Archimedes' spiral strongly correlates with age in healthy subjects [11].

Since there is a lack of research characterizing handwriting kinetic tremor due to pathological neurodegeneration in respect of normal-aging physiological tremor and the results are inconsistent, further studies are needed to better comprehend their differences. Thus, this preliminary and exploratory study aims at characterizing handwriting tremor in PD patients and healthy elderly. For this purpose, we used spectral analysis, alongside classical kinematic analysis, to identify features able to highlight possible differences between the two groups.

2 Materials and Methods

2.1 Subjects and Tasks

This study encompasses 35 subjects, 16 PD patients on antiparkinsonian medications (aged 62–88, mean 77.0 ± 6.4 years) and 19 healthy age-matched elderly control subjects, HC (aged 60–84, mean 71.0 ± 7.7 years). The subjects performed two different exercises: an ingoing, clockwise Archimedes' Spiral (AS) drawn following a given template, and repetition of overlapped Circles (C). Subjects were required to draw AS accurately with no time limits and C as fast as possible for a duration of 15 s. Participants were instructed to execute the exercises without pen lift and keeping the arm leaned on the table, otherwise the response was excluded from the analysis. Thus, 34 C samples (15 PD patients, 19 HC) and 27 AS samples (11 PD patients, 16 HC) were eventually considered. All the subjects released their written informed consent.

2.2 Handwriting Acquisition and Analysis

Handwriting was acquired by means of a commercial digitizing tablet (Wacom, Inc., Vancouver, WA, Model Intuos 3.0), using an ink pen thus providing visual feedback. The pen displacement was sampled at 200 Hz and acquired with a spatial resolution of 0.02 mm. The horizontal and vertical pen positions were filtered separately using a second-order low-pass Butterworth filter (15 Hz cut-off frequency) and the velocity and acceleration profiles were derived. For each test, the handwriting features were calculated and analysed by using an ad hoc custom program written in MATLAB® [12].

The following kinematic parameters were calculated: mean pressure (P), mean duration of strokes (D_s), mean curvilinear velocity of strokes (Vc_s), stroke number normalized by total track length (N_s/L), and normalized jerk (J_N). The stroke is here defined as a single writing movement comprised between two curvilinear velocity minima. J_N and N_s/L represent measures of fluidity; the smaller their values, the less fragmented and more fluid a movement is [13]. Power Spectral Density (PSD) of both velocity and acceleration profiles in their horizontal, vertical and curvilinear components was estimated by using Welch's method, with a Hamming window on intervals of 5 s and a 50% overlap. In order to analyse the power distribution related to different movement-associated phenomena, two frequency bands were selected: a band concerning voluntary Movement Execution required by the task (B_{ME}), ranging from 0.2 to 4 Hz, and a band associated with involuntary Tremor (B_T), ranging from 4.0 to 12 Hz. B_T includes the frequencies associated with both kinetic parkinsonian tremor and physiological tremor. For each subject, the following spectral parameters were selected: ratio of relative spectral powers, quantified by dividing the absolute power in each frequency band by their sum (rSP-B_{ME} and rSP-B_T) and subsequently calculating their ratio (rSP_{BME}/rSP_{BT}); frequency at the spectral power peak in B_T (F_P); bandwidth in B_T, defined as the frequency range in which the power is above the 10% of the peak value (BW-B_T).

For each task, the median value and the interquartile range of parameters were calculated in the two groups; the difference between them was assessed by the Wilcoxon Rank sum test, with a significance level of 5%. The statistical analysis did not include any correction for multiple testing since the study is oriented toward features selection. The

Bonferroni correction would not offer the flexibility required in such exploratory stage that has the purpose of emphasizing what parameters better characterize the tremor of the two groups rather than evaluating if the groups are different in all tested parameters [14].

Table 1. I. Median values and Interquartile Range (Iqr) of kinematic and spectral parameters in the two groups and p-values of their comparison, for Circles and Archimedes' Spiral (in bold, p-value < 0.05).

| | | | CIRCLES | | | | | ARCHIMEDES' SPIRAL | | | | |
| | | | HC | | PD | | | HC | | PD | | |
			Median	Iqr	Median	Iqr	p-value	Median	Iqr	Median	Iqr	p-value
Kinematic Parameters		D_S (ms)	133.00	14.88	143.00	22.50	0.054	131.00	12.50	145.50	10.50	**0.040**
		Vc_S (mm/s)	81.32	70.09	53.16	145.56	0.755	39.82	19.65	38.89	20.26	0.824
		N_S/L (mm^{-1})	0.08	0.10	0.11	0.15	0.755	0.18	0.07	0.18	0.08	0.863
		J_N	2.08	1.00	3.45	2.66	**0.003**	2.15	1.32	2.91	1.54	0.191
		P (A.U.)	281.83	190.88	238.36	140.12	0.445	287.64	145.17	276.81	118.38	0.604
Spectral Parameters	Vh	rSP_{BME}/rSP_{BT}	65.06	49.12	39.29	58.77	0.118	86.78	124.41	50.24	66.05	0.175
		BW-B$_T$	3.32	2.49	2.73	1.66	0.095	4.98	1.95	4.10	1.51	0.075
	Vv	rSP_{BME}/rSP_{BT}	61.43	46.09	16.98	20.65	**0.003**	83.60	123.41	29.53	73.44	0.080
		BW-B$_T$	2.92	2.92	2.73	1.56	0.465	5.27	1.86	3.52	2.29	**0.048**
	Vc	rSP_{BME}/rSP_{BT}	3.32	2.06	1.49	1.19	**0.020**	8.89	12.08	3.61	5.59	**0.025**
		BW-B$_T$	3.51	2.34	4.29	1.41	0.626	4.98	2.05	3.91	2.34	0.347
	Ah	rSP_{BME}/rSP_{BT}	1.94	5.21	0.41	5.1	0.199	0.53	0.61	0.21	0.24	**0.019**
		BW-B$_T$	4.29	2.44	3.32	0.73	0.338	6.45	2.73	3.91	0.73	**0.013**
	Av	rSP_{BME}/rSP_{BT}	1.75	4.42	0.26	3.17	0.056	0.41	0.36	0.18	0.28	**0.019**
		BW-B$_T$	3.51	2.63	3.12	1.61	0.305	5.86	3.13	3.71	3.13	**0.045**
	Ac	rSP_{BME}/rSP_{BT}	0.21	0.22	0.07	0.09	**0.016**	0.36	0.50	0.11	0.19	**0.017**
		BW-B$_T$	4.49	2.97	3.90	1.70	0.305	5.57	2.73	3.52	2.73	**0.021**

3 Results

Median and range values of kinematic and spectral parameters for PD patients and HC, as well as the p-values of their comparison, are reported in Table 1. Kinematic analysis reveals that D_S is higher in PD patients compared to HC in both tasks but significant only in AS. Other stroke parameters (Vc_S, N_s/L and J_N) show only slight differences in AS. On the contrary, in C task, PD patients present a reduced stroke velocity and a greater fragmentation, as indicated by higher J_N and N_s/L values. Furthermore, mean pressure is always smaller in PD patients although the statistics do not reveal significance in either task. Regarding spectral analysis, PD patients show lower power in B_{ME} and higher power in B_T compared to HC in all velocity and acceleration signal components resulting in smaller rSP_{BME}/rSP_{BT} values (Table 1). PD tremor bandwidth is always narrower compared to HC, except for curvilinear velocity in C task.

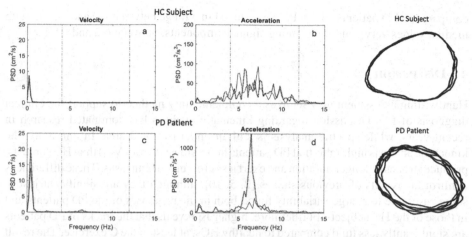

Fig. 1. PSD of horizontal (solid line) and vertical (dotted line) components of Velocity and Acceleration signals in a HC subject (a, b) and in a PD patient (c, d). For the HC subject, the spectral activity in the frequency range of tremor was distributed over a broader range. By contrast, the parkinsonian patient produced a consistent spectral peak. Both participants drew tremulous tracks (the corresponding tests are shown on the right).

Figure 1 shows the PSD of horizontal and vertical components of velocity and acceleration in a HC subject and in a PD patient and the corresponding C test tracks. The example highlights the different power distribution in B_T with the presence of a clear peak in vertical components of velocity and acceleration in the PD patient.

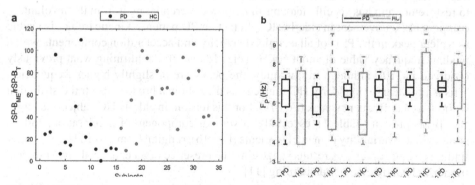

Fig. 2. (a) Distribution of rSPBME/rSPBT values of vertical velocity obtained from C exercise in each subject of both groups. (b) Boxplots of AS frequencies at peak in horizontal (Vh, Ah), vertical (Vv, Av), and curvilinear (Vc, Ac) components of Velocity and Acceleration signals; PD = PD patients, HC = healthy controls.

Figure 2a illustrates the distribution of rSP_{BME}/rSP_{BT} vertical velocity values for each subject in the C task. A clear separation of the two groups is appreciable. Figure 2b displays boxplots of tremor band F_P, at group level and for each signal component, in AS task. Though F_P is variable in both groups, HC subjects always show a higher variability compared to PD patients whose F_P are included in a range between 4.0 and 7.5 Hz with median values very consistent among signal components, between 6.2 and 6.8 Hz.

4 Discussion

Handwriting assessment may serve as a complementary method to support the clinical diagnosis of PD. Discussion regarding kinematic analysis has dominated research in recent years, while spectral analysis is still an under-explored area. In our study, the kinematic analysis highlights that PD patients move slower (lower Vc_s) than HC subjects, produce strokes of longer duration and exert less pressure in both tasks. These differences confirm the results of previous studies [2, 5, 10], although they are significant just in some cases due to a large variability found both in the responses of the PD patients and in those of the HC subjects. Furthermore, higher J_N reveals that the tracks of PD patients are significantly less fluid compared to healthy HCs, at least in the C exercise. The result is confirmed by a higher fragmentation (N_s/L) in PD patients. The loss of fluency has already been assessed in PD handwriting and it is attributed to impairment in fine motor control due to a deterioration of finger-wrist coordination ability [13]. The reason our data highlight a different fragmentation between the two tasks may be due to the different modalities (fast vs accurate) employed for C and AS execution. We hypothesize that task nature may influence the response, but more data are needed to verify this possibility.

On the other hand, the spectral analysis offers very consistent results. Whether the statistical significance is present or not, the data always follow a pattern. In general, for both tasks, the trend is clear and coherent. The outcome of statistical analysis confirms our hypothesis about the different character of kinetic tremor in parkinsonian patients and in healthy subjects. In PD, this tremor manifests at higher frequencies in comparison to rest tremor and has specific features that allow differentiating it from the involuntary component of movement in elderly HCs. In fact, in PD patients, kinetic tremor is visible as a clear peak in the PSD of all examined velocity and acceleration components with a median frequency value of about 6.5 Hz (Fig. 1d and 2b), confirming what previously observed in [10], although in our study, the peaks are at slightly higher frequencies. This is not the case in elderly HC subjects, as they show a broader spectral distribution without a clear frequency peak (Fig. 1b). For this reason, in elderly HC subjects, a larger $BW-B_T$ is present (Table 1), especially in vertical component of acceleration, and F_P shows greater variability than in PD patients (Fig. 1b), ranging from 4 to 10 Hz. The latter findings confirm previous results suggesting the presence of an enhanced physiological tremor in healthy elderly handwriting [11].

5 Conclusions

The outcomes of this study illustrate that the features extracted from spectral analysis offer a valid inquiring approach to characterize parkinsonian motor behavior, since they can distinguish between the groups even when kinematic analysis shows weak differences. These results support the hypothesis that, at group level, PD patients show handwriting-related kinetic tremor and that it is distinguishable from the involuntary movement of elderly HC subjects that is, on the contrary, due to age-related enhanced tremor. The accurate task seems to be the most sensitive to kinetic tremor detection, especially at the level of the acceleration signal, leading to the conclusion that the emergence of tremor, and its characteristics, are task-dependent. Further studies including more tasks, to establish what signal component better brings out the motor impairment in different conditions, and a larger examined population are needed to support or discard our findings.

The natural development of this feature selection step would be to perform a confirmatory study aiming at testing if the PD patients and the control group differ in all tested variables. This research line could support the implementation of spectral analysis as a tool for differential diagnosis of tremor-presenting patients but, to evaluate to which extent the spectral analysis can be used for early diagnosis of PD, a better characterization of patients' diagnosis is needed, including information about since how many years the patients have been diagnosed and the severity of the disease.

References

1. Mazzoni, P., Shabbott, B., Cortés, J.C.: Motor HC abnormalities in Parkinson's disease. Cold Spring Harbor Perspectives in Medicine (2012)
2. Vessio, G.: Dynamic handwriting analysis for neurodegenerative disease assessment: a literary review. Appl. Sci. **9**(21), 4666 (2019)
3. Pullman, S.L.: Spiral analysis: a new technique for measuring tremor with a digitizing tablet. Mov. Disord. **13**(SUPPL. 3), 85–89 (1998)
4. Letanneux, A., Danna, J., Velay, J.L., Viallet, F., Pinto, S.: From micrographia to Parkinson's disease dysgraphia. Mov. Disord. **29**(12), 1467–1475 (2014)
5. Thomas, M., Lenka, A., Kumar Pal, P.: Handwriting analysis in Parkinson's disease: current status and future directions. Mov. Disord. Clin. Pract. **4**(6), 806–818 (2017)
6. Kraus, P.H., Lemke, M.R., Reichmann, H,: Kinetic tremor in Parkinson's disease - an underrated symptom. J. Neural Transm. **113**(7), 845–853 (2006). https://doi.org/10.1007/s00702-005-0354-9
7. Mansur, P.H.G., et al.: A review on techniques for tremor recording and quantification. Crit. Rev. Biomed. Eng. **35**(5), 343–362 (2007)
8. Szumilas, M., Lewenstein, K., Ślubowska, E., Szlufik, S., Koziorowski, D.: A multimodal approach to the quantification of kinetic tremor in Parkinson's disease. Sensors **20**(1), 1–18 (2020)
9. Toffoli, S., et al.: A smart ink pen for spiral drawing analysis in patients with Parkinson's disease, pp. 6475–6478 (2021)
10. Aly, N.M., Playfer, J.R., Smith, S.L., Halliday, D.M.: A novel computer-based technique for the assessment of tremor in Parkinson's disease. Age Ageing **36**(4), 395–399 (2007)
11. Almeida, M.F.S., Cavalheiro, G.L., Pereira, A.A., Andrade, A.O.: Investigation of age-related changes in physiological kinetic tremor. Ann. Biomed. Eng. **38**(11), 3423–3439 (2010). https://doi.org/10.1007/s10439-010-0098-z
12. Accardo, A., et al.: A device for quantitative kinematic analysis of children's handwriting movements. In: Proceedings of MEDICON 2007, Lubljiana, 26–30 June 2007, pp. 445–448 (2007)
13. Teulings, H.L., Contreras-Vidal, J.L., Stelmach, G.E., Adler, C.H.: Parkinsonism reduces coordination of fingers, wrist, and arm in fine motor HC. Exp. Neurol. **146**(1), 159–170 (1997)
14. Bender, R., Lange, S.: Adjusting for multiple testing–when and how? J. Clin. Epidemiol. **54**(4), 343–349 (2001)

Exploration of Various Fractional Order Derivatives in Parkinson's Disease Dysgraphia Analysis

Jan Mucha[1]([✉])[iD], Zoltan Galaz[1][iD], Jiri Mekyska[1][iD],
Marcos Faundez-Zanuy[2][iD], Vojtech Zvoncak[1][iD], Zdenek Smekal[1][iD],
Lubos Brabenec[3][iD], and Irena Rektorova[3,4][iD]

[1] Department of Telecommunications, Faculty of Electrical Engineering
and Communication, Brno University of Technology, Brno, Czech Republic
mucha@vut.cz
[2] Escola Superior Politecnica, Tecnocampus, Mataro, Barcelona, Spain
[3] Applied Neuroscience Research Group, Central European Institute
of Technology – CEITEC, Masaryk University, Brno, Czech Republic
[4] First Department of Neurology, Faculty of Medicine and St. Anne's University
Hospital, Masaryk University, Brno, Czech Republic
irena.rektorova@fnusa.cz

Abstract. Parkinson's disease (PD) is a common neurodegenerative disorder with a prevalence rate estimated to 2.0% for people aged over 65 years. Cardinal motor symptoms of PD such as rigidity and bradykinesia affect the muscles involved in the handwriting process resulting in handwriting abnormalities called PD dysgraphia. Nowadays, online handwritten signal (signal with temporal information) acquired by the digitizing tablets is the most advanced approach of graphomotor difficulties analysis. Although the basic kinematic features were proved to effectively quantify the symptoms of PD dysgraphia, a recent research identified that the theory of fractional calculus can be used to improve the graphomotor difficulties analysis. Therefore, in this study, we follow up on our previous research, and we aim to explore the utilization of various approaches of fractional order derivative (FD) in the analysis of PD dysgraphia. For this purpose, we used the repetitive loops task from the Parkinson's disease handwriting database (PaHaW). Handwritten signals were parametrized by the kinematic features employing three FD approximations: Grünwald-Letnikov's, Riemann-Liouville's, and Caputo's. Results of the correlation analysis revealed a significant relationship between the clinical state and the handwriting features based on the velocity. The extracted features by Caputo's FD approximation outperformed the rest of the analyzed FD approaches. This was also confirmed by the results of the classification analysis, where the best model

This work was supported by grant no. NU20-04-00294 (Diagnostics of Lewy body diseases in prodromal stage based on multimodal data analysis) of the Czech Ministry of Health and by Spanish grant of the Ministerio de Ciencia e Innovación no. PID2020-113242RB-I00 and by EU grant Next Generation EU (project no. LX22NPO5107 (MEYS)).

C. Carmona-Duarte et al. (Eds.): IGS 2021, LNCS 13424, pp. 308–321, 2022.
https://doi.org/10.1007/978-3-031-19745-1_23

trained by Caputo's handwriting features resulted in a balanced accuracy of 79.73% with a sensitivity of 83.78% and a specificity of 75.68%.

Keywords: Fractional order derivatives · Fractional calculus · Parkinson's disease · Online handwriting · Handwriting difficulties

1 Introduction

Fractional calculus (FC) is a name of the theory of integrals and derivatives of an arbitrary order [28]. It has been developed simultaneously with the well-known differential calculus [16] and its principles have been successfully used in modern engineering and science in general [18, 32, 37]. The advances of FC have been employed in the modeling of different diseases as well, like the human immunodeficiency virus (HIV) [2] or malaria [27]. In addition, the FC has been widely utilized in several computer vision disciplines such as the super-resolution, motion estimation, image restoration or image segmentation [34]. Furthermore, in our recent research we developed new handwriting features extraction techniques based on the application of the fractional order derivatives (FD) [11, 21–25].

Parkinson's disease (PD) is a chronic idiopathic disorder, with the prevalence rate estimated to be approximately 2.0% for people aged over 65 years [12]. It is characterized by the progressive loss of dopaminergic neurons in the *substancia nigra pars compacta* [6, 13], which is a major cause of the symptoms linked with the PD. Primary PD motor symptoms are tremor at rest, muscular rigidity, progressive bradykinesia, and postural instability [3, 14]. One of the essential motor symptoms of PD is PD dysgraphia [17, 36]. Additionally, a variety of nonmotor symptoms such as cognitive impairment, sleep disturbances, depression, etc. may arise.

PD dysgraphia includes a spectrum of neuromuscular difficulties like motor-memory dysfunction, motor feedback difficulties, graphomotor production deficits and others [17, 31]. These disabilities leads to a variety of handwriting difficulties manifesting as dysfluent, shaky, slow, and less readable handwriting. The most commonly observed handwriting abnormality in PD patients is micrographia. Micrographia represents the progressive decrease of letter's amplitude or width [20]. Some PD patients never develop micrographia, but they still exhibit other handwriting difficulties. Accordingly, the consequences of PD dysgraphia significantly affect a person's quality of life. Starting with slow and less legible handwriting and often progressing to lower self-esteem, poor emotional well-being, problematic communication and social interaction, and many others. Nowadays, the most advanced approaches of the PD manifestations quantification contained in the handwriting are based on digitizing tablets [9, 21, 35]. These devices can acquire x and y trajectories along with temporal information, therefore the temporal, kinematic, or dynamic characteristics can be processed together with the spatial features. Handwritten signal acquired by the digitizing tablet is called online handwriting.

In the past decades, researchers have been exploring the effect of several handwriting/drawing tasks in PD dysgraphia analysis, including the simplest ones (loops, circles, lines, Archimedean spiral) together with more complex ones (words, sentences, drawings, etc.) [7–9, 21–23, 26]. Drotar et al. [7–9] reported classification accuracy up to 89% using a combination of kinematic, pressure, energy or empirical mode decomposition features. The diagnosis of PD with accuracy of 71.95% based on the kinematic and entropy features extracted from the sentence task was reported by Impedovo et al. [15]. Taleb et al. [35] reported up to 94% accuracy of PD severity prediction using kinematic and pressure features in combination with adaptive synthetic sampling approach (ADASYN) for model training. Rios-Urrego et al. [30] achieved classification accuracy of 83.3% using the kinematic, geometric, spectral and nonlinear dynamic features. New kinematic features utilizing the discrete time wavelet transform, the fast Fourier transform and a Butter/adaptive filter introduced by Aouraghe et al. [1] resulted in classification accuracy of 92.2%.

Finally, in our recent works [21–23, 25] we introduced and evaluated a new advanced approach of PD dysgraphia analysis employing the FD as a substitution of the conventional differential derivative during the basic kinematic feature extraction. Newly designed handwriting features achieved classification accuracy up to 90%, using the Grünwald-Letnikov approach only. In addition to PD dysgraphia analysis, we explored the FD-based handwriting features in analysis of graphomotor difficulties in school-aged children, where we examined three different FD approaches [24]. The results suggests that the employment of various FD approximations brings major differences in kinematic handwriting features. Therefore, as a next logical step, this study aims to:

1. extend our previous research in PD dysgraphia analysis by the utilization of various FD approaches,
2. explore the differences of various FD approaches in the analysis of PD dysgraphia,
3. compare the power of the FD-based handwriting features extracted by several FD approximations to distinguish between the PD patients and healthy controls (HC).

2 Materials and Methods

2.1 Dataset

For the purpose of this study, we used the Parkinson's disease handwriting database (PaHaW) [7]. The database consists of several handwriting or drawing tasks acquired in 37 PD patients and 38 healthy controls (HC). The participants were enrolled at the First Department of Neurology, St. Anne's University Hospital in Brno, Czech Republic. All participants reported Czech language as their native language and they were right-handed. The patients completed their tasks approximately 1 h after their regular dopaminergic medication (L-dopa). All participants signed an informed consent form approved by the local ethics committee. Demographic and clinical data of the participants involved in this study can be found in Table 1. For the purpose of this study, we selected the repetitive loop handwriting task. This task is missing for several participants of the PaHaW dataset, therefore, we processed 31 PD patients and 37 HC only.

Table 1. Demographic and clinical data of the participants.

Gender	N	Age [y]	PD dur [y]	UPDRS V	LED [mg/day]
Parkinson's disease patients					
Females	15	70.2 ± 8.4	7.9 ± 3.9	1.9 ± 0.4	1129.7 ± 572.9
Males	16	65.9 ± 13.1	7.0 ± 3.9	2.4 ± 0.9	1805.7 ± 743.3
All	31	68.0 ± 11.1	7.4 ± 3.9	2.2 ± 0.8	1478.6 ± 739.8
Healthy controls					
Females	17	61.6 ± 10.2	–	–	–
Males	20	63.3 ± 12.5	–	–	–
All	37	62.9 ± 11.5	–	–	–

N – number of subjects; y – years; PD dur – PD duration; UPDRS V – Unified Parkinson's disease rating scale, part V: Modified Hoehn & Yahr staging score [10]; LED – L-dopa equivalent daily dose.

2.2 Data Acquisition

The PaHaW database [7] consists of nine handwriting tasks. For the purpose of this study we selected the repetitive loop task only. An example of the repetitive loop task for a PD patient and a HC can be seen in Fig. 1. During the acquisition of the handwriting tasks, the participants were rested and seated in a comfortable position with a possibility to look at a pre-filled template. In case of some mistakes, they were allowed to repeat the task. A digitizing tablet (Wacom Intuos 4M) was overlaid with an empty paper and the participants wrote on that using the Wacom Inking pen. Online handwriting signals were recorded with $f_s = 150$ Hz sampling rate, and the following time sequences were acquired: x and y coordinates ($x[t]$, $y[t]$); time-stamp (t); on-surface and in-air movement status ($b[t]$); pressure ($p[t]$); azimuth ($az[t]$); and tilt (also called altitude; $al[t]$).

2.3 Fractional Order Derivative

The main subject of this study is the exploration of the various FD approximations as a substitution of the conventional differential derivatives in the handwriting feature extraction process. We utilized three different FD approximations, namely: Grünwald-Letnikov (GL), Riemann-Liouville (RL), and Caputo (C), implemented by Valério Duarte in Matlab [38–40].

First approach employed in this study was developed by Grünwald and Letnikov. A direct definition of the derivation of the function $y(t)$ by the order α – $D^{\alpha}y(t)$ [28] is based on the finite differences of an equidistant grid in $[0, \tau]$, assuming that the function $y(t)$ satisfies certain smoothness conditions in every finite interval $(0, t), t \leq T$, where T denotes the period. Choosing the grid

$$0 = \tau_0 < \tau_1 < ... < \tau_{n+1} = t = (n+1)h, \tag{1}$$

with

$$\tau_{k+1} - \tau_k = h, \tag{2}$$

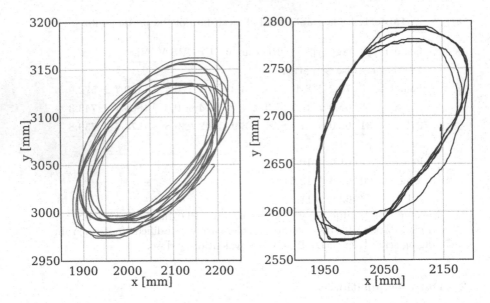

Fig. 1. Example of the repetitive loop task for a HC (left) and a PD patient (right).

and using the notation of finite differences

$$\frac{1}{h^\alpha}\Delta_h^\alpha y(t) = \frac{1}{h^\alpha}\left(y(\tau_{n+1}) - \sum_{v=1}^{n+1} c_v^\alpha y(\tau_{n+1-v}) \right),\qquad(3)$$

where

$$c_v^\alpha = (-1)^{v-1}\binom{\alpha}{v}.\qquad(4)$$

The Grünwald–Letnikov definition from 1867 is defined as

$$^{GL}D^\alpha y(t) = \lim_{h\to 0}\frac{1}{h^\alpha}\Delta_h^\alpha y(t),\qquad(5)$$

where $^{GL}D^\alpha y(t)$ denotes the Grünwald-Letnikov derivatives of order α of the function $y(t)$, and h represents the sampling lattice.

Second approach used in this study has been given by Riemann-Liouville. The left-inverse interpretation of $D^\alpha y(t)$ by Riemann-Liouville [18,28] from 1869 is defined as

$$^{RL}D^\alpha y(t) = \frac{1}{\Gamma(n-\alpha)}\left(\frac{\mathrm{d}}{\mathrm{d}t}\right)^n \int_0^t (t-\tau)^{n-\alpha-1}y(t)\,\mathrm{d}t,\qquad(6)$$

where $^{RL}D^\alpha y(t)$ denotes the Riemann-Liouville derivatives of order α of the function $y(t)$, Γ is the gamma function and $n-1 < \alpha \le n, n \in \mathbf{N}, t > 0$.

Third and last FD approach involved in this study was developed by M. Caputo [4]. In contrast to the previous ones, the improvement hereabouts lies in the unnecessity to define the initial FD condition [18, 28]. The Caputo's definition from 1967 is

$$^{C}D^{\alpha}y(t) = \frac{1}{\Gamma(n-\alpha)} \int_{0}^{t} (t-\tau)^{n-\alpha-1} y^{n}(t) \, dt, \tag{7}$$

where $^{C}D^{\alpha}y(t)$ denotes the Caputo derivatives of order α of the function $y(t)$, Γ is the gamma function and $n - 1 < \alpha \leq n, n \in \mathbf{N}, t > 0$.

2.4 Feature Extraction

Considering the nature of the selected task, on-surface handwriting features were extracted only. Since we did employ three FD approaches in the feature extraction process, three sets of the handwriting features were created. Digitizing tablet rarely omits 3–4 samples during the acquisition, therefore the in-signal outliers removal was performed (outliers were considered as elements more than three scaled median absolute deviations from the median). If not pre-processed, the differentiation of this gap would leave significant peaks in the output handwriting feature. All handwriting features were computed for α in the range of 0.1–1.0 (with the step of 0.1), where $\alpha = 1.0$ is equal to the full derivation. Furthermore, the statistical properties of all extracted handwriting features were described by the mean and the relative standard deviation (relstd). To sum up, each feature set consists of 180 computed kinematic features.

2.5 Statistical Analysis and Machine Learning

Firstly, the normality test of the handwriting features using the Shapiro-Wilk test was performed [33]. Since most of the features were found to come from normal distribution, we did not apply any normalization on a feature basis. To control for the effect of confounding factors (also known as covariates), we controlled for the effect of age and gender of the subjects.

Next, Spearman's (ρ) and Pearson's (r) correlation coefficient with the significance level of 0.05 were computed to assess the strength of the monotonous and linear relationship between the handwriting features and the subject's clinical status (PD/HC). Finally, to control for the issue of multiple comparisons, p-values were adjusted using the False Discovery Rate (FDR) method.

Consequently, binary classification models were built in order to distinguish between the PD patients and HC utilizing the extracted handwriting features. An ensemble extreme gradient boosting algorithm known as XGBoost [5] (with 100 estimators) was used for this purpose. The XGBoost algorithm was selected due to its ability to find complex interactions among features as well as the possibility of ranking their importance and its robustness to outliers. Hyperparameter space optimization (1000 iteration) by the randomized search strategy (stratified 5-fold cross-validation with 10 repetitions) was performed to optimize balanced accuracy. The set of hyper-parameters that were optimized can be found in the following table (Table 2).

Table 2. Hyper-parameters set.

Hyper-parameter	Values
Learning rate	[0.001, 0.01, 0.1, 0.2, 0.3]
Gamma	[0, 0.05, 0.10, 0.15, 0.20, 0.25, 0.5]
Maximum tree depth	[6, 8, 10, 12, 15]
Subsample ratio	[0.5, 0.6, 0.7, 0.8, 0.9, 1.0]
Columns subsample ratio at each level	[0.4, 0.5, 0.6, 0.7, 0.8, 0.9, 1.0]
Columns subsample ratio for each tree	[0.4, 0.5, 0.6, 0.7, 0.8, 0.9, 1.0]
Balance between positive and negative weights	[1, 2, 3, 4]
Minimum weights required in a child node	[0.5, 1.0, 3.0, 5.0, 7.0, 10.0]

The classification performance was evaluated by the following classification metrics: Matthew's correlation coefficient [19] (MCC), balanced accuracy (BACC), sensitivity (SEN) also known as recall (REC), specificity (SPE), precision (PRE) and F1 score (F1). These metrics are defined as follows:

$$\text{MCC} = \frac{TP \times TN + FP \times FN}{\sqrt{N}}, \tag{8}$$

$$\text{BACC} = \frac{1}{2}\left(\frac{TP}{TP + FN}\frac{TN}{TN + FP}\right), \tag{9}$$

$$\text{SPE} = \frac{TN}{TN + FP}, \tag{10}$$

$$\text{PRE} = \frac{TP}{TP + FP}, \tag{11}$$

$$\text{REC} = \frac{TP}{TP + FN}, \tag{12}$$

$$\text{F1} = 2\frac{PRE \times REC}{PRE + REC} \tag{13}$$

where $N = (TP + FP) \times (TP + FN) \times (TN + FP) \times (TN + FN)$, TP (true positive) and FP (false positive) represent the number of correctly identified PD patient and the number of subjects incorrectly identified as PD patient, respectively. Similarly, TN (true negative) and FN (false negative) represent the number of correctly identified HC and the number of subjects with PD incorrectly identified as being healthy.

For a better illustration, the overview of the performed analysis from the handwriting task selection to the evaluation of the results can be found in Fig. 2.

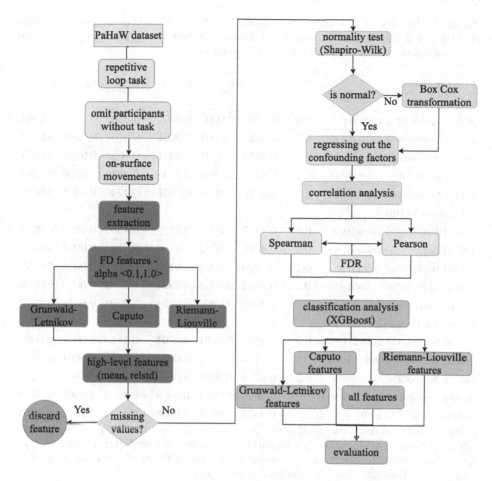

Fig. 2. Flow overview of the performed experiments.

3 Results

The results of the correlation analysis can be seen in Table 3, where the top 5 features per FD approximation according to the p-values of Spearman's correlation are shown. The most significant correlation (after the FDR adjustment) with the clinical state (PD/HC) of the participants was identified in the features extracted by the Caputo's FD approach. Nevertheless, all FD approaches provided the handwriting features that pass the selected significance level ($p < 0.05$), while features extracted by Caputo's and Riemann-Liouville's achieved the p-values very close to 0. Most of the top selected handwriting features are based on horizontal velocity, and all of them have α different from 1, which confirms the positive impact of the FD in PD dysgraphia analysis.

The results of the classification analysis are summarized in Table 4. In total, 4 models were trained: one model per each FD approach and one model com-

Table 3. Results of the correlation analysis between the subjects' clinical status (PD/HC) and the computed handwriting features ranked by the adjusted p-value (and the correlation coefficient) of Spearman's correlation.

Feature name	ρ	p_s	p_s^*	r	p_p	p_p^*
Caputo						
relstd horizontal velocity-$\alpha = 0.6$	−0.5408	0.0001	0.0001	−0.5456	0.0001	0.0001
relstd horizontal velocity-$\alpha = 0.5$	−0.5122	0.0001	0.0001	−0.5204	0.0001	0.0001
relstd horizontal velocity-$\alpha = 0.4$	−0.4912	0.0001	0.0001	−0.5024	0.0001	0.0001
mean horizontal velocity-$\alpha = 0.3$	0.4791	0.0001	0.0001	0.4049	0.0006	0.0051
mean horizontal velocity-$\alpha = 0.4$	0.4716	0.0001	0.0001	0.4240	0.0003	0.0036
Grünwald-Letnikov						
relstd horizontal velocity-$\alpha = 0.8$	−0.4475	0.0001	0.0180	−0.4332	0.0002	0.0240
relstd horizontal velocity-$\alpha = 0.9$	−0.4310	0.0002	0.0180	−0.4184	0.0004	0.0240
relstd horizontal velocity-$\alpha = 0.7$	−0.4220	0.0003	0.0180	−0.4162	0.0004	0.0240
relstd horizontal velocity-$\alpha = 0.6$	−0.3964	0.0008	0.0324	−0.3682	0.0020	0.0720
relstd vertical velocity-$\alpha = 0.9$	−0.3949	0.0009	0.0324	−0.3801	0.0014	0.0630
Riemann-Liouville						
mean horizontal velocity-$\alpha = 0.2$	0.4882	0.0001	0.0001	0.3869	0.0011	0.0060
relstd horizontal velocity-$\alpha = 0.2$	−0.4716	0.0001	0.0001	−0.4643	0.0001	0.0013
mean horizontal velocity-$\alpha = 0.3$	0.4716	0.0001	0.0001	0.4240	0.0003	0.0022
relstd vertical velocity-$\alpha = 0.2$	−0.4686	0.0001	0.0008	−0.4654	0.0001	0.0013
relstd vertical velocity-$\alpha = 0.3$	−0.4475	0.0001	0.0008	−0.4483	0.0001	0.0013

ρ – Spearman's correlation coefficient; p_s – p-value of Spearman's correlation; p_s^* – adjusted p-value of Spearman's correlation; r – Pearson's correlation coefficient; p_p – p-value of Pearson's correlation; p_p^* – adjusted p-value of Pearson's correlation; relstd – relative standard deviation; h. – horizontal; v. – vertical.

bining all the features. The best classification performance was achieved by the Caputo's FD approach with BACC = 0.7973, SEN = 0.8378, SPE = 0.7568, PRE = 0.7750 and F1 = 0.8052. However, the highest SEN and SPE were achieved by the Riemann-Liouville approach (SPE = 0.8378, PRE = 0.8065).

Next, in Fig. 3 the comparison of the horizontal velocity function for $\alpha = 0.6$ across all of the utilized FD approximations is visualized. The handwriting features were extracted from the performance of the PD patient with high PD severity. And finally, an example of the dependency of the mean of horizontal velocity on the FD order α for all three FD approaches is shown in Fig. 4.

4   Discussion

The main goal of this study is to explore various FD approximations and their differences in the analysis of the PD dysgraphia by online handwriting. For better illustration and more understanding of the differences as well as the common

Table 4. Results of the classification analysis.

FD approach	MCC	BACC	SEN	SPE	PRE	F1
C	**0.5966**	**0.7973**	**0.8378**	0.7568	0.7750	**0.8052**
RL	0.5204	0.7568	0.6757	**0.8378**	**0.8065**	0.7353
GL	0.4867	0.7432	0.7297	0.7568	0.7500	0.7397
ALL	0.5135	0.7568	0.7568	0.7568	0.7568	0.7568

MCC – Matthew's correlation coefficient; BACC – balanced accuracy; SEN – sensitivity; SPE – specificity; PRE – precision; F1 – F1 score; GL – Grünwald-Letnikov; C – Caputo; RL – Riemann-Liouville; ALL (combination of all feature-types, i. e. 540 features).

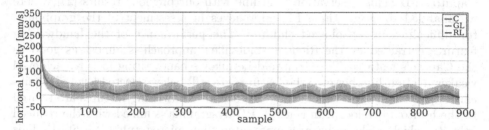

Fig. 3. Comparison of the horizontal velocity function ($\alpha = 0.6$) across all of the FD approximations (PD patient; C – Caputo; GL – Grünwald-Letnikov; RL – Riemann-Liouville).

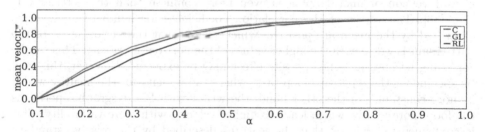

Fig. 4. Mean of horizontal velocity depending on FD order α (PD patient; C – Caputo; GL – Grünwald-Letnikov; RL – Riemann-Liouville).

characteristics, the comparison of the identical handwriting feature extracted for all three FD approaches can be found in Fig. 3. The feature is extracted from the handwritten product of a PD patient and the feature represents the horizontal velocity for $\alpha = 0.6$. The velocity function extracted by the Riemann-Liouville's approximation dominates by its oscillatory nature in comparison to the other two approaches. Nevertheless the envelope of Riemann-Liouville's approach follows the local maximums and minimums of the functions computed by the Caputo's and Grünwald-Letnikov's approximation. A minor shift of the velocity function can be noticed between the Caputo's and Grünwald-Letnikov's approaches. This is due to the nature of the Caputo's FD approach, which differentiates input data before the convolution operation, so the temporal memory is applied to the velocity afterwards. Regarding the visualization in Fig. 3, we can confirm the differences in the same handwriting feature extracted by various FD approximations. Additionally, the dependency comparison of the mean of horizontal velocity on the order α is provided in Fig. 4. The oscillatory behaviour of the Riemann-Liouville's function results in the wider gap from the Caputo's and Grünwald-Letnikov's functions. Nevertheless, all three FD approaches converge to the same point as the order α is closer to 1.0. This behaviour is expected, because the full derivation has to be the same for all approaches.

Regarding the results of the correlation analysis, the most significantly correlated handwriting features (after the FDR adjustment) were extracted by the Caputo's FD. This observation is in line with our previous results [24], where we analysed the same three FD approaches in assessment of the graphomotor difficulties in school-aged children. The performance of the handwriting features extracted by the Riemann-Liouville's approach is almost as good as the Caputo's features. The Grünwald-Letnikov's handwriting features achieved weaker relationship, however the features are still below selected level of significance ($p < 0.05$). Most significantly correlated handwriting features are related to the horizontal velocity. In general, PD dysgraphia is linked with the reduced velocity, which could occur even more often than micrographia [15,29,31]. This strong relationship is reasonable due to the cardinal symptoms of PD, such as bradykinesia or rigidity, which have a significant impact on fine motor skills, including handwriting/drawing. Moreover, some studies suggest that the horizontal version of micrographia is even more common than the vertical version [36]. The values of the correlation coefficients for handwriting features described by the mean are positive, which means that the performance of the participant is worse with the higher values of the horizontal velocity. This can be confusing because just the opposite effect may be expected. However, this may be specific for the repetitive loop task, where the velocity for the healthy writer is more constant. On the other hand, the writer with PD dysgraphia performs the loop more jerkily, which leads to higher velocity with more variability. This is confirmed by the fact that the features described by the relative standard deviation are negative, which means that the handwriting performance is better with the lower variability of the horizontal velocity.

Based on the results of the classification analysis, the best classification performance was obtained by the handwriting features computed by Caputo's FD. The resulting balanced accuracy was 79.73% with SEN = 83.78% and SPE = 75.68%. In our similar study [21] we achieved classification accuracy of 80.60% with SEN = 79.4% and SPE = 80.56% using all of the handwriting tasks from the PaHaW database, but only the Grünwald-Letnikov FD was employed. In comparison to this study, we can conclude that the exploration of the various FD approaches improved the classification analysis, considering that we achieved almost the same performance only by one handwriting task and using the on-surface kinematic features only. The balanced accuracy of the Riemann-Liouville and Grünwald-Letnikov FD is approximately 5% lower while the sensitivity is lower up to 15% in comparison to the Caputo's FD. Considering the reported results, we can conclude that the Caputo's approach is the most suitable FD approximation of the kinematic analysis of the PD dysgraphia by online handwriting.

5 Conclusion

To the best of our knowledge, this is one of the first studies performing an investigation of the various FD approaches in the computerized analysis of the PD dysgraphia by online handwriting. For that reason, the outcomes should be considered as being rather exploratory and pilot in nature. Based on the reported results, Caputo's FD approximation outperformed the rest of the analysed FD approaches in all experiments. The correlation analysis resulted in the significant relationship between the clinical state and the handwriting features based on the velocity, which is in line with our previous findings. Additionally, the best classification model achieved the balanced accuracy of 79.73% with SEN = 83.78% and SPE = 75.68%, which is a comparable result to our previous studies.

This study has several limitations and possible parts, that could be further improved. The processed dataset is relatively small in terms of the statistical validity of the achieved results. Next, the α order should be explored more sensitively (e.g. with a step of 0.01 or even less) in order to identify the optimal range for PD dysgraphia analysis. Additionally, other feature types, such as temporal, spatial, and dynamic, should be included in future comparisons. Moreover, the comparison of the various FD-based features with the conventionally used handwriting features should be performed. Besides, all handwriting tasks included in the PaHaW database have to be investigated by the various FD approaches. And finally, various machine learning models should be trained and compared in future studies.

References

1. Aouraghe, I., Alae, A., Ghizlane, K., Mrabti, M., Aboulem, G., Faouzi, B.: A novel approach combining temporal and spectral features of Arabic online handwriting for Parkinson's disease prediction. J. Neurosci. Methods **339**, 108727 (2020). https://doi.org/10.1016/j.jneumeth.2020.108727
2. Arshad, Sadia, Baleanu, Dumitru, Bu, Weiping, Tang, Yifa: Effects of HIV infection on CD4$^+$ T-cell population based on a fractional-order model. Adv. Differ. Eq. **2017**(1) (2017). Article number: 92. https://doi.org/10.1186/s13662-017-1143-0
3. Brabenec, L., Mekyska, J., Galaz, Z., Rektorova, I.: Speech disorders in Parkinson's disease: early diagnostics and effects of medication and brain stimulation. J. Neural Transm. **124**(3), 303–334 (2017). https://doi.org/10.1007/s00702-017-1676-0
4. Caputo, M.: Linear models of dissipation whose Q is almost frequency independent-II. Geophys. J. Int. **13**(5), 529–539 (1967). https://doi.org/10.1111/j.1365-246X.1967.tb02303.x
5. Chen, T., Guestrin, C.: XGBoost: a scalable tree boosting system. In: Proceedings of the 22nd ACM SIGKDD International Conference on Knowledge Discovery and Data Mining, pp. 785–794. ACM (2016)

6. Dickson, D.W.: Parkinson's disease and parkinsonism: neuropathology. Cold Spring Harb. Perspect. Med. **2**(8), a009258 (2012)
7. Drotar, P., Mekyska, J., Rektorova, I., Masarova, L., Smekal, Z., Faundez-Zanuy, M.: Evaluation of handwriting kinematics and pressure for differential diagnosis of Parkinson's disease. Artif. Intell. Med. **67**, 39–46 (2016). https://doi.org/10.1016/j.artmed.2016.01.004
8. Drotar, P., Mekyska, J., Rektorova, I., Masarova, L., Smekal, Z., Zanuy, M.F.: Decision support framework for Parkinson's disease based on novel handwriting markers. IEEE Trans. Neural Syst. Rehabil. Eng. **23**(3), 508–516 (2015). https://doi.org/10.1109/tnsre.2014.2359997
9. Drotar, P., Mekyska, J., Smekal, Z., Rektorova, I., Masarova, L., Faundez-Zanuy, M.: Contribution of different handwriting modalities to differential diagnosis of Parkinson's disease. In: 2015 IEEE International Symposium on Medical Measurements and Applications (MeMeA), pp. 1–5 (2015)
10. Fahn, S., Elton, R.L.: UPDRS Development Committee (1987) Unified Parkinson's Disease Rating Scale. Recent Developments in Parkinson's Disease. Macmillan, Florham Park (1987)
11. Galaz, Z., et al.: Advanced parametrization of graphomotor difficulties in school-aged children. IEEE Access **8**, 112883–112897 (2020). https://doi.org/10.1109/ACCESS.2020.3003214
12. Heinzel, S., et al.: Update of the MDS research criteria for prodromal Parkinson's disease. Mov. Disord. **34**(10), 1464–1470 (2019)
13. Hornykiewicz, O.: Biochemical aspects of Parkinson's disease. Neurology **51**(2 Suppl 2), S2–S9 (1998)
14. Hughes, A., Daniel, S., Lees, A.: The clinical features of Parkinson's disease in 100 histologically proven cases. Adv. Neurol. **60**, 595 (1993)
15. Impedovo, D., Pirlo, G., Vessio, G.: Dynamic handwriting analysis for supporting earlier Parkinson's disease diagnosis. Information **9**(10) (2018). https://doi.org/10.3390/info9100247. http://www.mdpi.com/2078-2489/9/10/247
16. Lazarević, M.: Further results on fractional order control of a mechatronic system. Sci. Tech. Rev. **63**(3), 22–32 (2013). ISSN: 206
17. Letanneux, A., Danna, J., Velay, J.L., Viallet, F., Pinto, S.: From micrographia to Parkinson's disease dysgraphia. Mov. Disord. **29**(12), 1467–1475 (2014)
18. Luchko, Y., Gorenflo, R.: An operational method for solving fractional differential equations with the Caputo derivatives. Acta Math. Vietnam **24**(2), 207–233 (1999)
19. Matthews, B.W.: Comparison of the predicted and observed secondary structure of T4 phage lysozyme. Biochim. Biophys. Acta (BBA) **405**(2), 442–51 (1975)
20. McLennan, J., Nakano, K., Tyler, H., Schwab, R.: Micrographia in Parkinson's disease. J. Neurol. Sci. **15**(2), 141–152 (1972)
21. Mucha, J., et al.: Analysis of Parkinson's disease dysgraphia based on optimized fractional order derivative features. In: 2019 27th European Signal Processing Conference (EUSIPCO), pp. 1–5 (2019)
22. Mucha, J., et al.: Advanced Parkinson's disease dysgraphia analysis based on fractional derivatives of online handwriting. In: 10th International Congress on Ultra Modern Telecommunications and Control Systems and Workshops (ICUMT) (2018)
23. Mucha, J., et al.: Identification and monitoring of Parkinson's disease dysgraphia based on fractional-order derivatives of online handwriting. Appl. Sci. **8**(12), 2566 (2018)

24. Mucha, J., et al.: Analysis of various fractional order derivatives approaches in assessment of graphomotor difficulties. IEEE Access **8**, 218234–218244 (2020). https://doi.org/10.1109/ACCESS.2020.3042591
25. Mucha, J., et al.: Fractional derivatives of online handwriting: a new approach of Parkinsonic dysgraphia analysis. In: 2018 41st International Conference on Telecommunications and Signal Processing (TSP), pp. 214–217. IEEE (2018)
26. Nackaerts, E., et al.: Handwriting training in Parkinson's disease: a trade-off between size, speed and fluency. PLoS One **12**(12), e0190223 (2017). https://doi.org/10.1371/journal.pone.0190223
27. Pinto, C.M., Machado, J.T.: Fractional model for malaria transmission under control strategies. Comput. Math. Appl. **66**(5), 908–916 (2013). https://doi.org/10.1016/j.camwa.2012.11.017. http://www.sciencedirect.com/science/article/pii/S0898122112006785. Fractional Differentiation and Its Applications
28. Podlubny, I.: Fractional Differential Equations an Introduction to Fractional Derivatives, Fractional Differential Equations, to Methods of Their Solution and Some of Their Applications. Academic Press, San Diego (1999)
29. Ponsen, M.M., Daffertshofer, A., Wolters, E.C., Beek, P.J., Berendse, H.W.: Impairment of complex upper limb motor function in de novo Parkinson's disease. Parkinsonism Relat. Disord. **14**(3), 199–204 (2008)
30. Rios-Urrego, C., Vásquez-Correa, J., Vargas-Bonilla, J., Nöth, E., Lopera, F., Orozco-Arroyave, J.: Analysis and evaluation of handwriting in patients with Parkinson's disease using kinematic, geometrical, and non-linear features. Comput. Methods Programs Biomed. **173**, 43–52 (2019). https://doi.org/10.1016/j.cmpb.2019.03.005
31. Rosenblum, S., Samuel, M., Zlotnik, S., Erikh, I., Schlesinger, I.: Handwriting as an objective tool for Parkinson's disease diagnosis. J. Neurol. **260**(9), 2357–2361 (2013). https://doi.org/10.1007/s00415-013-6996-x
32. Samko, S.G., Kilbas, A A., Marichev, O.I., et al.: Fractional Integrals and Derivatives. Theory and Applications, p. 44. Gordon and Breach, Yverdon (1993)
33. Shapiro, S.S., Wilk, M.B.: An analysis of variance test for normality (complete samples). Biometrika **52**(3/4), 591–611 (1965)
34. Sun, H., Zhang, Y., Baleanu, D., Chen, W., Chen, Y.: A new collection of real world applications of fractional calculus in science and engineering. Commun. Nonlinear Sci. Numer. Simul. **64**, 213–231 (2018). https://doi.org/10.1016/j.cnsns.2018.04.019. http://www.sciencedirect.com/science/article/pii/S1007570418301308
35. Taleb, C., Khachab, M., Mokbel, C., Likforman-Sulem, L.: A reliable method to predict Parkinson's disease stage and progression based on handwriting and re-sampling approaches. In: 2018 IEEE 2nd International Workshop on Arabic and Derived Script Analysis and Recognition (ASAR), pp. 7–12. IEEE (2018)
36. Thomas, M., Lenka, A., Kumar Pal, P.: Handwriting analysis in Parkinson's disease: current status and future directions. Mov. Disord. Clin. Pract. **4**(6), 806–818 (2017). https://doi.org/10.1002/mdc3.12552. https://onlinelibrary.wiley.com/doi/abs/10.1002/mdc3.12552
37. Uchaikin, V.V.: Fractional Derivatives for Physicists and Engineers, vol. 2. Springer, Heidelberg (2013). https://doi.org/10.1007/978-3-642-33911-0
38. Valério, D.: Variable order derivatives. https://www.mathworks.com/matlabcentral/leexchange/24444-variable-order-derivatives
39. Valério, D., Sá da Costa, J.: Ninteger: a fractional control toolbox for Matlab. In: Fractional Differentiation and Its Applications, Bordeaux (2004)
40. Valério, D., Sá da Costa, J. (eds.): An Introduction to Fractional Control. IET, Stevenage (2013)

Lognormal Features for Early Diagnosis of Alzheimer's Disease Through Handwriting Analysis

Nicole Dalia Cilia[2,4], Tiziana D'Alessandro[3], Cristina Carmona-Duarte[1], Claudio De Stefano[3], Moises Diaz[1], Miguel Ferrer[1], and Francesco Fontanella[3(✉)]

[1] IDeTIC: Instituto para el Desarrollo Tecnológico y la Innovación en Comunicaciones, Universidad de Las Palmas de Gran Canaria, Las Palmas, Spain
[2] Department of Computer Engineering, University of Enna "Kore", Cittadella Universitaria, Enna, Italy
[3] Department of Electrical and Information Engineering (DIEI), University of Cassino and Southern Lazio, Via G. Di Biasio 43, 03043 Cassino, FR, Italy
fontanella@unicas.it
[4] Institute for Computing and Information Sciences, Radboud University, Toernooiveld 212, 6525 EC Nijmegen, The Netherlands

Abstract. Alzheimer's disease causes most of dementia cases. Although currently there is no cure for this disease, predicting the cognitive decline of people at the first stage of the disease allows clinicians to alleviate its burden. Clinicians evaluate individuals' cognitive decline by using neuropsychological tests consisting of different sections, each devoted to test a specific set of cognitive skills. The sigma-lognormal model allows complex movements to be represented as a summation of simple time-overlapped movements, and has been used in several fields to model numerous human movements such as, for example, handwriting and speech. Recently, this theory has been also used for detecting and monitoring neurodegenerative disorders. In this paper, we present the results of a preliminary study aimed at exploring the use of lognormal features to classify patients affected by Alzheimer's disease. The promising results achieved confirms that lognormal features can be used to support Alzheimer's diagnosis.

1 Introduction

Neurodegenerative diseases (NDs in the following) are incurable and debilitating, caused by progressive degeneration of nerve cells, affecting movements and/or mental skills. Alzheimer's disease (AD) is the most common among them, and because of worldwide lifespan lengthening, it is expected that its incidence will dramatically increase in the coming decades.

AD produces a slow and progressive decline in mental functions such as memory, thought, judgment, and learning abilities. The predominant symptom

C. Carmona-Duarte et al. (Eds.): IGS 2021, LNCS 13424, pp. 322–335, 2022.
https://doi.org/10.1007/978-3-031-19745-1_24

in the early stages of AD is the episodic memory impairment, whereas later stages are characterized by progressive amnesia and deterioration in other cognitive domains.

Unfortunately, there is no cure for AD, but its symptoms can be managed during their progression. This creates a critical need for the improvement of the approaches currently used for diagnosing them as early as possible. As cognitive and motor functions are both involved in planning and execution of movements, and because handwriting requires a precise and properly coordinated control of the body [20], the analysis of handwriting dynamics might provide a cheap and non-invasive method for evaluating the disease progression [10]. Furthermore, it has been observed that the application of machine learning methods to motor function has shown promise in decreasing the time taken to perform clinical assessments [1,12]. To this aim, cheap and widely used graphic tablets can be used to administer handwriting tests, which include simple and easy-to-perform handwriting/drawing tasks [10], and to record kinematic and dynamic information of the performed movements. For this reason, researchers are showing an increasing interest in developing and using machine learning based methodologies to support both the diagnosis and the treatment of NDs, and several methods have been proposed for the diagnosis of both AD [24].

The Kinematic Theory of rapid movements, together with the use of the Sigma-Lognormal model, allows the decomposition of a complex movement into a vector summation of simple time-overlapped movements [15–17]. This theory has been applied in several fields to model numerous human movements such as, handwriting [14], speech [2], head and trunk movement [11], etc. However, it has been barely applied to the detection and monitoring of neuromuscular disorders [13,19]. Specifically, this model has been used to classify parkinsonian patients in this pair of papers [8,9]. The authors found competitive performance by combining this model with other velocity-based features like Maxwell-Boltzmann distribution, Fourier, and Cepstrum transforms.

In this paper, we present the results of a preliminary study aimed at exploring the use of lognormal features to classify patients affected by AD, on the basis of their ability to accomplish six handwriting tasks. Those tasks were introduced in [4], and are described later in this paper. We collected the data produced by 174 participants (89 AD patients and 85 healthy people). To the best of our knowledge, this is the largest dataset containing handwriting data related to AD. Starting from the lognormal parameters computed to represent the handwriting contained in this data, we have identified fourteen features that can be used to characterize the handwriting of people affected by AD. We assessed the effectiveness of the features extracted We used seven well-known and widely used classifiers to asses the effectiveness of the features proposed. The promising results achieved confirms that lognormal features can be used to support AD diagnosis.

The organization of this paper is as follows. Section describes the Sigma-lognormal model used for the representation of handwriting. In Sect. 3 we present the tasks used to collect handwriting data and the features extracted using the

Sigma-lognormal model. Section 4 details some experimental results. Concluding remarks and possible future investigations are outolined in Sect. 5.

2   The Sigma-Lognormal Model

Based on lognormal movement decomposition, there are several studies about the normative range of variations in the lognormal parameters, which give a notion of how ideal a movement could be [18]. To parametrizing the human movement velocity and trajectory by the Kinematic Theory, different algorithms have been developed, as Robust XZERO [5,14] and IDeLog [6]. In this work we based on the IDeLog algorithm [6].

Sigma-Lognormal model considers the resulting velocity of each simple fast movement primitive as a lognormal function (Λ), being each peak of velocity between two speed minima modeling by a lognormal. The lognormal parameters, t_{0_j}, μ_j and σ_j^2 are calculated finding the less minimimun error between the velocity profile and the obtained lognormal from successive interactions and the trajectory original profile and the reconstructed one. The lognornormal function that model each velocity peak or "simple movement" or "stroke" can be defined as:

$$v_j(t; t_{0_j}, \mu_j, \sigma_j^2) = D_j \Lambda(t; t_{0_j}, \mu_j, \sigma_j^2) = \frac{D_j}{\sigma_j \sqrt{2\pi}(t - t_{0_j})} exp\{ \frac{[-ln(t - t_{0_j}) - \mu_j]^2}{2\sigma_j^2}$$

$$(1)$$

where t is the time basis, D_j the amplitude , t_{o_j} the time of occurrence, μ_j the time delay and σ_j the response time, both on a logarithmic time scale.

In case a complex movement, a succession of simple movements or strokes as can be observed in Fig. 1, the velocity profile $v_n(t)$ is given by the time superposition of the M previous lognormals.

$$v_n(t) = \sum_{j=1}^{M} v_j(t; t_{0_j}, \mu_j, \sigma_j^2) = \sum_{j=1}^{M} D_j \begin{bmatrix} \cos(\Phi_j(t)) \\ \sin(\Phi_j(t)) \end{bmatrix} \Lambda(t; t_{0_j}, \mu_j, \sigma_j^2) \qquad (2)$$

where $\Phi_j(t)$ is the angular position given by:

$$\Phi_j(t) = \Theta_{s_j} + \frac{(\Theta_{e_j} - \Theta_{s_j})}{2} [1 + erf(\frac{ln(t - t_{0_j}) - \mu_j}{\sigma_j \sqrt{2}})] \qquad (3)$$

being Θ_{s_j} and Θ_{e_j} are the starting and the end angular direction of the jth simple movement or stroke.

3   Tasks and Features

Following subsections detail the data collection procedure, the tasks used, and the features extracted.

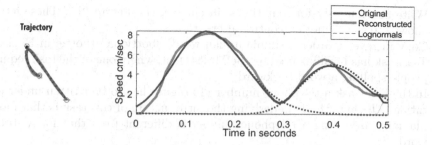

Fig. 1. An example of lognormal.

3.1 Data Collection

Nowadays it is known that alteration in handwriting is one of the first signs of AD, that is why data acquisition step for this work focus on the recording and collection of handwriting samples. Those samples comes from the execution of a protocol [4] composed of different kinds of handwriting tasks. Every participant executed all the tasks with a special pen on A4 paper sheets fixed to a graphic tablet, that allow the recording of the handwriting in terms of x-y-z coordinates for each point, acquired at a constant sampling rate, equal to 200 Hz. The first two coordinates are spatial ones and represent the point position in the two-dimensional surface where the writing is produced, while the third one is a measure of the pressure exerted by the subject at that point. This last measure assumes positive values when the pen is on the sheet, while a null value when it is detached, up to a maximum distance of 3 cm from the sheet, beyond which the system is not able to receive information. The protocol was administered to a group of 174 participants: 89 patients at the first stages of AD and a control group of 85 people. Both the AD patients and the control group were recruited with the support of the geriatrics department, Alzheimer's unit, of the "Federico II" hospital in Naples. Both groups were selected according to a recruiting criteria based on standard clinical tests, such as the Mini-Mental State Examination (MMSE), the Frontal Assessment Battery (FAB) and the Montreal Cognitive Assessment (MoCA).

3.2 Tasks

In this study we considered only the handwriting samples relative to six tasks of the protocol:

1. Join two points with a vertical line continuously for four times. The up-down vertical movements require the finger joint and wrist movements. This task is useful to investigate elementary motor functions [27];
2. Trace a circle continuously for four times. The circle diameter has to be 6 cm. This task allows to test the automaticity of movements and the regularity and coordination of the sequence of movements [21];

3. Write continuously for four times, in cursive, the bigram 'le'. These letters allow to test the motion control alternation;
4. Copy in reverse order a simple italian word: "bottiglia" (bottle in English). This task has been inspired by the MMSE test, where one of the task requires people spelling a word backward;
5. In the fifth task a telephone number (10 digits) has to be written under dictation. The hypothesis underlying the introduction of this task is that motor planning in writing a telephone number is different from that for writing a word;
6. The sixth task is the Clock Drawing Test (CDT). In [26] the authors found that CDT shows a high sensitivity for mild AD.

The first two tasks belong to the category of graphic tasks, whose objective is to test the patient's ability in: (i) writing elementary traits; (ii) joining some points; (iii) drawing figures (simple or complex and scaled in various dimensions). The third and the fourth tasks are copy and reverse Copy tasks, whose objective is to test the person's abilities in repeating complex graphic gestures, which have a semantic meaning, such as letters, words and numbers (of different lengths and with different spatial organizations). The fifth is a dictation task, whose purpose is to investigate how the writing varies (with phrases or numbers) in which the use of the working memory is necessary throughout the execution. The sixth task is a graphic task whose purpose is not only to test the dynamic ability of a person, but also his cognitive skills, the spatial dysfunction and lack of attention. This test requires verbal understanding, memory and spatially coded knowledge in addition to constructive skills [25].

3.3 Lognormal Features

The feature engineering process allowed us to identify a set of features that according to our domain of knowledge were good candidates to discriminate the handwriting of people affected by AD from that of healthy people. The Sigma-Lognormal model, defined in Sect. 2 was applied to the data acquired as stated in Sect. 3.1. The result of this procedure was the decomposition of each task into a vector summation of simple time-overlapped movements, from which it was possible to extract a set of Sigma-Lognormal parameters $P_j = [D_j, t_{0_j}, \mu_j, \sigma_j, \Theta_{s_j}, \Theta_{e_j}]$. In particular, for every point (x, y) acquired during the execution of the tasks, one or more overlapping lognormals were found, so their parameters and the percentage of contribution were stored for every point. The term "First lognormal" is used to refer to the lognormal that most contributes for a certain point. Once the Sigma-Lognormal parameters were obtained for every task and every participant, it was possible to compute a set of fourteen features, described in Table 1.

Table 1. Summary of computed features

Name	Description
num_seg	Total number of segments generated by the execution of the task
avg_log	Average of the number of overlapped lognormals for every point
tot_log	Total number of lognormals extracted from the entire trace of the task
avg_D	Average of D parameter of the first lognormal for every point
D_max	Max of D parameter found among the first lognormals of all the points
P_first_log	Average of the percentage of contribution of the first lognormal for all the points
σ_stability	Variance of the sigma parameter of the first lognormal for all the points
diff_logs	Average of the differences between the percentage of contribution of the first and the second lognormal on all points
var_log	Variance of the percentage of contribution of the first lognormal on all points
avg_t_o	Average of the t_o parameter of the first lognormal on all points
avg_σ	Average of the σ parameter of the first lognormal on all points
avg_μ	Average of the μ parameter of the first lognormal on all points
avg_Θ_s	Average of the Θ_s parameter of the first lognormal on all points
avg_Θ_e	Average of the Θ_e parameter of the first lognormal on all points

The aim of this procedure is to use those computed features to distinguish between patients and healthy controls, the two groups of participants involved. From this section on, those features will be referred as "Lognormal Features".

4   Experimental Results

This section shows the results obtained by applying several classification approaches according to the input data. Specifically, lognormal features are classified through six well known ML algorithms, while RGB images are used to feed three different kinds of CNNs.

We used the lognormal features (see Sect. 3.3) with standard machine learning algorithms: k-Nearest Neighbors (K-NN), Random Forest (RF), Decision Tree (DT), Support Vector Machine (SVM), Logistic Regression (LR), Gradient Boosting (GB), XGboost (XGB). We used the scikit-Learn library. The settings of their hyperparameters were left at the default values provided by scikit-Learn. The only exceptions regard the SVM classifiers, for which we used a linear kernel, and the KNN classifier, for which a the number of neighbours was set to 3. In order to obtain statistically significant results, we performed 30 runs for each classifier. For each run, the dataset was randomly shuffled and a 5-fold classification strategy was adopted. In order to evaluate the performance of the mentioned models we considered the following metrics: accuracy (acc), Sensitivity (True Positive Rate, TPR), Specificity (True Negative Rate, TNR), Precision, False Negative Rate (FNR), and Area Under the Curve (AUC).

Since we performed 30 runs for each classifier, the above mentioned parameters were computed for each run and their average and standard deviation (in parentheses) are shown in the following tables. All the metrics are expressed in percentages, except for the AUC and bold values highlight the best performance achieved.

Looking at the accuracies in Table 2 it is worth noting that we achieved the best performance on task 3 with a value of accuracy equal to 74.66% (SVM), whereas the worst performance was obtained on the task 1 with an accuracy of 58.24% (DT). The best performing algorithm was SVM, except for tasks 2 and 4 where RF achieved higher values. The DT classifier, on the contrary, achieved the worst performances for almost every task.

Looking at the table, we can observe a general trend: the first two tasks have worse performances than the others. An explanation to this phenomenon can comes from the analysis of the considered tasks. As mentioned in Sect. 3 the first two tasks are graphic and test the dynamics of simple movements and the motor control of the person who executes them, without requiring an important cognitive attention. The other tasks are words, numbers and the clock drawing test and they indeed require cognitive attention, as some of them have semantic meanings, include descending and ascending traits, requiring greater coordination, control skills and the use of the working memory. These considerations suggest that the use of the lognormal features is more effective on tasks with a semantic meaning instead of graphic tasks and it better brings out the difference between patients and healthy controls.

Table 3 shows the sensitivity values obtained during the experimental process. The sensitivity is a very important metric to consider when facing problems in the medical field, as it gives information about the number of patients correctly recognized. The best sensitivity score is obtained by RF on the fourth task (77.47%), while the worst by DT on the first task (59.29%). According to this table, RF and LR classifiers achieved good sensitivity values, but this doesn't mean they are the best classifiers, because looking at the accuracy the best is SVM. Despite SVM is the best classifier, this table shows that other classifiers are better able to recognize patients correctly.

From Table 4 we can see the specificity values obtained. The best specificity measure is achieved by SVM on the third task (82.03%), while the worst by RF on the second task (54.06%). This measure is linked to the sensitivity as it gives information about the healthy control participants correctly classified. As we said SVM was the best classifier according to the accuracy, but didn't achieve the higher sensitivity values, the specificity table, as a consequence, show high values of this metric for the SVM classifier. It means SVM is the best classifier according the accuracy, but, taking into account the considerations on sensitivity and specificity, it seems to better recognize healthy controls instead of patients, among our participants.

Table 5 shows that the best precision value is achieved from SVM on the third task (80.36%), while the worst by DT on the first task (59.89%). Though according to the sensitivity SVM wasn't the better classifier in recognising patients, this table shows that it is the most precise.

The FNR values obtained during the experimental process are shown in Table 6, where we can see that the best value is obtained with RF on the fourth task (22.52%), while the worst by DT on the first task (40.71%). FNR is a metric linked to Sensitivity, in fact they are complementary measures. FNR represents the number of patients that are erroneously classified and of course it should be at the lowest possible value. This is a fundamental information in the medical field, because an error in classifying a patient is a more serious problem than an error on a healthy person.

Table 7 shows the AUC values. AUC measures the area under the ROC curve, which illustrates the diagnostic ability of a binary classifier as its discrimination threshold is varied with the higher value the better. From the table we can observe that LR on the third task achieved the best result (0.83), whereas the worst was obtained by DT on the first task (0.58).

Table 2. Average Accuracy achieved on 30 runs for every ML algorithm on lognormal features

T	Accuracy						
	KNN	RF	DT	SVM	LR	GB	XGB
1	64.3 (2.7)	63.8 (2.2)	58.2 (3.1)	**66.9** (2.2)	63.9 (1.5)	61.5 (2.3)	61.3 (2.9)
2	62.7 (2.4)	**63.9** (2.6)	60.8 (3,2)	59.4 (2.0)	61.3 (2.1)	63.3 (3.7)	62.0 (3.0)
3	62.7 (2.0)	72.9 (2.2)	67.0 (2.7)	**74.6** (1.5)	74.2 (1.5)	69.7 (2.7)	71.2 (2.4)
4	64.6 (2.6)	**72.0** (2.0)	62.1 (3.5)	68.7 (1.8)	70.4 (1.4)	69.9 (3.5)	70.5 (2.7)
5	66.8 (2.3)	71.8 (1.8)	63.5 (2.8)	**73.6** (1.9)	72.6 (1.9)	69.7 (3.2)	69.6 (2.9)
6	67.0 (2.8)	67.1 (3.0)	61.1 (3.9)	**72.6** (2.8)	71.5 (2.3)	68.4 (2.9)	70.1 (3.0)

Table 3. Average Sensitivity achieved on 30 runs for every ML algorithm on lognormal features

T	Sensitivity						
	KNN	RF	DT	SVM	LR	GB	XGB
1	67.2 (2.6)	64.3 (3.0)	59.2 (4.2)	64.5 (2.7)	**67.3** (2.1)	62.6 (2.5)	62.5 (3.1)
2	66.6 (3.5)	**72.0** (3.9)	63.5 (4.2)	62.5 (3.5)	64.5 (3.2)	70.5 (4.3)	67.9 (3.6)
3	63.5 (2.0)	68.0 (3.7)	66.3 (4.1)	67.3 (1.8)	**70.1** (2.0)	66.3 (4.2)	68.6 (3.5)
4	67.7 (3.0)	**77.4** (2.1)	66.1 (5.4)	68.8 (3.0)	73.4 (2.7)	75.5 (3.5)	75.9 (3.1)
5	62.4 (3.1)	**70.1** (3.0)	62.3 (4.1)	68.6 (2.8)	68.5 (2.1)	67.6 (4.2)	68.2 (4.3)
6	70.5 (3.5)	69.6 (4.6)	62.0 (6.2)	75.1 (3.4)	**75.2** (3.6)	71.1 (4.8)	72.5 (5.3)

4.1 Comparison Findings

To test the effectiveness of the lognormal features extracted, we compared the results shown in the above tables with those achieved by some deep neural networks (DL) trained on synthetic images generated from the raw data described

Table 4. Average Specificity achieved on 30 runs for every ML algorithm on lognormal features

T	Specificity						
	KNN	RF	DT	SVM	LR	GB	XGB
1	61.1 (4.5)	63.2 (4.8)	57.1 (5.9)	**69.5** (3.5)	60.3 (2.7)	60.4 (4.3)	59.9 (5.0)
2	**58.0** (3.1)	54.0 (3.0)	57.4 (4.2)	55.6 (3.4)	57.3 (2.4)	54.3 (4.7)	54.8 (4.8)
3	61.9 (3.6)	77.8 (2.0)	67.6 (5.5)	**82.0** (2.6)	78.4 (2.0)	73.0 (3.2)	73.8 (3.3)
4	60.7 (4.0)	65.0 (3.9)	56.9 (6.4)	**68.5** (2.5)	66.5 (2.4)	62.8 (5.1)	63.8 (5.0)
5	71.3 (2.6)	73.4 (2.7)	64.8 (4.7)	**78.7** (2.9)	76.9 (3.1)	71.8 (3.5)	71.0 (3.9)
6	63.1 (3.6)	64.0 (4.0)	60.1 (5.0)	**69.8** (4.7)	67.1 (3.7)	65.4 (4.7)	67.3 (3.7)

Table 5. Average Precision achieved on 30 runs for every ML algorithm on lognormal features

T	Precision						
	KNN	RF	DT	SVM	LR	GB	XGB
1	65.3 (3.0)	65.7 (2.8)	59.8 (3.4)	**69.7** (2.7)	64.9 (1.7)	63.2 (2.7)	62.9 (3.1)
2	**66.3** (2.6)	66.2 (2.4)	65.0 (3.3)	63.8 (2.0)	65.2 (2.0)	65.9 (3.3)	65.4 (3.0)
3	63.2 (2.3)	76.4 (1.9)	68.5 (3.3)	**80.3** (2.5)	77.6 (2.0)	72.1 (2.8)	73.6 (3.0)
4	69.2 (2.6)	74.4 (2.5)	66.7 (3.7)	**74.5** (2.0)	74.3 (1.7)	72.8 (3.5)	73.2 (2.8)
5	69.6 (2.7)	73.8 (2.3)	64.8 (3.8)	**77.3** (2.8)	76.0 (2.9)	71.6 (3.6)	71.1 (3.0)
6	69.0 (3.1)	69.6 (3.1)	64.3 (3.9)	**74.6** (3.1)	72.8 (2.6)	71.1 (2.9)	72.3 (2.7)

Table 6. Average FNR achieved on 30 runs for every ML algorithm on lognormal features

T	FNR						
	KNN	RF	DT	SVM	LR	GB	XGB
1	32.7 (2.7)	35.6 (3.0)	40.7 (4.2)	35.4 (2.7)	**32.6** (2.1)	37.3 (2.5)	37.4 (3.1)
2	33.3 (3.5)	**27.9** (3.9)	36.4 (4.2)	37.4 (3.5)	35.4 (3.2)	29.4 (4.3)	32.0 (3.6)
3	36.4 (2.0)	31.9 (3.7)	33.6 (4.1)	32.6 (1.8)	**29.8** (2.0)	33.6 (4.2)	31.3 (3.5)
4	32.2 (3.0)	**22.5** (2.1)	33.8 (5.4)	31.1 (3.0)	26.5 (2.7)	24.4 (3.7)	24.0 (3.1)
5	37.5 (3.1)	**29.8** (3.0)	37.6 (4.1)	31.3 (2.1)	31.4 (2.1)	32.3 (4.2)	31.7 (4.3)
6	29.4 (3.5)	30.3 (4.6)	37.9 (6.2)	24.8 (3.4)	**24.7** (3.6)	28.8 (4.8)	27.4 (5.3)

Table 7. Average AUC achieved on 30 runs for every ML algorithm on lognormal features

T	AUC						
	KNN	RF	DT	SVM	LR	GB	XGB
1	0.66 (0.02)	0.70 (0.01)	0.58 (0.03)	**0.72** (0.02)	0.71 (0.01)	0.66 (0.02)	0.67 (0.02)
2	0.65 (0.02)	**0.68** (0.02)	0.60 (0.03)	0.63 (0.04)	0.65 (0.02)	0.67 (0.03)	0.66 (0.03)
3	0.69 (0.01)	0.82 (0.01)	0.66 (0.02)	0.82 (0.01)	**0.83** (0.01)	0.79 (0.02)	0.78 (0.02)
4	0.68 (0.02)	0.78 (0.01)	0.61 (0.03)	0.78 (0.01)	**0.79** (0.01)	0.76 (0.02)	0.77 (0.02)
5	0.69 (0.01)	**0.78** (0.01)	0.63 (0.02)	0.77 (0.01)	0.76 (0.01)	0.75 (0.02)	0.75 (0.02)
6	0.68 (0.02)	0.72 (0.03)	0.74 (0.02)	**0.76** (0.02)	0.75 (0.02)	0.73 (0.03)	0.74 (0.02)

in Sect. 3.1. The image generation process and the comparison between the our approach and DL are detailed in the following.

RGB Images. Starting from the raw data acquired as described in Sect. 3.1 and stored in terms of x-y coordinates and pressure at a frequency of 200 Hz, we generated synthetic images to feed Convolutional Neural Networks (CNN). The traits of these images are obtained by considering the points (x_i, y_i) as vertices of the polygonal that approximates the original curve. We encoded kinematic information in the RGB channels and as the tools used for the acquisition step allow us to record in air movements too, these images contains both in air and on paper information. In particular, they were obtained by considering the triplet of values (z_i, v_i, j_i) assumed as RGB color components for the $i-th$ trait, delimited by the couple of points (x_i, y_i) and (x_{i+1}, y_{i+1}). The triplet is obtained as follows:

- z_i is the pressure value at point (x_i, y_i) and it is assumed constant along the i-th trait;
- v_i is the velocity of the i-th trait, computed as the ratio between the length of the i-th trait and interval time of 5 ms corresponding to the period of acquisition of the tablet;
- j_i is the jerk of the i-th trait, defined as the second derivative of velocity.

The values of the triplet (z_i, v_i, j_i) have been normalized into the range [0, 255] in order to match the standard 0–255 color scale, by considering the minimum and the maximum value on the entire training set for these three quantities. For further details about the generation of these images, we suggest checking out our recent publication [3]. We selected three CNN models that accept input images that are automatically resized to 256×256 for VGG19 [22], to 224×224 for ResNet50 [7], to 299×299 for InceptionV3 [23] respectively. Taking into account these constraints for both type of images, the original x, y coordinates have been resized into the range [0, 299] for each image, in order to provide ex-ante images of suitable size and minimize the loss of information related to possible zoom in/out.

ML/DL Comparison. As mentioned above, lognormal features can be given in input to standard ML algorithms, whereas RGB images contain dynamic information encoded into the three color channels and can be used to feed a different CNN. Table 8 shows the accuracy performances achieved by the two approaches. From the table we can observe that in most cases ML outperformed DL, especially with the SVM classifier. DL only won on the second task with the VGG19 net. For the sake of comparison, for each task we plotted the ROC curves of the classification algorithms/nets that outperformed the others in at least one task, namely LR and SVM among the ML classifiers, and VGG19 among the CNNs (see Table 8). Looking at these two different sources of evaluation, we can observe that the deep approach (RGB images) outperformed the lognormal-based one on the graphic tasks (Tasks #1 and #2). On the contrary, the lognormal features confirmed their effectiveness in dealing with handwriting and cognitive tasks (see Fig. 2).

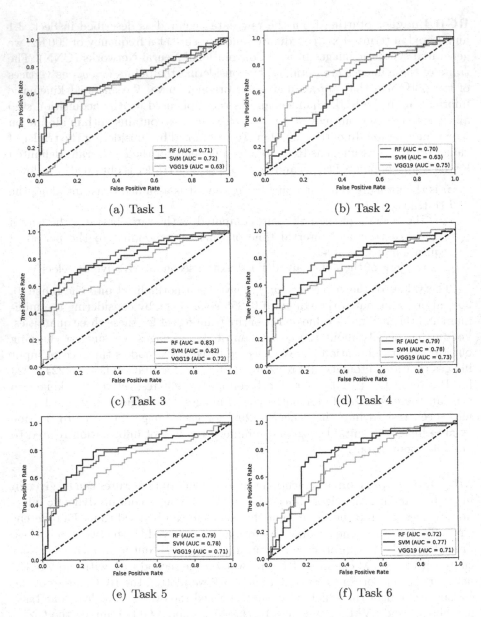

Fig. 2. Comparison of ROC curves obtained from RF, SVM and VGG19 for every task.

Table 8. Comparison results.

T	ML							Deep		
	KNN	RF	DT	SVM	LR	GB	XGB	VGG19	ResNet50	Inc.V3
1	64.34	63.83	58.24	**66.92**	63.98	61.56	61.33	61.62	62.64	62.20
2	62.77	63.97	60.83	59.47	61.31	63.30	62.05	**72.19**	65.90	71.25
3	62.79	72.97	67.01	**74.66**	74.25	69.73	71.27	66.83	62.09	70.81
4	64.67	**72.03**	62.11	68.72	70.43	69.97	70.59	66.82	58.62	63.97
5	66.87	71.80	63.58	**73.69**	72.68	69.70	69.63	66.01	62.43	70.37
6	67.09	67.10	61.14	**72.66**	71.50	68.45	70.10	66.48	64.07	65.39

5   Conclusions and Future Work

Neurodegenerative disease is a cognitive impairment that can be manifested through the graphonomics lack of skills. Alzheimer's and Parkinson's are the two most common diseases observed in handwriting. This paper analyzes the writing of patients and healthy people with kinematic features extracted from the kinematic theory of rapid movement. To study the skill levels of participants, we used a dataset with healthy people and patients at the early stage of AD. Their handwriting included signatures, letters, and drawings following a well-established protocol for Alzheimer's [4]. Our preliminary results confirm that lognormal features model handwriting better than graphic tasks. In particular, we achieved the best results (ACC > 70%) with the following tasks:

- 'le' (repeated four times);
- Word 'bottiglia' backward;
- Dictated telephone number;
- Clock drawing test.

It is worth noting that we did not apply any parameter optimization in this work. We expect that a grid search procedure will allow us a significant improvement in our future outcomes. Furthermore, these results align with those achieved using standard kinematic features (velocity, acceleration, etc.). We also plan to analyze which tasks lognormal/deep features perform better. This would allow us deepening for each task which features (approach) achieve the best classification performance. Finally, similar to related works, there is room to improve our final prediction by combining the responses from the single classifiers (one per task).

References

1. Albu, A., Precup, R., Teban, T.A.: Results and challenges of artificial neural networks used for decision making and control in medical applications. Facta Univ. Ser. Mech. Eng. **17**(3), 285–308 (2019)

2. Carmona-Duarte, C., Ferrer, M., Plamondon, R., Gómez-Rodellar, A., Gómez-Vilda, P.: Sigma-lognormal modeling of speech. Cogn. Comput. **13**(2), 488–503 (2021). https://doi.org/10.1007/s12559-020-09803-8
3. Cilia, N., D'Alessandro, T., De Stefano, C., Fontanella, F., Molinara, M.: From online handwriting to synthetic images for Alzheimer's disease detection using a deep transfer learning approach. IEEE J. Biomed. Health Inform. **25**(12), 4243–4254 (2021). https://doi.org/10.1109/JBHI.2021.3101982
4. Cilia, N.D., De Stefano, C., Fontanella, F., Di Freca, A.S.: An experimental protocol to support cognitive impairment diagnosis by using handwriting analysis. Proc. Comput. Sci. **141**, 466–471 (2018)
5. Djioua, M., Plamondon, R.: A new algorithm and system for the characterization of handwriting strokes with delta-lognormal parameters. IEEE Trans. Pattern Anal. Mach. Intell. **31**(11), 2060–2072 (2009)
6. Ferrer, M.A., Diaz, M., Carmona-Duarte, C., Plamondon, R.: IDeLog: iterative dual spatial and kinematic extraction of sigma-lognormal parameters. IEEE Trans. Pattern Anal. Mach. Intell. **42**(1), 114–125 (2020)
7. He, K., Zhang, X., Ren, S., Sun, J.: Deep residual learning for image recognition. In: 2016 IEEE Conference on Computer Vision and Pattern Recognition (CVPR), pp. 770–778 (2016)
8. Impedovo, D.: Velocity-based signal features for the assessment of parkinsonian handwriting. IEEE Signal Process. Lett. **26**(4), 632–636 (2019)
9. Impedovo, D., Pirlo, G., Balducci, F., Dentamaro, V., Sarcinella, L., Vessio, G.: Investigating the sigma-lognormal model for disease classification by handwriting. In: The Lognormality Principle and its Applications in E-Security, E-Learning and E-Health, pp. 195–209. World Scientific (2021)
10. Impedovo, D., Pirlo, G., Vessio, G.: Dynamic handwriting analysis for supporting earlier Parkinson's disease diagnosis. Information **9**(10), 247 (2018)
11. Lebel, K., Nguyen, H., Duval, C., Plamondon, R., Boissy, P.: Capturing the craniocaudal signature of a turn with inertial measurement systems: methods, parameters robustness and reliability. Front. Bioeng. Biotechnol. **5**, 51 (2017). https://doi.org/10.3389/fbioe.2017.00051
12. Myszczynska, M.A., et al.: Applications of machine learning to diagnosis and treatment of neurodegenerative diseases. Nat. Rev. Neurol. **16**, 440–456 (2020)
13. O'Reilly, C., Plamondon, R.: Design of a neuromuscular disorders diagnostic system using human movement analysis. In: 2012 11th International Conference on Information Science, Signal Processing and their Applications, ISSPA 2012, pp. 787–792 (2012). https://doi.org/10.1109/ISSPA.2012.6310660. Cited by: 28
14. O'Reilly, C., Plamondon, R.: Development of a sigma-lognormal representation for on-line signatures. Pattern Recogn. **42**(12), 3324–3337 (2009). https://doi.org/10.1016/j.patcog.2008.10.017. new Frontiers in Handwriting Recognition
15. Plamondon, R.: A kinematic theory of rapid human movements - part II. Movement time and control. Biol. Cybern. **72**(4), 309–320 (1995). https://doi.org/10.1007/BF00202786
16. Plamondon, R.: A kinematic theory of rapid human movements: part I. Movement representation and generation. Biol. Cybern. **72**(4), 295–307 (1995)
17. Plamondon, R.: A kinematic theory of rapid human movements: part III. Kinetic outcomes. Biol. Cybern. **78**(2), 133–145 (1998). https://doi.org/10.1007/s004220050420
18. Plamondon, R., O'Reilly, C., Rémi, C., Duval, T.: The lognormal handwriter: learning, performing, and declining. Front. Psychol. **4** (2013). https://doi.org/10.3389/fpsyg.2013.00945, https://www.frontiersin.org/article/10.3389/fpsyg.2013.00945

19. Plamondon, R., Pirlo, G., Anquetil, É., Rémi, C., Teulings, H.L., Nakagawa, M.: Personal digital bodyguards for e-security, e-learning and e-health: a prospective survey. Pattern Recogn. **81**, 633–659 (2018). https://doi.org/10.1016/j.patcog.2018.04.012
20. Precup, R.E., Teban, T.A., Albu, A., Borlea, A.B., Zamfirache, I.A., Petriu, E.M.: Evolving fuzzy models for prosthetic hand myoelectric-based control. IEEE Trans. Instrum. Meas. **69**(7), 4625–4636 (2020)
21. Schröter, A., Mergl, R., Bürger, K., Hampel, H., Möller, H.J., Hegerl, U.: Kinematic analysis of handwriting movements in patients with Alzheimer's disease, mild cognitive impairment, depression and healthy subjects. Dement. Geriatr. Cogn. Disord. **15**(3), 132–42 (2003)
22. Simonyan, K., Zisserman, A.: Very deep convolutional networks for large-scale image recognition. CoRR arXiv:1409.1556 (2015)
23. Szegedy, C., Vanhoucke, V., Ioffe, S., Shlens, J., Wojna, Z.: Rethinking the inception architecture for computer vision. In: 2016 IEEE Conference on Computer Vision and Pattern Recognition (CVPR), pp. 2818–2826 (2016)
24. Tanveer, M., et al.: Machine learning techniques for the diagnosis of Alzheimer's disease: a review. ACM Trans. Multimed. Comput. Commun. Appl. **16**(1s), 1–35 (2020)
25. Tseng, M.H., Cermak, S.A.: The influence of ergonomic factors and perceptual-motor abilities on handwriting performance. Am. J. Occup. Ther. **47**(10), 919–926 (1993)
26. Vyhnálek, M., et al.: Clock drawing test in screening for Alzheimer's dementia and mild cognitive impairment in clinical practice. Int. J. Geriatr. Psychiatry **32**(9), 933–939 (2017)
27. Yan, J.H., Rountree, S., Massman, P., Smith Doody, R., Li, H.: Alzheimer's disease and mild cognitive impairment deteriorate fine movement control. J. Psychiatr. Res. **42**(14), 1203–1212 (2008)

Easing Automatic Neurorehabilitation via Classification and Smoothness Analysis

Asma Bensalah[1]([✉])(iD), Alicia Fornés[1](iD), Cristina Carmona-Duarte[2](iD), and Josep Lladós[1](iD)

[1] Computer Vision Center, Computer Science Department,
Universitat Autònoma de Barcelona, Barcelona, Spain
{abensalah,afornes,josep}@cvc.uab.es
[2] Universidad de Las Palmas de Gran Canaria, Las Palmas, Spain
cristina.carmona@ulpgc.es

Abstract. Assessing the quality of movements for post-stroke patients during the rehabilitation phase is vital given that there is no standard stroke rehabilitation plan for all the patients. In fact, it depends basically on the patient's functional independence and its progress along the rehabilitation sessions. To tackle this challenge and make neurorehabilitation more agile, we propose an automatic assessment pipeline that starts by recognising patients' movements by means of a shallow deep learning architecture, then measuring the movement quality using jerk measure and related measures. A particularity of this work is that the dataset used is clinically relevant, since it represents movements inspired from Fugl-Meyer a well common upper-limb clinical stroke assessment scale for stroke patients. We show that it is possible to detect the contrast between healthy and patients movements in terms of smoothness, besides achieving conclusions about the patients' progress during the rehabilitation sessions that correspond to the clinicians' findings about each case.

Keywords: Neurorehabilitation · Upper-limb · Movement classification · Movement smoothness · Deep learning · Jerk

1 Introduction

Neurological disorders result in cognitive and motor impairments. The stroke survivors in particular may face deficits in motor functions in one side of the body. These function deficits are addressed through rehabilitation sessions to partially or fully recover the functional independence of the patient [1]. One of the central challenges, during this phase, is the assessment of the patient's evolution. Essentially, notable progress in post-stroke patient cases happens during the first weeks namely the critical windows of heightened neuroplasticity [2]. After that, the non-linear recovery function reaches asymptotic levels. For all above reasons, both timing and treatment intensity in that critical period of time should be optimised. Thus it is indispensable to monitor patient's progress continuously

© Springer Nature Switzerland AG 2022
C. Carmona-Duarte et al. (Eds.): IGS 2021, LNCS 13424, pp. 336–348, 2022.
https://doi.org/10.1007/978-3-031-19745-1_25

and accurately, in order to maximise the patient's recovery by the end of the critical window. For long years, the way to proceed has been to use specific clinical scales [3]. In practice, the patients' motor functions are evaluated once or twice in ten days. Ergo, the drawback of such an approach is that the patient's evolution is not assessed whenever patient is out of the rehabilitation room. In fact, its the patient's daily activities performance that best reflect his functional independence.

One way to cope with this limitation is to automatize the assessment in order to help clinicians to asses efficiently the patient. Many issues arise when automatizing: firstly, determining the movement nature throughout a continuous recording for hours; secondly, finding out which measures describe best the movement quality.

To address the previous mentioned issues, we propose a framework to automatically assess patients' movements. The framework has two parts:

- The first part consists of movements' classification via a shallow deep learning architecture into four key movements classes;
- The second part is an assessment module based on the jerk measure to ascertain the contrast between patients and healthy individuals' signals, as well as estimating the patients' evolution along the different sessions. Contrary to other existing kinematic algorithms that need more memory space and computational resources due to the number of kinematic parameters [4], jerk is easier to implement in an embedded device.

Along the rest of this paper, we give an overview of related works in Sect. 2, then we describe our classification deep learning architecture in Sect. 3. In Sect. 4, we give an overview of movement smoothness measurements. Next, we describe our setup in Sect. 5. Then, we present our results and findings in Sect. 6.

2 Related Work

Spotting a sequence in a signal aims to retrieve the signal or parts of it that are relevant for a given query. Depending on the nature of the query, many sequence spotting tasks arise [5–7]. If the signal is a series of one or many different modalities and the query is an action, activity, motion or gesture, then we're addressing a Human Activity Recognition (HAR) task.

HAR has benefited greatly from the deep learning boom. HAR has been performed using different modalities: RGB images [8], skeleton [9], acceleration [10], wifi [11]...

Acceleration is a broadly exploited modality for action recognition due to the fact that it is an non-invasive sensing method thus there are no privacy constraint issues. HAR through acceleration is possible because often humans perform a movement in the same qualitative way [12]. HAR is either performed using traditional learning algorithms, for instance, support vector machines [13], k-nearest neighbors [14] or employing deep learning models such as Convolutional Neural Networks (CNN) [15], Recurrent Neural Networks (RNNs) [16] or Long short-term memory (LSTM) [17]. According to [18], 22% of the HAR works were dedicated to health applications.

On the other hand, to assess recognized movements particularly for stroke patients there is no general agreement on how to obtain a movement smoothness indicator or what measure describes it best [19]. One reason for that is the vague understanding of the neurophysiology behind movements' quality, as it is the case for upper limb movements [20]. According to [21], works about smoothness measures for stroke patients fall mainly in five different categories: trajectory related metrics [22], velocity related metrics [23,24], acceleration related metrics [25,26], jerk related metrics [27] and other metrics [28]. As explained above, HAR tasks have been tackled in many ways, as well as the assessment movement quality question. In our work, and given the few available data, we opt for a shallow deep learning architecture for HAR; moreover, we explore the use of jerk measure for assessing patients quality movements.

3   Movement Classification

We got inspired from Supratak's model [29] that was designed to tackle the Polysomnography challenges, which is one of the ways to assess sleep quality [30]. Traditionally, Polysomnography is performed by a group of experts that annotate recorded data, using a sleep stage scoring.

To alleviate the previous limitations the architecture implements a data augmentation module and less signal processing steps in the pipeline.

3.1   Architecture

The model is fed with epochs of our raw acceleration signal (see Fig. 1). We classify the movements into one of the four key movement classes: M1, M2, M3, M4. The first component of the model is composed of four CNN layers with the aim of extracting time-invariant features from the raw signal. A max-pool and a dropout layers are introduced after the first CNN layer and the last one,

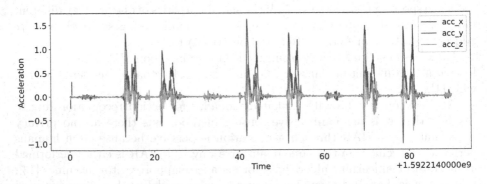

Fig. 1. Raw acceleration signal of a healthy individual.

as exemplified in Fig. 2. The second component is designed to learn temporal dependencies of the raw signal (sequence learning). This is done via one LSTM layer followed by a dropout layout, and together they form a unidirectional RNN. The unidirectional RNN is supposed to learn time transition rules. The unidirectionality of the LSTM results in eliminating the forward pass, hence, reducing the number of hyperparameters and the computational resources.

Fig. 2. Model architecture.

Since our dataset is balanced, the weighted cross-entropy loss is set to 1 for all classes. Furthermore, to address the scarce data issue, a data augmentation is performed on the original data, every training epoch. Data augmentation is carried out by shifting the signal through the time axis, the shifting span is from a certain range of the epoch duration. The model is pretrained with the Sleep-EDF dataset [31].

4 Movement Smoothness

Following the description of the classification architecture, we present the movements' smoothness measurements next. Quantifying a movement quality can be performed in many ways. Measuring the position relative to time, is one of them. Velocity $\vec{v}$ (Eq. 1), acceleration $\vec{a}$ (Eq. 2), jerk $\vec{j}$ (Eq. 3) and snap $\vec{s}$ (Eq. 4) are respectively the first, second, third and fourth derivative of the trajectory $\vec{x}$ with respect to time, are the most widespread used measuring quantities [32]. Those are the same measures used by the human body to manage its balance. More specifically, this is handled by the sensorial functions of the vestibular system that provides information such as body position together with gravity direction [33]. If an object is in motion, it experiences velocity. When velocity is not constant, the object is said to have an acceleration which is not equal to zero. If acceleration is varying over time, then emerges a sensation of jerkiness of the movement. Since attention was brought back to jerk in [34], it has had many applications in the science and technology fields [35–37]. Jerk should always take into account when vibrations occur, also whenever an abrupt transition happens [35]. For example, jerk is considered when designing railways to ensure a smooth motion whenever train changes from a straight line to a curved one, equally when ensuring that an industrial tool fails too soon because of fast acceleration changes.

When analysing a human movement by looking at its acceleration, it is axis orientation dependent. A small rotation of the wrist while recording data can result in a lot of noise in an axis acceleration. Hence, in this work, we focus on jerk as a movement quality measure, in particular, as a smoothness indicator. Ultimately, jerk is easier to implement in a an embedded device, unlike other existing kinematic algorithms that need more space due to the number of kinematic parameters.

$$\vec{v}(t) = \frac{d\vec{x}(t)}{dt} \tag{1}$$

$$\vec{a}(t) = \frac{d\vec{v}(t)}{dt} \tag{2}$$

$$\vec{j}(t) = \frac{d\vec{a}(t)}{dt} \tag{3}$$

$$\vec{s}(t) = \frac{d\vec{j}(t)}{dt} \tag{4}$$

5   Setup

5.1   Dataset

The dataset used was recorded as a part of *3D kinematics for remote patient monitoring* (RPM3D) project[1], aiming to build an automatic pipeline for stroke patients. A dataset for stroke patients and healthy subjects along with a classification baseline was published [38]. Patients and healthy individuals were given a smartwatch in each hand. Healthy individuals were recorded once while patients were recorded during four different sessions. The time interval between patients' sessions is between one or two weeks. Initially, to assess a stroke patient upper limb motor functions, an assessment is performed once in a week or ten days. The best-known scale to asses sensorimotor impairments within stroke patients is the Fugl-Meyer Assessment [39]. For this reason, authors were inspired from the Fugl-Meyer movements to design their set of key movements $\mathcal{M}_i, i \in [1, 4]$, thusly:

- Movement $\mathcal{M}_1$: shoulder extension/flexion.
- Movement $\mathcal{M}_2$: shoulder abduction.
- Movement $\mathcal{M}_3$: external/internal shoulder rotation.
- Movement $\mathcal{M}_4$: elbow flexion/extension.

Scenarios. The experiments were held into two different setups: a constrained scenario L1 and unconstrained one L2. These are described as follows:

- Scenario L1: it represents a constrained scenario, where individuals perform four key movements $\mathcal{M}_i$: once with the dominant hand, second using the non-dominant one and lastly with both hands.
- Scenario L2: it represents the unconstrained scenario, composed of a sequence of key movements $\mathcal{M}_i$ along with a set of other non-target movements $\mathcal{R}_j$, $j \in [1, 19]$. $\mathcal{R}_i$ movements are a list of usual daily activities such as: drinking, setting on a chair, ... The movements are carried out in a random order.

---

[1] http://dag.cvc.uab.es/patientmonitoring/.

5.2   Pipeline

We start by classifying movements into the four main classes: M1, M2, M3, M4 (shoulder extension/flexion, shoulder abduction, external/internal shoulder rotation, elbow flexion/extension).Then we compute the jerk value for a signal that represents performing one movement, for several times, such as shown in Fig. 3 to inspect the global acceleration patterns of a movement.

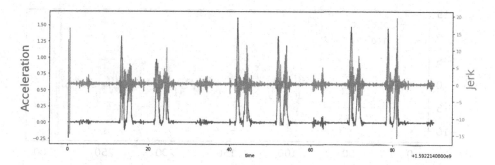

Fig. 3. Acceleration and jerk for a repetition of movements - Healthy individual.

After that, we compute the jerk for a smaller fragment of the previous signal (one well segmented movement), for a more accurate smoothness estimation.

6   Results

Results below are related to the classification of L1 movements and their smoothness analysis.

6.1   Classification

For the experiments, the data is divided into 80% for training, and 20% for testing. The testing accuracy reaches an average of 77,01%. We experience a decrease of accuracy in some epochs, which we believe is due to the small size of the training data set.

6.2   Smoothness

In Table 1 we give information about the jerk values for well segmented movements of healthy and patient individuals, along axis x. Theoretically, the jerk
value should be lower in the case of healthy individuals compared to patients,
because their ability to move and perform the movements in a smoother way is
superior, thus their movements are less jerky (see Fig. 4) [21].

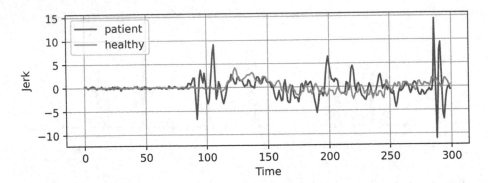

Fig. 4. Jerk values for a patient and healthy individual performing the same movement.

As observed in Table 1, this is the case for M2, M3, M4. For instance, regarding movement M3, the absolute value of the jerk mean for patients is 0.7 times
the absolute value of the jerk mean for healthy subjects. Simultaneously, the
trend in Table 1 is that the maximum of jerk within the healthy population is
greater than the patients' one, for all four movements M1, M2, M3, and M4.

Table 1. Jerk measures for patients and healthy individuals, along axis x.

| Axis x | Jerk measure | | | | | |
| | Mean | | Max | | Min | |
	Healthy	Patient	Healthy	Patient	Healthy	Patient
M1	0,00500712	−0,006998	497,99	145,54	−1,96E+02	−138,99182
M2	−0,0004051	−0,001621	157,56	69,46	−186,062127	−152,652
M3	−0,0023341	0,0016529	102,74	84,58	−1,27E+02	−62,973556
M4	0,00031141	0,0006176	161,04	107,14	−1,50E+02	−114,20477

The jerk represents the change in acceleration. In that sense, to gain more
understanding of the movements' smoothness, we went for jerk related measures,
which are calculated based on the absolute value of the jerk. In this work, we
focus on the squared jerk measure. Table 2 shows the mean, maximum and minimum values of the squared jerk measure. Notice that the trend in Table 1 is

that the mean jerk within healthy individuals is lower, which corresponds to the theory premises' that the jerkier and less smooth the movement is, the higher is the jerk value. Hence, patients should have higher jerk values. Nonetheless, this is not the case for the squared mean jerk. The general pattern in Table 2 is that the healthy population's squared jerk mean is higher than patients. We think that this could be related to the fact that a patient signal is noisier than healthy individual one because patients are slower, thus a patient's signal has more peaks and more cumulative noise (see Fig. 5).

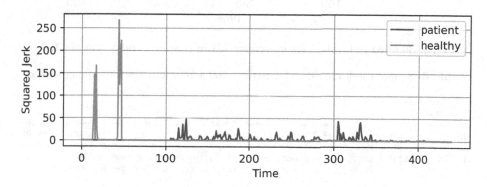

Fig. 5. Healthy vs patient signal.

Table 2. Squared jerk measures for patients and healthy individuals, along axis x.

| | Squared jerk measure | | | | | |
| | Mean | | Max | | Min | |
Axis x	Healthy	Patient	Healthy	Patient	Healthy	Patient
M1	19,96	7,65	247993,61	21182,96	8,93E−12	2,22E−12
M2	18,11	5,76	34619,12	23302,63	0	8,42E−10
M3	14,40	3,75	16056,08	7153,85	3,55E−11	0
M4	26,19	4,48	25934,96	13042,73	8,93E−12	0

Tables 3, 4, 5, and 6 provide information about the squared jerk measure for four patients, namely: 100, 101, 102, 103. It indicates the evolution of four patients through four sessions, along axis x. Table 3 gives information about the squared jerk measures: mean, maximum and minimum for patient 100. Patient's performance for movement M1 is better in sessions 3 and 4. Figure 6 shows a less jerky M1 in session 3 compared to the first session. At the same time patient 100 reaches the most significant improvement for M3 and M4 in the third session. Yet, movement M2 squared jerk mean values present no improvement during the four sessions.

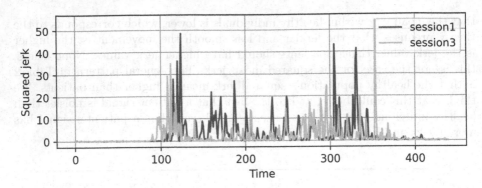

Fig. 6. Squared jerk values for movement M1 in session 1 and 3- Patient 100.

Table 3. Squared jerk measures for patient 100 across four sessions, along axis x.

	Patient 100											
	Mean				Max				Min			
Axis x	Session 1	Session2	Session3	Session4	Session 1	Session2	Session3	Session4	Session 1	Session2	Session3	Session4
M1	12,88	13,04	5,09	10,16	18882,36	12129,74	4166,80	21182,96	8,38E−09	1,67E−08	1,75E−07	2,30E−09
M2	4,17	9,07	12,74	19,92	715,66	1246,53	23302,63	7364,52	9,35E−08	4,49E−08	8,42E−10	1,88E−08
M3	9,16	6,25	4,65	8,28	3738,07	2385,56	976,07	7153,85	8,53E−10	2,05E−10	5,18E−09	3,94E−08
M4	6,28	30,45	4,80	7,14	1804,63	13042,73	1246,78	670,45	1,98E−08	1,28E−08	1,20E−08	0

As for Patient 101 (see Table 4), the mean squared jerk values have increased during the four rehabilitation sessions, as illustrated in Fig. 7. The Figure shows a less smooth M4 movement in the last session, except for movement M1, which experiences a decrease in the mean squared jerk value compared to the first session.

Table 5 depicts patient's 102 data, in which movements M1, M2, M3 witness a gradual decrease of squared jerk mean until the last rehabilitation session. Contrary, the M1 mean squared jerk stops lessening after the second session.

It is clear that the three patients 100, 102, 103 have reached lower squared jerk means than those of their first sessions, for at least three movements.

Table 4. Squared jerk measures for patient 101 across four sessions, along axis x.

	Patient 101											
	Mean				Max				Min			
Axis x	Session 1	Session2	Session3	Session4	Session 1	Session2	Session3	Session4	Session 1	Session2	Session3	Session4
M1	7,61	2,62	4,63	5,23	1357,01	445,53	581,59	968,97	1,64E−07	2,22E−12	4,59E−08	3,55E−11
M2	2,03	2,16	7,52	5,20	267,21	484,64	3781,94	1086,66	1,04E−07	1,05E−08	2,22E−08	2,82E−09
M3	2,14	4,05	3,21	8,03	406,89	2257,01	604,45	3965,67	6,13E−08	8,39E−09	4,69E−09	3,60E−08
M4	0,58	0,73	2,88	2,49	44,56	163,14	1068,82	1034,61	2,24E−09	1,52E−08	8,85E−10	5,00E−10

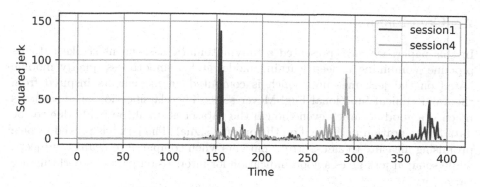

Fig. 7. Squared jerk values for movement M4 in session 1 and 4- Patient 101.

How Good is Jerk as a Smooth Indicator? Overall, it is not trivial to compare the jerk values of healthy individuals to the ones of the patients owing to the way the patients performed the movements. In particular, when patients have difficulties to perform the movements in a consistent way, it implies that a simple comparison of healthy movements' jerk values and patients ones is not always conclusive. For example, in the case of movement M1, the jerk mean value is higher within healthy samples than the patient samples. Despite that, the mean squared jerk values provide interesting insights concerning the evolution of patients across the four sessions. Our conclusions do align with the clinicians' closures: most patients' smoothness improved when compared to the first session. Additionally, for patient 101, the patient that presented more motor function issues during the sessions, we observed the least improvement in terms of squared jerk mean values.

Table 5. Squared jerk measures for patient 102 across four sessions, along axis x.

| Patient 102 | | | | | | | | | | | |
| Axis x | Mean | | | | Max | | | | Min | | | |
	Session 1	Session2	Session3	Session4	Session 1	Session2	Session3	Session4	Session 1	Session2	Session3	Session4
M1	4,27	1,18	4,82	7,09	5256,19	49,80	3829,05	7841,56	1,61E−08	2,90E−09	1,50E−08	8,84E−12
M2	2,89	4,61	2,21	1,78	473,36	2788,06	353,56	739,78	5,98E−09	4,09E−08	8,61E−10	3,77E−08
M3	1,03	1,56	1,03	0,58	88,71	405,24	117,23	81,77	1,26E−09	0	3,21E−08	6,56E−09
M4	1,90	1,25	1,67	0,84	306,19	165,53	184,44	125,36	1,22E−08	1,77E−09	3,01E−08	2,59E−09

Table 6. Squared jerk measures for patient 103 across four sessions, along axis x.

| Patient 103 | | | | | | | | | | | |
| Axis x | Mean | | | | Max | | | | Min | | | |
	Session 1	Session2	Session3	Session4	Session 1	Session2	Session3	Session4	Session 1	Session2	Session3	Session4
M1	8,57	16,17	9,97	9,47	2570,08	19318,73	2733,30	1991,19	2,35E−08	2,79E−08	5,36E−11	7,71E−08
M2	2,80	4,34	1,88	3,79	500,42	2143,84	222,50	1488,18	2,18E−07	1,73E−09	1,29E−09	4,98E−08
M3	1,66	2,14	1,86	1,34	1039,28	707,50	297,98	331,72	8,53E−09	2,33E−10	2,86E−08	3,82E−08
M4	3,18	4,12	2,11	2,52	4304,22	2560,54	1628,78	713,06	4,45E−10	8,66E−09	3,60E−08	4,36E−01

7   Conclusion

In this paper, we have presented a fully automatic assessment stroke patients pipeline, combining a deep learning model and a smoothness quality module based on the jerk measure, which is computed on movements inspired from the valid clinical functional Fugl-Meyer scale. The classification of movements reached a good accuracy even though the dataset is small, probably due to the data augmentation performed on the original signal. The jerk has proved to be a promising measure to assess stroke patients when compared to healthy subjects, while squared jerk gives a good indication for intersession patient's performance variability.

Alike all vision and machine learning tasks that are not image or NLP related, the data available for our task is few. Hence, in the future work will be directed toward enhancing available data and exploiting more robust smoothness measures.

Acknowledgment. This work has been partially supported by the Spanish project RTI2018-095645-B-C21, the CERCA Program/Generalitat de Catalunya and the FI fellowship AGAUR 2020 FI-SDUR 00497 (with the support of the Secretaria d'Universitats i Recerca of the Generalitat de Catalunya and the Fons Social Europeu).

References

1. Dobkin, B.H.: 60 - rehabilitation and recovery of the patient with stroke. In: Grotta, J.C., et al. (eds.) Stroke, 7th edn, pp. 879–887.e2. Elsevier, Philadelphia (2022)
2. Ballester, B., et al.: A critical time window for recovery extends beyond one-year post-stroke. J. Neurophysiol. **122**, 350–357 (2019)
3. Bosch, J., et al.: Functional abilities of an international post-stroke population: standard assessment of global everyday activities (SAGEA) scale. J. Stroke Cerebrovasc. Dis. **31**(4), 106329 (2022)
4. Stenum, J., Rossi, C., Roemmich, R.T.: Two-dimensional video-based analysis of human gait using pose estimation. PLoS Comput. Biol. **17**(4), 1–26 (2021)
5. van der Westhuizen, E., Kamper, H., Menon, R., Quinn, J., Niesler, T.: Feature learning for efficient ASR-free keyword spotting in low-resource languages. Comput. Speech Lang. **71**, 101275 (2022). Query date: 2022-03-07 13:17:34
6. Giotis, A.: Keyword spotting in handwritten document images using supervised and unsupervised representations. National Documentation Centre (EKT) (2021). Query date: 2022-03-07 13:23:13
7. Pan, H., Xie, L., Wang, Z.: Spatio-temporal convolutional attention network for spotting macro- and micro-expression intervals. In: Proceedings of the 1st Workshop on Facial Micro-Expression: Advanced Techniques for Facial Expressions Generation and Spotting (2021). Query date: 2022-03-15 13:24:42
8. Dritsas, E., Trigka, M.: A methodology for extracting power-efficient and contrast enhanced RGB images. Sensors **22**(4), 1461 (2022)
9. Memmesheimer, R., Häring, S., Theisen, N., Paulus, D.: Skeleton-DML: deep metric learning for skeleton-based one-shot action recognition. In: 2022 IEEE/CVF Winter Conference on Applications of Computer Vision (WACV), pp. 837–845 (2022)

10. Zhou, C., Yang, L., Liao, H., Liang, B., Ye, X.: Ankle foot motion recognition based on wireless wearable sEMG and acceleration sensors for smart AFO. Sens. Actuators, A **331**, 113025 (2021)

11. Li, C., Liu, M., Cao, Z.: WiHF: gesture and user recognition with WiFi. IEEE Trans. Mob. Comput. **21**(2), 757–768 (2022)

12. Rahmani, H., Bennamoun, M., Ke, Q.: Human action recognition from various data modalities: a review (2021)

13. Chaabane, S.B., Hijji, M., Harrabi, R., Seddik, H.: Face recognition based on statistical features and SVM classifier. Multimed. Tools Appl. **81**, 8767–8784 (2022). Query date: 2022-02-22 13:16:18

14. Malik, N.U.R., Abu Bakar, S.A.R., Sheikh, U.U.: Multiview human action recognition system based on OpenPose and KNN classifier. In: Mahyuddin, N.M., Mat Noor, N.R., Mat Sakim, H.A. (eds.) Proceedings of the 11th International Conference on Robotics, Vision, Signal Processing and Power Applications. LNEE, vol. 829, pp. 890–895. Springer, Singapore (2022). https://doi.org/10.1007/978-981-16-8129-5_136

15. Khalid, H.-U.-R., Gorji, A., Bourdoux, A., Pollin, S., Sahli, H.: Multi-view CNN-LSTM architecture for radar-based human activity recognition. IEEE Access **10**, 1 (2022). Query date: 2022-02-23 12:56:18

16. Zhu, Q., Chen, Z., Soh, Y.C.: A novel semisupervised deep learning method for human activity recognition. IEEE Trans. Ind. Inform. **15**(7), 3821–3830 (2019)

17. He, J.-Y., Xiao, W., Cheng, Z.-Q., Yuan, Z., Jiang, Y.-G.: DB-LSTM: densely-connected Bi-directional LSTM for human action recognition. Neurocomputing **444**, 319–331 (2021)

18. Gupta, N.: Human activity recognition in artificial intelligence framework: a narrative review. Artif. Intell. Rev. **55**, 4755–4808 (2022)

19. Refai, M.I.M.: Moving on: measuring movement remotely after stroke. Ph.D. thesis. University of Twente, Netherlands (2021)

20. Buma, F., Kordelaar, J., Raemaekers, M., van Wegen, E., Ramsey, N., Kwakkel, G.: Brain activation is related to smoothness of upper limb movements after stroke. Exp. Brain Res. **234**, 07 (2016)

21. Scheltinga, B.L.: Suitable metrics for upper limb movement smoothness during stroke recovery (2019)

22. Bigoni, M., et al.: Does kinematics add meaningful information to clinical assessment in post-stroke upper limb rehabilitation? A case report. J. Phys. Therapy Sci. **28**, 2408–2413 (2016)

23. Rohrer, B., et al.: Movement smoothness changes during stroke recovery. J. Neurosci.: Official J. Soc. Neurosci. **22**, 8297–304 (2002)

24. Liebermann, D.G., Levin, M.F., McIntyre, J., Weiss, P.L., Berman, S.: Arm path fragmentation and spatiotemporal features of hand reaching in healthy subjects and stroke patients. In: 2010 Annual International Conference of the IEEE Engineering in Medicine and Biology Society (EMBC), pp. 5242–5245. IEEE (2010)

25. Pila, O., Duret, C., Laborne, F.-X., Gracies, J.-M., Bayle, N., Hutin, E.: Pattern of improvement in upper limb pointing task kinematics after a 3-month training program with robotic assistance in stroke. J. Neuroeng. Rehabil. **14**, 10 (2017)

26. Rahman, H.A., Khor, K., Fai, Y., Su, E., Narayanan, L.: The potential of iRest in measuring the hand function performance of stroke patients. Bio-Med. Mater. Eng. **28**, 105–116 (2017)

27. Laczko, J., Scheidt, R., Simo, L., Piovesan, D.: Inter-joint coordination deficits revealed in the decomposition of endpoint jerk during goal-directed arm movement after stroke. IEEE Trans. Neural Syst. Rehabil. Eng. **PP**, 1 (2017)

28. Irfan, M., et al.: Smoothness metrics for reaching performance after stroke. Part 1: which one to choose? J. NeuroEng. Rehabil. **18**, 10 (2021)
29. Supratak, A., Guo, Y.: TinySleepNet: an efficient deep learning model for sleep stage scoring based on raw single-channel EEG. In: 2020 42nd Annual International Conference of the IEEE Engineering in Medicine Biology Society (EMBC), pp. 641–644 (2020)
30. Wang, X., Zhou, Y., Zhao, C.: Heart-rate analysis of healthy and insomnia groups with detrended fractal dimension feature in edge. Tsinghua Sci. Technol. **27**(2), 325–332 (2022)
31. Kemp, B., Zwinderman, A.H., Tuk, B., Kamphuisen, H.A.C., Oberye, J.J.L.: Analysis of a sleep-dependent neuronal feedback loop: the slow-wave microcontinuity of the EEG. IEEE Trans. Biomed. Eng. **47**(9), 1185–1194 (2000)
32. Van Dam, J., Tanous, K., Werner, M., Gabbard, J.L.: Calculating and analyzing angular head jerk in augmented and virtual reality: effect of AR cue design on angular jerk. Appl. Sci. **11**(21), 10082 (2021)
33. Oliveira, S.M.S., et al.: The balance concept on unilateral vestibular hypofunction patients changes the balance and quality of life. Health Sci. J. **15**(5), 1–5 (2021)
34. Schot, S.H.: Jerk: the time rate of change of acceleration. Am. J. Phys. **46**, 1090–1094 (1978)
35. Hayati, H., Eager, D., Pendrill, A.-M., Alberg, H.: Jerk within the context of science and engineering—A systematic review. Vibration **3**(4), 371–409 (2020)
36. Hostler, D., Schwob, J., Schlader, Z.J., Cavuoto, L.: Heat stress increases movement jerk during physical exertion. Front. Physiol. **12**, 748981 (2021)
37. Alpers, B.: On fast jerk–, acceleration– and velocity–restricted motion functions for online trajectory generation. Robotics **10**(1), 25 (2021)
38. Bensalah, A., Chen, J., Fornés, A., Carmona-Duarte, C., Lladós, J., Ferrer, M.Á.: Towards stroke patients' upper-limb automatic motor assessment using smartwatches. In: Del Bimbo, A., et al. (eds.) ICPR 2021. LNCS, vol. 12661, pp. 476–489. Springer, Cham (2021). https://doi.org/10.1007/978-3-030-68763-2_36
39. Nakazono, T., et al.: Reliability and validity of Japanese version of Fugl-Meyer assessment for the lower extremities. Top. Stroke Rehabil. **29**, 1–8 (2021). PMID: 33724162

Signature Execution in Alzheimer's Disease: An Analysis of Motor Features

Carina Fernandes[1,2](✉), Gemma Montalvo[1], Michael Pertsinakis[3,4,5], and Joana Guimarães[6]

[1] Instituto Universitario de Investigación en Ciencias Policiales,
Universidad de Alcalá, Alcalá de Henares, Spain
cafernandes@ncforenses.pt
[2] NCForenses Institute, Porto, Portugal
[3] Chartoularios PC Institute of Questioned Document Studies, Athens-Crete, Greece
[4] MBS College of Crete, Crete, Greece
[5] City Unity College, Athens, Greece
[6] Faculty of Medicine of the University of Medicine, Porto, Portugal

Abstract. The analysis of signatures attributed to individuals with Alzheimer's disease (AD) poses special challenges to Forensic Handwriting Examiners (FHEs) and research on the subject has been scarce. The aim of the study was to assess how AD impacts motor features in signature execution through kinematic analysis. The study included 10 individuals with mild AD, 10 individuals with moderate AD and 10 healthy controls matched by age, education and gender. Eight hybrid signatures were collected from each participant using a digitizer and NeuroScript's MovAlyzeR® software. The study revealed no statistically significant intergroup differences regarding average absolute velocity, absolute jerk, normalized jerk and average pen pressure in the text-based that were produced. Findings suggest that, in text-based signatures, motor features are relatively preserved in the initial and moderate stages of Alzheimer's disease. Therefore, at these stages of the illness, FHEs should not expect significant changes in such features for this signature type. These results also support the hypothesis that motor programs responsible for the creation/execution of text-based signatures are not significantly impaired in the initial and moderate stages of the illness, due to the automation and lower cognitive demands of well-trained signatures.

Keywords: Signature execution · Alzheimer's disease · Dementia · Dynamic features · Digitally captured signatures · Motor programs

1 Introduction

Forensic Handwriting Examination is a complex discriminatory process that requires the analysis, comparison and evaluation of handwriting patterns [1]. The analysis of handwriting attributed to a signatory with Alzheimer's disease poses special challenges to Forensic Handwriting Examiners (FHEs), since this irreversible neurodegenerative disease progressively impairs several cognitive domains [2, 3] and hence is susceptible

© Springer Nature Switzerland AG 2022
C. Carmona-Duarte et al. (Eds.): IGS 2021, LNCS 13424, pp. 349–354, 2022.
https://doi.org/10.1007/978-3-031-19745-1_26

of affecting handwriting. Moreover, simulations and handwriting changes due to illness may share common characteristics, such as tremor, lack of fluency, retouching and a higher number of pen lifts [4, 5], thus making the evaluation of the findings more intricate.

Research on how Alzheimer's disease (AD) affects motor features in signature execution has been scarce, particularly from a FHE's perspective. Behrendt [6], in 1984, described the preservation of writing skill despite cognitive decline. However, the author also highlighted that when deterioration occurs it may progress rapidly. These findings were confirmed in a study conducted by Caligiuri and Mohammed [7], using digitizers. The authors found no significant differences between signatures produced by AD participants with moderate dementia and the control group regarding stroke duration, amplitude, velocity, pen pressure and fluency, although there was an increase in the natural variation of handwriting [7]. Despite these findings, other forensic studies using conventional pen and paper signatures described lower line quality in AD individuals with more severe dementia due to tremor and hesitations [8, 9], whereas velocity and pressure were considered similar [7].

Non forensic studies also suggest changes in motor features of signatures in AD. Research by Pirlo et al. [10] extracted dynamic features from signatures using a Sigmalognormal model. In this study, the bagging CART classification tree allowed the differentiation between AD participants and healthy controls with an error rate of 3%. Wang et al. [11] also reported that the signatures of individuals with AD, when compared to healthy controls, had lower information content in the time sequences of pressure and pen altitude angles. The authors found significant differences in the way AD subjects hold the pen, due to lower muscle tonus. However, whether these findings have forensic relevance and therefore can be applied in Forensic Handwriting Examination warrants further research.

In this context, the aim of the study was to assess how Alzheimer's disease impacts motor features in signature execution through kinematic analysis, thereby providing more information for FHEs dealing with such cases.

2   Material and Methods

2.1   Participants

The study included 20 subjects with a previous medical diagnosis of probable AD according to the DSM-5 criteria [12], recruited from hospitals and dementia day care centers located in Porto, Portugal. These subjects were divided into two groups according to dementia severity, as 10 individuals had mild stage AD and 10 were in the moderate stage, based on the criteria of the clinical dementia rating (CDR) [13]. The study also included a control group with 10 healthy matched individuals, recruited from day care centers or through senior associations, who underwent neuropsychological testing to confirm the absence of cognitive deficits and non-dementia status. Inclusion criteria for the study subjects were the following: all individuals were Portuguese, right-handed, had normal or corrected hearing and eyesight, and knew how to read and write, as the minimum level of education was the 4th grade, taking into consideration the literacy levels for this age group in the Portuguese population [14]. In the Alzheimer's disease groups, subjects with additional medical conditions that further impaired cognition or motor control, or individuals with signs of parkinsonism were excluded. In the control group, subjects with any medical condition that could adversely affect cognition or motor control were also excluded. A description of the demographic characteristics for each group and the scores obtained in the Mini-Mental State Examination Test (MMSE), adapted to the Portuguese population by Guerreiro et al. [15], is presented in Table 1.

Table 1. Description of the three groups (Control, Mild AD and Moderate) regarding age, education, gender and MMSE scores.

	Control group	Mild AD	Moderate AD
Participants	10	10	10
Age (years)	80 ± 6	80 ± 5	78 ± 9
Education (years)	6 ± 3	5 ± 2	6 ± 3
Gender (f/m)	6/4	6/4	5/5
MMSE Scores	28 ± 2	23 ± 4	19 ± 3

Age, Education and MMSE scores are means $\pm$ Standard deviation (SD)

This study was approved by the Ethics Committee of the University of Alcalá, as well as by the Ethics Committees of the Institutions involved. Informed consent was obtained from all the study subjects or their legal representatives prior to the beginning of the experiment.

2.2 Equipment and Procedure for Signature Collection

Participants wrote with an electronic inking pen (Wacom inking pen KP-130-01) on an A4 sized unlined form, affixed to the surface of a Wacom Intuos Pro M digitizing tablet (active area 22.4 cm × 14.8 cm, sampling rate 133 Hz, accuracy 0.01 cm) with sticky tape. With this procedure, for each signature that was produced, researchers obtained simultaneously a digital representation and a conventional pen and paper signature sample. The digitizing tablet was connected to a laptop PC with NeuroScript's MovAlyzeR® software (Version 6.1.), which was the software used to conduct the experimental procedure and record handwritten signature data. For signature collection, participants were seated with the digitizing tablet placed on top of the table in front of them. Subjects were allowed to adjust the position of the digitizer and their own writing position. Participants were instructed to write their signature eight times on the forms (only one signature per form), as naturally as possible, and were given the opportunity to practice prior to the trials, in order to familiarize themselves with the equipment.

2.3 Data Analysis

The motor features included in the present study were: average absolute velocity, absolute jerk, normalized jerk and average pen pressure, which was measured in tablet pressure units that vary from 0 to 1023. Data extraction and analysis was performed with NeuroScript's MovAlyzeR® software (Version 6.1.0.0), using the following segmentation criteria: first segment added at any rate, last segment added at any rate and the entire trial was regarded as one stroke. Prior to statistical analysis, all trials were reviewed to ensure that discontinuities or recording errors were not present. All the statistical analysis in this study were performed using SPSS Statistics 17.0, with a level of significance of 0.05. Intergroup differences regarding demographics and MMSE scores were first explored. Age analysis was conducted using one-way analysis of variance (ANOVA), since this variable met the criteria for normal distribution. Educational level was examined using Kruskal-Wallis H test, as this variable was not normally distributed (Shapiro-Wilk test: p ≤ 0.05). Gender differences were evaluated using Fisher´s Exact Test, given the number of study subjects.

As for the kinematic parameters, differences between the three groups regarding average absolute velocity, absolute jerk and average pen pressure were examined using ANOVA, as these variables were normally distributed. Normalized jerk were analyzed using the non-parametric Kruskal-Wallis H test, since this variable was not normally distributed (Shapiro-Wilk test: p ≤ 0.05).

3   Results and Discussion

The signatures produced by all the participants in this study were text-based, since all of the allographs that composed the various names were clearly recognizable. This is an expected result, as this is the most common signature form for this age group, in the Portuguese population.

The analysis of demographic characteristics showed no statistically significant differences between healthy controls, mild AD subjects and moderate AD subjects regarding age (ANOVA test; $F = 0.36$; $p = 0.70$), educational level (Kruskal-Wallis H test; $\chi 2 = 1.27$; $p = 0.53$) and gender (Fisher's Exact Test $= 0.38$; $p = 1.00$). However, MMSE scores did reveal significant intergroup differences, with the control group exhibiting the highest scores and the moderate AD group the lowest ones (ANOVA test; $F = 26.42$; $p = 0.00$).

Table 2 summarizes the descriptive statistics for each of the examined motor features in the control, mild and moderate AD groups. One-way analyses of variance (ANOVA), executed with SPSS Statistics 17.0 with a level of significance of 0.05, showed no statistically significant differences between the three groups in average absolute velocity ($F = 0.24$; $p = 0.79$), absolute jerk ($F = 0.44$; $p = 0.65$) and average pen pressure ($F = 0.02$; $p = 0.98$). Moreover, the Kruskal-Wallis H test didn't reveal statistically significant intergroup differences concerning normalized jerk (Chi-square $= 0.79$; $p = 0.68$).

The results of the study suggest that, in text-based signatures, motor features are relatively preserved in the initial and moderate stages of Alzheimer's disease. Therefore, these findings support the hypothesis that motor programs responsible for the creation/execution of text-based signatures are not significantly impaired in the initial and moderate stages of the illness. This may be attributed to the automatization of well-trained signatures and the fact that they are programmed as a single unit, hence being less cognitively demanding than other forms of handwriting, such as text [16, 17]. However,

Table 2. Descriptive statistics for the motor features in the three groups (Control, Mild AD and Moderate), shown as means ± standard deviation

	Control group	Mild AD	Moderate AD
Average absolute velocity (cm/s)	3.1 ± 0.6	3.4 ± 0.9	3.2 ± 1.3
Absolute jerk (cm/s³)	15150 ± 7830	17955 ± 5251	16156 ± 7017
Normalized jerk	1.38E6 ± 1.07E6	1.97E6 ± 1.69E6	1.38E6 ± 7.87E5
Average pen pressure (tablet pressure units)	317 ± 144	313 ± 108	324 ± 133

it should also be noted that there is a very high variation of average normalized jerk in all the three groups, suggesting that there may be an age effect.

These results are in agreement with the findings of Behrendt [6] and Caligiuri and Mohammed [7], but differ from the results presented by Fernandes and Lopes Lima [8] and Birincioglu et al. [9]. The differences that were encountered could be due to the fact that the latter studies included subjects in more severe stages, who exhibited higher degrees of cognitive impairment.

It is worth noting that the present study has limitations, given the small number of subjects per group, the restricted number of dynamic features that were examined and the fact that only eight signatures were collected per participant. As such, further research should be conducted with a larger sample and, in connection to both forensic and non-forensic studies [10, 11], include additional dynamic characteristics.

4 Conclusion

According to the results of the present study, Forensic Handwriting Examiners should not expect significant changes in motor features of text-based signatures, in early and moderate stages of Alzheimer's disease. Moreover, the motor programs involved in the creation/execution of such signatures appear to be relatively preserved in early and moderate stages of the disease.

References

1. Huber, R., Headrick, A.: Handwriting Identification: Facts and Fundamentals, 1st edn. CRC Press, Boca Raton (1999)
2. Lane, C.A., Hardy, J., Schott, J.M.: Alzheimer's disease. Eur. J. Neurol. **25**(1), 59–70 (2018)
3. Nussbaum, R.L., Ellis, C.E.: Alzheimer's disease and Parkinson's disease. N. Engl. J. Med. **348**(14), 1356–1364 (2003)
4. Harralson, H.: Developments in Handwriting and Signature Identification in the Digital Age. Anderson Publishing, Oxford (2013)
5. Walton, J.: Handwriting changes due to aging and Parkinson's syndrome. Forensic Sci. Int. **88**(3), 197–214 (1997)

6. Behrendt, J.E.: Alzheimer's disease and its effect on handwriting. J. Forensic Sci. **29**(1), 87–91 (1984)
7. Caligiuri, M.P., Mohammed, L.: Signature dynamics in Alzheimer's disease. Forensic Sci. Int. **302**, 109880 (2019)
8. Fernandes, C., Lopes Lima, J.M.: Alzheimer's disease and signature execution. J. Forensic Doc. Examination **27**, 23–30 (2017)
9. Birincioglu, I., Uzun, M., Alkan, N., Kurtas, O.: Handwriting changes due to Alzheimer disease: a case report. Forensic Sci. Int. **136**, 78 (2003)
10. Pirlo, G., Diaz, M., Ferrer, M.A., Impedovo, D., Occhionero, F., Zurlo, U.: Early diagnosis of neurodegenerative diseases by handwritten signature analysis. In: Murino, V., Puppo, E., Sona, D., Cristani, M., Sansone, C. (eds.) ICIAP 2015. LNCS, vol. 9281, pp. 290–297. Springer, Cham (2015). https://doi.org/10.1007/978-3-319-23222-5_36
11. Wang, Z., Abazid, M., Houmani, N., Garcia-Salicetti, S., Rigaud, A.S.: Online signature analysis for characterizing early stage Alzheimer's disease: a feasibility study. Entropy **21**(10), 956 (2019)
12. A.P. Association: Diagnostic and statistical manual of mental disorders (DSM-5®). American Psychiatric Publisher (2013)
13. Morris, J.C.: The Clinical Dementia Rating (CDR): current version and scoring rules. Neurology **43**(11), 2412–2414 (1993)
14. Gonçalves-Pereira, M., et al.: The prevalence of dementia in a Portuguese community sample: a 10/66 Dementia Research Group study. BMC Geriatr. **17**(1), 261 (2017)
15. Guerreiro, M., Silva, A.P., Botelho, M.A., Leitão, O., Castro-Caldas, A., Garcia, C.: Adaptação à população portuguesa da tradução do Mini Mental State Examination (MMSE). Revista Portuguesa de Neurologia **1**(9), 9–10 (1994)
16. Caligiuri, M., Mohammed, L.: The Neuroscience of Handwriting: Applications for Forensic Document Examination. CRC Press, Boca Raton (2012)

Correction to: Prodromal Diagnosis of Lewy Body Diseases Based on the Assessment of Graphomotor and Handwriting Difficulties

Zoltan Galaz⬤, Jiri Mekyska⬤, Jan Mucha⬤, Vojtech Zvoncak⬤,
Zdenek Smekal⬤, Marcos Faundez-Zanuy⬤, Lubos Brabenec⬤,
Ivona Moravkova⬤, and Irena Rektorova⬤

Correction to:
Chapter "Prodromal Diagnosis of Lewy Body Diseases Based on the Assessment of Graphomotor and Handwriting Difficulties" in: C. Carmona-Duarte et al. (Eds.): *Intertwining Graphonomics with Human Movements*, **LNCS 13424, https://doi.org/10.1007/978-3-031-19745-1_19**

In an older version of this paper, the acknowledgment was missing. This has now been inserted.

The updated original version of this chapter can be found at
https://doi.org/10.1007/978-3-031-19745-1_19

Author Index